AQA Psychology AS and A-level Year 1 Book

BRILLIANT EXAM NOTES

The Complete Study and Revision Notes

Nicholas Alexandros Savva

Published by Educationzone Ltd

London N21 3YA United Kingdom

© 2021 Educationzone Ltd

British Library Cataloguing in Publication Data:

A catalogue record for this publication is available from the British Library.

Visit our website for exam questions and answers, teaching resources, books and much more:
www.psychologyzone.co.uk

Email us for further information:
info@psychologyzone.co.uk

ISBN 978-1-906468-96-5

Contents

Topic 1 Social influence

Topic 2 Memory

Topic 3 Attachment

Topic 4 Approaches in Psychology

Topic 5 Biopsychology

Topic 6 Psychopathology

Topic 7 Research Methods

*   A-level only

** Mainly A-level apart from the following information, which applies to both AS and A-level:

Introduction to statistical testing; the sign test. When to use the sign test; calculation of the sign test.

Topic 1
Social influence

AQA specification for Topic 1: Social influence (AS and A-level)

- Types of conformity: internalisation, identification and compliance. Explanations for conformity: informational social influence and normative social influence, and variables affecting conformity, including group size, unanimity and task difficulty as investigated by Asch.

- Conformity to social roles as investigated by Zimbardo.

- Explanations for obedience: agentic state and legitimacy of authority, and situational variables affecting obedience, including proximity and location, as investigated by Milgram, and (the effect of) uniforms. Dispositional explanation for obedience: the Authoritarian Personality.

- Explanations of resistance to social influence, including social support and locus of control.

- Minority influence including reference to consistency, commitment and flexibility.

- The role of social influence processes in social change.

AQA specification: Social influence

- Types of conformity: internalisation, identification and compliance.

◆ Introduction

Social psychology is the study of human social behaviour – how humans interact with each other. A branch of social psychology that you will be learning about is called social influence – how other people's thoughts, feelings and behaviour can influence how we behave. How people would behave in a given situation is not always how they would normally behave – social psychology experiments have proven this. Research studies into social influence have challenged some of our most deep-seated beliefs, by demonstrating that our behaviour is not always based on the consequences of our own free, personal choices, but is often under the influence of others.

◆ Key terms

- Social influence. A term that refers to how people can influence each other's behaviour, attitudes and values. Conformity and obedience are an example of social influence.

- Conformity. Conformity is a form of social influence that results in an individual or a small group of people changing their behaviour, attitudes and values to fit in with the view of a larger social group (majority group) they have been exposed to, even if it goes against their own personal judgement. For example, a person who alters their behaviour merely to fit in with a peer group is said to be conforming.

◆ Types of conformity

Psychologists, such as Herbert Kelman (1958), have identified that there is not one, but three different types of conformity to the majority. They are *compliance*, *identification* and *internalisation*. Types of conformity tend to be defined by the 'social condition' that leads to that type of conformity – how people conformed, although it can also be used to explain why people conform.

Compliance

- Compliance occurs when an individual changes their behaviour, attitude or opinion to that of the majority group. They do this in order to 'fit in' with the group because they want to avoid disapproval or gain approval (e.g. for 'reward' purposes). Compliance means 'going along with others' in public, but privately not agreeing with the group, and does not result in the individual changing their underlying attitude or opinion. As a result, the change in behaviour/opinion is superficial (not long-lasting) and often lasts as long as the group pressure is present but disappears in the absence of group pressure. Compliance tends to be the result of *normative social influence*.

Example of compliance

Your group of friends at college say they do not like a particular person and refuse to talk to them. You may agree with them, but privately you do like that person and when your friends are not around you do talk to them.

Identification

- Identification occurs when individuals adjust their behaviour or opinions to those of a group, because they want to be like them. This is a stronger type of conformity than compliance because the person alters their behaviour/opinions in private, as well as demonstrating public acceptance. However, these changes are generally temporary and is not maintained when individuals leave the group, for example, when they finish school.

Example of identification

A student at university adopts the beliefs of their flatmates (e.g. being vegetarian or holding certain political beliefs), but on leaving university life, they adopt new behaviours and opinions again, for example, eating meat.

Internalisation

- Internalisation occurs when individuals genuinely accept the behaviour, attitude, or opinions of the majority group because they have accepted the group's views as being right. This can often be because the majority position is consistent with their own values or the majority's position may convince the individual that they, the individual are wrong, and the majority is right. Accepting the view of the majority as right often leads to an acceptance of the majority position both publicly and privately. Even when the influence of the group is absent, the individual will continue to accept the view of the majority. Internalisation is the most permanent form of conformity and tends to be the result of informational social influence

Example of internalisation

A person who takes on a new religious faith will accept, both publically and privately, the values and norms of the religious group and will continue to accept these, regardless of whether the group is there to influence the individual or not.

Practice exam questions

1. The following statements are related to conformity. In the table below, enter the correct letter (A, B or C) to match the type of conformity to the statement. **[3 marks]**

   A The individual conforms in public with the group but in private they disagree with them.

   B The individual sees the views of the group are right and these views become part of his or her belief system.

   C The individual is doing what the group does in order to be liked by them.

   →

Type of conformity	Statement (e.g. A B or C)
Conformity	
Internalisation	
Compliance	

2. Explain what is meant by 'identification' in the context of conformity. [3 marks]

3. Explain what is meant by 'internalisation' in the context of conformity. [3 marks]

4. Explain what is meant by 'compliance' in the context of conformity. [3 marks]

5. Explain the difference between internalisation and compliance [3 marks]

6. Aisha and Bushra have just started sixth form college and have made a group of new friends. All their friends wear a headscarf for religious reasons. Aisha had listened to their point of view and now she also wears a headscarf. Bushra was also happy to wear a headscarf at college. They have now finished college and have started university. Aisha continues to wear a headscarf but Bushra does not. Both girls conformed, but for different reasons. Explain which type of conformity each girl was showing. [4 marks]

AQA specification: Social influence

- Explanations for conformity: informational social influence and normative social influence.

◆ Explanations for conformity

According to Deutsch and Gerard (1955), there are two main explanations of why individuals conform to the majority – *informational social influence* and *normative social influence*.

Informational social influence

- **Informational social influence (ISI)** is when a person conforms to the behaviour or opinion of the majority because they see others as a source of the correct information and use this to guide their personal decisions. This is likely to occur when the situation is ambiguous (unclear) and a person is unsure of the correct response. They will then look to others to lead their response, believing the majority to be correct. An example would be during a crisis when people often panic and are uncertain what to do; it is then natural to see how others are responding and follow their example. Another example would be when expert knowledge is required and we trust other people's judgment to be more correct. Therefore, ISI conformity is due to cognitive reasons rather than emotional reasons.

Example of informational social influence

One example would be a person who has started at a new job and the fire alarm goes off and the person watches his colleague's behaviour to see how he should behave.

A sad example is the 9/11 attack on the World Trade Center. Some people remained in the South Tower building, even after observing the first plane hitting the North Tower of the World Trade Centre. In this ambiguous situation, some people turned to their colleagues' behaviour (who remained in the building), as a reference point to guide their own behaviour; sadly, this may have cost them their lives.

ISI leads to a type of conformity called internalisation. This means a person genuinely believes that the views of the others are right, which results in a change in their behaviour or view in public, showing public compliance, and in private, showing private acceptance. One example would be joining a religious group because you believe their ideas are right.

Normative social influence

- **Normative social influence (NSI)** is when a person changes their behaviour/view to that of the majority (i.e. conforms), in order to be liked and accepted by the group and avoid the group's disapproval. Therefore, NSI is often due to emotional reasons rather than a cognitive (thinking about it) process. Although the individual may publicly change their behaviour/views (i.e. showing 'public conformity'), in private they may not agree. This type of conformity is also known as compliance.

Example of normative social influence

An example would be a teenage girl who conforms to deviant behaviour (e.g. shoplifting) with her friends, so she can fit in, but privately she knows this is wrong.

◆ Evaluation

For ISI

Strength

✔ **Research support for ISI.** A strength of this theory is that there is supporting research evidence for ISI. A classic study by Jenness (1932) investigated the effect on 101 American students. The aim was to investigate whether individual judgements of the number of jellybeans in a jar were influenced by group discussion. Jenness asked participants to estimate in private how many jellybeans were in a jar. He then grouped the participants and got them to discuss their estimates. After the discussion, the group estimates were created. Then, the participants made a second individual private estimate. Jenness found that private second estimates were closer to the group decision than the initial estimates. This showed that individual judgements were affected by the majority opinion, especially in an ambiguous situation, and thus people were more likely to conform due to ISI.

Weakness

✘ **Social identities can influence ISI.** A weakness of the ISI theory is it cannot be replicated reliably. Abrams et al. (1990) found that in an ambiguous situation, people are more likely to conform with others they they feel they share a common social identity with, known as the 'in-group', compared to those they do not have things in common with, the 'out group'. Examples of in-groups would be friends, people of the same ethnicity, religion, work colleagues, or a badminton club. This produces an in-group bias (tendency to favour one's in-group over an out-group). As a result, people are more likely to conform by internalising the opinions and views of friends than those of a stranger. This shows that the processes that determine informational influence are much more complex, suggesting that ISI as an explanation is over-simplified.

For NSI

Strength

✔ **Research support for NSI.** The strength of this theory is supporting research evidence that people conform as a result of NSI. Asch (1956, see next exam notes for study) carried out an experiment that required a group of 7-9 American male participants, seated around a table, to look at three vertical lines (A, B and C) and judge them, by calling out which line was the same length as the 'standard line'. In each group, there was only one genuine participant (naive participant), the others were confederates, who knew about the study and were told to give a wrong answer. Asch found on average about 32% of the naive participants conformed to the incorrect majority answer (about one-third of them) and about 75% of the naive participants conformed at least once. The study showed that conformity displayed by individuals can be explained by NSI. Even in a situation where the answer is clearly obvious, people will yield to group pressure and conform to the majority view to avoid being ridiculed.

Weakness

✗ **Individual differences.** A limitation of NSI as an explanation for conformity is that it does not consider individual differences. For example, people who care more about being liked by others are known as nAffiliators and are more likely to be affected by NSI. McGhee and Teevan (1967) found that students who were assessed as nAffiliators were more likely to conform. The desire to be liked underlies conformity for some people more than others. This shows that NSI as an explanation does not cover the fact there are differences in people, which may influence why they conform.

Both ISI and NSI

Weakness

✗ **NSI and ISI work together.** A limitation of NSI and ISI as explanations for conformity is that this is an over-simplification. This is because these two explanations, NSI and ISI, work independently from each other - conformity is either due to NSI or ISI. However, some psychologists suggest that, in fact, the two work together in influencing levels of conformity. For example, in another experiment by Asch, conformity was reduced when there was a dissenter (a person who disagrees) in the group. It could be argued that this dissenter may have reduced the influence of NSI (by providing social support) or reduced the influence of ISI (because they were an alternative source of information). This shows that it is difficult to know when a person is subject to ISI or NSI.

Practice exam questions

1. Explain what is meant by informational social influence. **[3 marks]**

2. Explain what is meant by normative social influence. **[3 marks]**

3. Explain the difference between informational social influence and normative social influence. **[3 marks]**

4. Outline one study that has demonstrated informational social influence. **[5 marks]**

5. Outline one study that has demonstrated normative social influence. **[5 marks]**

6. Georgina and Tina met at work and have now become really good friends. Georgina finds that when they do meet up, a lot of the time they spend together is with Tina's friends smoking marijuana. They asked Georgina if she would like to join them. She agrees even though she does not like it.

7. Identify whether Georgina is demonstrating normative social influence or informational social influence. Justify your answer. **[3 marks]**

8. Outline and evaluate explanations of conformity. **[16 marks]**

9. Discuss what psychological research has told us about why people conform. **[16 marks]**

AQA specification: Social influence

- Variables affecting conformity including group size, unanimity and task difficulty as investigated by Asch.

◆ Introduction

In the 1950s, Solomon Asch carried out a number of experimental tests, which showed that people would deny the evidence of their own eyes and give the wrong answer to a task in order to conform with the majority group, even when that answer was unambiguous (the correct answer was obvious). Below is Asch's original classic study that investigated conformity.

AN 'EYE' ON THE STUDY

A study into normative social influence
The line-judgement task (Asch, 1956)

Aim

- To see whether people's behaviour is influenced by the majority view even when the answer to an experimental task is unambiguous. Asch wanted to see if people conformed to the majority as a result of normative social influence.

Method/procedures

- The study involved a sample of 123 American male university students. In each test, a group of 7-9 students sat around a table in a classroom. The experimenter told them they would be taking part in a vision test (the cover story) by comparing the length of vertical lines.

- In each group, there was only one participant who was genuine, called the naive participant, all the others were confederates of the experimenter – they knew the true aim of the experiment and were told how to respond in the test. The genuine participant was led to believe that the other participants were also real.

- The task required the participants to look at two white cards. One card showed a single dark vertical line and the other card showed three dark vertical lines of different lengths, labelled A, B, and C (see Figure 1 below). The participants were asked to call out in turn, in the order they were seated, which of the three lines (A, B or C) was the same length as the 'standard line'. The correct answer was always obvious. The naive participant was seated last around the table and was the last, or second from last, to give his opinion.

- Each line test was called a 'trial' and there were 18 trials altogether. The confederates were instructed to give the correct answer on six of the 18 trials, called *neutral trials*, and to give the wrong answer on 12 of the trials, called *critical trials*.

Findings

- Asch found that in the 12 critical trials, the naive participants conformed to the incorrect answer 32% of the time. This means that in approximately four out of the 12 critical trials, each participant conformed to the wrong answer. This is significant; if we compare this against the neutral trials (with no confederates giving the wrong answer), the participants answered incorrectly 0.7% (less than 1%) of the time.

→

- Asch also found that 75% of the participants conformed at least once to the wrong answer. This means 25% of the naive participants never conformed at all - they gave the correct answer on all 12 critical trials.

Conclusions

- The study showed that conformity displayed by some individuals can be explained by normative social influence. Even in a situation where the answer is clearly obvious, people will yield to group pressure and conform to the majority view to avoid being ridiculed.

- The study also showed that a quarter of the naive participants gave the correct answer, resisting the pressure of the majority influence and thus demonstrating independent behaviour.

Figure 1

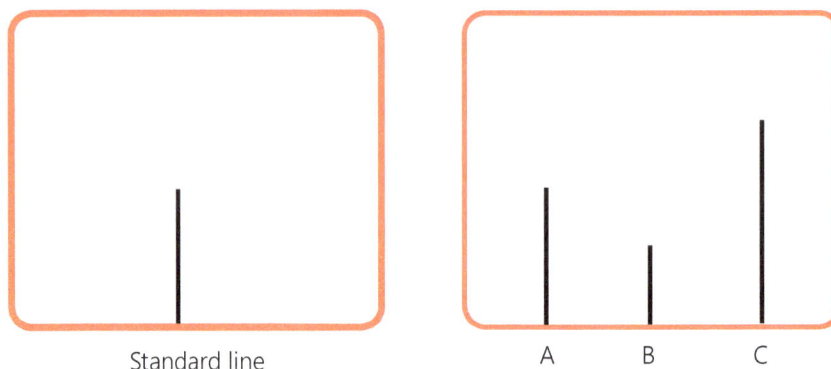

Standard line   A   B   C

◆ Evaluation

For NSI

Weaknesses

✗ **Explanation for the high level of conformity found in Asch studies.** One limitation is that Asch's findings may be unique because of the period of US history (McCarthyism) in which the study took place, which may explain the high level of conformity found. The 1950s was a time where increasing tension between America and the Soviet Union, led to a social climate of anti-communist feelings known as the 'McCarthyism' period (instigated by the anti-communist politician called Joseph McCarthy). American people were fearful of expressing their own opinions, in case they were accused of being a 'communist sympathiser', so it was safer to conform and show solidarity with your peers than be different. This may explain the high levels of conformity found. Perrin and Spencer (1980) repeated Asch's study in the UK and found just one conforming response in 396 trials. Such findings may reflect a change in social attitudes in society (less conformist), which may explain why conformity levels have decreased. This suggests that Asch's findings are not consistent over time, so conformity behaviour is not an enduring feature of human behaviour.

✗ The above explanation is supported by Bond and Smith (1996), who conducted a meta-analysis of experiments using Asch's line-judgement experiment. They identified 97 studies that were conducted in the United States and looked at changes over time between 1950 and the early 1990s. They found a decline in overall conformity in these studies; the early Asch-type studies showed higher conformity levels whereas the later studies showed lower levels of conformity. This suggests that social changes have taken place in society, which may account for the different findings in conformity levels.

✗ **Asch overstated the amount of conformity.** A criticism of Asch's study is that it is used to overstate the amount of conformity demonstrated. In fact, 25% of the naive participant never conformed at all - they gave the correct answer on all 12 critical trials, demonstrating independent behaviour. These participants felt confident in their judgement, despite the pressure of a unanimous majority that gave a different answer. This shows that although many people were influenced strongly by a unanimous majority, some people remained independent in the same conditions.

✗ **Biased sample.** A limitation of Asch's study is that it was based on a biased sample of people – male university students from one particular culture – the USA. This means the findings can only be applied to males in America. Studies that have replicated the Asch experiment have found greater conformity in women than men (Eagly and Carli, 1978). Neto (1995) suggested that women might be more conformist because they are more concerned with social relationships and being accepted. Furthermore, conformity varies between individualist and collectivist cultures. Smith et al. (2006) found the average conformity rate for studies carried out in collectivist cultures was much higher (37%) than for individualist cultures (25%). They argue that conformity rates are higher in collectivist cultures (e.g. China) because these cultures are more concerned with group needs and collective responsibility than individualist cultures (e.g. USA, UK), which place more emphasis on individual freedom and expression. This suggests that the effect of conformity varies depending on the culture.

✗ **Asch's task was artificial.** Another criticism of Asch's study is about the experimental setting used to investigate conformity. Critics argue that the situation and task were artificial and therefore lacked mundane realism (did not reflect true-life situation). The trivial task of judging the length of a line is an unlikely task to be asked to complete with strangers in real life, suggesting that the study may lack ecological validity. Furthermore, Williams and Sogon (1984) argued that Asch's research only assesses conformity among strangers and people may behave differently with friends. They carried out a similar experiment and found that conformity was much greater amongst friends than with strangers, suggesting the effect of conformity varies depending on circumstances.

✗ **Unethical.** The study by Asch also raises ethical issues. The participants did not provide full informed consent because they were misled about the true aim of the study, this was deception and was therefore unethical. Furthermore, the study placed the participants in a difficult and embarrassing position when the confederates gave the wrong answer, meaning that they have experienced some forms of (mild) stress and this can also be considered unethical.

◆ Variables affecting conformity

Research into majority influence has identified several *situational* variables, those qualities of an environment that influence levels of conformity – the degree to which individuals conform. In further research based on his his original study, Asch tested several variations of his procedure of the line judgement task, in order to determine which factors influenced conformity levels. These factors included group size (the number of people in a social group), unanimity (to what degree the group of people are in agreement with each other), and task difficulty (how obvious the correct answer/decision was when regarding a task).

Situational variables

• **Group size.** Asch found there was very little conformity when the majority consisted of just one or two confederates. With one confederate and one real participant, conformity was low at just 3%, rising to 13%

with two confederates on the critical trials. When the number of confederates increased to three, conformity rose to about 32%. Further increases in the size of the majority did not significantly increase this level of conformity, suggesting that there comes a cut-off point in the influence of group size on conformity e.g. a group of three people is about as influential as groups of 16.

Campbell and Fairey (1989) found that group size has a different effect depending on the type of judgement being made and the motivation of the person. They found that the size of the group is not so important when responses are ambiguous (the judgment is difficult). In an ambiguous situation where the person is concerned about fitting in, they may be swayed by fewer people. However, when there is an objectively correct response that is not ambiguous (the judgment is easy), the power of the group size is important - the larger the majority size, the greater the chance of conformity.

- **Unanimity.** Research has shown that conformity declines when the majority group is not unanimous – the people in the group do not agree with each other. Asch (1956) found that if there was one confederate who went against the others and gave the right answer before the genuine participants answered, conformity dropped from around 32% (original study) to 5.5%. This shows that when a person has a 'supporter' in the group, the person no longer feels alone and conformity levels decrease significantly. In another experimental test, where the dissenting confederate gave an answer that was a different wrong answer to the one given by the majority, conformity levels also decreased to 9%. Asch believed that it was breaking the group's unanimous position that was the major contributing factor in conformity reduction.

- **Task difficulty.** Greater conformity rates are seen when task difficulty increases, as the correct answer becomes less obvious. This means that individuals will look to others for guidance in making the correct response. In one experimental test, Asch made the line-judgement task more difficult by making the difference between the line lengths smaller and therefore appear more similar, so that the task was more ambiguous. The results of this study showed that, as the rate of conformity increased, participants were increasingly likely to conform to wrong answers (Asch did not report a percentage). This demonstrated the effect of task difficulty on conformity. The reason for the increase in conformity in line with task difficulty is likely due to informational social influence, as individuals look to others for guidance when carrying out an ambiguous task, in order to be right.

◆ Evaluation

Weaknesses

✗ **Who's in the group is just as important.** A limitation of research into group size on conformity is that conformity also depends on *who* is in the majority group, as well as *how many* are in the group. Abrams et al. (1990) found that, in ambiguous situations, we are more likely to be influenced by other people's opinions when we feel we share a common social identity with them (known as the 'in-group'), than by those with whom we do not share a common social identity (known as the 'out-group'). This produces an in-group bias (tendency to favour one's in-group over the out-group). As a result, people are more likely to internalise the opinions and views of friends, and thus show conformity, and less likely to internalise a stranger's views.

✗ **Social characteristics of the supporter.** Another limitation of research into 'unanimity' on the effects of conformity is that it ignores the effects of the social characteristics of the supporter (dissenter in the group). For example, Melamed and Savage (2013), found that the education, race and sex of the 'supporter' can influence whether a person will resist conforming to the group or not. If the 'supporter' is perceived to be different (e.g. education or class), then they are less likely to have an effect. This suggests that conformity depends on the characteristics of the supporter rather than simply on her/his presence.

✗ **Ignores individual differences.** A limitation of research into 'task difficulty' on the effects of conformity is that it ignores the role of individual differences. For example, Lucas et al. (2006) found that the influence of task difficulty was affected by the individual's confidence in their own abilities (i.e. their self-efficacy). They found that participants with high self-efficacy remained more independent in their judgements, showing less conformity than participants with low self-efficacy, even under conditions of high task difficulty. Task difficulty also depends on the skills and abilities of the participants, rather than the difficulty of the task itself. For example, a given problem in mathematics might prove hard for most people but not for an expert. This suggests situational differences (task difficulty) and individual differences (e.g. self-efficacy, skills) are both important in determining conformity.

✗ **Alpha bias.** A limitation of Asch's studies is that they were based on males, which means the findings can only apply to males. The problem with carrying out studies on just males is that results can be influenced by 'beta bias'. This means Asch's findings may have minimised the differences between male and female behaviour in relation to conformity, where there could be a difference. Neto (1995) suggested that women might be more conformist, possibly because they are more concerned about social relationships and being accepted.

✗ **Demand characteristics.** A further criticism of the study by Asch is the possibility that the naive participants may have experienced demand characteristics (i.e. subtle cues about how to behave). For example, in the study of group size and conformity, the naive participant may have become suspicious about the entire experiment, when so many other people were holding the same opinion, which differed from their own. This may explain why increasing group size to five or more participants has the same effect as a group of two or three people. This suggests that the findings into group size may not be totally valid.

Practice exam questions

1. Describe the procedure and findings of Asch's research into conformity.   **[6 marks]**

2. Identify three variables affecting conformity and outline how each of these was investigated in Asch's experiment.   **[6 marks]**

3. Explain the role of 'group size' as a variable affecting conformity.   **[6 marks]**

4. Discuss at least two factors that have been shown to affect conformity. Refer to evidence in your answer.   **[16 marks]**

5. Outline and evaluate research into conformity.   **[12 marks AS, 16 marks A-level]**

AQA specification: Social influence

- Conformity to social roles as investigated by Zimbardo.

AN 'EYE' ON THE STUDY
The Stanford prison experiment (SPE)

Background

Philip Zimbardo's study was an attempt to understand the brutal and dehumanising behaviour found in prisons, and was motivated by the violent prison riots reported on a regular basis in the American media. Two widely differing explanations were to be explored. First, there was the *dispositional hypothesis* that the violence and degradation of prisons were due to the 'nature' of the people found within the prison system – both guards and prisoners were both 'bad seeds' possessed of sadistic, aggressive characteristics, which naturally led to brutality. Second, there was the *situational hypothesis* that saw violence and degradation as due to the environment of the prison. In other words, it was the brutalising and dehumanising environment of prison that led to the brutal behaviour of all concerned (prison guards and prisoners).

To separate the effects of the prison environment from those within the prison system, Zimbardo built a 'mock prison' that used 'average' people with no record of violence or criminality to play both prisoners and guards, roles that were determined purely randomly. If no brutality occurred, the dispositional hypothesis would be supported, but if brutality was seen then it must be situational factors that were driving normal, law-abiding people to such behaviour.

Aims

- To investigate the extent to which people would conform to the roles of guard and prisoner in a role-playing simulation of prison life.

- To test the *dispositional* versus *situational* hypotheses that saw prison violence as either due to the sadistic personalities of guards and prisoners or the brutal conditions of the prison environment.

Procedure

- *Participants* – Zimbardo set up a 'mock prison' in the basement of the psychology department at Stanford University in California and made it as realistic as possible. Participants were recruited by newspaper adverts asking for volunteers to be part of a study into prison life, paying $15 a day. They recruited 24 psychologically healthy, male students, determined by psychological testing. These men were randomly assigned to play the role of either prisoners or guards and given appropriate uniform to wear (10 as guards and 11 as prisoners). Zimbardo himself played the role of the prison 'superintendent'. To make the experience as realistic as possible, the prisoners were arrested at their homes by the real local police and delivered to the 'prison' where they were blindfolded, fingerprinted, stripped, and deloused.

- *Setting* – To make the 'mock prison' as real as possible, the design simulated a real prison cell holding three prisoners. Once the participants were in the mock prison setting, *dehumanisation* (the removal of individual identity) took place. Prisoners had to wear garments with an ID number on them (the prisoners were referred to by their ID number, not their name), nylon stocking caps (to simulate shaved heads), and a chain around one ankle. Guards wore khaki uniforms and reflective sunglasses (to prevent eye contact)

→

and were issued with handcuffs, keys, whistles and truncheons (although physical punishment was not permitted).

The prisoners' daily routines were heavily regulated (mealtimes, toilet trips, visiting hours, parole, bedtime, etc.) in order to reflect a real-life environment in prison. There were 16 rules to follow, enforced by guards working in shifts, three at a time. Three times per day, the prisoners were required to line up for a 'count', which would last for 10 minutes and include a test on the rules of the prison. The study was planned to run for two weeks.

Findings

- Both guards and prisoners settled quickly into their social roles. However, within the first two days, Zimbardo observed that the guards grew increasingly tyrannical and abusive toward the prisoners. The prisoners rebelled against their treatment. They ripped their uniforms and shouted and swore at the guards, who retaliated with fire extinguishers. Guards harassed the prisoners constantly by conducting frequent headcounts, sometimes in the middle of the night, or they woke the prisoners in the middle of the night and forced them to clean the toilets with their bare hands.

- After the rebellion was put down, the prisoners were showing signs of anxiety and depression. They also showed signs of passiveness, an acceptance of their lowly position, whilst the guards progressively increased their brutality and aggression every day. Five prisoners were released early because they showed signs of psychological disturbance (crying, rage and acute anxiety) and one prisoner went on hunger strike. The study had to be stopped after six days rather than the planned 14 days, as Zimbardo realised the extent of the harm that was occurring to the prisoners and observed the increasingly aggressive nature of the guards' behaviour. In later interviews, both guards and prisoners said they were surprised at the uncharacteristic behaviours they had shown.

Conclusions

- The situational hypothesis is favoured over the dispositional hypothesis, meaning that the power of the situation can influence people's behaviour. The environment of the mock prison and the social roles it demanded the participants play, led to their uncharacteristic behaviour (none of the participants had ever shown such character traits or behaviour before the study). When the guards were placed in a position of power, they began to behave in ways they would not usually act in their everyday lives. The prisoners, placed in a situation where they had no real control, became passive and depressed.

- Individuals conform quite readily to the social roles that are demanded by the situation, even when such roles override an individual's values and moral beliefs. Both guards and prisoners demonstrated social roles gained from media sources (e.g. prison films) and learned models of social power (e.g. parent-child, teacher-student).

◆ Evaluation

Strength

✔ **Control over variables.** A strength of the SPE is that the methodology allowed Zimbardo to have control over many variables of the experimental situation, for example by recruiting 'emotionally stable participants' who were then randomly assigned either as the role of guard or prisoner. The guards and prisoners had those roles only by chance. This eliminates the possibility of the participant's personality being the cause of their behaviour. This means their behaviour was due to the pressures of the situation and not their personalities. Control increases the study's internal validity, meaning that we can be more confident in drawing conclusions about the influences of social roles on behaviour.

✔ **Real-life application.** A further strength of the SPE study is that the findings have real-life applications. Zimbardo's findings have often been used to explain the effects of institutionalisation, such as the abusive behaviour in prisons and the military (e.g. the notorious Abu Ghraib prison in Iraq). The study has shown that it is not personal character but the environment - situational factors- that has a strong influence on people's behaviour. The results have been used by the criminal justice system and the military to educate those authority figures working in such potentially dangerous environments. This study has also helped alter the way US prisons are run. For example, prisons now minimise the differences in social roles between prisoners and guards, and young prisoners are no longer kept with adult prisoners to prevent the bad behaviour perpetuating.

Weaknesses

✘ **SPE lacks realism.** A limitation of the SPE is a lack of realism. Banuazizi and Mohavedi (1975) suggested that participants were play-acting – a case of demand characteristics. Their performances reflected stereotypes of how prisoners and guards are supposed to behave. One guard based his role on a character from the film Cool Hand Luke. Prisoners rioted because they thought that is what real prisoners did, and not because of the environmental conditions being tested. If demand characteristics could explain the findings of the study, this means the study has low ecological validity and therefore we cannot generalise the findings to real-life prison settings.

✘ **SPE lacks ecological validity.** Another criticism of the SPE is that some psychologists have further questioned the ecological validity of the study. For ethical reasons, many aspects of real prison life were absent (for instance, rape, racism, beatings, etc.) and the maximum sentence was two weeks. Furthermore, real prisons are rarely monitored by an entire staff of guards with no experience or training and prisoners are rarely (we hope) imprisoned for no reason. Consequently, we should be cautious about generalising findings to the real world of prison systems.

✘ **Sample bias.** The study can also be criticised for sample bias. Since the experiment was conducted using 24 normal, healthy, male, American college students who were predominantly middle class and white, we must be careful generalising the study's findings beyond the sample, to female prisons or those from other countries. For example, America is an individualist culture (where people are generally less conforming), so the results may be different in collectivist cultures (such as communist countries).

✘ **Ethical issues with SPE.** A limitation is that there were major ethical issues with the SPE. One major issue was the lack of protection for the prisoners from psychological and physical harm. Participants playing the role of prisoners were not protected from psychological harm (e.g. humiliation, stress, anger, and distress). A student who wanted to leave the study spoke to Zimbardo, who responded as a superintendent worried about the running of his prison rather than as a researcher. This limited Zimbardo's ability to protect his participants from harm because his superintendent role conflicted with his lead researcher role. However, Zimbardo argued that he debriefed the participants with follow-up questionnaires monitoring for any permanent harm, many years after the study. These revealed no lasting effects and Zimbardo felt that the impact of the findings justified the ethical breaches.

✗ Dispositional factors are important. Fromm (1973) argued that Zimbardo understated dispositional influences. Individual differences (people's personalities) are important in the outcome of this study. Only a third of the guards behaved brutally, another third applied the rules fairly to the prisoners, and the rest supported the prisoners, offering them cigarettes and reinstating privileges. Fromm concluded that the degree to which participants conformed to social roles may be over-stated, exaggerating the power of the situation. The differences in the guards' behaviour showed that they could exercise right and wrong choices, despite situational pressures to conform to a role.

Practice exam questions

1. Outline the procedures and findings of Zimbardo's research into conformity to social roles. **[4 marks]**

2. Describe Zimbardo's research into conformity to social roles. **[6 marks]**

3. Briefly discuss two reasons why people have criticised Zimbardo's prison study. **[6 marks]**

4. Discuss research into the conformity of social roles. **[12 marks AS, 16 marks A-level]**

AQA specification: Social influence

- Obedience as investigated by Milgram.

◆ Key term

- **Obedience.** This refers to a type of social influence whereby an individual carries out an act in response to an order given from a figure recognised to be in authority. Obedience can also imply an individual is acting upon an order because they feel they have no choice, even though they may personally not wish to have carried out that order.

◆ Obedience

Obedience plays an important role in society. Obedience to the laws and rules of society helps people to co-exist, otherwise society would fall into disorder and conflict. Unfortunately, obedience can also be very destructive. History is marked with repeated examples of atrocities and genocides all in the name of obedience – in Germany, Vietnam, Armenia, Rwanda, and Cambodia. These examples were the result of soldiers obeying orders, from those in authority, to carry out immoral acts such as torture or murder. It has been claimed that people who commit such atrocities must either be immoral or have a sadistic personality to be so obedient. This is not the case; psychological research such as Milgram's famous study (see below) demonstrates that even ordinary people can be persuaded to commit an immoral act when ordered to by an authority figure.

Differences between obedience and conformity

- **Influence versus direct order:** Obedience and conformity are both forms of social influence. Conformity is where a person changes their behaviour due to the influence of the majority group (e.g. informational social influence or normative social influence), without having been told to change; whereas obedience is when an individual's behaviour changes, as the result of a direct order by an authority figure (e.g. we are told what to do).

- **Difference in social status:** Obedience and conformity often differ in terms of social status. With obedience, those who carry out the orders tend to have a lower social status than those giving the orders (e.g. sergeant and solider); whereas with conformity, the group has similar social status to the individual that is being influenced (e.g. friends).

AN 'EYE' ON THE STUDY

Research study into obedience
Milgram's original shock experiment (Milgram, 1963)

Aim

- The aim of the experiment was to investigate the level of obedience a person would show when told by an *authority* figure, to carry an unjust order of administering increasingly harmful electric shocks to another person.

→

Method/procedures

- Milgram advertised (e.g. in a local newspaper) for male volunteers aged between 20 and 50 years to take part in a memory and learning study (the cover story) for about an hour at Yale University. The experimenter selected 40 volunteers and paid them $4.50 each on arrival for taking part. Participants were told that the money was theirs no matter what happened (i.e. even if they decided to quit during the experiment).

- Each experiment involved three people: two confederates (accomplices, who were in on the study and knew what it was about) and one naive participant (a real person who responded to the advertisement). One of the confederates played the experimenter (a stern-looking 31-year-old high school teacher of biology – the 'authority' figure) and was dressed in a grey laboratory coat. The other confederate pretended to be another participant that volunteered to the advertisement (a likeable 47-year-old accountant).

- When the naive participant arrived, the experimenter told them that another 'volunteer', (the confederate) would also be part of the study. The naive participant was also told specifically that the experiment was to test the effects that *punishment has on learning*, and it required one of them to be the teacher and the other the learner. The participants were asked to draw a slip of paper from a hat to determine they would play. The draw was rigged so the naive participant was always the 'teacher' and the confederate was always the 'learner'.

- The teacher and learner were then taken to a room, where the 'learner' was strapped into a chair by the experimenter and his wrists were attached to an electrodes. Both participants were told that the electrodes were wired to a shock generator in the adjacent room, which delivered electric shocks. The experimenter then led the teacher into the adjacent room, where he was seated in front of the shock generator and shown how to operate the equipment. The shock generator consisted of 30 switches in a horizontal row, with each switch clearly labelled with the voltage level from 15 to 450 volts. There was a 15-volt increment from one switch to the next, going from left to right (15 volts, 30 volts, 45 volts and so on). In addition, every four sets of switches was labelled going from left to right: Slight Shock; Moderate Shock; Strong Shock; Very Strong Shock; Intense Shock; Extreme Intensity Shock, and Danger: Severe Shock. The final two switches (435 and 450 volts) were labelled "XXX." (See Figure 2 below). Each naive participant was given a sample shock by pressing the third switch of the generator (45 volts, which is quite painful) to convince them that the generator was real, so that they understood that a much higher voltage level would be fatal. In fact, the shock came from a hidden battery wired inside the generator. The shock generator was not real and therefore incapable of delivering shocks; in other words, it was a dummy which the naive participant was not aware of.

- The teacher was instructed to read out a list of word pairs to the learner (e.g. 'tree-needle', 'cloud-hat', 'horse-rock') and the learner was instructed to memorise the pair. The teacher then read the first word of each pair (e.g. 'tree' from 'tree-needle'), plus four possible responses for the learner (e.g. 'axe', 'needle', 'stick', or 'blade'). The learner had to choose which of the four words had originally been paired with the first word (in this case 'needle'), by pressing one of four switches labelled 1, 2, 3, and 4. This action lit up one of four numbered lights located at the top of the shock generator, which the teacher was able to see.

- If the answer was wrong, the teacher was instructed to press the first voltage-level switch (15 volts) and to call out the voltage shock they were administering. For every subsequent incorrect answer, the teacher was instructed to move one shock level higher. The learner gave no vocal response or other sign of protest after receiving a shock for an incorrect answer, until the shock level reached 300 volts. The learner was given predetermined responses to the word-pair test. At 300 volts, the learner kicked loudly at the wall and, at 315 volts, the learner became silent and gave no further answers. The experimenter instructed the teacher to treat the absence of a response as a wrong answer and to increase the shock level by one increment each time the learner failed to respond. The learner had been instructed to deliberately gave wrong answers to see how long the teacher would administer the electric shocks.

- During the whole experiment, the teacher was supervised by the experimenter. If the teacher asked the experimenter for advice on whether to continue administering shocks or gave some other indication that he did not wish to go on, the experimenter encouraged him to continue by using a sequence of standardised 'prods', such as:

  "Please continue" or "Please go on".

  "The experiment requires that you continue."

  "It is absolutely essential that you continue."

  "You have no other choice, you must go on."

- Obedience was measured by how far the teacher went up on the shock generator, before refusing to obey the commands of the experimenter.

The 'shock generator'.

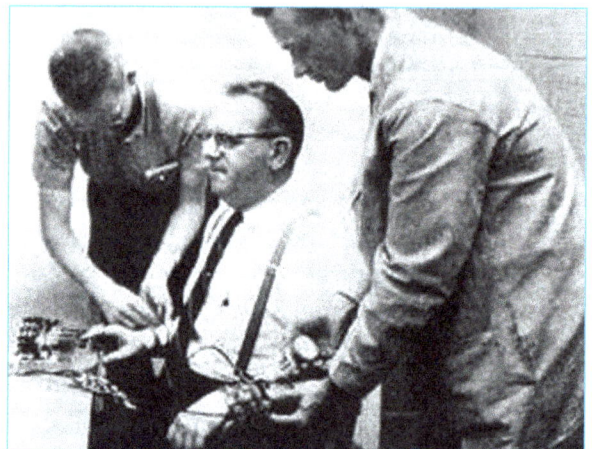
The learner is strapped in to the chair and electrodes are attached to his wrists.

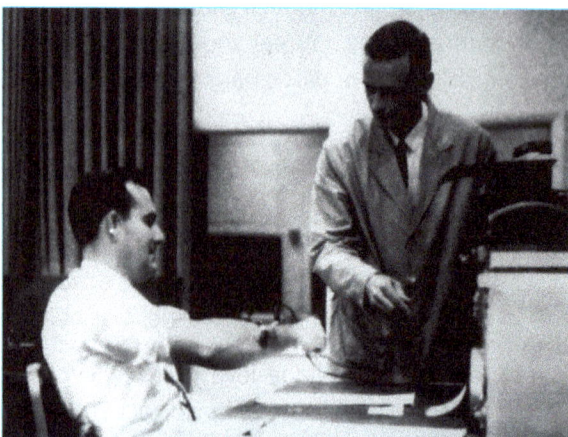
The experimenter gives the teacher a sample shock from the generator.

The four numbers located above the shock generator.

Figure 2: Milgram's shock experiment

Findings

- Before the research began, Milgram carried out a survey on a number of psychiatrists, psychology students and adults, who were given a description of the experiment. They were asked to predict how many of 100 hypothetical participants (teachers) would administer shocks all the way to the highest level (e.g. 450 volts). The survey group predicted, on average, that one out of the 100 participants would go all the way and administer 450 volts.

- Milgram found that all 40 of the participants obeyed the experimenter and delivered shocks up to 300 volts, the point at which the learner first objected to receiving the shocks. At 300 volts, five (12%) of the participants disobeyed the experimenter and refused to carry on giving shocks. Then, 14 of the participants stopped obeying the teacher between 300 and 375 volts. The main finding was that 26 of the 40 (65%) participants continued to the maximum shock level of 450 volts.

- Milgram also found that many participants showed a high level of tension and stress (sweating, trembling, stuttering, biting their lips, groaning, digging their fingernails into their skin, or nervous laughing fits), but they still continued.

Conclusion

- Milgram's study showed a high level of obedience to *authority* from ordinary people even when the order required committing an immoral act. However, he did find that the participants showed a great amount of distress in obeying an unjust order, indicating that this went against their better moral judgement. *So, one explanation why obedience was high is that we are more likely to be obedient to those whom we regard as authority figures.*

◆ Evaluation

Strengths

✔ **Replication.** A strength of the Milgram study is that he used a laboratory experiment to investigate obedience. This meant that the study could be repeated (which Milgram did as well as other researchers) using the same experimental conditions and procedures to assess the reliability of the findings – whether they got similar results – which they did.

✔ **Control of variables.** Another strength of Milgram's study is the use of a laboratory experiment, which meant he could alter one variable at a time to test effects on obedience. This means independent variables (IV) such as the social setting, proximity, or group size could be tested, while other variables were kept constant/controlled. The control of other experimental settings and the manipulation of the IV, mean that we can be more certain that changes in obedience were caused by the variable manipulated (e.g. proximity), enabling us to establish a cause-and-effect relationship.

Weakness

✘ **Milgram study lacks internal and external validity.** Milgram's study has been criticised because it lacks internal validity. Orne and Holland (1968) claimed that the participants did not believe that they were really giving electric shocks. They were aware of the deception, and therefore simply went along with the 'role play', and they may have pretended to show signs of distress just to please the experimenter. This could explain why the obedience levels found in the study were so high. This suggests that Milgram's experiment did not measure obedience, as the participants were not genuine in their behaviour and were reacting to the demand characteristics of the experiment. Furthermore, Orne and Holland also challenged the generalisability of Milgram's findings. The laboratory setting (rooms at Yale University) and the actual task for testing obedience (giving someone 450 volts of electric shocks!) are artificial measures of obedience and bear little resemblance to real-life situations where obedience is required.

Strengths

✔ **Others argue it does have internal validity.** The view that the Milgram study lacks internal validity has been criticised. In another study, Sheridan and King (1972) asked participants to administer real electric shocks to puppies whenever the puppies made a mistake on a training task. Participants were led to believe that the shocks were becoming increasingly severe. In fact, the puppy was getting a small shock each time, just enough to make it jump and show obvious signs of receiving a shock. Eventually, the puppy received an anaesthetic gas to put it to sleep, making the participants think they had killed it. They found that even after the dog 'seemed dead', 54% of the male participants and all females continued to obey the command and administer the maximum shock voltage of 450 volts. Furthermore, when interviewed, 70% of Milgram's participants thought the shocks were genuine. This suggests that Milgram's study did have internal validity.

✔ **Evidence shows Milgram study has external validity.** Hofling et al. (1966) carried out a field experiment in a number of hospital settings to see whether the level of obedience observed by the Milgram laboratory experiment could be applied to real life. The study involved 22 real nurses, who were unaware they were participating in the study. The nurses were completing their routine night duties alone on a ward, when they received a phone call from an unknown doctor, 'Dr Smith' (not a real doctor). The 'doctor' instructed each nurse to administer 20mg of a drug called Astroten (really a placebo drug) to a patient immediately. This broke hospital regulations as nurses were not allowed to take instructions over the phone. Also, the dose of medication was twice the recommended amount (the maximum for that drug is 10mg- clearly stated on the label of the bottle). The researchers found that 95% (21 out of 22) of the nurses obeyed the doctor's orders. As the nurses were not aware of the study, it shows high-level obedience does occur in real-life settings and it also proves that Milgram's experimental study does have external (ecological) validity.

Weakness

✗ **Ethical issues with Milgram's study.** Baumrind (1964) criticised Milgram's study for even taking place because of the many ethical issues raised, for example, participants experienced psychological harm – some were very distressed by the experience (as supported by video evidence). They displayed physical effects such as sweating and trembling, and some of the participants even had full-blown seizures. There was also the issue of deception, for example, the participants were told the study was about the effects of punishment on learning when in fact it was on obedience. Milgram also deceived the participants into believing that they had an equal chance of being the teacher or learner, when in fact it was rigged, and the learner was really a confederate of the experimenter. Finally, Milgram deceived the participants into believing that the electric shocks were real when they were not.

Strength

✔ **Milgram's response to ethical issues.** Milgram (1974) argued that without deception the experiment could not have taken place. Telling the participants the shocks were not real would have altered their behaviour drastically and thus rendering the study meaningless (i.e. it would lack internal validity). He argued that the deception was dealt with appropriately, as the participants were thoroughly *debriefed* afterwards about the true aim of the experiment.

Milgram rejected Baumrind's criticism that the experiment was unethical due to the severe stress it caused in the participants. Milgram argued that he did not anticipate prior to the study the high level of stress the participants would experience. In addition, Milgram argued that the follow-up questionnaire revealed that 84% were 'very glad' or 'glad' to have taken part in the study and 74% of the participants felt they had learnt something of personal importance about human nature. So, according to the participants, the psychological harm was minimal. Also, a psychiatric examination one year after the experiment revealed no evidence of psychological harm.

Practice exam questions

1. Explain what is meant by the term 'obedience'. **[3 marks]**

2. Explain the difference between conformity and obedience. **[4 marks]**

3. Outline the procedure of one study into obedience. **[6 marks]**

4. Outline what research has shown about obedience. **[6 marks]**

5. Milgram's experiment into obedience has been criticised for being unethical. Describe two ways in which his study is unethical. **[2 marks + 2 marks]**

6. Apart from ethical issues, give one strength and one limitation of Milgram's methodology. **[2 marks + 2 marks]**

7. Explain why Milgram's experiment into obedience may lack validity. **[6 marks]**

8. Outline and evaluate research studies into obedience. **[12 marks AS, 16 marks A-level]**

AQA specification: Social influence

- Explanations for obedience: situational variables affecting obedience, including proximity and location, as investigated by Milgram, and the effect of uniforms.

◆ Situational variables – the external explanation

Situational variables form an *external explanation* for obedience. Situational variables are features of the environment (an aspect of the situation) affecting obedience. Milgram (1974) carried out further variations on his original study of obedience. He changed the procedure to see which factors would increase or decrease the level of obedience. He identified three important situational factors that can influence obedience: proximity, location, and uniforms.

- **Proximity.** In one of the proximity experiments, Milgram found that if the learner and teacher are placed in the same room (1 metre away from each other), only 40% of the participants went all the way to 450 volts, a drop in the obedience level compared to the original experiment (65%). A possible explanation for the fall in obedience is that the physical closeness may have distressed the teacher, because they could hear the screams and moans of the learner more clearly. In another proximity experiment, when the experimenter was absent from the room and instructions to the teacher were given via the telephone, 20.5% of the participants administered the full 450 volts, showing that 79.5 % of the participants showed a high level of resistance to obedience. The findings suggest that distance seemed to act as a buffer to obedience: the greater the distance from (or the absence of) an authority figure, the less obedience people displayed to an unjust order.

- **Location**. The location of an environment can be relevant to the amount of perceived legitimate authority that the person giving orders is seen to have. In locations that add to the perceived legitimacy of the authority, obedience rates will be higher. Obedience rates are often the highest in institutional settings where obedience to authority figures is instilled in members. When Milgram conducted his original study in the laboratory at Yale University, he found that 65% of participants gave the maximum 450-volt shock. However, when he repeated the study in the less prestigious location of a run-down office, above a shop in a deprived area that had no obvious links with Yale University, he found that 48% of participants administered the maximum shock. Milgram concluded that the prestigious setting of Yale University may have contributed to the high level of obedience in the original study. This suggests that the lower the perceived legitimacy of the authority (based on location), the less likely we will obey (disobedience). However, although the location of the study was an important factor, it did not reduce obedience as much as proximity alterations.

- **Uniforms.** The wearing of uniforms can give the perception of added legitimacy for authority figures when delivering orders, and thus increase obedience rates. In Milgram's original experiment, the confederate researcher wore a lab coat to give him to give an air of authority. In Milgram's location experiment, the experimenter was called away to a telephone call at the start of the procedure and an ordinary man who appeared to be a participant (confederate) in everyday clothes (rather than a lab coat) took over the experimenter role. Milgram found that this had a dramatic effect: obedience rates dropped down to 20%. This shows that uniforms can influence obedience, as power and authority can become symbolised in the uniform itself. Bickman (1974) found that when his research assistant ordered people in a New York street to pick up rubbish, loan a coin to a stranger, or move away from a bus stop; 19% would obey when the assistant was dressed in civilian clothes, 14% when he was dressed as a milkman, but 38% obeyed when he wore a security guard's uniform. These results show that uniforms can have an influence on obedience, as power and authority can become symbolised in the uniform itself.

◆ Evaluation

✔ **Supporting evidence for situational variables**. A strength of Milgram's theory is supporting research evidence for situational variables. Bickman (1974), found that when his research assistant ordered people in a New York street to pick up rubbish, loan a coin to a stranger, or move away from a bus stop, 19% would obey when the assistant was dressed in civilian clothes, 14% when he was dressed as a milkman, but 38% obeyed when he wore a security guard's uniform, demonstrating that uniforms can influence obedience levels. This supports Milgram's conclusion that a uniform conveys authority and is a situational factor producing obedience.

✔ **Control of variables.** Another strength of Milgram's study was that the use of a laboratory experiment allowed him to have control over the variables. These meant that independent variables (IV) such as location, proximity, and uniform could be systematically manipulated to see the effects on obedience, while other variables were controlled. This gives us more confidence that the changes in obedience were caused by the manipulated variable (e.g. proximity), enabling us to establish a cause-and-effect relationship.

Weaknesses

✗ **Milgrams variation studies lack internal validity.** A limitation is that Milgram's variations studies may lack internal validity. Orne and Holland (1968) argued that participants in Milgram's variations were even more likely to realise the procedure was faked because of the extra experimental manipulation. In the proximity variation study, where the experimenter was replaced by 'a member of the public', even Milgram recognised that this may have led to demand characteristics, where some participants may have worked out the procedure was faked. This suggests that it is unclear whether the results are due to obedience or because the participants saw the deception and 'play-acted'.

✗ **Milgram's research provides an excuse.** Mandel (1998) criticised Milgram's conclusions because they provide an 'obedience alibi'. This means Milgram's findings are an 'excuse' for Holocaust Nazi war criminals who were 'just following orders' out of obedience to their superiors and were not responsible for their actions. This 'obedience alibi' – to suggest that the Nazis simply obeyed orders and were victims of situational factors beyond their control – is offensive to Holocaust survivors (and our memories of the victims). Mandel argues that Milgram's situational theory is dangerous; he believes the over-simplified explanation of 'just following orders' for the Holocaust as being the dominant view in psychology textbooks ignores the roles that discrimination, racism and prejudice played in the Holocaust.

Practice exam questions

1. Milgram investigated situational variables affecting obedience to authority figures. Identify two of these variables and explain how each of them affects obedience. **[3 marks + 3 marks]**

2. Identify two factors that have been shown to affect obedience to authority. Briefly discuss how each of these factors affects obedience to authority. **[6 marks]**

3. Evaluate Milgram's research into the effects of situational variables on obedience. **[6 marks]**

4. Outline research into the effect of situational variables on obedience and discuss what this tells us about why people obey. **[12 marks AS, 16 marks A-level]**

AQA specification: Social influence

- Explanations for obedience: agentic state and legitimacy of authority.

◆ Key terms

- **Agentic state.** This is a state of feeling controlled by an authority figure and therefore lacking a sense of personal responsibility for our actions.

- **Legitimate authority.** The person giving the order is seen to have the right to do so because they are seen as justified in having power over others.

◆ Explanations of why people obey

Below are two reasons why people obey.

Agency theory

After World War II, Nazi war criminal Adolf Eichmann was arrested for war crimes. Eichmann had been in charge of the Nazi death camps and his defence was the 'obedience alibi', that he was "just following orders" from those above him. As a consequence of the trial and the findings from experimental studies, this led Milgram to develop the agency theory.

- One explanation of obedience to authority is the agentic state theory. This is when an individual does not see themselves as being responsible for their own actions and believes that the person in authority will take responsibility for their behaviour. Milgram described this process of shifting responsibility onto another person, often an authority figure, as an agentic shift where the individual is now an 'agent' acting on behalf of the authority figure. The agentic shift involves moving from an autonomous state, where you feel you are responsible for your own actions, to an agentic state, carrying out someone else's wishes. Milgram suggested that the agentic shift occurs only when we perceive someone else as an authority figure. A person in an agentic state can often experience high anxiety ('moral strain') when they realise that what they are doing is wrong but feel powerless to disobey the person, who they perceive as having greater power because of their position in a social hierarchy.

As a note

'Autonomy' means to be independent or free. So, a person in an autonomous state is free to behave according to their own principles and therefore feels a sense of responsibility for their own actions. People, in their everyday lives, usually operate in an autonomous state. When we are in an autonomous state, we are more likely to behave within the boundaries of our moral values.

- Milgram observed that many of the participants in his experimental studies spoke as if they wanted to quit but seemed unable to do so. What kept them in this agentic state (especially if they knew they were doing wrong)? Milgram explains that an individual remains in this agentic state because of binding factors. Binding factors are aspects of a situation that the person can use to ignore, or minimise the damaging effects of their behaviour and reduce the 'moral strain' they feel. Milgram proposed a number of strategies the individual uses. Examples of binding factors could be shifting the responsibility to the victim, 'he was foolish to volunteer' or 'denying' the damage they were doing to the victims.

Legitimate authority

- **Socialised to accept authority.** Milgram (1974) observed that most societies are structured in a hierarchical way. This means that some people are assigned positions of authority over others, such as parents, police officers and teachers. The authority they hold is 'legitimate' as it is agreed by society. Most of us accept that authority figures should exercise social power over others for society to have order and run smoothly. Without obedience, there would be challenges to this social order resulting in chaos and societal breakdown. Milgram believes that we are socialised to accept obedience to authority at a young age (e.g. by our family and the education system). Parents often use a system of rewards and punishments to encourage obedience and discourage dissent in young children. Sanctions and rewards are also institutional within the educational and legal systems and so perform a large role in ensuring that we develop as subordinates within our society.

- **The perception of legitimate authority** plays an important role in obedience and is the first condition needed for a person to shift to the agentic state. There is a tendency for people to accept definitions of a situation that are provided by a legitimate authority (e.g. uniforms, symbols, formal dress, social settings). If an authority figure's commands are potentially harmful or destructive, then for them to be perceived as legitimate they must occur within some sort of institutional structure. For example, in Milgram's original study, the experimenter was seen as a legitimate authority figure because he wore a grey lab coat (uniform) and his status was indicated by the social setting, the prestigious Yale University. This explains why participants were more obedient when the study was conducted at Yale University than when it was conducted in run-down office buildings, as the experimenter's authority was perceived to be lower in a non-academic setting compared to Yale University.

◆ Evaluation

Agentic state

Strength

✔ **Support from Milgram's study.** A strength of Milgram's agency theory is that it is supported by his own research findings. During Milgram's original obedience experiments, the participant (teacher) would often require reassurance that the experimenter would be held responsible for the effects the shocks had on the learner. For example, when participants were reminded that they had responsibility for their own actions, almost none of them were prepared to obey. In contrast, many participants who were refusing to go on, did proceed if the experimenter said that he would take responsibility.

Legitimate authority

Strength

✔ **Cultural differences.** A strength of legitimate authority as an explanation for obedience is that it is a useful explanation of cultural differences in obedience. For example, Kilham and Mann (1974) replicated Milgram's research in Australia and found that only 16% of participants went up to the full voltage (450 volts), whereas Mantell (1971) found that with German participants, the obedience level was 85%. This is a strength because it supports the idea that legitimate authority is dependent on the influence of individuals that belong to a society and this reflects the way in which children are socialised to perceive authority figures. As a result, these cross-cultural findings increase the validity of the explanation of legitimacy of authority for obedient behaviour.

Both agentic state and legitimate authority

Strengths

✔ **Supporting research evidence.** There is strength for the legitimate authority and agentic state theories from supporting research evidence. In Hofling et al. (see Exam Note 5), the researchers found that 95% (21 out 22) of the nurses obeyed the request of a doctor when asked to administer a dose of medication that was twice the recommended amount. Against the hospital policy, the 'doctor' informed the nurse that she (the doctor) would sign the prescription later. This study supports the legitimate authority explanation because several of the nurses justified their behaviour by stating that the orders came from a legitimate authority, from a doctor established in a legitimate organisation i.e. hospital. It also supports the agency theory because the majority of nurses displaced their personal responsibility onto the doctor and thus were in an agentic state.

✔ **Real-life evidence.** There is also real-life evidence to support the agency theory. Milgram sees the high level of obedience displayed by Nazi soldiers during the Holocaust atrocities, as evidence of the soldiers being in an 'agentic state'. The excuse the soldiers gave is that they were 'just following orders'. The 'just following orders' excuse is often used to explain more recent war crimes, atrocities, and genocides committed by soldiers. Examples of these are the My Lai massacre during the Vietnam war, events in Bosnia and Rwanda, and the infamous torturing of prisoners at Abu Ghraib prison. These real-life examples offer some support for the agency theory, demonstrating a displacement of responsibility. On the other hand, Kelman and Hamilton (1989) suggested that the My Lai massacre (Vietnam War) could be explained by the 'legitimate authority' justification. The army is seen to have legitimate authority, recognised by the US government and the law. Soldiers assumed that orders given by the hierarchy were legal, even orders to kill, rape, and destroy villages. The legitimacy of authority explanation can provide reasons why destructive obedience is committed.

Weaknesses

✘ **Partial explanation.** A weakness of the agentic shift as an explanation for obedience is that it only offers a limited explanation. Although Milgram's first obedience experiment provides evidence for the agency theory by demonstrating that 65% of participants were willing to obey an authority figure and potentially seriously harm an innocent person; it cannot explain why some of the participants (35%) showed resistance to obedience by refusing to administer the full 450 volts. Equally, the legitimate authority explanation fails to explain why some people are less influenced than others by legitimate authority. Some reasons can be related to personality type, age, gender and situation and experience. This means the agency theory and legitimacy of authority explanation are limited as they cannot account for all situations of obedience, which demonstrates that obedience is a more complex process than can be explained by these two theories.

Practice exam questions

1. Outline 'agentic state' as an explanation for why people obey. **[4 marks]**
2. Outline 'legitimacy of authority' as an explanation for why people obey. **[4 marks]**
3. Describe research into the agentic state explanation for obedience. **[4 marks]**
4. A teacher enters a classroom and tells Adam and his friends to 'keep their voices down' as there are examinations going on next door. They are more likely to agree to this request, than if another student tells them to lower their voices.

   Use your knowledge of why people obey to explain this behaviour. **[4 marks]**
5. Outline and evaluate one or more explanations of why people obey. **[12 marks AS, 16 marks A-level]**

AQA specification: Social influence

- Explanations for obedience: Dispositional explanation for obedience to the Authoritarian Personality.

◆ Key terms

- **Authoritarian personality.** This is the type of personality that holds rigid conventional values about society, has an exaggerated respect for authority, and expresses contempt for people of inferior social status or non- conventional social groups.

AN 'EYE' ON THE STUDY

The Authoritarian Personality
(Theodor Adorno, 1950)

Like Milgram, Theodor Adorno and his colleagues (1950) wanted to understand how the Holocaust occurred during the Nazi period in Germany. Notably, Adorno wanted to investigate whether Germans in this period of history had a certain type of personality that made them more obedient to authority.

Adorno felt that high levels of obedience can be explained by dispositional factors (personality characteristics), rather than by situational factors as suggested by Milgram. He argued that the characteristics that make up an authoritarian personality make people more likely to obey the orders of an authority figure. He found such individuals have the following characteristics:

- *Respect for authority.* He found people with an authoritarian personality have an exaggerated respect for authority; they obey their superiors without question and have submissive attitude towards authority.

- *Enjoy being in authority.* Authoritarian personalities like being an authority figure and have hostility toward people that they perceive as inferior, such as minority groups and non-conventional people (e.g. in Nazi Germany: homosexuals).

According to Adorno, the authoritarian personality is servile to those of superior status and hostile to those of inferior status and minority groups. If given an order by someone of high social status and legitimate authority, the authoritarian personality is more likely to obey than other personality types.

Why are authoritarian personality types so obedient?

- Adorno theorised that the authoritarian personality forms during childhood through harsh and extremely strict upbringing, such as demanding high levels of obedience, standards, and expectations. The child acquires the same authoritarian attitudes from their parents through the process of learning and imitation. Adorno argues that this type of upbringing creates unconscious bitterness and hostility (resentment) in the child. In later life, such children act submissively towards authority figures and project the hostility they had towards their parents to minority groups and socially inferior persons in the form of prejudice.

The authoritarian personality is believed to develop when children grow up in a family which places a strong emphasis on obedience.

→

F-scale test

- Adorno et al. (1950) developed a number of psychometric tests (various questionnaires) that measure people's attitudes. The most important test was called the F-scale ('F' stands for fascism), which measured the 'fascist attitudes' that make up an authoritarian personality. He administered the F-scale test to more than 2000 middle-class, white Americans. He found that people with an authoritarian personality scored high on the F-scale (and other measures), identified with strong people, and held excessive respect and submissiveness to authority, as well as holding prejudicial views towards perceived inferior, minority or weak groups. This led Adorno to conclude that individuals with an authoritarian personality were more likely to be obedient to authority figures and hostile to those of inferior groups, which he believes can account for the high level of obedience found in Nazi Germany, and the subsequent Holocaust atrocities.

Elms and Milgram's (1966) study

- Elms and Milgram (1966) wanted to see if the obedient participants in Milgram's original study were more likely to display an authoritarian personality, in comparison to disobedient participants. They assessed the 20 most obedient participants who administered the full 450 volts and the 20 most defiant participants, who refused to continue in the experiment. Each participant completed several personality questionnaires, including Adorno's F-Scale questionnaire, to measure their level of an authoritarian personality. They found that the obedient participants scored higher on the F-scale in comparison to the disobedient participants. Furthermore, the obedient participants were more distant from their fathers during childhood and admired the experimenter in Milgram's study, which was quite the opposite for disobedient participants, suggesting a link between the authoritarian type personality and obedience. Although Milgram (1974) found the 'power of the situation' as a major force for explaining obedience, he also suggested that disposition (authoritarian personality) can also explain high levels of obedience.

  However, it must be noted that the findings of Elms and Milgram are correlational and therefore psychologists are unable to establish whether or not authoritarian personality traits cause obedience, or obedience causes personality traits. Therefore, while it was concluded that the obedient participants in Milgram's original research displayed more characteristics of the authoritarian personality, these results should be treated with caution. We are unable to conclude whether one causes the other, we only know that the two factors are linked.

◆ Evaluation

Weaknesses

✗ **F-scale to support authoritarian personality has been criticised.** A limitation is that the authoritarian personality, as an explanation for obedience, is based on a flawed research methodology. Greenstein (1969) suggested that the F-scale is 'a comedy of methodological errors'. For example, items are worded in the same 'direction' so the scale just measures the tendency to agree to everything. This means it is possible that the F-scale suffers from response bias. This is because people could be agreeing for the sake of it and not paying attention to what the actual question is asking. It is possible to get a high score for authoritarianism, just by ticking the same line of boxes down one side of the page. As a result, the data collected lacks credibility, which means the authoritarian personality as an explanation of obedience may lack validity.

✗ **Evidence is only correlational.** A further limitation of Milgram and Elm's psychometric test is that the evidence can only prove a correlation (a link) between obedience and authoritarian personality. This link does not prove that an authoritarian personality actually caused high levels of obedience and as a result, it is impossible to draw a definitive conclusion. It is possible that a 'third factor' is involved. Perhaps both obedience and authoritarian personality are associated with a lower level of education, for instance, and are not directly linked with each other at all (Hyman and Sheatsley, 1954).

✗ **Dispositional explanations cannot explain obedience in entire societies.** The authoritarian explanation for obedience has been criticised. In pre-war Germany, millions of individuals displayed obedient, racist and anti-Semitic behaviour, but these millions did not all have the same personality and therefore it is unlikely they all had the same 'authoritarian personality'. An alternative explanation, and a more realistic one, is the 'social identity theory', which states that during this period and regime most Germans identified with the anti-Semitic Nazi state and adopted its views towards the Jews.

✗ **F-scale is politically biased.** Christie and Jahoda (1954) argued that the F-scale is a politically biased interpretation of authoritarian personality. This is because the F-scale aims to assess a tendency towards extreme right-wing ideology (political views). This is simplistic because left-wing authoritarian personalities also exist, for example, Russian Bolshevism or Chinese Maoism insist on complete obedience to political authority. Therefore, Adorno's theory is not a comprehensive dispositional explanation of obedience to authority because it doesn't explain obedience that stems from left-wing authoritarianism, i.e. it is politically biased.

✗ **Ignores situational influences.** A limitation of the authoritarian explanation for obedience is that it ignores situational factors. For example, Milgram's obedience study showed that social context is more important than someone's personality, as the obedience level changed depending on things such as location and proximity. Explaining obedience through authoritarianism cannot account for these variations in obedience levels, as they have nothing to do with the personality of the participants.

Practice exam questions

1. Explain what is meant by an 'authoritarian personality'. **[2 marks]**

2. Outline the authoritarian personality explanation of obedience. **[6 marks]**

3. Briefly explain two limitations of the authoritarian personality as an explanation for obedience. **[2 marks + 2 marks]**

4. Outline and evaluate one research study relating to the authoritarian personality as an explanation of obedience. **[6 marks]**

5. Discuss the authoritarian personality as an explanation for obedience. **[12 marks AS, 16 marks A-level]**

AQA specification: Social influence

- Explanations of resistance to social influence, including social support and locus of control.

◆ Key terms

- **Resistance to social influence** is the ability of a person to withstand the social pressure to conform to the majority or to obey authority.

- **Social support** is when a person in a particular situation resists the social pressure to conform or obey and will help others who are there to do the same and remain independent.

- **Locus of control** refers to the degree to which people believe they have control over their own behaviour or events that happen in their lives (e.g. exam grades, success, or being rich or poor).

◆ Social support

- **Conformity.** *Social support* is one factor that can help people to resist conformity. A person is more likely to resist conforming to the majority if they see another person disagreeing within the group, known as a **dissenter**. The dissenter helps break up the unanimity of the group and shows that there are other possible ways of thinking or responding. The dissenter represents/is seen as a form of social support because they make it easier for another individual to have confidence in their own view.

- **Obedience.** *Social support* can also help people resist obedience. The pressure to obey can be reduced if there is another person who is seen to disobey. A disobedient model reduces the unanimity of a group making it easier for an individual to act independently.

◆ Locus of control

In some cases, people can resist the pressure to conform or obey because of their **personality** type. Julian Rotter (1966) developed the concept of a **locus of control (LOC)**, which is a personality characteristic that refers to how much a person believes they have control over their behaviour and events that influence their lives. Rotter devised a LOC questionnaire to measure a person's perception of control, using a continuum scale with an internal locus of control at one end of the scale and an external locus of control at the other.

- **Internal locus of control.** People who are referred to as having an *internal locus of control* (known as 'internals') believe they have a high level of control over their own behaviour and take responsibility for the outcome of life circumstances that occur in their lives (what happens to them). Internals see the outcome of events as a consequence of their own ability and effort.

- **External locus of control.** People with a high external locus of control (known as 'externals') feel they have low control over their behaviour and life events – what happens in their lives. This is because they see external factors such as fate, luck, or other people, as influencing the outcome.

Locus of control and resistance to social influence

- Research has shown that individuals with a *high internal locus of control* rely less on the opinions or social approval of others, have higher intelligence, and are more likely to show greater independence in thought and behaviours. As a result, they are more likely to resist the pressures of social influence (e.g. conformity and obedience).

- People with a *high external locus* of control tend to approach events with a more passive and fatalistic (accepting things/events as inevitable) attitude than internals and are therefore less likely to show independent behaviour. This means they are more likely to accept the influence of others and less able to resist social influence.

Figure 3: Locus of control

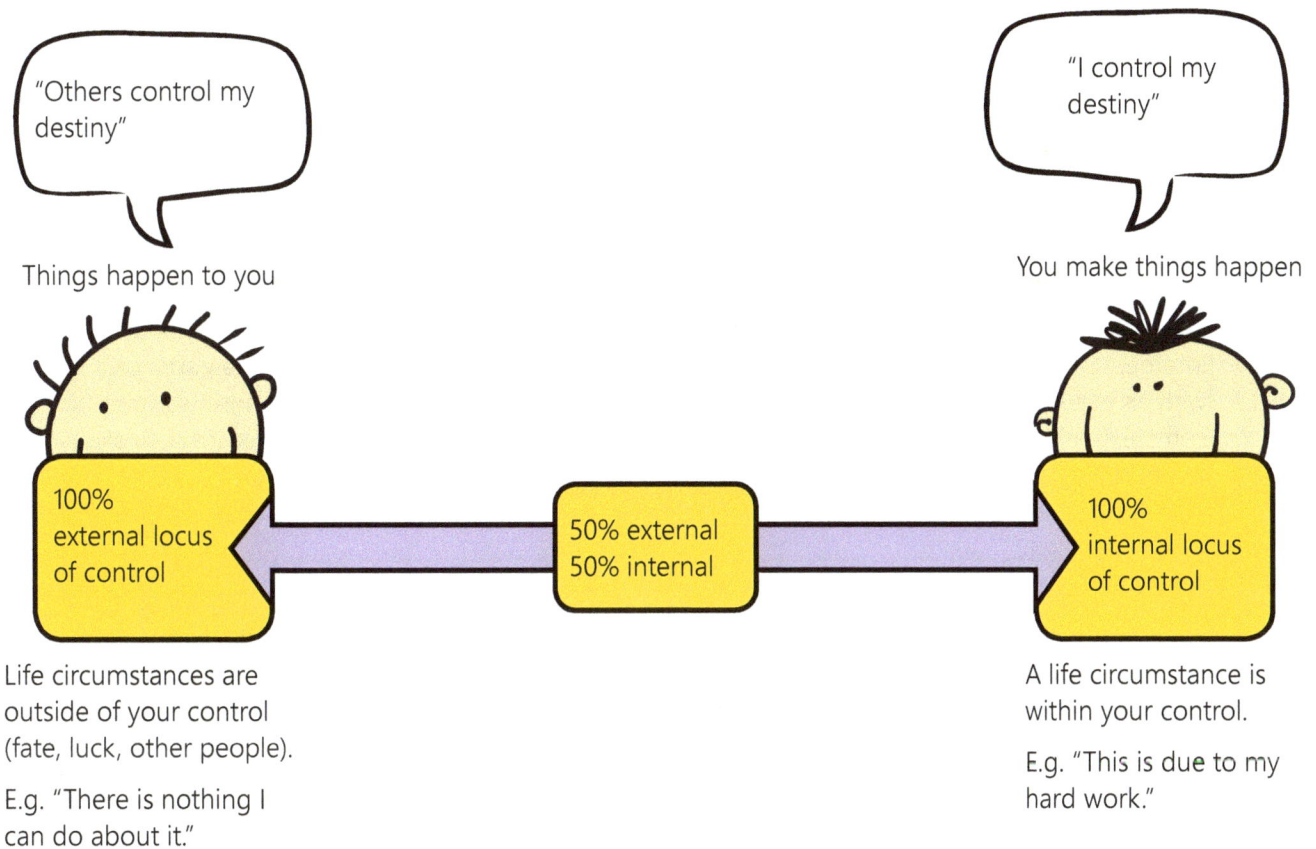

"Others control my destiny"

Things happen to you

100% external locus of control

Life circumstances are outside of your control (fate, luck, other people).

E.g. "There is nothing I can do about it."

50% external 50% internal

"I control my destiny"

You make things happen

100% internal locus of control

A life circumstance is within your control.

E.g. "This is due to my hard work."

◆ Evaluation

Social support

✔ **There is supporting research evidence for the social support explanation**. Asch found in one of his line-judgement conformity experiments, that when another person disagreed (dissenter) with the majority, the level of conformity drastically dropped from 33% to 5%. Research has also shown that social support does not have to be correct/effective. Allen and Levine (1971) found resistance to conformity increased, even if the dissenter wore thick glasses and said he had problems with vision (he couldn't judge the line lengths). This suggests that resistance is not motivated by following what someone else says, but it enables others to be free of pressure from the group. In Milgram's shock experiment, if the participant (teacher) was paired with another two teachers (confederates) who refused to give shocks (i.e. dissenters) beyond 240 volts, 90% of participants were disobedient, resisting the pressures to obey. It seems the dissenter's disobedience frees the participant to act from their own moral conscience.

✔ **Real-life application.** There is real-life evidence that using social support can help resist social influence. For example, in 1943, when female German protesters demanded the release of 2000 Jewish men to whom they were related, the Gestapo (Nazi secret police) agents threatened to open fire if the women did not disperse. The support the women gave each other led to the Gestapo letting their family members go. This supports Milgram's finding that a disobedient confederate gives a person the confidence and courage to resist obeying. Furthermore, this example gives Milgram's research ecological validity as it happened outside of the laboratory conditions.

Locus of control

Strengths

✔ **Research evidence that internals are more resistant to obedience.** There is supporting evidence of a link between locus of control (LOC) and resistance to obedience. Holland (1967) carried out three experiments that were similar to Milgram's shock experiment, to see if obedience levels are affected by internal and external LOC. He found that 37% of the participants with an internal LOC did not administer the strongest electric shock, compared to 23% of the participant with an external LOC. This study shows that participants with an internal LOC are more resistant (to some extent) to the pressures to obey than externals. As a result, this research increases the validity of the LOC as an explanation of resistance to social influence.

✔ **Research evidence that 'internals' are less conforming.** Avtgis (1998) carried out a meta-analysis to see the effects of LOC on the different forms of social influence and conformity. Avtgis found a significant positive correlation for the relationship between LOC and scores on measures of persuasion, social influence, and conformity. Those who scored higher on external LOC tended to be more easily persuaded, more influenced, and more conforming than those who scored higher on internal LOC. As a result, the findings support the validity of the LOC explanation for resisting social influence.

Weaknesses

✘ **No link between LOC and conformity.** There is research that does not support the link between LOC and resistance to conformity. Williams and Warchal (1981) examined this relationship by administering Rotter's internal-external locus of control scale to 30 university students, who also carried out a range of conformity task, similar to that of the Asch-type line-judgement task. The researchers failed to find a link between conformity and LOC. The students who were either internal or external locus of control did not score differently in the conformity task, showing that conformity is not related to locus of control.

✗ **Internal or external LOC depends on social situation.** A criticism of locus of control is that it is not a stable personality characteristic, an internal will always show more resistance to social influence than an external. However, this is clearly not the case, as individuals can act as both internals and externals depending on the environment, the group and their own personal feelings, for example, they may feel confident, have high esteem or have past experience in the ongoing debate. There is research evidence that supports this view to some extent. Twenge et al. (2004) carried out a meta-analysis on research studies that investigated locus of control scores in young Americans between 1960-2002. They found that, over a 40-year period, people have become increasingly more resistant to obedience but also more external than internal. Hamid (1994) showed that Western cultures (e.g. America) tend to have a higher locus of control than collectivist cultures (e.g. Japan), suggesting that Western societies are more likely to resist social influence. This suggests locus of control is not an accurate predictor of human behaviour, as it depends on the situation in which people find themselves.

Practice exam questions

1. Explain how locus of control can help people to resist social influence. **[4 marks]**

2. Explain how social support can help people to resist social influence. **[4 marks]**

3. Using your knowledge of psychology, give two explanations why some people might resist pressures to obey authority. **[2 marks + 2 marks]**

4. Amy has just started university and many of her friends spend most of their time socialising in a pub drinking alcohol. Amy does not drink alcohol but some of the girls are putting pressure on her to start drinking.

   Using what you have learned from studying conformity, suggest one way Amy might resist the pressure to conform. **[3 marks]**

5. Nina passed her English GCSE exam and got a grade A, whereas Tom failed and could only manage a grade E. Nina believes the reason why she did so well is because she worked very hard for it. Tom on the other hand, blames the teacher for the reason why he failed, as they did not get on.

   A. What type of locus of control does Nina show? **[1 mark]**

   B. What type of locus of control does Tom show? **[1 mark]**

   C. Which one of the two students is most likely to resist pressures to conform? Use your knowledge of psychology to explain your choice. **[3 marks]**

6. Discuss locus of control as an explanation of resistance to social influence. **[8 marks]**

7. Outline and evaluate two explanations or resistance to social influence. **[12 marks AS, 16 marks A-level]**

AQA specification: Social influence

- Minority influence including reference to consistency, commitment and flexibility.

◆ Key term

Minority influence is another type of social influence where an individual or a small group influences the larger group, the majority, to accept the minority's beliefs, attitudes or behaviour. Minority influence is most likely to lead to internalisation. This is because both public behaviour and private beliefs are changed if the majority needs to accept the minority as 'right' and to reject the dominant majority.

◆ Minority influence

There are three processes that make minorities more likely to convince majorities of their view: consistency, commitment, and flexibility.

Consistency

- According to Moscovici (1969), one of the key ingredients for the minority to influence the majority is if they are *'consistent'* in their view, especially over time. For Moscovici, consistency has two components:

  - Synchronic consistency means that individuals within the minority should hold the same views (be saying the same thing) and thus this shows stability across the group.

  - Diachronic consistency means that the minority group must hold these views consistently over a period of time.

Hogg and Vaughan (1988) argued that if the minority are consistent in their view, this creates doubt and uncertainty in the majority, which can lead them to re-think their own views, e.g. 'Maybe they have a point if they keep saying it.'

AN 'EYE' ON THE STUDY

Serge Moscovici et al. (1969): Minority influence (consistency)

Moscovici et al. (1969) carried out a well-known experiment investigating the 'consistency' of a minority group to see the effect on the majority group.

Aim

- Moscovici wanted to see if a consistent minority of participants could influence a majority of naive participants to give an incorrect answer in a colour perception task.

Method

- A group of 172 female participants were told that they were taking part in a colour perception task. The participants were placed in groups of six and shown 36 slides, which were all varying shades of blue. Two of the six participants were confederates. The participants had to state out loud, in turn, the colour of each slide.

→

There were three conditions:

1. Confederates consistently said that all the 36 slides were green (consistent minority group).
2. Confederates were inconsistent about the colour of the slides (inconsistent minority group) saying that 24 of the slides were green and 12 were blue.
3. No confederates (control group).

Findings

- Moscovici found that in the consistent minority condition, naive participants agreed on 8.2% of the trials. In the inconsistent minority condition, the naive participants only agreed on 1.25% of the trials. In the control group, the naive participants wrongly identified colour in 0.25% of the trials.

Conclusion

- Moscovici's results show that a consistent minority is more effective than an inconsistent minority and thus consistency is an important factor in exerting minority influence.

Commitment

- If the minority group's activities show commitment by putting themselves in harm's way for their cause, their influence becomes even more augmented (even more 'powerful', known as the 'augmentation principle'). This means the majority group will consider the minority group's views more seriously, as they are even risking their lives for their cause.

Flexibility

- Minorities are often relatively powerless, so they need to be flexible in their approach. Nemeth (1986), argued that being consistent and repeating the same arguments and behaviours will be seen as too dogmatic (inflexible) and uncompromising. This can be interpreted negatively by the majority and thus is unlikely to result in any conversions to the minority position. Instead, the minority should be prepared to adapt their point of view and accept reasonable counter-arguments.

◆ The process of change

- All three factors above *(consistency, commitment, flexibility)* will make people think about the views of the minority more seriously. This is because they allow for deeper processing, which is important in the process of converting to a different, minority view. Over time, the majority will convert to the view of the minority, with increasing numbers of people switching from the majority position to the minority position. The more this happens, the faster the rate of conversion; this is called the snowball effect. The snowball effect explains how this change gathers momentum and the minority view becomes the majority view. Minority influence seems to have a permanent effect because people have been converted to their belief. This means they have privately and publicly changed their beliefs, compared to conformity and obedience where publicly they may comply but privately they reject such beliefs.

◆ Evaluation

Strength

✔ **Historical evidence to support minority influence.** There is real-life evidence to support minority influence. History is littered with minority individuals/groups that have challenged and questioned the values and norms of society. For example, Martin Luther King and Nelson Mandela, who led civil right movements against white apartheid, faced many years of being persecuted and criminalised for their beliefs. It could be argued their commitment to the cause led to the change in the majority view and subsequently led to the abolition of apartheid in America and South Africa.

Weaknesses

✗ **Minority group too radical to be effective.** One criticism is that if the minority message is too radical for the majority, then a change in behaviour or beliefs is unlikely to occur. For example, this can be seen in cases such as extreme political or religious groups that go against the values and norms of society. Furthermore, some critics argue that minority influence is also not successful due to consistency or flexibility. Often, change is the result of physical acts of protest such as the massive civil rights demonstrations by African Americans in the 1950s and 1960s and the uprising of eastern Europeans, who overthrew the communist regimes in 1989, rather than the processes of minority influence.

✗ **Biased sample.** A methodological weakness of Moscovici study is that he used just 172 female participants from America, which makes this a biased sample – only females and only Americans. This means that we are unable to generalise the results to male participants or other cultures, and therefore we cannot conclude that male participants would respond to minority influence in the same way, demonstrating the experiment has low population validity.

✗ **Artificial task.** A limitation of minority influence research is that many of the experimental tasks are artificial – such as the one by Moscovici whereby the participants had to identify the colour of a slide. The experimental task of identifying colour is not how minorities attempt to change the behaviour of majorities in real life. In cases such as jury decision-making and political campaigning, the outcomes are vastly more important, sometimes even literally a matter of life and death, and people may act differently under such issues. This means the findings of minority influence research lack external validity and are limited in what they can tell us about how minority influence works in real-life social situations.

✗ **When minority influence is not influential.** A limitation of minority influence research is that it may not be applied to the real world. Many studies make a clear distinction between a 'minority' group and a 'majority' group when investigating minority influence. However, in real life it is not as simple as this – it is not just about 'size' (number), there are other factors involved. For example, Latane and Wolf's (1981) social impact model found that the effect of 'consistency' may be limited to some degree. This because the minority effect can only occur under certain conditions, such as the size, strength (status and power), and immediacy (either physical or psychological closeness) of the majority. For example, if the size of the majority is large, it is less likely the minority will be able to exert pressure on them, which suggests that social change may be ineffective, regardless of the persistence of the minority. So, the research findings by Moscovici and other studies may lack ecological validity, because they do not take into consideration other factors that can influence people's behaviour.

Practice exam questions

1. Explain what is meant by the term 'minority influence'. **[2 marks]**

2. Name three behaviours that enable a minority to influence a majority. **[3 marks]**

3. Outline the procedure and findings of one study into minority influence. **[6 marks]**

4. Lucy wants to persuade her group of friends to stay in the UK for Christmas but her friends want to spend Christmas in Australia because the weather is hot.

   Briefly suggest how Lucy might use the three behaviours to persuade her friends to stay in the UK for Christmas.

5. Outline and evaluate research into minority influence. **[12 marks AS, 16 marks A-level]**

AQA specification: Social influence

- The role of social influence processes in social change.

◆ Key terms

- **Social change** is the process by which society changes beliefs, attitudes and behaviour over time to accept a new way of thinking and behaving that then becomes the accepted social norm. Social change refers to the changes that occur to society as a whole and not at an individual level. Examples are the suffragettes, the anti-apartheid movement in South Africa and gay rights.

- **Processes.** In the context of the AQA specification 'social influence processes in social change', 'processes' refers to the psychological mechanism that brings about social change. In other words, how does conformity work (i.e. what are the processes that bring about social change)? Or how does minority influence work to bring about a social change – what is the element that helps contribute to these changes?

◆ Introduction

Typically, an exam question will ask you to explain how social influence helps to bring about social change. In simple terms, you are asked to address the three areas of social influence you have studied:

- How does minority influence help bring about social change?

- How does obedience help bring about social change?

- How does conformity help bring about social change? (i.e. changes to society behaviour/attitude?)

We will look at each one in turn.

◆ Minority influence and social change

Moscovici (1980) and Nemeth (1986) showed how a minority group can bring about social changes at a societal level. Below are the 'conditions' (mechanisms) necessary for social change. Moscovici refers to this process as 'conversion'. We can roughly break this down into a number of stages by which minority influence leads to successful social change:

1. **Drawing attention to the issue.** A minority group often attempts to bring about a social change by drawing the attention of the majority group that holds a different view to the issue (e.g. the suffragette movement, Civil Rights movement). This can be done by educational campaigns, marches, and political and militant tactics to bring awareness to the public.

2. **Cognitive conflict.** Secondly, if the majority holds a different view, this creates cognitive conflict in the majority by making them think more deeply about the issues being challenged. For example, the suffragettes created a conflict between a patriarchal society that only allowed men to vote and the position advocated by the suffragettes – that women should be allowed to vote. This resulted in the majority thinking more deeply about the issues. This deep thinking is the first step in the process of changing views towards the minority view.

3. **Consistency.** Thirdly, minorities are more likely to be successful when they express their arguments consistently, with each other (synchronic consistency) and over time (diachronic consistency). This makes the majority reassess their belief and consider the issue more carefully.

4. **The argumentation principle.** Fourthly, if the minority's activities show commitment by putting themselves in harm's way or making personal sacrifices for their cause, their influence becomes even more augmented (even more 'powerful', known as the 'augmentation principle'). This means the majority will consider their views more seriously, as the minority are risking their lives for their cause.

5. **Snowball effect.** The minority influence will have a small effect on the majority, but over time, their influence will spread as more and more people begin to change their opinion. As more people change their view, this gathers momentum, leading to a 'tipping point', which leads to wide-scale social change. This process is called the 'snowball effect'.

6. **Social cryptomnesia.** Often, the majority knows that a social change has occurred, but they fail to know how it happened or the people who led this change. This is known as social cryptomnesia (e.g. suffragettes). Social change is a slow, gradual process. Through the process of the gradual snowball effect and people having no memory that social change has happened, gradually the minority turns into the majority. This benefits society, as it allows for change to occur in a gradual manner that is not too disruptive to social order, because rapid change may cause conflict within society and social change may not occur.

◆ Conformity and social change

- Research into conformity has also shown that the majority can influence social change. For example, the Asch line-judgement task showed the importance of normative social influence – people change their behaviour to fit in with the group norm (majority). This study has contributed to our understanding of social change because if people perceive something to be the norm, then they are more likely to alter their behaviour to fit that norm. For example, environmental and health campaigners exploit majority influence, by drawing attention to what other people are doing, giving the impression it is the norm, e.g. "Bin it – others do".

- Also, social change can occur through informational social influence, which is when a person conforms to gain knowledge, or because they believe that someone else is 'right'. For example, government, scientists and doctors who tell us that smoking or certain foods are bad for our health can bring about a social change for the majority of people.

- However, conformity (and obedience) generally serve to help maintain the existing social order in society. Therefore, as social change occurs, conformity/obedience will serve to oversee and uphold the new social order.

◆ Obedience and social change

- Governments, lawmakers or dictators use obedience to bring about social change through their use of legitimate power and authority. For example, changes to the laws will require certain behaviour to be adopted by the public. This leads to groups of people changing their behaviour because of the fear of punishment or consequences of not obeying. However, this does not mean that the people accept these changes, there may be public acceptance but private rejection.

- Milgram's research studies into obedience (e.g. the shock experiment study) led him to develop the agency state theory. The agency theory says that people will obey an authority when they believe that the authority will take responsibility for the consequences of their action. This theory may explain how obedience can cause a social change to occur. The theory explains, for example, why soldiers are willing to inflict unjust harm at the request of authority to bring about social changes - they are 'just following orders' from their superiors.

◆ Evaluation

Minority influence

Strengths

✔ **Real-life example.** There is real-life historical evidence that shows how social change happens through minority influence. History is littered with minority individuals/groups that have challenged and questioned the values and norms of society. For example, Martin Luther King and Nelson Mandela, who led civil right movements, remained consistent in their view against apartheid for many years, and made the personal sacrifice of being persecuted and criminalised for their beliefs (e.g. imprisonment). This commitment to the cause helped bring about social change – the abolition of apartheid in America and South Africa. Notably, these examples showed the conditions (consistency, commitment) and snow-ball effect (gradual change) required for such changes. Such real-life evidence gives validity to research into minority influence.

✔ **Supporting research evidence for minority influence**. There is supporting research evidence that minority influence can lead to social change. Moscovici et al. (1969) carried out an experiment to investigate if a minority of participants could influence a majority of participants to give an incorrect answer in a colour perception test. He found that if the minority views were consistent, they influenced the majority views. The relevance of this research into minority influence shows that consistency is an important factor to help bring about social change.

Weakness

✘ **When minority influence cannot bring about social change.** However, it could be argued that minority influence might not be totally effective if the message for change is too radical, which means social change is unlikely to occur. For example, extreme political or religious groups whose views are too extreme and go against the values and norms of society are unlikely to cause social change even if they use tactics of consistency and commitment. Kruglanski (2003) claimed that such minority groups have to resort to the use of 'terrorism acts' as a strategy to bring about social change.

Conformity

Strength

✔ **Research support that conformity can influence social change.** There is supporting research evidence that conformity can influence social change. Nolan et al. (2008) hung messages regarding reducing energy consumption on the doors of houses in California for one month, with the main message explaining that most people were already doing this. They found significant decreases in energy usage as a result. This study shows that when people think others are doing something, they are more likely to change their behaviour so as not to feel left out or isolated (normative influences). This shows that conformity can lead to social change.

Obedience

Strength

✔ **Agency theory has ecological validity.** There is ecological validity for the agency state theory bringing about social change. This theory explains how governments can abuse their power, by implementing blind obedience in soldiers to bring about devastating and destructive social changes. For example, the Nazi regime during World War II demanded military obedience from its soldiers to implement the 'Final Solution', which required them to carry out the systematic extermination of ethnic and social groups (e.g. Jews, homosexuals, gipsies, Africans) across Europe. This is a strength of the agency theory, because it explains how destructive social changes can occur when an obedient military, which knows what they are doing is wrong and yet continues to do so, claims that they are 'just following orders'. As a result, the explanatory power of the agency state theory has real-life applications as it is able to explain how destructive changes can occur.

General

Weakness

✘ **Methodological issues with studies.** Research studies by Asch, Milgram and Moscovici, which have shown how social influence can bring about social change, have been criticised because most of the evidence is based on experimental tasks that are artificial. For example, the study by Moscovici where the participants had to identify the colour of a slide does not reflect the social dynamic of the minority group's attempts to change the attitudes of the majority in real life. This means we need to be cautious of psychological explanation of how social influence processes contribute to social change, because the studies they are based on may not be completely valid.

Practice exam questions

1. Explain what is meant by 'social change' in reference to social change. **[2 marks]**

2. Using an example, outline how the role of social influence processes help contribute to social change. **[6 marks]**

3. How has social influence research helped our understanding of social change? **[4 marks]**

4. Explain how a minority can bring about social change. **[4 marks]**

5. Social attitudes towards eating have changed over the years. In the past, many people paid little attention to the type of food they ate, but in recent years people have become much more health-conscious. For example, when shopping in supermarkets many people now choose food products with less fat and reduced sugar.

   Using your knowledge of the psychology of social change, explain how this social change has occurred. **[6 marks]**

6. Discuss how social influence processes contribute to social change. **[12 marks AS, 16 marks A-level]**

7. Discuss research into the role of social influence processes in social change. **[12 marks AS, 16 marks A-level]**

Topic 2

Memory

AQA specification for Topic 2: Memory

- The multi-store model of memory, sensory register, short-term memory and long-term memory. Features of each store: coding, capacity and duration.

◆ Key terms for multi-store model

Before we look at the multi-store model of memory, it is important to become familiar with these key terms that make up the multi-store model.

- **Memory:** This is a mental process where information is coded, stored, and retrieved when requested. Memory can be distinguished between the sensory register (store of sensory memory), short-term memory (STM) and long-term memory (LTM). These storage systems differ in terms of how the information is coded, the amount stored (capacity) and the length of time held (duration).

- **Sensory register:** This storage system (also known as sensory memory or SM) receives information from the environment through the senses (e.g. eyes, ear, etc.), and has a very high capacity for storing information and a very limited duration of 250 milliseconds – 2 seconds.

- **Short-term memory (STM):** A storage system that holds information for a very short period of time. Duration of information in STM is approximately about 18-30 seconds if the information does not receive attention, e.g. it has not been rehearsed. STM also has a limited capacity, of approximately 7±2 digits.

- **Long-term memory (LTM):** A memory storage system where information is held for a long time, or permanently. LTM differs from STM, as it has potentially unlimited capacity and a duration that can last for a lifetime.

- **Multi-store model (MSM):** The multi-store model attempts to explain how information is processed, retained and recalled in the brain. It is called the multi-store model because it suggests that memory consists of several different mental storage systems. This model was developed by Richard Atkinson and Richard Shiffrin in 1968.

- **Coding:** This is the process of converting information into memory traces (code) so it can be stored and remembered successfully (e.g. like changing a Microsoft Word document file into a Portable Document Format (PDF).). Research suggests that the sensory register is modality-specific: information remains in the same form as it entered the senses. Short-term memory tends to code information acoustically (i.e. information is stored as sounds). In long-term memory, information tends to be coded semantically rather than acoustically.

- **Capacity:** This refers to how much information can be held in the memory store. The STM has a limited capacity, 7±2 digits or items, whereas the LTM has an unlimited capacity.

- **Duration:** This is the amount of time the information is held in the memory store. The STM has a very limited duration, up to 18-30 seconds, whereas the LTM has a very long duration, possibly permanent.

◆ Multi-store model

Atkinson and Shiffrin (1968) first proposed the multi-store model (MSM) to explain how information is processed and flows from one memory store to another.

This theory of memory suggests that information must be successfully processed through all three storage systems in order to be stored and recalled over long periods of time. According to this theory, SM, STM and LTM differ in terms of:

- **Encoding** – How information is converted as a code to be stored successfully in memory.
- **Duration** – The length of time the information is stored for.
- **Capacity** – The amount of information that is stored.

The three different memory storage systems in the MSM are:

Sensory Register [SR]	→	Short-term memory [STM]	→	Long-term memory [LTM]

◆ The sensory register

Information initially enters memory through the sensory register (also know as the sensory memory or SM). We hold an exact copy of what we saw or heard for a few seconds, or less, before it decays (fades). For example, if you look at an object such as a car and then close your eyes, you will see an image of the car for about half a second before it fades away.

Coding

- Atkinson and Shiffrin (1968) suggested that encoding of information in the SM is modality-specific, that is, information is stored in the way it is received. The main forms of modality-specific encoding are iconic storage (of visual memories) and echoic storage (of auditory memories). Information in the SM is retained in separate stores for a very brief time and then fades if we do not give it attention. If we do, then the information is transferred into the STM.

Capacity

- The amount of information stored in the SM is claimed to be very high because it needs to register virtually all the incoming information from the senses.

Duration

- Information is stored in the SM for the shortest time of any memory system in this theory, between 0.25 milliseconds and 2 seconds.

◆ Short-term memory

Once information is transferred from SM to STM, it is processed again. Psychologists have carried out numerous experiments to show how information is processed in STM.

Duration

- The STM store tends to encode information acoustically (as sound) even when the information is presented *visually*.

Capacity

- Research suggests that the amount of information that STM can hold is limited.

Duration

- Information cannot remain in the STM for very long without verbal rehearsal (without repeating it).

AN 'EYE' ON THE STUDY

Coding in STM
(Conrad, 1964)

In this laboratory experiment, participants were quickly **shown** a sequence of six consonant letters of the alphabet that were acoustically similar (they sounded the same, e.g. D, P, T, B, L, V) or acoustically dissimilar (such as K, Z, W, R, Y, F). The participants had to immediately write down as many letters as possible in the order they were given. Conrad found that people made more mistakes recalling the order of acoustically *similar* letters but, acoustically dissimilar letters were remembered better. This is because when the letters sounded similar, it was harder to remember which of the similar sounds came first, for example, B was mistaken for V or D because they all sound like 'ee'. This study supports the MSM because it shows that STM attempts to code information acoustically – even when it is presented **visually**. This is known as the acoustic similarity effect.

AN 'EYE' ON THE STUDY

Capacity in STM
(Jacobs, 1887)

In this laboratory experiment, the capacity of STM was tested using the serial digit span technique. Participants were presented with a sequence of digits (numbers) and were required to repeat them back in the same order. The participants had to repeat one, then two, then three digits, and so on. When they made a mistake, the experimenter assessed them on additional sequences of the longest length they had correctly recalled. If they recalled 4-5 sequences correctly, this was considered their "digit span". Jacobs found that the average adult digit span is between five and nine digits. This is supported by Miller (1956) who claimed that STM can hold 7 ± 2 digits or items (e.g. between five and nine), whether those items are numbers, letters, or words. He called this "the magic number seven plus or minus two". Miller also found that if we chunk (group) items together in a meaningful way, we can increase the amount of information we can store in our STM. For example, recalling the sequence 1 9 5 8 1 9 6 7 1 9 7 0 as 12 separate numbers would be challenging to most people, but chunked as three meaningful items, such as three dates (1958, 1967, 1970), the sequence could have meaning, for example, if the three chunks related to the birth dates of family members. In this way you can effectively remember 12 individual numbers, but if they were unrelated you could only recall 7 ± 2 of them. Furthermore, Simon (1974), found that participants tended to recall fewer chunks if the chunks themselves were larger, and could recall more, smaller chunks. This suggests that the amount of information in each *chunk size* can affect the overall capacity in STM.

Duration in STM
(Peterson and Peterson, 1959)

This experiment investigated how long information remains in STM without verbal rehearsal (without repeating it). In a laboratory experiment, 24 students were briefly presented with a nonsense trigram (e.g. three letters such as CLD, NWQ), immediately followed by a three-digit number (e.g. 882). They were then asked to count backwards in threes from the specified number (e.g. 882, 879, 876) until they were told to stop. This was to prevent them from repeating the three letters (maintenance rehearsal). After intervals of 3, 6, 9, 12, 15 or 18 seconds, participants were asked to recall the nonsense trigram in the correct order. They found that participants were able to correctly recall over 80% of the trigrams after a 3-second interval and 50% of them after a 6-second interval. After 18 seconds, fewer than 10% of trigrams were recalled correctly. Based on these results, Peterson and Peterson suggested that if verbal rehearsal is prevented, information in STM rapidly fades, and almost completely by 18 seconds. This study supports the MSM because it shows that memory is made up of separate memory stores. STM has a limited duration, while LTM arguably has an unlimited duration. This method of investigating duration is referred to as the Brown–Peterson technique.

◆ Long-term memory

How do we remember information from the past if our STM has a limited capacity and duration? If the information in our STM is acted on, through maintenance rehearsal (repeating) for long enough, then the information can be transferred into our LTM. A more effective way of transferring information into LTM is through elaborative rehearsal, encoding information semantically (see Figure 4 on page 52). In terms of encoding, capacity and duration, LTM differs from STM in the following ways:

Coding

- Information from STM entering LTM tends to be transferred semantically (making the information meaningful) rather than acoustically. However, evidence has shown that LTM can also store information acoustically and in a visual form (Paivio, 1986).

Capacity

- Information storage in LTM seems to be unlimited, but it is very difficult, perhaps impossible, to test the true capacity of LTM using experimental methods.

Duration

Information in the LTM can potentially last a whole lifetime. See the study below.

AN 'EYE' ON THE STUDY

Capacity in LTM
(Bahrick et al., 1975)

Bahrick et al. (1975) conducted a natural experiment to investigate how long information is held in LTM. This study used a sample of nearly 400 Americans who all attended the same high school and had left between 3 months and 48 years ago (the age of ex-students varied between 17 years to 74 years). The students were shown photographs from their high-school yearbook. The participants were organised into two groups:

- **Recall group** – The participants carried out a free recall test in which they were asked to remember and list as many names of their ex-classmates as possible.

- **Recognition group** – The participants were given a name-matching recognition test. They were given the names of their ex-classmates and asked to match the names with the photos.

Bahrick et al. found that participants in the recognition group were 90% correct even 15 years after graduation. Those who had graduated 48 years before accurately matched 80% of the names to faces. In the recall group, memory performance was significantly worse: 60% correct after 15 years and only 30% after 48 years. These results provide strong evidence that information is held in LTM for a very long time. It also shows that there is some memory loss over time, especially when attempting to freely recall information (such as remembering names). However, memory recall is better when presented with a visual memory cue (as demonstrated by the photo recognition test).

According to Atkinson and Shiffrin (1968), the multi-store model consists of three memory stores: the sensory register (also known as sensory memory or SM), short-term (STM) and long-term memory (LTM). Their model explains how information is processed and transferred from one store to another. This process also tells us how information is remembered and forgotten.

- In SM, encoding of information tends to be modality-specific (stored in the way format it is received). The SM has unlimited capacity, but a limited duration (250 milliseconds to 2 seconds) before it fades out. Information constantly enters the SM for a very brief amount of time and quickly fades if attention is not given to it. If attention is directed toward the information, it is then transferred to short-term memory STM. This is the first process step of remembering encoding information.

- For information to be successfully transferred from SM to STM it needs to be encoded acoustically, turning images or written words into a verbal code (sound). To prevent information fading in STM, a process of maintenance (verbal) rehearsal (verbal rehearsal) is needed. If it is not encoded correctly or verbally rehearsed sufficiently, the information will quickly fade away, often within 18 seconds or so, showing that STM has a limited duration. This can be seen as the second process step of remembering encoding for a short period of time. Research evidence also suggests that STM has a limited capacity of between five and nine items of information, which. This can be increased by breaking the information into meaningful chunks.

- Information can be transferred to LTM if it has been sufficiently rehearsed/repeated the information in STM has been continuously rehearsed. It can also be transferred by elaborative rehearsal, where the information is remembered in a meaningful way. This is the final stage step of remembering encoding information for a long period of time. Evidence also shows that, in the absence of injury or disease, LTM has unlimited capacity and unlimited duration of up to a lifetime.

Figure 4: Maintenance rehearsal

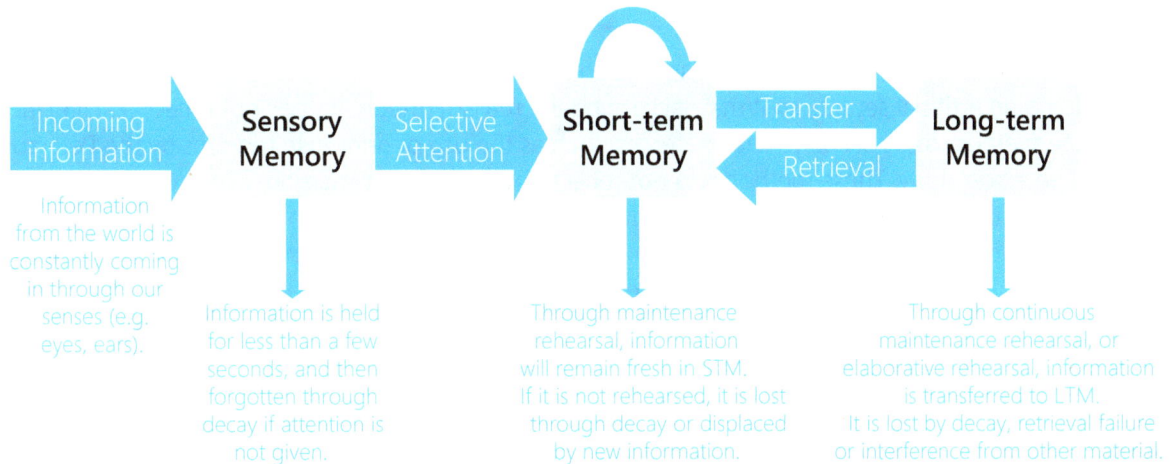

| | Incoming information | | Sensory Memory | | Selective Attention | | Short-term Memory | Transfer / Retrieval | Long-term Memory |

Incoming information — Information from the world is constantly coming in through our senses (e.g. eyes, ears).

Sensory Memory — Information is held for less than a few seconds, and then forgotten through decay if attention is not given.

Short-term Memory — Through maintenance rehearsal, information will remain fresh in STM. If it is not rehearsed, it is lost through decay or displaced by new information.

Long-term Memory — Through continuous maintenance rehearsal, or elaborative rehearsal, information is transferred to LTM. It is lost by decay, retrieval failure or interference from other material.

Differences between the memory stores

Memory	Encoding	Capacity	Duration
SM	Modality-specific	Very large	Very brief Less than 2 seconds
STM	Acoustic (sound) Acoustic similarity effect *(Conrad, 1964)*	Limited (5–9 items) Serial digit span technique *(Jacobs, 1887)* Chunking 7 ± 2 *(Miller, 1959)*	Limited Approx. 18 seconds *(Peterson and Peterson, 1959)*
LTM	Semantic (meaning)	Unlimited	Unlimited High school study *Bahrick et al. (1975)*

◆ Evaluation

Strengths

✔ **Controlled experiments.** A strength of the MSM is that controlled laboratory studies (e.g. Peterson and Peterson) on capacity, duration, and coding, support the existence of separate short and long-term stores, which make up the MSM. Furthermore, neuroimaging studies have also demonstrated a difference between STM and LTM. For example, Beardsley (1997) found that the prefrontal cortex is active during STM tasks, but not during LTM tasks, and Squire et al. (1992) found the hippocampus is active when LTM is engaged.

✔ **Study to support STM and LTM are different memory stores.** The MSM is further supported by research showing STM and LTM are separate. For example, Conrad (1966) found that we tend to mix up words that sound similar when using STM. We also mix up words that have similar meanings when we use our long-term memory. This clearly shows that coding in STM is acoustic and in LTM it is semantic. This supports the MSM's view that these two memory stores are separate and independent.

Weaknesses

✗ **Low ecological validity.** Research evidence to support the MSM is based on laboratory experiments, which is an artificial setting, so it may lack mundane realism (that is, it does not reflect real life). Some of the memory tasks used artificial materials, such as the use of nonsense trigrams by the Peterson and Peterson study. These methods do not reflect how we use our memory in our day-to-day real life. The participants may have found this activity meaningless and may not have performed as well as they might have if the experiment was something they could relate to. In everyday life, we form memories related to all sorts of useful things – people's faces, their names, facts, places, etc. Research findings may reflect how memory works with meaningless material in laboratory testing but may not reflect how memory works in everyday life. Therefore, although there is evidence for the MSM, it mainly comes from artificial environments and may not stand true in the real world.

✗ **Elaborative rehearsal more effective than maintenance rehearsal.** A further criticism of the MSM is that it suggests that maintenance rehearsal determines the likelihood that the information will pass into the LTM. However, Craik and Watkins (1973) suggest that elaborative rehearsal is more effective in transferring information from the STM to the LTM. This is because the information that is processed more deeply/richly is more memorable than facts that are just repeated (maintenance rehearsal). Furthermore, a study by Tulving (1967) found that maintenance rehearsal is not necessary to transfer information to LTM. Overall, rehearsal in STM may be helpful but not essential to transfer information to LTM, and making links with existing knowledge is a more effective method.

✗ **Too simplistic.** A criticism of the MSM is that it is too simplistic. For example, the MSM oversimplifies LTM by saying it is a single unitary store; however, research shows that there are different storage systems within LTM, and each behaves differently. For instance, there are storage systems for procedural memories (e.g. how to ride a bike), semantic memories (e.g. the capital of France), and episodic memories (e.g. your eighth birthday party). This shows that the MSM is limited because it does not reflect these different types of LTM.

Practice exam questions

1. Explain what is meant by the terms 'encoding', 'capacity' and 'duration'. **[2 marks + 2 marks + 2 marks]**

2. Describe two differences between short-term and long-term memory. **[2 marks + 2 marks]**

3. Explain one strength of the multi-store model of memory. **[3 marks]**

4. Explain two weaknesses of the multi-store model of memory. **[3 marks + 3 marks]**

5. Describe one or more studies that investigated short-term memory. **[6 marks]**

6. Describe one or more studies that investigated long-term memory. **[6 marks]**

7. Tom was getting ready to go to the supermarket to shop for his mum. His older brother Adam shouted out 'Don't forget to buy Benny's chocolate chip cookies, otherwise, you're dead, you little squirt!' On his way to the shops, Tom kept on repeating to himself 'Benny's chocolate chip cookies'. At the pay counter, Tom just remembered that Adam also wanted something – but he could not for the life of him remember what it was! Using your knowledge of what you have learnt about the multi-store model, explain why the above scenario would be used to criticise the model. **[4 marks]**

8. Outline and evaluate the multi-store model of memory. **[12 marks AS, 16 marks A-level]**

AQA specification for Topic 2: Memory

- Types of long-term memory: episodic, semantic, procedural.

◆ Types of long-term memory

The multi-store model and working memory model are primarily explanations of how short-term memory works, and say very little about long-term memory (LTM). Endel Tulving, a cognitive psychologist, was critical of the multi-store model view of LTM as too simplistic and inflexible. In 1985, Tulving proposed that there were three LTM stores called episodic memory, semantic memory and procedural memory.

Episodic LTM

- Tulving first described episodic long-term memory in 1972. Episodic LTM are memories of your personal life events/experiences. This is also called autobiographical memory. One example would be when you remember what happened on the first day at school, university or your friend's wedding. Episodic memory allows you to travel mentally back in time and experience the event all over again.

- Episodic memories are 'time-stamped', in other words, you remember the 'time' this specific event happened.

- Each episode often contains several elements of what occurred during the event – people and places, objects, behaviours and associated emotions – all linked to form one single 'episode'. For example, imagine that you are having a conversation with a friend about a concert that you attended last week. You tell her the name of the artist, the time of the concert, the location of the concert, and how you enjoyed watching the singer perform her latest hits. The information is stored in your episodic LTM. Episodic memory does not usually start to function until around age four, explaining why the majority of people do not have personal memories before this age.

- The prefrontal cortex is associated with the initial coding of episodic memories. Memories of the different aspects of the event are located in the different areas of the brain but are connected together in the hippocampus to create a memory of an episode.

Sematic LTM

- Sematic LTM contains all learned knowledge (e.g. facts, concepts, meanings, and functions). It has been likened to an encyclopaedia or dictionary. Examples of semantic LTM are the names of objects/people, the meaning of words, the taste of food, the function of objects such as what a screwdriver does.

- Semantic memories are not 'time-stamped', in other words, we do not remember where we first learnt them. Semantic knowledge is less personal and not based on experiences and is more about the facts we all share about the world. Semantic memories are linked to episodic memories, as new knowledge tends to be learned from experiences, and therefore, episodic memories underpin semantic memories. However, over time, there will be a gradual move from episodic memory to semantic memory with knowledge becoming divorced from the events/experiences it was learned from.

- There is controversy over which part of the brain is responsible for semantic LTM. Some evidence suggests it is mainly related to the prefrontal cortex/hippocampus, while others believe that semantic knowledge is widely distributed across all brain areas.

Procedural LTM

- Procedural memory is a memory store of how to do things (e.g. motor skills/actions/muscle memories). As the name implies, procedural memory stores information on how to perform certain procedures, such as walking, talking, or driving a car. Procedural LTM does not involve conscious thought or effort to recall these things and allows people to simultaneously perform other cognitive tasks at the same time, for example, being able to drive and change gear without actively recalling the procedure and also talking to a friend at the same time.

- Procedural memories are encoded and stored by the cerebellum, prefrontal cortex and motor cortex, which are all engaged early in learning motor skills. Procedural memories do not appear to involve the hippocampus.

◆ Evaluation

Strengths

✔ **Research evidence for different types of LTM.** Much of this research has been done by looking at adults with specific brain injuries and associated memory changes. One example is Clive Wearing, who suffered brain damage from a virus that made his brain swell. Following this infection, Wearing could not encode any new personal information – he was permanently trapped in 1985. However, his procedural and semantic memory were still fully intact, so he could still play the piano to concert hall standard. This case study is a strength of Tulving's research into LTM because it suggests that there are different memory stores. One store can be damaged (in this case, Clive's episodic memory) but leave the others unaffected (procedural and semantic). This gives credibility to Tulving's research and theories of multiple types of LTM.

✔ **Evidence for neuroimaging.** Further strength for the explanations into different types of LTM is that they are supported by strong empirical evidence from neuroimaging studies. For example, in a study by Tulving et al. (1994), participants performed various memory tasks while their brain activity was scanned using a positron emission tomography (PET) scanner. They found that the episodic and semantic memory tasks both activated an area of the brain known as the prefrontal cortex. This area is divided into two, with one on each side (hemisphere) of the brain. The left prefrontal cortex was active in recalled semantic memories and the right was active in recalled episodic memories. These findings provide neuroanatomical support to the theory that LTM has different stores for multiple types of information, and those stores may be in physically different areas of the brain.

Weaknesses

✗ **Low population validity.** A weakness of the research that supports the different types of LTM is that it has low population validity. This is because a large body of supporting evidence is based on case studies of patients with brain damage. This is a criticism because the sample used in this research, such as Clive Wearing, may not be representative of the wider population. For example, just because Clive Wearing's, memory was selectively damaged doesn't mean that other people who suffer brain damage in the same areas of the brain would present with the same memory problems. Before his illness, Clive Wearing was a highly intelligent, articulate and professional man in his early 40's. Therefore, we cannot generalise the findings of this case study to the wider population. As a result, this reduces the credibility of Tulving's research evidence to support the different types of LTM.

✗ **How different are episodic and semantic memories?** A further criticism is that episodic and semantic memories may not be totally distinct memory types. Although research suggests different brain areas for semantic and episodic memories, there is a lot of overlap between the two memory systems. This is because many semantic memories originate as an episodic memory. This is an issue because we cannot be sure that a transformation of an episodic memory into semantic means a change in a different type of memory system. Cohen and Squire (1980) argued that episodic and semantic memories are stored together in one LTM store called declarative memory (memories that can be consciously recalled). Cohen and Squire do agree that procedural memory is a distinctly different kind of memory to semantic/episodic and call it non-declarative memory. It is important to get the distinction between semantic and episodic memories right because the way we define them influences how memory studies are researched.

Practice exam questions

1. Using an example, explain what is meant by the term 'episodic memory'. **[2 marks]**

2. Using an example, explain what is meant by the term 'semantic memory'. **[2 marks]**

3. Using an example, explain what is meant by the term 'procedural memory'. **[2 marks]**

4. Two types of long-term memory are procedural memory and episodic memory. Explain two differences between procedural memory and episodic memory. **[4 marks]**

5. Outline and evaluate types of long-term memory. **[12 marks AS, 16 marks A-level]**

AQA specification for Topic 2: Memory

- The working memory model: central executive, phonological loop, visuo-spatial sketchpad and episodic buffer. Features of the model: coding and capacity.

◆ Key term

- Working memory model (WMM): Baddeley and Hitch's (1974) working memory model is an attempt to explain the structure and function of memory. The model consists of four components: the central executive, the phonological loop system, the visuo-spatial sketchpad and the episodic buffer. The model describes how each component processes and stores different types of information.

◆ Working memory model

- Baddeley and Hitch (1974) proposed an alternative explanation of memory (from the multi-store model or MSM), called the working memory model (WMM). Rather than viewing STM as a single passive storage system holding and passing information to LTM (as suggested by MSM), these authors proposed a system where information is analysed, evaluated, and processed. So in this sense, the information is being 'worked on', hence the working memory model. The WMM consists of four systems (components), each dealing with different types of information:

  - Central executive (allocates and controls the flow of information)

  - Phonological loop (deals with sound information)

  - Visuo-spatial sketchpad (deals with visual information)

  - Episodic buffer (blends information together from the other slave systems).

Figure 5: Basic diagram of the working memory model

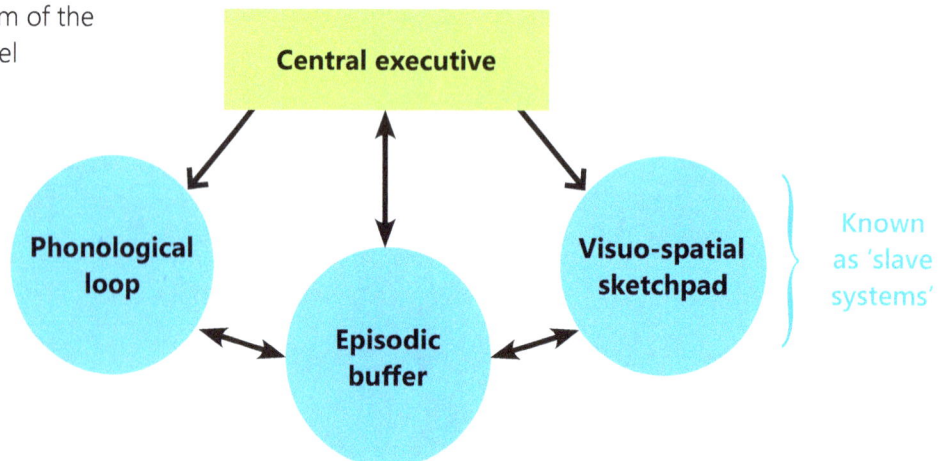

Known as 'slave systems'

◆ The central executive

- The central executive is in overall charge (hence 'executive') of the other three 'slave systems'; the phonological loop, visuo-spatial sketchpad and episodic buffer. Some of the functions that the central executive carries out are:

  - Allocation: It decides which information should receive attention and allocates the information to an appropriate slave system to be processed.

- Control: It controls the flow of information to and from the slave systems and LTM and blends the information from the phonological loop and visuospatial sketchpad so our memories are integrated (see 'Episodic buffer' on page XX).

- Processes: It can process information in any sensory modality (any senses) and from different types of cognitive tasks (e.g. mental arithmetic, reasoning, recollection of events from LTM, etc.). Evidence suggests that information can fade quickly (suggesting a limited duration) and the central executive cannot deal with a large amount of information (suggesting a limited capacity).

◆ Phonological loop

- The phonological loop is a system that receives, holds and processes phonological material (sound information). The phonological loop can be further subdivided into the phonological store and the articulatory loop, which each have a different function.

  - The phonological store is referred to as the 'inner ear'. It is a storage system for receiving and holding verbal/sound information for a short while.

  - The articulatory control process is referred to as the 'inner voice'. It performs two main functions:

1. Production of sound: First, the articulatory loop helps with the creation of sound by converting written information into a sound format, for example, it converts the inner voice we create when reading from a book silently. Once a sound is created, this is then deposited in the phonological store.

2. Rehearsal: Second, the articulatory control process allows us to rehearse the sound information held in the phonological store to prevent it from decaying. If rehearsal is continuous, the sound information will be transferred into LTM. Rehearsal can either happen by repeating the information out loud or through sub-vocal rehearsal. This is where our inner voice silently repeats the information before saying it out loud, for example, silently repeating a telephone number you have just heard, whilst looking for a pen and paper to write it down. Evidence suggests that the duration and capacity of the phonological loop are very limited; it can only hold information that can be said (or rehearsed) in 2 seconds, otherwise, the information will decay.

◆ Visuo-spatial sketchpad

- The visuo-spatial sketchpad is known as the 'inner eye' and deals with visual and spatial information (e.g. objects, places, dimensions). Mental images are created or retrieved from the LTM. The visuo-spatial sketchpad can also process verbal or sound information by converting it into a mental image (e.g. formulating mental images of characters when reading a book). The 'spatial' aspect means we can 'visualise' the distance or layout of mental images. For example, if you attempt to explain to your friend the direction to your home from school, your friend will manipulate the layout, spaces, and distances of images from the geographical environment.

◆ Episodic buffer

- The working memory model could not adequately explain how we are able to remember events as a single unified representation (combining visual, spatial and sound information), as none of the slave systems had the ability to do this. So, Baddeley (2000) modified the WMM to include an additional memory slave system called the episodic buffer. This is a temporary storage system, which interacts with the other components by manipulating and combining material from the central executive, the phonological loop, the visual-spatial sketchpad and LTM to create a single integrated representation (hence 'episode'). For example, remembering a particular movie scene is a single episode created from a range of information. (See Figure 6 below for a summary of the WMM, including the episodic buffer.)

Figure 6: A summary of the working memory model.

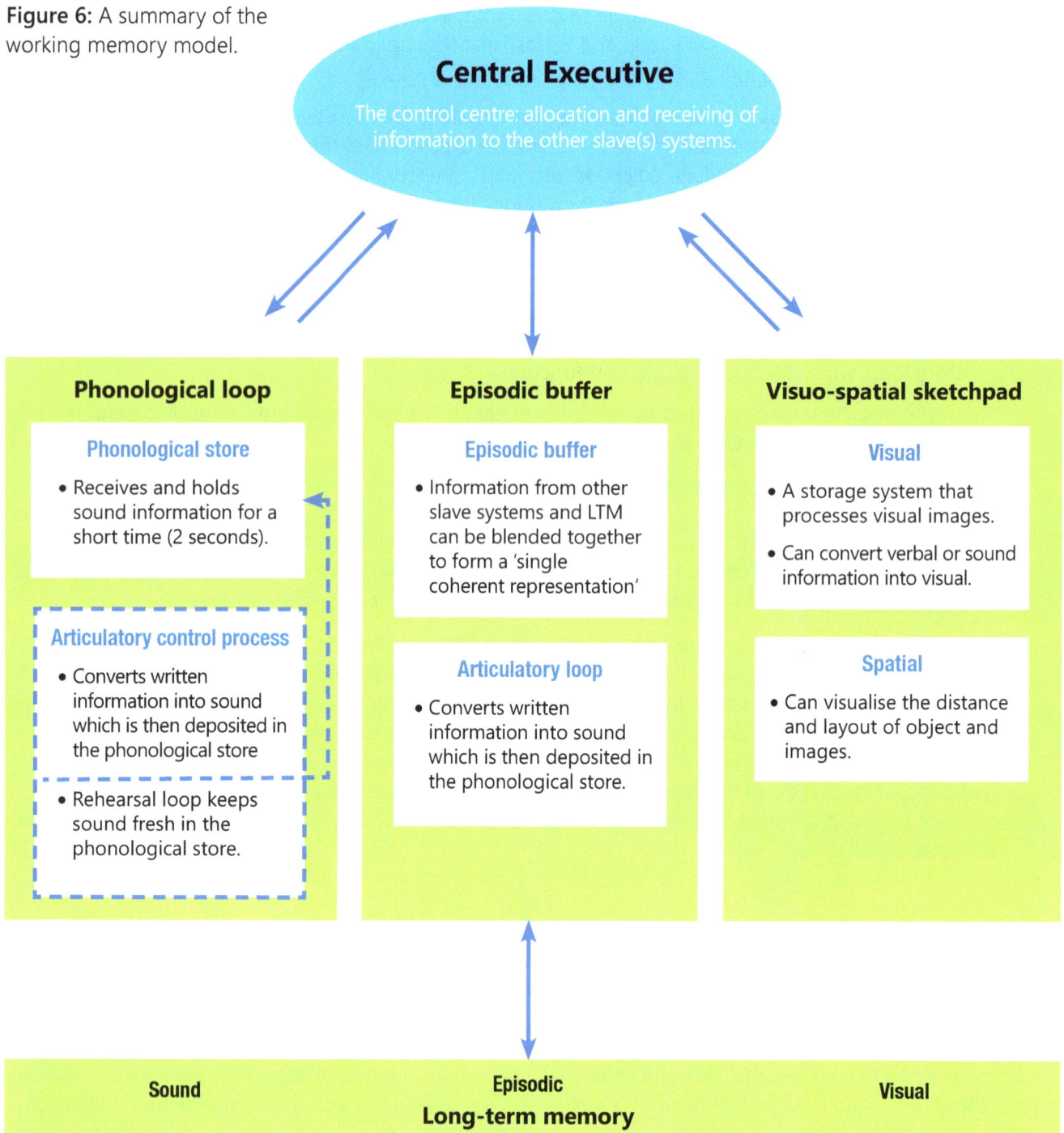

Central Executive
The control centre: allocation and receiving of information to the other slave(s) systems.

Phonological loop

Phonological store
- Receives and holds sound information for a short time (2 seconds).

Articulatory control process
- Converts written information into sound which is then deposited in the phonological store
- Rehearsal loop keeps sound fresh in the phonological store.

Episodic buffer

Episodic buffer
- Information from other slave systems and LTM can be blended together to form a 'single coherent representation'

Articulatory loop
- Converts written information into sound which is then deposited in the phonological store.

Visuo-spatial sketchpad

Visual
- A storage system that processes visual images.
- Can convert verbal or sound information into visual.

Spatial
- Can visualise the distance and layout of object and images.

Sound	Episodic	Visual
	Long-term memory	

◆ Evaluation

Strengths

✔ **A detailed explanation.** The working memory model (WMM) can offer a more detailed explanation of how memory works than the multi-store model (MSM). The WMM has shown memory to be a more complex processing system capable of performing more than one function at the same time, whereas the MSM suggests that information enters STM and then transfers to LTM. Therefore, the WMM theory is more complex and nuanced.

✔ **Phonological loop.** Baddeley et al. (1975) provided evidence for the phonological loop in their word-length-effect experiment. They found that, on average, participants can recall lists of words more effectively if the words are short (e.g. sun, belt), rather than long (e.g. aluminium, university). This supports the theory of articulatory loop because it shows it has a limited duration/capacity. We can rehearse more short words in a period of time than long words, meaning we remember more short than longer words. The longer words cannot be rehearsed as easily by the phonological loop because they take more space/time.

✔ **Visuo-spatial sketchpad.** Baddeley et al. (1973) provided evidence for the visuo-spatial sketchpad. Participants were asked to carry out a visual tracking task (following a moving spot of light with a pointer) at the same time as completing an imaginary visual task requiring them to describe all the angles in capital block letter such as 'F', 'E', etc. Starting at the bottom-left corner of each letter, participants were asked to confirm 'yes' or 'no', according to whether each right angle of the letter touched the top or bottom line of the letter. The participants found carrying out these tasks very difficult because both tasks required the use of the visuo-spatial sketchpad, hence the poor performance. However, when the participants performed a list of verbal reasoning tasks where they had to answer true or false as quickly as possible (e.g. B is followed by A – *true or false*, A follows B – *true or false*) and a visual tracking task; they found no difficulty performing both tasks at the same time. This is because they had to use different slave systems (visual and verbal). This supports the WMM as it shows that memory has different components for different types of memory tasks.

✔ **Support from brain-imaging studies.** A further strength of the model is support from neuroimaging studies. These studies have suggested that different parts of working memory use different areas of the brain. For example, tasks involving the phonological loop show activation of Wernicke's area of the brain, which deals with processing speech/sound. Articulatory processing tasks activate Broca's area, which deals with speech production. Visuo-spatial sketchpad tasks activate the occipital lobe, which processes visual information. Such experimental tasks support the view that there are separate systems as suggested by the WMM.

Weaknesses

✘ **Low internal validity.** The Baddeley et al. (1975) word-length-effect study has been criticised for low internal validity. It is possible that the participants would have been more familiar with the short words, but not so familiar with the longer words, which may explain why participants found it harder to recall longer words and easier to recall shorter words. Therefore, caution is needed when generalising laboratory findings to the real world with regards to memory processing.

✘ **No discussion of LTM.** The WMM tells us very little about how the working memory system relates to the long-term storage of information. This means the WMM is limited as it only gives us a partial explanation of how memory works.

✗ **Central executive function is vague.** A limitation of the WMM is that there is still little real understanding of the role and function of the central executive, which is probably the most crucial part of the model. Exactly what it does and how it works, remains speculative. Part of the reason is that there is little experimental support to test the functionalities of the central executive. For example, the central executive is said to have limited capacity, but the actual capacity has not been established. Eysenck (1986) suggested that the central executive might really be a single STM store on its own. Again, the model can only give a partial explanation of memory because it cannot explain adequately how the central executive operates.

Practice exam questions

1. Outline the main features of the working memory model.   **[6 marks]**

2. Explain two strengths of the working memory model.   **[2+2 marks]**

3. Explain two weaknesses of the working memory model.   **[2+2 marks]**

4. Alan is attempting to read the newspaper but, at the same time, he is listening to his wife moaning on the phone to his sister about his attitude to household duties. Alan finds that he can't really remember much of what he has just read from the newspaper or his wife's conversation.

   A. Using your knowledge of the working memory model, explain why Alan found it difficult to recall any of the information.   **[5 marks]**

5. Ben is drawing his favourite cartoon character from his comic book and listening to his teacher Mrs Annabel talk at the same time. Mrs Annabel soon realises what Ben is doing and immediately tells him off. To prove a point that he was not paying attention, she asks him to recall what she has just been saying. She is surprised to find that Ben can recall most of what she was just talking about.

   B. Using the working memory model, explain why Ben's memory recall is quite impressive.   **[5 marks]**

3. Describe the working memory model.   **[12 marks AS, 16 marks A-level]**

AQA specification for Topic 2: Memory

- Explanations for forgetting: proactive and retroactive interference and retrieval failure due to the absence of cues.

◆ Explanations for forgetting

Forgetting can be defined as the inability to recall information. Experimental research suggests that forgetting in LTM is mainly due to two explanations: interference theory and retrieval failure theory.

◆ Interference theory

- **Interference theory.** According to the interference theory, forgetting occurs because two sets of information that are relatively similar become confused (i.e. interfere) with each other, resulting in forgetting or distorting of one or both. The more similar the information is, the more likely interference will occur. There are two types of interference that have been found.

- **Proactive interference:** Proactive interference is when past information interferes with new information, causing us to forget or poorly recall the new information. For example:
  - If you change your telephone number, every time you attempt to recall the new number, the old number will disrupt your attempts.
  - A teacher confuses the names of his past psychology students with his current class. We call a new boyfriend by an old boyfriend's name.

- **Retroactive interference:** Retroactive interference is when new information interferes with previously learned information, causing us to forget or poorly recall the information already learned. For example:
  - A student understood a psychology concept last week but can no longer understand the concept correctly, because he confuses it with another, newer concept studied since that time.
  - A teacher learns the names of his new psychology class but cannot remember the names of his previous students.

◆ Retrieval failure theory

- **Retrieval failure theory.** According to this theory, forgetting in LTM is mainly due to retrieval failure. That is when information is stored in LTM but is not accessible because of the absence of, or insufficient, appropriate cues (clues) to trigger our memory.

- Tulving and Thomson (1973) proposed that memory recall is most effective if the cues that were present at encoding (learning) are also present at the time of retrieval. They proposed the encoding specificity principle, which states that when new information is encoded (learned), the associated cues are also stored in memory. If these cues are not available at the time of recall, it may appear as if you have forgotten the information, but this is due to retrieval failure – the lack of cues means the information cannot be triggered. According to the encoding specificity principle, the cue doesn't have to be exactly the same, but the closer the cue it is to the original item when it was initially encoded, then the more likely we will remember the information. There is evidence that cues which been explicitly or implicitly encoded at the time of learning often have a meaningful connection to the learning material. For example, the cue 'magic 7+/- 2' may lead you to recall all sorts of information about the capacity of short-term memory.

- Other cues can also be encoded at the time of learning but not in a meaningful way; this is as a *context-dependent failure* and *state-dependent failure*.

  - **Context-dependent failure.** Context-dependent failure states that forgetting is more likely to occur when the external/environment cues (e.g. the location, weather, people) are different at recall from the time of encoding. We do not have the benefit of the familiar location acting as a cue, therefore, we are less likely to recall the material. One example is getting a lower score in a test when sitting in an unfamiliar room than when sitting the test in your normal room.

  - **State-dependent failure.** State-dependent failure suggests that forgetting is more likely to occur when internal cues, that is the individual internal psychological state of mind (e.g. feeling upset, happy, drunk, etc.) are dissimilar at recall to when information was initially encoded. In other words, we need to be in a similar state or mood when attempting to recall information, as when we first learnt that information. For example, Goodwin et al. (1969) found that heavy drinkers who learn things in drunken states are more likely to recall them in a drunken state than if they were sober.

◆ Evaluation

Interference theory

Strength

✔ **Research evidence for proactive interference.** There is experimental research to support the proactive interference explanation for forgetting. Keppel and Underwood (1962) carried out an experiment similar to the Peterson and Peterson (1959) duration study. They found that when participants were presented with a list of meaningless three-letter consonant trigrams (e.g. XVW) that the students had previously learned, the more likely they were to forget the new task (recalling a nonsense syllable). This demonstrates that proactive interference occurred: a memory for the earlier consonants, which had transferred to LTM, was interfering with the memory for new consonants, due to the similarity of the information presented.

✔ **Real-life evidence for retroactive inference theory.** There is experimental research to support the retroactive interference explanation for forgetting. McGeogh and McDonald (1931) gave participants lists of words to learn until they could recall them with 100% accuracy. After 10 minutes, they were then given a new list to learn. The new material varied in the degree to which it was similar to the old original words, depending on the group.

> Group 1 – words had the same meanings as the originals.
>
> Group 2 – words had opposite meanings to the originals.
>
> Group 3 – words unrelated to the original ones.
>
> Group 4 – nonsense syllables.
>
> Group 5 – three-digit numbers.
>
> Group 6 – no new list.

After learning both lists, the participants were tested on their recall of the first list. They found that the performance of the original words depended on the nature of the second list. The recall was worse in Group 1 than Group 5. This shows that retroactive interference affected recall, as it indicates that the more similar the later word, the more of the original information participants would forget.

Weaknesses

✗ **Contradictory research evidence.** A limitation of the interference explanation is that there is opposing research evidence. Tulving and Psotka (1971) gave participants five lists to remember. Each list contained 24 words and was organised by category (e.g. fruits, animals, etc.). Recall was about 70% for the first list, but this fell as each additional list was learned, presumably due to interference. However, when the participants were given a cued recall test (told the names of the categories), recall rose again to about 70%. This shows that the memories of the words were stored in LTM, but interference prevented access to them. When given a cue, participants found it easier to access the forgotten words.

✗ **Low ecological validity.** One weakness of the theory of interference is that research into it has low ecological validity. For example, because the majority of the research was carried out in a lab, the materials used were usually lists of words, with a task attached to learn them. This material differs from things we try to learn every day e.g. people's faces, their birthdays, class information for an exam. This is an issue because these materials are artificial compared to everyday life, meaning that it is difficult to generalise these findings to real life. This manipulation of variables makes interference much more likely to occur in a lab. As a result, the ecological validity of these pieces of research is questioned, which in turn casts doubt over the explanatory power of interference for forgetting in everyday life.

✗ **Information similar?** Another criticism of interference theory is that it only really explains forgetting when two sets of information are similar, for example when someone is simultaneously learning two languages, such as French and Spanish. This does not happen very often and so interference cannot explain forgetting in the majority of real-life situations when information is not similar.

Retrieval failure theory

Strengths

✓ **Supporting research evidence.** A strength of retrieval failure theory is that it has supporting research evidence. Godden & Baddeley (1975) asked underwater divers to learn and recall a list of words. The conditions were:

Group 1: Learn on land – recall on land.

Group 2: Learn on land – recall underwater.

Group 3: Learn underwater – recall on land.

Group 4: Learn underwater – recall underwater.

Groups 1 and 4 had matching encoding and recall conditions, and Groups 2 and 3 had non-matching conditions. The authors found that recall was 40% lower in the non-matching environmental context conditions (Groups 2 and 3), than when the environment did match (Groups 1 and 4). This study showed that context-dependent forgetting occurred because the information was not accessible – participants forgot when context at recall did not match context at learning.

✔ **Evidence from experimental is reliable.** A further strength of retrieval failure is that the research on which it is based is repeatable. Research into the nature of forgetting in LTM is carried out in a laboratory environment where the effects of extraneous variables can be controlled. As a result, this type of research is scientific and the results of such research when repeated are likely to be the same. This increases the credibility of the retrieval failure as a valid explanation for forgetting LTM.

Weaknesses

✗ **Contradictory evidence.** A weakness of retrieval failure as an explanation for forgetting is that there is contradictory evidence. Baddeley (1997) argued that the actual ability of the 'context' to influence recall is not very strong, especially in real life. Baddeley argued that the different contexts have to be very different before they can have an impact (e.g. land versus underwater as an extreme example). Learning something in one room then recalling it another is unlikely to result in much forgetting because these environments are not sufficiently different. This is a weakness because it means that the real-life examples of retrieval failure due to contextual cues don't actually explain all instances of forgetting. As a consequence of this argument, the overall credibility of the theory of retrieval failure theory is weakened.

✗ **Laboratory experiments are artificial**. A weakness of retrieval failure theory is that most of the research has been carried out in laboratory environments. Such situations are not similar to a real-life experience of memory and thus may be low in ecological validity. For example, procedural memories (knowing how to do things) are not related to cue-dependent recall, because you can ride a bike or drive a car even in a different context to where you first learned.

Practice exam questions

1. Outline one explanation of forgetting in long-term memory. **[3 marks]**

2. Choose one study in which the effects of interference were investigated. Briefly outline what the participants had to do in the study. **[2 marks]**

3. Choose one study in which the effects of retrieval failure were investigated. Briefly outline what the participants had to do in the study. **[2 marks]**

4. Briefly discuss one limitation of interference as an explanation of forgetting. **[3 marks]**

5. Briefly discuss one limitation of retrieval failure as an explanation of forgetting. **[3 marks]**

6. Describe and evaluate interference as an explanation for forgetting. **[12 marks AS, 16 marks A-level]**

7. Describe and evaluate retrieval failure as an explanation for forgetting. **[12 marks AS, 16 marks A-level]**

8. Describe and evaluate two explanations for forgetting. **[12 marks AS, 16 marks A-level]**

AQA specification for Topic 2: Memory

- Factors affecting the accuracy of eyewitness testimony: misleading information, including leading questions and post-event discussion; anxiety.

◆ Factors affecting the accuracy of eyewitness testimony

- Most people assume that eyewitness testimony (e.g. witnessing a criminal event) is a reliable source of evidence – 'I saw it with my own eyes!' Unfortunately, this is not true. Eyewitness testimony (EWT) can be an unreliable source of evidence and is often prone to cognitive errors (e.g. distortion or false memories). In fact, in recent years thousands of people have been proved to have been wrongly convicted based on misidentification of eyewitness accounts alone, and up to 70% have now been cleared because of DNA evidence. Several factors have been identified as affecting the accuracy of EWT. One factor is known as misleading information. This refers to incorrect information given to the eyewitness usually after the event in the form of leading questions and post-event discussion. Another factor that can affect the accuracy of EWT is anxiety (see next exam notes).

◆ Leading questions

Research by Elizabeth Loftus (1974) found that an eyewitness account about an event can be affected by how questions are worded to the witness. The main issue is a leading question, which refers to a question that has been phrased in a particular way that suggests a certain answer. For example, asking someone 'What colour was the man's hat?' suggests that he was wearing a hat! Below, you can find more information about Elizabeth Loftus' famous study on leading questions.

AN 'EYE' ON THE STUDY

Leading questions in EWT
(Loftus and Palmer, 1974)

Loftus and Palmer (1974) carried out a number of laboratory experiments to see whether asking participants leading questions would affect the accuracy of their recall. In one of their experiments, a sample of 45 American students from Washington University were asked to watch a video of a car accident. They were then given a questionnaire with many questions about the incident. Each group's questionnaire differed in the wording of only one question, 'About how fast were the cars going when they XXX into each other?' The different groups had the words: smashed, hit, collided, bumped, or contacted, in the question. The average speed of the cars guessed by the students was found to be affected by the verb used. Their findings (in the table below) show that use of more 'severe' verbs in the question led the participants to give a higher estimation of the speed at which the car was travelling before the accident. Loftus and Palmer concluded that leading questions can distort original memory accounts and thus affect the accuracy of recall.

Verb	Mean speed estimation (mph)
Smashed	40.8
Collided	39.3
Bumped	38.1
Hit	34.0
Contacted	31.8

Explanations for the effect of leading questions

- **Response-bias explanation.** The response-bias explanation suggests that the actual wording of the question does not change the participant's memories of the event, but influences how they decide to answer.

- **Substitution explanation.** The substitution explanation disagrees with the response bias explanation and suggests that the wording of the question actually changes the participant's memories of the event. Loftus and Palmer (1974) conducted a second experiment that supported the substitution explanation. They found that participants who originally heard 'smashed' were more likely to report seeing broken glass in the clip, than those who heard 'hit', suggesting high speed led to the glass being broken. This because they assumed that that the verb used actually changed the memory for the incident.

◆ Post-event discussion

In terms of eyewitness testimony (EWT), post-event discussion is another form of misleading information that can affect the accuracy of recall i.e. distortion of information or recalling false information. Post-event discussion is when co-witnesses to a crime accident discuss the event with each other, potentially exchanging information and contaminating memories and EWT. This is because they combine misinformation from other witnesses with their own memories.

AN 'EYE' ON THE STUDY

A study on post-event discussion
(Gabbert et al., 2003)

Gabbert et al. (2003) investigated the effect of post-event discussion on the accuracy of eyewitness testimony. The study consisted of 60 students from the University of Aberdeen and 60 older adults, recruited from a local community. Participants watched a video of a girl stealing money from a wallet. The participants were either tested individually (control group, who watched the film on their own) or in pairs (co-witness group). The participants in the co-witness group were told that they had watched the same video, however, they had in fact seen a different viewpoint (angle) of the same crime. For example, only one of the participants could see the title of a book being carried by a young woman. Participants in the co-witness group discussed what they had seen, before individually completing a test of recall. All of the participants then completed a questionnaire that tested their memory of the event. Gabbert et al. found that 71% of the witnesses in the co-witness group recalled information they had not actually seen in the video but had picked up in the discussion. The corresponding figure in the control group where there was no discussion was 0%. Gabbert et al. concluded that witnesses often agree with others in a phenomenon known as memory conformity (see below).

Explanations for the effects of post-event discussions

- **Misinformation effect.** One explanation for why witnesses (and people) in general are prone to making an error in recall could be that these discussions or misinformation are more recent in the memory, so they became 'blended in' with the fading original event. The eyewitness then has difficulty in deciding which of the two memory sources is the true one and which is a later addition. This confusion leads to the eyewitness wrongly 'attributing' the post-information as being part of the original event, and thus forms part of their recall of the original event: known as the misinformation effect.

- **Memory conformity.** Another reason for these effects is that people integrate other people's opinions and knowledge into their own experiences. This could be to win social approval or because people believe that the other witnesses are right. Therefore, the underlying reason why distortions of memory occur could be due to conformity.

◆ Evaluation

✔ **Well-controlled experiment allows replication.** Loftus' laboratory studies took place in a highly controlled setting. This meant that the experimenter could control or eliminate any potential extraneous (unwanted) variables such as demand characteristics, the time allowed to answer and individual differences among the students (e.g. in their age and gender). This ensured that the unwanted variables would not affect the respondents' answers. The researchers, therefore, were confident in establishing a causal relationship between the misleading question and the accuracy of memory recall in terms of the speed of the car. This means the study can be easily be repeated by other researchers, using the same experimental conditions and procedures to see whether they get similar results. Other researchers have shown similar results, suggesting that these studies are reliable and valid.

✔ **Real-life application.** Research into misleading information has real-life applicability and importance. The results have important practical uses for police officers and investigators because the consequences of inaccurate EWT can be very serious. Loftus (1975) claimed that leading questions can have such a distorting influence on memory, that police officers need to be careful about how they phrase questions when interviewing eyewitnesses. Research into EWT is one area where psychologists can make an important difference to the lives of real people, e.g. by improving how the legal system works and acting as expert witnesses.

Weaknesses

✗ **Low in ecological validity.** Loftus' experimental research into EWT may be low in ecological validity because it lacks mundane realism (real life). Witnessing a video of a crash in a laboratory is different from experiencing one in real life. It could be argued that the participants were aware that something interesting was going to be shown to them, and thus their attention level would have been higher than normal. In real life, eyewitnesses are often taken by surprise, and often fail to pay close attention to the event or incident. As a consequence, we cannot be sure that misleading information does in fact impact eyewitness testimony in real life, as we cannot generalise the results outside the lab setting. As a result, this reduces the overall credibility of the research evidence.

✗ **Demand characteristics.** Loftus' experimental design into EWT may have given the participants clues as to what the research hypothesis was about, so they may have acted in a way that they thought would please the researchers. For example, in Loftus' study on car speed, the participants may have guessed the experiment was about 'speed' and therefore may have adjusted their answers to fit with the expectations of the researcher. In the study by Gabbert et al., the findings could have been contaminated by demand characteristics. Whilst Gabbert's research used an independent groups design, it could still have been obvious that participants were expected to put details of their partner's accounts in their own recollections when responding to the questionnaire. As a consequence, this reduces the explanatory power of research into the effect of post-event discussion on eyewitness testimony.

✗ **Limited sample type.** Loftus' laboratory studies were based on a narrow sample type. University students differ from the general population in terms of their age and education level. Also, students are in an environment where they are continually memorising information, so they are probably good at remembering things. This means that the research findings cannot be generalised to the wider population. However, the study by Gabbert et al. tested two different populations, university students and older adults, and found little difference between these two conditions. Therefore, these results provide good population validity and allow us to conclude that post-event discussion affects younger and older adults in a similar way.

Practice exam questions

1. Explain what is meant by the term 'eyewitness testimony'. **[1 mark]**

2. Identify which of the following two questions (A or B) is a leading question and explain why it is a leading question.

   A. 'Did you see a girl jump from the car?' **[1 mark]**

   B. 'Did you see the girl jump from the car?' **[2 marks]**

3. Identify three factors affecting the accuracy of eyewitness testimony. **[3 marks]**

4. Describe one or more studies that investigated the effects of misleading information on eyewitness testimony. **[6 marks]**

5. Explain why research studies into eyewitness testimony have been criticised for lacking validity. **[5 marks]**

6. Outline and evaluate research (theories and/or studies) into the effects of misleading information on eyewitness testimony. **[12 marks AS, 16 marks A-level]**

AQA specification for Topic 2: Memory

- Factors affecting the accuracy of eyewitness testimony: anxiety.

◆ Eyewitness testimony and anxiety

- Studies on crime, especially violent or dangerous crime (such as those involving weapons) , show that it can have an impact on the accuracy of eyewitness recall. A victim or witness of a crime will undoubtedly experience high levels of anxiety or stress that can influence their account of events. Below, we describe studies that have investigated the relationship between anxiety and the memory recall of eyewitnesses account, but it is not clear whether these effects make recall better or worse.

Anxiety has a negative effect on memory recall

- **Weapon focus effect.** Loftus (1987) offered an explanation why heightened anxiety reduces the accuracy of recall, known as the weapon focus effect. The presence of a dangerous weapon (e.g. gun or knife) heightens anxiety levels, which then increase our attention on the weapon, so that we 'focus in'. This draws our attention away from other details of the crime (e.g. facial features, clothing, details of the crime scene). This explains why recall of the events is sometimes poor while descriptions of the weapon are good.

- **Heated conversation laboratory experiment.** Johnson and Scott (1976) carried out a laboratory experiment to investigate the effect of a weapon on memory recall. The participants were exposed to two conditions. In a 'no weapon' condition, they sat outside a room waiting to participate in an experiment and could overhear an everyday conversation taking place in the next room. Then they witnessed a man emerge from the room holding a pen, with grease on his hands. In the 'weapon' condition, the participants overheard a heated conversation in the next room, together with crashing sounds. They witnessed the same man emerge from the room holding a paper knife and with his hands covered in blood. When the participants were asked to identify the man from a set of 50 photographs sometime later, 49% in the 'no weapon' condition accurately identified him, compared to 33% in the 'weapon' condition. The study shows that anxiety arising from the presence of a weapon distracts attention from other details and therefore reduces the accuracy of witness recall. From this, Johnson and Scott concluded that attention narrows in to focus on a weapon because it is a source of anxiety.

Anxiety has a positive effect on memory recall

- **Real-life armed robbery study.** Real-life research contradicts the evidence from laboratory experiments as carried out by Johnson and Scott (1976). Two psychologists, Yullie and Cutshall (1986), examined a real-life crime in which 21 people witnessed the stressful event of an armed thief holding up a gun shop in Canada. The shop owner shot the thief dead. Out of the 21 witnesses, 13 agreed to take part in this study. Yullie and Cutshall interviewed the witnesses 4-5 months after the incident and these were compared with the original police interviews made at the time of the shooting. Accuracy was determined by the number of details reported in each account. The witnesses were also asked to rate how stressed they had felt at the time of the incident using a 7-point scale, and asked if they had any emotional problems since the event, such as sleeplessness. They found that the witnesses were very accurate in their accounts and there was little change in the amount of accuracy with an average of 88% accuracy recalling events that matched their initial detailed report to the police. Some details were less accurate, such as recollection of the colour of items and age/height/weight estimates. More noticeably, those participants who reported the highest levels of stress showed the most accurate recall. This real-life example questions the tunnel theory (weapon effect) because it shows that even in a highly stressful situation, recall can still be accurate–even after a long period of time.

◆ Explaining the contradictory findings

- **Yerkes-Dodson law.** One possible explanation for why there has been contradictory evidence has been provided by Yerkes and Dodson (1908). They proposed that an inverted "U" relationship (i.e. ∩) exists between the two variables - stress and memory recall - known as the Yerkes-Dodson law. This law suggests that memory recall is at its highest when there is a moderate level of anxiety (known as an optimum point) and then memory recall declines if the anxiety levels increase above or below the optimum point, suggesting that too high or low levels of anxiety can affect memory recall.

◆ Evaluation

Weaknesses

✗ **Explanation of the weapon-focus effect questioned.** Valentine et al. (2003) investigated real-life crimes and the presence of a weapon by analysing data from a questionnaire completed by 640 real eyewitnesses, who attempted to identify the suspects in 314 line-ups organised by the Metropolitan Police in London. They found that the presence of a weapon had no effect on the outcome of correctly identifying the suspect. The findings show that the presence of a weapon does not reduce recall accuracy. As a result, this undermines the weapon-focus effect as an explanation of why the accuracy of EWT may be poor.

✗ **Low internal validity for Johnson and Scott's study.** A limitation of the research is that the weapon-focus effect may not be caused by anxiety. Pickel (1998) argued that Johnson and Scott's research may have been testing 'surprise' rather than anxiety. To test this, she conducted an experiment for participants to watch a thief enter a hairdressing salon carrying scissors (high threat, low surprise), a handgun (high threat, high surprise), a wallet (low threat, low surprise) or a raw chicken (low threat, high surprise. She found that identification was least accurate in the high surprise conditions, rather than the high threat conditions. This suggests that the weapon-focus effect is due to unusualness (surprise) rather than anxiety. As a result, this reduces the explanatory power of Johnson and Scott's research into the effect of anxiety on EWT.

✗ **The inverted-U explanation is too simplistic.** The inverted-U explanation has been criticised because it is too simplistic. Anxiety is difficult to define and measure because it has many elements – cognitive, behavioural, emotional, and physical. The inverted-U explanation assumes that one of these (physical) is linked to performance. The explanation fails to account for other factors, such as the effect of the emotional experience of witnessing a crime (e.g. terror, fear) on the accuracy of memory.

✗ **Low internal validity for Johnson and Scott's study.** One issue with Johnson and Scott's research into the effect of anxiety on EWT is that it is low on internal validity. Pickel (1998) argued that Johnson and Scott's research may be testing 'surprise' rather than anxiety. For example, he conducted an experiment using scissors, a handgun, a wallet or a raw chicken as the handheld items in a hairdressing salon video. Eyewitness accuracy was significantly poorer in the unusual conditions (chicken and handgun). This suggests that the weapon focus effect is due to unusualness (surprise) rather than anxiety and therefore tells us nothing specific about the effect of anxiety on EWT. As a result, this reduces the explanatory power of Johnson and Scott's research into the effect of anxiety on EWT.

✘ **Low external validity for Johnson and Scott's study.** Johnson and Scott's research study has also been criticised for lacking ecological validity. Although the participants were waiting in the reception area outside the laboratory, they may have anticipated that something was going to happen, which could have affected the accuracy of their judgements. Therefore, care is needed before generalising such findings to the real world.

✘ **Low internal validity for Yuille and Cutshall's study.** A weakness of Yuille and Cutshall's research is that it has low internal validity. This is because they had little control over any extraneous variables that may have occurred. For example, they would not have had control during the 4-5 month period after the crime had happened, on variables such as witnesses discussing with others what the thief looked like, what the shop owner said, and whether he was provoked or not. Also, the questions asked by the police may have had an impact on the accuracy of what happened. This is a problem for the study because if witnesses had conferred, they may have induced false memories and believed they saw something which may not have happened. Additionally, we know from previous research that if the police had not followed protocol and asked leading questions, this too can affect the accuracy of the eyewitness testimony (EWT). If the majority of witnesses had the same answer, this could have influenced others to change their memory of the gun crime incident. This would then have impacted the accuracy of EWT, in which case, researchers would not be measuring whether real-life crime and anxiety do lead to a more accurate recall. As a result, this lowers the credibility of Yuille and Cutshall's research into the effect of anxiety on the accuracy of EWT.

Practice exam questions

1. Describe one study that has investigated the effects of anxiety on eyewitness testimony. **[6 marks]**

2. Outline how anxiety may be a factor affecting the accuracy of eyewitness testimony. **[4 marks]**

3. Outline and evaluate research [theories and/or studies] into the effects of anxiety on eyewitness testimony. **[12 marks AS, 16 marks A-level]**

AQA specification for Topic 2: Memory

Improving the accuracy of eyewitness testimony, including the use of the cognitive interview.

◆ The cognitive interview

Elizabeth Loftus' research into misleading questions has shown how these can distort memory recall, making the information provided unreliable. One way to improve memory recall is to make the process of interviewing more effective. Fisher and Geiselman (1984) devised the cognitive interview (CI) technique. The aim of the cognitive interview technique is to help the police in the process of interviewing, by reducing recall error and improving the accuracy of memory recall of the witness. There are four components to the cognitive interviewing techniques, designed to encourage retrieval cues to help memory recall. The cues should be given in this order to the witness:

1. Context reinstatement (CR). Context reinstatement requires the witnesses to mentally recreate an image of the situation, including details of the environment such as the weather conditions, and the individual's emotional state, including their feelings at the time of the incident. The notion is based on the context-dependent forgetting theory. If the context and feelings of the individual are similar for recall to the original situation these will act as cues and help trigger more information from memory recall.

2. Report everything (RE). The witness is encouraged not to hold back any information but to report everything they can remember about the incident, regardless of how unimportant the information may seem to them. Reporting trivial matters is important as it may help trigger more information from memory. This is because memories are interconnected with one another, so that recollection of one item may then cue (trigger) a whole lot of other memories.

3. Recall in reverse order (RO). As well as recalling events in their natural sequence from beginning to end, the witness is asked to describe the scene in a different chronological order, in other words, to work backwards in time through the events they witnessed. This is done to prevent people from reporting their 'expectations' of how the events must have happened, rather than what happened. It also prevents dishonesty, as it is harder for people to produce an untruthful account if they have to reverse it.

4. Changed perspective (CP). The witness is asked to try to imagine how the incident would have appeared from the viewpoint of another witness. Changed perspective is believed to help increase the accuracy of recall by reducing/disrupting the eyewitness's use of prior knowledge, expectations and schemas when asked to recall. For example, the schema you have for a particular setting (e.g. going into a shop) generates expectations of what would have happened, so the existing schema is recalled rather than what actually happened.

◆ Enhanced cognitive interview

Subsequent research by Fisher et al. (1987) led them to refine the cognitive interview, as the enhanced cognitive interview (ECI). The main additional features of the ECI are:

- Minimised distractions
- Reduced witness anxiety
- Encouraging witness to speak slowly
- Allowing a pause between responses and the next question
- Adapting the language to suit the witness's understanding.

Differences between the cognitive interview and standard interview

Standard interview (SI)	Cognitive interview (CI)	Enhanced cognitive interview (ECI)
Less information collected	**More information is collected**	**More information is collected**
SI does not use different retrieval cues so limited information is recalled.	CI is an effective technique as it uses different retrieval cues to increase the ability to extract more information from the witness.	ECI minimises distractions and reduces witness anxiety.
Unstructured format	**Structured format**	**Structured format**
SI uses an unstructured question format (Who? What? Where? How?) that increases the possibility of (mis)leading questions being asked, resulting in a greater chance of recall error.	The four components are structured in a way that reduces (mis)leading questions from the interviewer because questions are open-ended. This helps reduce recall error.	ECI encourages the witness to speak slowly. It allows a pause between the witness's response and the next question. It adapts the language of questions to suit the witness's understanding.

◆ Evaluation

Strengths

Strengths

✔ **Laboratory experiment.** Supporting research evidence for CI comes from Geiselman et al. (1986). They carried out a laboratory experiment comparing the effectiveness of the original CI with a standard police interview. Participants initially viewed a simulated violent crime film and 48 hours later they were interviewed, face-to-face, by police officers using a CI or SI. They found that the CI produced an average of 17% more correct information than the SI. The findings suggest that under laboratory conditions, CI is more effective than the SI for enhancing both the amount of information and the accuracy of eyewitness recall.

✔ **Comparing ECI with CI.** There is further support that ECI is more effective than CI. Fisher et al. (1987) interviewed university students either using the original CI or ECI two days after having viewed a stimulated violent crime film. The researchers found that the ECI extracted 45% more correct information compared to the original CI.

✔ **Ecological validity.** To avoid the criticisms of the findings from the above two studies being under controlled artificial laboratory conditions, Fisher et al. (1990) carried out a real-life study. Detectives from the Miami Police Department tape-recorded several interviews with eyewitnesses/ victims to a real-life crime. The detectives were then assigned to one of two conditions, namely untrained detectives using SI or trained detectives using ECI. The findings showed that the ECI extracted approximately 47% more information than SI, with 94% of the recall of information being accurate. This shows the effectiveness of ECI techniques in a real-life setting and prove that it has high ecological validity.

Limitations

✗ **Increase in recall error.** The CI procedure is designed to enhance the quantity of correct recall without compromising the quality of that information but the main effect may have been on quantity. Kohnken et al. (1999) carried out a meta-analysis of over 53 studies and found an average 33% increase in correct recall using CI compared with SI. However, there was also an increase in recall error, with 17% more incorrect details reported with CI than with SI. Therefore, police officers need to take this into account when evaluating EWT as the CI may not guarantee accuracy.

✗ **Ineffective for identification.** CI procedure does not help with face recognition and person identification. For example, Newlands et al. (1999) found that the descriptions of criminals using the CE/ECI technique were no better than those resulting from SI.

✗ **Unsuitable for young children.** Geiselman's (1999) review of previous studies suggested that CI was not very effective with children under the age of six. Young children have difficulty understanding the requirements of the CI procedure, for example, they struggled with the 'change perspective' instruction. This suggests that CI is only effective for use after a certain age – with older children and adults.

✗ **Time-consuming.** A final limitation of the CI is that it is time-consuming. Police officers are reluctant to use the CI because it takes much more time than the SI. More time is needed to establish rapport with the witness to allow them to relax. Kebbell and Wagstaff (1997) pointed out that the CI also requires special training that many forces have not been able to provide. This means it is unlikely that the 'proper' version of the CI is actually used. This may explain why the police report low enthusiasm/interest in CI and the use of the CI has not been widespread.

Practice exam questions

1. Explain what is meant by the term 'cognitive interview'. **[3 marks]**

2. Identify two techniques used in the cognitive interview and explain how this can improve the accuracy of eyewitness recall. **[2 marks + 2 marks]**

3. Explain two differences between a cognitive interview and a standard interview. **[2+2 marks]**

4. Explain one weakness in the use of the cognitive interview. **[3 marks]**

5. Outline and evaluate research into the use of cognitive interviews. **[12 marks AS, 16 marks A-level]**

Topic 3
Attachment

AQA specification for Topic 3: Attachment (AS and A-level)

- Caregiver-infant interactions in humans: reciprocity and interactional synchrony. Stages of attachment identified by Schaffer. Multiple attachments and the role of the father.

- Animal studies of attachment: Lorenz and Harlow.

- Explanations of attachment: learning theory and Bowlby's monotropic theory. The concepts of a critical period and an internal working model.

- Ainsworth's 'Strange Situation'. Types of attachment: secure, insecure-avoidant and insecure-resistant. Cultural variations in attachment, including van Ijzendoorn.

- Bowlby's theory of maternal deprivation. Romanian orphan studies: effects of institutionalisation.

- The influence of early attachment on childhood and adult relationships, including the role of an internal working model.

AQA specification for Topic 3: Attachment

- Caregiver-infant interactions in humans: reciprocity and interactional synchrony.

◆ Key term

- **Attachment:** Attachment is an emotional connection between the infant and the main caregiver. This is displayed through mutual affection, frequent interaction, a desire for proximity (to be close) and selectivity (the child wants to be with the caregiver rather than anyone else e.g. displaying stranger anxiety and separation anxiety, when separated from the caregiver).

◆ Introduction

One of the most important events during the first year of life is the development of a close attachment bond with the mother. A mother-infant bond is not present at birth but develops later. Even though an infant cannot talk at this stage of its development, the non-verbal communication between the mother and infant has an important function. It helps to lay the foundation for the development of the attachment bond between the caregiver and infant. Two important mother-infant interactions are *reciprocity* and *interactional synchrony*.

◆ Reciprocity

- **Reciprocity** in attachment refers to a two-way interaction between caregiver and infant whereby they take it in turns (turn-taking) to respond to each other's behaviours/signals in a meaningful way, in order to sustain an interaction. The behaviour of each party elicits a response from the other (turn-taking), for example, when the baby stretches its arms, the mother picks up the baby, or the mother smiles back when the baby smiles. Brezelton et al. (1975) described this interaction as a 'dance' because when a couple dance together, they each respond to one another's movements and rhythm. Likewise, reciprocity as a caregiver–infant interaction is where the interaction between both individuals flows back and forth. From around three months old, according to Feldman (2007), reciprocity increases in frequency as the infant and caregiver pay increasing attention to each other's verbal and facial communications. It is suggested that showing this sensitive responsiveness, whereby the caregiver pays attention sensitively towards the infant's behaviour, will lay the strong foundations for attachment to develop later between the caregiver and infant.

Study. Belsky et al. (1984) carried out a controlled observational study of mother-infant interactions when each infant was one, three and nine months of age. At the age of 12 months, the infant's attachment to the mother was assessed using the 'Strange Situation' technique. Belsky found that if the mothers demonstrated more reciprocal interactions, the infants were more securely attached to their mothers, compared to infants with low levels of reciprocal interactions with their mother, who tended to have an insecure attachment.

◆ Interactional synchrony

- **Interactional synchrony** is when the caregiver and infant **mirrors** (imitates) what the other is doing in terms of their facial expressions and behaviour (body movements). This mirroring of each other's facial and body movements occurs rapidly back and, for example, a baby moving her head in time with her mother or the mother imitating the sounds the baby makes. Research suggests that infants as young as 2-3 e weeks old can imitate specific facial and hand gestures. Interactional synchrony is best described as a sensitively tuned 'emotional dance' in which the interactions are mutually rewarding to the caregiver and infant. This interaction serves to sustain communication between the two individuals, which helps develop and eventually maintain a healthy attachment bond.

- Study. Meltzoff and Moore (1977) carried out a controlled observational study of interactional synchrony in infants as young as two weeks old. An adult model displayed one of three facial expressions (e.g. mouth opening or tongue protrusion) or gestures (e.g. hand movements). Following the display, the infant's responses were filmed. An association was found between the expression or gesture the adult had displayed and the actions of the infant. This suggests that an infant's imitation may indicate an innate ability (rather than learned) to aid the formation of attachment, especially when it was seen in infants younger than two weeks old.

◆ Evaluation of caregiver–infant Interactions

Strengths

✔ **Studies are well controlled.** A strength of the research into early caregiver-infant interactions is that it uses well-controlled procedures. Mother-infant interactions are usually filmed, often from multiple angles, which means that very fine details of behaviour can be recorded and analysed later by psychologists. This allows valid conclusions to be drawn because inter-rater reliability can be established by having independent observers re-watch the tapes and compare their findings to see if they were similar and thus reliable.

✔ **Supporting evidence for imitation being innate.** A strength of the research study conducted by Meltzoff and Moore is that there is further research to provide evidence that imitation behaviours by babies are innate (biological). For example, Murray and Trevarthen (1985) conducted a study using two-month-old infants. First, the infants interacted with their mothers via a video monitor in real-time. In the next part of the research, the video monitor played a tape recording of their mothers, so image on the screen did not respond to the infant's gestures. The result was acute distress; the infants tried to interact with their mothers but gaining no response, turned away. This suggests that imitation behaviour is innate; the infant is actively eliciting a response rather than exhibiting a response that has been rewarded. If there was an element of reward in the process, it would suggest the behaviour had been learnt. As a result, this strengthens the credibility of Meltzoff and Moore's original research and conclusion that reciprocal synchrony is innate, increasing the validity of this theoretical explanation.

Weaknesses

✘ **Problems with testing infant behaviour.** An issue with the research into early caregiver-infant interactions is that it is difficult to test the baby's behaviour in a reliable manner. For example, as in Meltzoff and Moore's and Brazelton's observational research, observing and measuring facial expression or hand movements that are constantly moving makes it difficult to distinguish between general activity and specific imitated behaviours. A study by Koepke et al. (1983) failed to replicate the findings of Meltzoff and Moore, which may suggest that the original findings were unreliable. Meltzoff and Moore argued that Koepke et al.'s research was less controlled. This suggests that more research is required. As a result, this reduces the validity of the research evidence into caregiver-infant interactions.

✗ The purpose of synchrony and reciprocity. A problem with the research into synchrony and reciprocity is that the findings do not tell us the reason why such behaviours in caregiver-infant interactions occur. All the study can do is describe what is happening between the mother and the infant. Other psychologists disagree with this view and offer several reasons why these behaviours occur. For example, Isabella (1989) demonstrated the importance of interactional synchrony, when he found high levels of synchrony were associated with a higher quality infant-mother attachment, suggesting that such behaviours are helpful in the development of attachment. However, Le Vine et al. (1994) reported that Kenyan mothers have little physical contact or interaction with their infants, but such infants still develop secure attachments. This suggests that reciprocity and interactional synchrony is not found in all cultures, which weakens the idea that they are necessary for the development of attachments. This would suggest further research evidence into caregiver-infant interactions is needed.

✗ Socially sensitive. A weakness of research (as in the study by Isabella) into early caregiver-infant interactions is that it is socially sensitive. This is because the implications of findings suggest that low levels of caregiver-infant interaction lead to insecure attachment, which may continue into adulthood. The findings not only poses a dilemma for working mothers, but also reinforce gender stereotypes that women should prioritise childcare over their career – they should stay at home. Some people may criticise this view because appears to discourage women from being mothers with a career.

Practice exam questions

1. Explain what is meant by the term 'reciprocity' and 'interactional synchrony' in the context of caregiver-infant interaction. **[2 marks + 2 marks]**

2. Outline research into reciprocity. **[4 marks]**

3. Outline research into interactional synchrony. **[4 marks]**

4. Outline and evaluate research into caregiver-infant interactions in humans. **[12 marks AS, 16 marks A-level]**

AQA specification for Topic 3: Attachment

- Stages of attachment identified by Schaffer. Multiple attachments.

◆ Stages of attachment

- Schaffer and Emerson (1964) investigated (see key study below) the stages of attachment development. They suggest that attachment follows a common pattern that can be divided into four distinct stages.

Stages of attachment	Descriptive features
Stage 1 **Asocial stage** *(from 0-2 months)*	• Baby behaviour during this stage towards people and innate objects (e.g. balloon) is quite similar, no real distinction between the two. • Babies are also happier when in the presence of other humans as opposed to being alone.
Stage 2 **Indiscriminate attachment** *(from 2-7 months)*	• Babies now show a preference for human company rather than inanimate objects. • They can discriminate between familiar and unfamiliar faces but can be comforted/cuddled by anyone and they do not show stranger anxiety. Attachment is 'indiscriminate' because the behaviour to known people (family) and strangers is the same.
Stage 3 **Specific attachment** *(from 7 months)*	• Babies can now form attachment and will have a preference for a specific attachment, the caregiver, known as the *primary attachment figure*. • Babies can now discriminate between the caregiver and other people. The evidence for this is through the child's behaviour: (a) the child will often stay close to his or her caregiver; (b) the child will show separation anxiety when separated from their caregiver; and (c) the child will display stranger anxiety (distress) when picked up or played with by a stranger.
Stage 4 **Multiple attachments** *(8/9 -12 months)*	• The child now begins to develop strong emotional ties with other major caregivers (e.g. father, grandparents, brothers and sisters). These caregivers are sometimes referred to as secondary (or multiple) *attachments* but the mother-figure attachment remains the strongest. • By the age of one year, the majority of infants have multiple attachments.

👁 AN 'EYE' ON THE STUDY

Key study: attachment development
(Schaffer and Emerson, 1964)

Aim

- The aim of the study by the psychologists Schaffer and Emerson (1964) was to find out at what age attachments begin.

→

- Their sample consisted of 60 babies (31 males and 29 females) from working-class families in Glasgow aged between 5–23 weeks at the start of the investigation. The researchers visited the babies in their homes, every month for the first 12 months and then once again at 18 months. The mothers kept a diary to measure the infant's behaviour in relation to separation and stranger anxiety in a range of everyday activities, and to identify to whom the protest was directed. This was rated on a four-point scale.

Method

- *Separation protest* was measured, for example, when the infant was left alone, left with others, or left in the pram outside the house, or left in the pram outside shops.

- *Stranger anxiety* was measured, for example, by the researcher starting each home visit by approaching the infant to see if this distressed the child.

Results

- *Approx. 6-8 months:* Around 50% of infants showed separation anxiety when parted from their attachment figure between 6-8 months, with stranger anxiety being shown a month later (as expected of the specific attachment stage).

- *Approx. 9 months:* Around 80% of the infants had a strong attachment to their mother by 9 months (as expected at the specific attachment stage). The researchers also found that feeding was not the most critical factor in the formation of attachment. It was noted that infants with the strongest attachment had carers who were more responsive to their signals and needs. Shaffer and Emerson called this sensitive responsiveness.

- *Approx. 18 months:* About 87% of infants developed multiple attachments to at least two attachments, with 31% of infants forming five or more attachments (as expected at the multiple stages of attachment).

- They also found that in 39% of infants, the prime attachment was not the main caregiver.

Conclusion

- The researchers concluded that feeding or the amount of time the person spent with the infant were not the most critical factors in the formation of attachment. The researchers observed that the mother had responded quickly and sensitively to their 'signals' (needs) and offered their child the most interaction. Shaffer and Emerson called this sensitive responsiveness.

◆ Evaluation of Shaffer's stages of attachment

Strength

✔ **High external validity.** A strength of Schaffer and Emerson's (1964) research into the development of attachment is that it has high external validity. For example, the study was carried out in the families' own homes and most of the observation was actually done by the parents during ordinary activities and reported to researchers later. This is a strength because it means the behaviour of the babies was unlikely to be affected by the presence of observers. This increases the chances of the babies behaving naturally in their own environments. As a result, this increases the credibility of the research that discovered the stages of attachment theory.

Weaknesses

✗ **Low population validity.** A weakness of Schaffer and Emerson's (1964) research into the development of attachment is that the sample was biased. They used 60 babies from the working-class population of Glasgow. This is an issue because the sample may not be representative of other social groups and therefore, we cannot generalise the findings that attachment develops in stages to other social groups. It may be that babies from more privileged backgrounds develop attachments in a different way, as a result of being cared for by a nanny or other privileges they would experience. As a result, Schaffer's stage theory of attachment may not be universally valid.

✗ **Low temporal validity.** Another weakness is that Schaffer and Emerson's study may suffer from low temporal validity. This is because it was conducted in 1964, over 50 years ago, and parental care of children has changed considerably since that time. More women go out to work, so many children are cared for outside the home, or fathers stay at home and become the main carer. Research shows that the number of dads who choose to stay at home and care for their children has quadrupled over the past 25 years (Cohn et al., 2014). This is an issue, as it is likely that if a similar study were conducted today, the findings might be different, which suggests that Schaffer's stage theory of attachment may not be applicable in modern times.

✗ **Social desirability bias.** A further weakness of Schaffer and Emerson's study is that it has been criticised on the grounds of a possibility of social desirability bias. Shaffer and Emerson interviewed the mothers about their children and some of them may not have reported accurate details about their children, in order to appear like 'better' mothers with secure attachments. This could cause a bias in the data that would reduce the internal validity of the findings, since natural behaviour may not have been recorded about the stages of attachment.

✗ **Schaffer's stages too fixed.** One criticism of Schaffer and Emerson's account of attachment development is that it suggests that attachment stages are fixed. This is because the theory claims that children must go through each stage at a particular age and must demonstrate particular types of attachment behaviour. Some psychologists argue that attachment development is more fluid than Schaffer has outlined, because children display different behaviours of attachment at different ages. This is a problem because these stages may become a standard by which families are judged and could lead to them being classed as abnormal.

Practice exam questions

1. Explain what is meant by the term 'multiple attachments'. **[2 marks]**

2. Name three of the stages of attachment identified by Schaffer. **[3 marks]**

3. Outline Schaffer's stages of attachment. **[6 marks]**

4. Explain two criticisms of Schaffer's stages of attachment. **[3 marks + 3 marks]**

5. Outline research into multiple attachments. **[6 marks]**

6. Describe and evaluate the stages of attachments as identified by Schaffer.
   [12 marks AS, 16 marks A-level]

AQA specification for Topic 3: Attachment

- Role of the father.

◆ Introduction

Traditional domestic roles meant that the role of the father was minor in the parenting of children. Fathers were seen as the breadwinners, going to work whilst the mothers stayed home and took care of the children. Society has now changed in its domestic arrangements, with many women also working. This means that the role of the father in parenting has also significantly changed. However, psychologists disagree over the exact role the father plays. In terms of being a primary attachment figure, some psychologists argue that men are not equipped to be a primary attachment figure or to develop the type of attachment bond that women can. Psychologists point to biological evidence which suggests that the hormone oestrogen underlies caring behaviour in women and the lack of oestrogen in men is why they are unable to form a close attachment. However, some psychologists argue that fathers can demonstrate sensitive responsiveness and respond to the needs of their children and therefore can form a strong emotional tie or bond with their child. Other researchers argue that fathers do not take on a caregiver role and in fact provide a different role as a playmate.

◆ The role of the father

- **Mothers best suited as primary attachment figures.** Schaffer and Emerson (1964) found that most babies did become attached to their mothers' first – with a primary attachment (around 7 months) – and weeks or months later formed secondary attachments to other family members including the father. In 75% of the infants studied, an attachment was formed with the father by the age of 18 months. This was determined by the fact that the infants protested when their fathers walked away – a sign of attachment. This showed that fathers were far less likely to become primary attachment figures than mothers.

- **Father's role less significant in child attachment type.** Grossman (2002) carried out a longitudinal study of 44 families by comparing and assessing the quality of the mother's and father's parenting behaviour (e.g. sensitive parenting), during the child's early years to see if this contributed to the children's attachment experiences towards the parents at six, 10 and 16 years. They found that the quality of infant-mother attachment was by far the best predictor of later attachment style in teenagers, even if the father provided sensitive parenting. This suggests that the infant-father attachment was less important.

- Lamb (1997) reported that studies have shown little relationship between the amount of time the father spends with the infant and the infant-father relationship, suggesting babies are more suited to forming a primary attachment to the mother. This might be because men lack the emotional sensitivity that women have. Heerman et al. (1994) found that fathers are less sensitive to infant cues than mothers.

- **Father more suited as playmate.** Grossman (2002), in his study above, did find the infant's attachment towards the father was related to the quality of the father's play behaviour with the infant. This suggests that fathers have a different role in attachment – one that is more to do with play and stimulation rather than nurturing. Lamb (1987) also found that children often prefer interacting with their father when in a positive emotional state and seeking stimulation but prefer their mother when they are when distressed and seeking comfort. This supports Grossman's idea of the father being preferred as playmate, but only in certain conditions.

◆ Evaluation of the role of the father

Weaknesses

✘ **Gender stereotyping.** One criticism of the claim that the father's role is not suited to become a primary attachment figure can be explained through traditional gender stereotyping. For example, Schaffer and Emerson's (1964) study was conducted over 50 years ago. The explanation for fathers not becoming the primary attachment figure could simply be due to traditional gender roles, at a time when women were expected/socialised by society to be more caring and nurturing than men. Even with the decline of traditional gender roles in modern society, it could be that female hormones (oestrogen) create higher levels of nurturing and therefore women are biologically pre-disposed to be the primary attachment figure. This is a strength as it confirms that such difference between mothers and fathers in the role of rearing children can be down to an individual's nature but also their experiences of nurture.

✘ **Fathers can also be suited as primary attachment figures.** There is opposing research that suggests that fathers can be primary attachment figures and adopt behaviours more typical of mothers. Field (1978) filmed 4-month-old babies in face-to-face interactions with primary caregiver mothers, secondary caregiver fathers and primary caregiver fathers. Primary caregiver fathers, like mothers, spent more time smiling, imitating, and holding infants than the secondary caregiver fathers. Since this behaviour appears to be important in building an attachment, the infant may then see the father as the primary attachment figure. The key to the attachment relationship appears to be the level of responsiveness of the parent and not their gender.

✘ **Biological difference supported by research.** Research by Hrdy (1999) found that fathers were less able to detect low levels of infant distress, in comparison to mothers. Their findings would seem to support the biological explanation for different parenting styles, suggesting that fathers are not equipped to form close attachments with their children. This suggests that the role of the father is, to some extent, biologically/societally determined and that a father's role is restricted because of who they are. This provides further evidence that fathers are not able to provide a sensitive and nurturing type of attachment.

✘ **Inconsistent findings in the role of the father.** Another criticism of research into the role of the father is that researchers are interested in different research questions when looking at the father-infant attachment. Some researchers are interested in understanding the role fathers have as secondary attachment figures, whereas others are more concerned with the father's role as a primary attachment figure. The former have tended to see fathers behaving differently from mothers and having a distinct role to play. The latter have tended to find that fathers can take on a 'maternal' role, and therefore can become a primary attachment figure. This is a problem because it means psychologists cannot easily answer the question, 'What is the role of the father?' The findings from research will be different and inconsistent, which means that we cannot draw firm conclusions.

✗ **Father's role not so important?** Another weakness is that some researchers oppose this and believe that fathers do not play a significant role. MacCallum and Golombok (2004) found that children growing up in single or same-sex parent families where the father is absent, do not develop any differently from those in two-parent heterosexual families, suggesting that the role of the father is not important. However, one study has found that the absence of a father has various negative effects on children, such as, lower levels of school achievement, heightened risk-taking behaviours, and higher levels of aggression in boys (McLanahan and Teitler, 1999).

Practice exam questions

1. Briefly explain the role of the father in relation to attachment. **[4 marks]**

2. Outline research relating to the role of the father in attachment. **[6 marks]**

3. Describe and evaluate research into the role of the father in attachment. **[12 marks AS, 16 marks A-level]**

AQA specification for Topic 3: Attachment

- Animal studies of attachment: Lorenz and Harlow.

◆ Introduction

Much earlier research into attachment was conducted with animals, based on the assumption that what is true for animals is also true for humans. Studying animals in the wild and in captivity might deepen our understanding to help develop theories and ideas on how attachments are developed and maintained. In fact, John Bowlby, the most eminent psychologist in this area, was influenced by such animal studies in forming his theory of monotropy (see Exam Notes 6) and maternal deprivation (see exam Exam Notes 9), which explain the effects of disrupting attachment bonds. Two of the most well-known animal studies were conducted by Konrad Lorenz and Harry Harlow.

AN 'EYE' ON THE STUDY

Imprinting
(Konrad Lorenz, 1935)

- Konrad Lorenz (1935) was a biologist who was interested in animal behaviour. He is best known for his discovery of attachment in animals, specifically, a certain type of attachment called imprinting. Konrad observed that when animals that are mobile from birth (like geese and ducks) are born, they will bond with the first moving object they see, known as imprinting. He carried out a famous study to investigate this further.

Aim

- To investigate attachment imprinting behaviour in newborn goslings.

Procedure

1. Lorenz (1935) randomly split a clutch of 12 greylag goose eggs into two batches. One batch of eggs was hatched by the mother goose in their natural environment (control group), the other batch was hatched in an incubator, with Lorenz making sure that he was the first moving object the goslings encountered (experimental group).

2. Lorenz next marked the goslings so that he knew whether they had hatched naturally or in the incubator. He then mixed the goslings up by placing them under an upturned box. The box was then removed, and the goslings' behaviour was recorded.

Findings and conclusion

- Immediately after birth, the naturally hatched baby goslings followed their mother about, whilst the incubator-hatched goslings followed Lorenz.

- When released from the upturned box, the naturally hatched goslings went straight to their mother whereas the incubator-hatched goslings went straight to Lorenz (showing no bond to their natural mother).

- Lorenz identified a critical period in which imprinting needs to take place: a short period of time after birth, between four and 25 hours. If imprinting did not occur within that time, the chicks did not attach themselves to the mother figure.

- These bonds proved to be irreversible (the naturally hatched goslings would only follow their mother, and the incubator-hatched goslings would only follow Lorenz).

Sexual imprinting

- Through further experiments, Lorenz attempted to learn about what he called sexual imprinting. This is when an animal starts developing a sexual preference (i.e. choice of mate) based on the species they have imprinted on, than on than their own species. In a case study, Lorenz (1952) describes a peacock that had been reared in the reptile house of a zoo, where the first moving object the peacock saw after hatching was a giant tortoise. An adult, this bird would only direct courtship behaviour towards the tortoises. Lorenz concluded that this meant the peacock had undergone sexual imprinting.

What have we learnt from these animal studies of attachment?

- The fact that imprinting must take place very quickly, as soon as animals are born, suggests that attachment has a critical time frame, otherwise attachments may not occur. Also, the importance of instinctively returning to the imprinted moving object would suggest that attachments are biologically programmed (part of genetic make-up). This is because such behaviour would increase the animal's chances of survival (food and protection from predators by the mother) at a vulnerable time of their lives.

- Imprinting also is important as it provides the ability for animals to recognise members of their own species, and learn life skills and specific behaviours (e.g. how to be a duck). This ensures that when it comes to mating, sexual behaviour is directed towards other animals of the same species. Therefore, imprinting is important for the survival of the species.

- The implication of attachment studies in animals is that formation of early attachments in humans is important for their social and cognitive development Also, the importance of forming attachments and the type of attachment you experience as a child may to some extent predict future bonds.

AN 'EYE' ON THE STUDY

Importance of contact comfort
(Harlow, 1958)

- The importance of early attachments can be learnt by studying monkeys. Harry Harlow carried out animal research and investigated attachment behaviour in rhesus monkeys in order to expand our understanding of attachment. Below, we have described a famous study he carried out.

Aim

- Harlow wanted to investigate whether feeding or comfort was important in the development of attachment.

Procedure

- Harlow created two wire-frame surrogate mothers, each with a different head. One wire mother was wrapped in soft cloth ('towelling mother'), and the other wire mother was left bare without any cloth, just the wire showing ('harsh wire mother'). Harlow used 16 infant rhesus monkeys, eight in each condition, and in both conditions both "mothers" were present:

    - In the first condition, the harsh-wire mother had a milk bottle for feeding, the towelling mother did not.

    - In the second condition, the towelling mother had a milk bottle for feeding, the harsh-wire mother did not.

- The amount of time each infant spent with the two different 'mothers' was recorded. The monkeys were also frightened with loud noises to test for mother preference during times of stress. The researchers also observed the infants' responses when frightened (e.g. by mechanical noise-making teddy bear).

→

- Harlow and colleagues also continued to study the monkeys who had been deprived of a 'real' mother into adulthood.

Findings

- All eight monkeys in each condition spent most of their time with the cloth-covered mother whether or not this mother had the feeding bottle. Those monkeys who fed on the wire mother only spent a short amount of time getting milk and then returned to the cloth-covered mother.

- When frightened, all monkeys clung to the cloth-covered mother rather than the wire mother. When playing with new objects, the monkeys often kept one foot on the cloth-covered mother for reassurance.

Conclusions

- *Food or comfort?* The findings suggest that infants do not develop an attachment to the person who feeds them but to the person offering them comfort.

- *Maternally deprived monkey in adulthood.* As the monkeys grew up, the effects of their early rearing continued. The monkeys exposed to the wire mothers developed more severe problems. The monkeys reared with wire mothers only were the most dysfunctional. Both wire and cloth-reared monkeys were socially abnormal; they were more aggressive and less sociable (they froze or fled when approached by other monkeys). They also did not display normal mating behaviour and did not cradle their own babies (even killing their infants in some cases).

- *The critical period for normal development.* Harlow also concluded that there was a critical period for this behaviour (like Lorenz). A mother figure had to be introduced to an infant monkey within 90 days for an attachment to form. After this time attachment was impossible and the damage done by early deprivation became irreversible.

What have we learnt from these animal studies of attachment?

- The preference of the infant rhesus monkeys to seek comfort rather than food would suggest that food is not as crucial as comfort when forming a bond. This suggests that attachment development is driven by providing emotional security more than food.

- Isolated monkeys displayed long-term dysfunctional behaviour. This suggests that early poor attachment experiences can predict long-term social development. The implication of animal studies in attachment theory is that poor attachment experiences in infancy may have permanent effects on social development later in life.

◆ Evaluation

Lorenz's study

Strengths

✔ **Deepen our attachment to human behaviour.** A strength of animal studies such as those by Lorenz, is that the findings have been influential in the field of developmental psychology. For example, the fact that imprinting is seen to be irreversible (as suggested in Lorenz's study), shows that attachment formation is under biological control and happens within a specific time frame. This is a strength because it led the developmental psychologist Bowlby to develop his attachment theory, which suggested that the attachment formation is an innate biological process that must take place during a critical period. Such theories have been highly influential in the way childcare and parenting is administered today.

✔ **Supporting evidence for imprinting.** A strength of Lorenz's study is that there is research evidence to support imprinting. Guiton (1966) demonstrated that leghorn chickens which were exposed to yellow rubber gloves for feeding during the first few weeks, subsequently imprinted on the gloves. This is a strength because it supports the view that young animals are not born with a predisposition to imprint on a specific type of object, but probably on any moving things that are present during the critical window of development. However, Guiton also observed that the chickens eventually learned through experience to prefer other chickens over yellow rubber gloves. As a result, this study strengthens the overall validity of Lorenz's research into imprinting, however, the impact of imprinting on mating behaviour may not be as permanent as Lorenz believed.

Harlow's study

Strength

✔ **Controlled experiment.** A strength of Harlow's study is that it was conducted in a controlled, laboratory setting. Harlow was able to control potential extraneous variables such as the monkeys being taken away from their mothers straight after birth and the infant monkeys not being exposed to any love or attention from their biological mothers. This is a strength because it means that Harlow was measuring what he intended to measure (i.e. factors that can affect the formation of attachment) and therefore, the study can be seen to have high internal validity allowing a cause-and-effect relationship to be established.

✔ **Practical value.** A strength of Harlow's (1959) research into attachment is that there is a great deal of practical application from its findings. For example, Howe (1998) reported that Harlow's research has helped social workers understand risk factors in child neglect and abuse and so intervene to prevent this happening. In addition, Harlow's research has influenced the care of captive monkeys; we now understand the importance of proper attachment figures for baby monkeys in zoos and also breeding programmes in the wild. This is a strength because it demonstrates how Harlow's research has influenced society. As a result, this increases the relevance of Harlow's research into the importance of comfort in attachment.

✔ **Humans and monkeys are similar.** A strength of Harlow's study is that it may be possible to generalise the findings to humans, unlike the Lorenz study. For example, Green (1994) stated that, on a biological level, all mammals (including rhesus monkeys) have the same brain structure as humans; the only differences relate to size and the number of connections. As a consequence, we may be able to extrapolate the findings from Harlow's research into attachments to humans.

Weaknesses

✗ **Lacks internal validity.** A criticism of Harlow's research is the lack of control of the two 'mothers'. The two wire-mothers varied in more ways than just being cloth-covered or not, as they also had different heads. Therefore, it could be that the infant monkeys preferred the cloth-covered monkey as it was more attractive. The two different heads could have acted as a confounding variable, suggesting that Harlow's research may have lacked internal validity.

✗ Generalisability to humans. A weakness of Lorenz's research into imprinting is that we cannot generalise his findings about imprinting to humans. This is because Lorenz conducted his study on greylag geese and humans and geese are physiologically different. The way a human infant develops an attachment with their primary caregiver could be very different to the way a greylag goose forms an attachment. For example, mammalian mothers show more emotional attachment to their young than birds and mammals may be able to form attachments at any time. As a consequence, we cannot extrapolate the findings from Lorenz's research to humans and thus, this casts doubt over the explanatory power of Lorenz's research on human attachment.

✗ Artificial study. A weakness of Harlow's study is that it was conducted in a controlled, artificial laboratory setting. The highly controlled laboratory setting was not reflective of real-life situations and may have caused the monkeys to behave in an artificial manner. This is a weakness because it means that Harlow wasn't necessarily measuring the real-life attachment formation and therefore the study can be criticised for lacking ecological validity.

✗ Ethical issues. A criticism of Harlow's study is that it has been accused of being unethical. The monkeys in Harlow's study showed great distress when they were removed from their biological mothers. In addition, after the study, these monkeys suffered lasting emotional harm, had difficulty forming relationships, showed distress in social situations and were unable to communicate with other monkeys, as well as neglecting their own offspring. However, some psychologists argue that the experiment can be justified in terms of the significant effect it had on our understanding of attachment. This suggests that the benefits of some animal research may outweigh the costs. However, others argue the study doesn't really tell us anything about the formation of human attachments (monkeys and humans are physiologically different). Therefore, psychologists would argue that the lack of generalisability from this research makes Harlow's study even more unethical.

Practice exam questions

1. Describe the findings and procedure of one animal study of attachment. **[6 marks]**

2. Describe Lorenz's animal studies of attachment. Refer in your answer to what he did and what he found. **[6 marks]**

3. Briefly evaluate Lorenz's animal studies of attachment. **[4 marks]**

4. Describe Harlow's animal studies of attachment. Refer in your answer to what he did and what he found. **[6 marks]**

5. Briefly evaluate Harlow's animal studies of attachment. **[4 marks]**

6. Describe and evaluate two animal studies of attachment. **[12 marks AS, 16 marks A-level]**

AQA specification for Topic 3: Attachment

- Explanations of attachment: learning theory.

◆ Introduction

- There have been several explanations put forward to explain why an infant-mother attachment develops in the first place and what keeps the attachment bond going. The two theories you need for the exam are the learning theory (this exam note) and Bowlby's theory (the following exam note). Before we give the two explanations, it is worthwhile to be able to identify certain behaviours in an infant that show that an attachment to the mother has developed.

Evidence of attachment formation

- Research has shown that from approximately seven months onwards, babies will begin to show a preference for the mother over other people, suggesting an attachment has been formed. Maccoby (1980) identified certain types of behaviours that demonstrate that the baby has formed an attachment towards the mother.

  - Proximity seeking: A baby will display *proximity-seeking behaviour* towards the mother, which means they want to stay physically close to her. In the presence of unfamiliar faces, the baby will become anxious or cry, this is known as stranger anxiety.

  - Separation anxiety: A baby separated from the mother will show distressed behaviour such as crying and an unwillingness to separate, although the baby is easily comforted when the mother returns.

  - Secure base: The mother is seen as a secure base, which means the baby feels secure enough to move away from the mother and explore the surrounding physical environment, knowing that the mother will be close by. From time to time, the baby will make contact with the mother for reassurance while exploring their environment.

◆ Learning theory of attachments

- Learning Theory (or Behavioural Theory) suggests that attachments are not innate, but babies learn to form an attachment to the mother through the experiences of feeding, that is, because the mother feeds them. The attachment is formed either by the process of classical conditioning or operant conditioning. This approach has often been called the 'Cupboard Love' theory, becomes cats often display 'sudden' attachment behaviour to their owners, when they see the owner going into the 'cupboard' to get their can of cat food. This theory states that children (and cats) learn to love whoever feeds them.

Classical conditioning

Classical conditioning suggests that babies form an attachment though the process of association. The mother is 'associated' with food and the baby will become attached to those who feed it. We have described the process below.

Food is known as the unconditioned stimulus (UCS) because this stimulates an involuntary reaction for the baby to salivate at the sight/smell of food when hungry. This reaction to salivate is known as the unconditioned response (UCR).

(Unconditioned response means the reflex response happens automatically, we do not have to make it happen)

⬇

When a baby is fed, she/he feels pleasure as this satisfies their hunger. The mother, who feeds the baby, is known as the neutral stimulus (NS). Over time, the mother becomes 'associated' with the unconditioned stimulus (food).

(The mother is a neutral stimulus because the infant does not react at the sight of the mother)

When the mother and the food are 'associated' together, the mother becomes a conditioned stimulus (CS) to the baby. This is because the baby has now been conditioned (learned) to associate the mother with food. This brings a reaction of pleasure to the baby, known as conditioned response (CR) regardless of whether food is present or not.

Through this process of *classical conditioning*, an attachment forms because the mother, who is the feeder, is now associated with pleasure.

Operant conditioning

Dollard and Miller (1950) explained attachment through the process of operant conditioning. The theory is that the baby attaches itself to the mother because they see the mother as a source of providing positive reinforcement (rewarding). The mother is able to reduce the baby's physiological discomfort (e.g. hunger, thirst, cold, etc.), which the baby finds satisfying. We have described the process below.

Food is seen as a primary reinforcer (rewarding) because the baby finds eating food a pleasing experience as this reduces the unpleasant feelings of hunger.

(Primary reinforcer means any behaviour/action that is rewarding and does not have to be learnt)

The mother is seen as a secondary reinforcer because she provides the baby with food which helps reduce the unpleasant feelings of hunger, which is rewarding.

(Secondary reinforcer means any behaviour/action that has been learnt to be rewarding)

Therefore, a baby becomes attached to the mother because she is seen as a source of reward (reduction of discomfort). Attachment-seeking behaviour (crying, smiling) brings positive responses to the baby, so such behaviour is more likely to be repeated.

Operant conditioning can explain why adults learn to form an attachment with babies too. Whenever a baby cries, this is unpleasant for the mother, who is likely to respond by feeding or cuddling them and this will eventually lead the baby to stop crying. Therefore, the mother responds to stop the child from crying, because crying acts as a negative reinforcer for the mother. Negative reinforcers mean certain acts or behaviours are carried out ('stamped in') to stop something unpleasant from continuing, in this case, the baby crying! Therefore, negative reinforcers make the mother's behaviour, feeding and cuddling, more likely to occur in the future as this will stop the crying, so this behaviour will be repeated again and again – it has been 'stamped in'.

◆ Evaluation

Strength

✔ **Laboratory experiment.** A strength of learning theory is that it has laboratory-based evidence to support the classical conditioning explanation for attachment. For example, Pavlov (1927) found that dogs would begin to salivate (in the absence of food or smell) whenever an assistant entered the room, suggesting salivation was a learned response. The dogs were responding to the sight of the research assistant's white lab coat, which the dog had come to associate with food. Therefore, this increases the validity of the classical conditioning explanation in the formations of attachment.

Weaknesses

✗ **Responsive parents, not food.** A weakness of this theory is that there is research evidence against the learning theory of attachment. Schaffer & Emerson (1964) observed Glaswegian babies and found that 40% of the infants were most attached to people who did not feed, bathe or change them, but who were more responsive and provided stimulation through play and touch. This contradicts the learning theory of attachment because if this theory were correct, 100% of the babies would have formed an attachment with the people who fed them. Therefore, this suggests that the formation of attachment bonds is not based solely on food but more on the responsiveness of the mother. As a result, this weakens the learning theory as an explanation of attachment.

✗ **Rhesus monkeys.** Further opposing research evidence comes from Harlow's (1959) famous experiment on rhesus monkeys. Eight monkeys were raised in isolation and deprived of their real mother. Each monkey was allocated a cage that contained two 'wire-mesh mothers' (not real monkeys). One bare wire-mesh mother had just a feeding bottle fitted, and a rectangular box-shaped face. The other was wrapped in soft cloth with no milk bottle (no food) and a monkey-like face. He found that the monkeys spent most of the time clinging to the cloth-covered mother, even though she provided no milk. This was especially true when the monkey was frightened and this demonstrated proximity-seeking behaviour indicating attachment. This is a weakness of the learning theory because the experiment suggests that food is not a crucial factor in the process of forming an attachment. The infant monkeys were more likely to form an attachment with those who provided comfort and security. As a consequence, this weakens the explanatory power of the learning theory of attachment.

✗ **Bowlby's theory of attachment.** Another criticism of learning theory is that Bowlby's theory may provide a better explanation of attachment. His theory can explain why attachments form, whereas learning theory can only explain how they form. Also, Bowlby's theory outlines the benefits of attachment, which learning theory does not. For example, Bowlby argues that attachments form because they are adaptive and promote survival. This means that Bowlby's theory provides a more complete explanation for attachment. In summary, learning theory does not offer a full account as to why attachments form and therefore the validity of the learning theory in explaining the formation of attachment is weakened.

✗ **Evidence on non-human research.** The research evidence to support the learning theory of attachments has been criticised on methodological grounds (the method is used to collect the evidence). Many of the experimental studies have been carried out on non-humans (i.e. animals), such as Harlow's rhesus monkey study. Although there may be some similarities, there are also clear differences between human and non-human interactions when it comes to attachments. This means it is difficult to apply the findings of experimental research-carried out on non-humans to attachment in human beings. Therefore, the learning theory may lack validity because it presents an oversimplified version of human behaviour.

✗ **Social learning theory**. There is a newer learning explanation based on social learning theory (SLT). Hay and Vespo (1988) suggested that parents teach children to love them by modelling attachment behaviours (e.g. hugging them and other family members) and also by rewarding them with approval when they display their own attachment behaviours ('that's a lovely smile', etc.). In this version, babies have learned attachment behaviours as a result of their interactions, which fits with research on the importance of interactional synchrony and reciprocity.

Practice exam questions

1. Describe the learning theory of attachments. **[6 marks]**

2. Briefly evaluate learning theory as an explanation of attachment. **[4 marks]**

3. Outline research findings that challenge the learning theory of attachment. **[4 marks]**

4. Outline and evaluate the learning theory of attachment. **[12 marks AS, 16 marks A-level]**

AQA specification for Topic 3: Attachment

- Explanations of attachment: Bowlby's monotropic theory. The concepts of a critical period and an internal working model.

◆ Bowlby's monotropic theory of attachments

John Bowlby's theory is probably the most influential explanation for the formation of attachments. He rejects the view that attachments are a learnt process (Learning Theory) and instead suggests that attachment formation is a biological process (that has evolved over thousands of years), in which babies are innately programmed (in their genes) to display attachment-seeking behaviour for survival and reproductive reasons.

- **Survival and reproductive value.** Babies who engage in proximity-seeking behaviour (staying close) enable the mother to offer greater protection and safety than those babies that do not. So, babies who display such behaviours increase their likelihood of survival. Babies that do survive are more likely to go on and ultimately reproduce themselves and pass on the 'attachment genes' (behaviours programmed to form an attachment) to the next generation ensuring their greater chance of continued survival. Attachments, therefore, also have a reproductive value. One of the innate behaviours that babies are born with is to display social releasers, such as smiling, crying and cooing. The aim is to provoke a sympathetic and caring reaction from the mother and thus increase their chance of survival.

- **Monotropy theory.** According to Bowlby, babies will bond with a number of attachment figures that will vary in degree of closeness (called hierarchy of attachments). However, the baby will have an innate drive to form a special bond to one particular primary attachment figure. This will often be to the one who responds in the most sensitive way to the baby's social releasers, usually the mother. This favouritism towards one attachment figure is called monotropy. According to Bowlby, the special formation of attachment between the mother and the baby must occur within 2½ to 3 years of the baby's life, called the critical period. After this time frame, an attachment will be unlikely to occur, which can have negative consequences on the baby's cognitive and social development later on in life.

- **Internal working model.** The type of relationship the baby experiences with the primary attachment figure (e.g. caring, secure, inconsistent) will provide the baby with their own expectations of what relationships should all be like. This is called the internal working model. Bowlby also proposed that the early type of attachment type that the child experiences will shape their emotional relationships later in life (e.g. secure or insecure relationships). Bowlby called this the continuity hypothesis. A study by Bailey (2007) questioned 99 teenage mothers with one-year-old babies about their attachment to their mothers. They also observed the participants with their own young children. They found that those mothers who reported insecure attachments to their own parents were much more likely to have children whose behaviour implied insecure attachment. Bailey's findings support Bowlby's theory that a pattern of insecure attachment was being passed from one generation to the next.

◆ Evaluation

Strength

✔ **Attachments have adaptive and survival value.** Bowlby's attachment theory has supporting research evidence that attachments are genetically programmed. Lorenz (1952) reared a batch of goose eggs in an incubator; when they hatched, the first thing they saw moving was Lorenz and their innate response was to start following him around. This is an animal version of attachment, ensuring that the young are genetically programmed to stay close in order to be fed and protected from danger. However, there is the issue of generalising findings from animal research and applying these to explain human behaviour. As a consequence, caution is required in using this research evidence to validate Bowlby's attachment theory.

✔ **Evidence for social releasers.** Further strength of Bowlby's theory is that there is clear evidence to support the existence and value of social releasers. For example, Brazelton (1975) asked mothers to ignore their baby's social releasers. He found that the babies became distressed quickly and some even curled up and became motionless, exhibiting signs of depression. These findings support Bowlby's idea that attachment depends on good quality care and the importance of responding to social releasers. As a result, this supports Bowlby's ideas about the significance of infant social behaviour eliciting caregiving from adults and the role of releasers in initiating social interaction.

✔ **Internal working model.** An additional strength is that there is research evidence to support Bowlby's internal working model. Hazan & Shaver (1987) designed a love quiz and found that securely attached infants tended to have secure loving relationships in adulthood, whereas insecurely attached infants found adult relationships more challenging, and were more likely to be divorced. This would support Bowlby's continuity hypothesis, suggesting that early attachment experience can have an effect on relationships later in life. This provides credible support for Bowlby's internal working model.

Weaknesses

✘ **Opposing research for monotropy theory.** Schaffer and Emerson (1964) carried out a longitudinal study on 60 Glasgow babies over a two-year period to see how attached infants were to various adults. They found that by seven months old, 29% (nearly one-third) had formed multiple attachments to two or more people. By 10 months old, this figure was 59% (more than half) and at 18 months, 87% had formed multiple attachments. These findings suggest babies do not necessarily have a preferred attachment figure, as claimed by Bowlby's monotropy theory.

✘ **Critical period.** A final criticism of Bowlby's theory is the concept of the critical period. Many studies, such as Rutter et al., have showed that a critical period is true to some extent, because whilst it appears less likely that attachments will form after this period, it is not impossible to form an attachment outside of the critical period. For example, a case study by Curtiss (1997) reported that Genie who was isolated and brought up by abusive parents up to the age of 12, did go on and develop a mild attachment behaviour to others. Tizard and Hodge's study of adopted children (assuming no attachment were formed prior to adoption), found that even children adopted later than the age of 2½ managed to form attachment bonds to their new parents. This means that researchers now use the term 'sensitive' period, instead of a 'critical' period, suggesting that Bowlby's original idea of a critical period isn't completely correct.

Practice exam questions

1. Explain what is meant by 'critical period' and 'internal working model'.   **[2 marks + 2 marks]**

2. Describe Bowlby's theory of attachments.   **[6 marks]**

3. Outline how the learning theory of attachments differs from Bowlby's theory of attachment.   **[4 marks]**

4. Outline two criticisms of Bowlby's theory of attachment.   **[2 marks + 2 marks]**

5. Outline research findings that challenge Bowlby's theory of attachment.   **[4 marks]**

6. Outline and evaluate Bowlby's theory of attachment.   **[12 marks AS, 16 marks A-level]**

AQA specification for Topic 3: Attachment

- Ainsworth's 'Strange Situation'. Types of attachment: secure, insecure-avoidant and insecure-resistant.

◆ Introduction

Explanations of attachment (e.g. learning theory and Bowlby's theory) deal with *why* attachments are formed between the baby and the mother, but do not offer reasons for the *different types* of attachments that can develop between the baby and mother. It is the extensive research by Mary Ainsworth et al. (1978) that has shown that different types of attachment exist, by using an experimental research procedure known as the 'Strange Situation'.

AN 'EYE' ON THE STUDY

Strange Situation experiment
(Ainsworth, 1978)

Aim

- The aim was to *test* and *classify* the different types of attachment that exists between the mother and the baby, using the 'Strange Situation' procedure.

Procedure

- The Strange Situation test was conducted in a laboratory experiment setting with a sample of 100 American babies aged between 12 and 18 months. They were placed in a playroom setting that contained toys, and left to play for approximately 20 minutes. During this time, the baby was exposed to eight separate episodes lasting about three minutes each, except for episode one, which lasted 30 seconds. The baby's behaviour was observed and recorded (controlled observation – the observers were behind a one-way mirror). The eight episodes were:

  Episode 1: Mother and baby are introduced to the experimental play room.

  Episode 2: Mother and baby are alone; the infant is left to explore and play with the toys.

  Episode 3: A stranger enters, talks with the mother, and approaches the baby. The mother leaves discreetly.

  Episode 4: The stranger continues to interact with the baby through play.

  Episode 5: Mother enters the room; the stranger leaves discreetly. The mother comforts the baby if in distress. The mother leaves again.

  Episode 6: Baby is left alone in the room.

  Episode 7: The stranger comes back and attempts to interact with the baby.

  Episode 8: The mother returns and greets the baby; the stranger leaves discreetly.

→

Findings and conclusion

The results showed individual differences in behavioural and emotional responses in the sample of babies observed. This led to a classification of three types of attachment.

- **Type B: securely attached (70%):** The baby with a secure attachment *will see the mother as a secure base* - the baby feels confident enough to explore and play in their environment but will seek proximity when required. The baby tends to show *moderate separation anxiety*, will be moderately upset when the mother departs, but is *easily comforted* upon the mother's return. Contact with strangers in the presence of the mother is fine - the baby is unaffected but will display *moderate stranger anxiety* when left alone with an unfamiliar face.

- **Type A: insecure-avoidant (20%):** A baby with this type of insecure attachment style tends to ignore or avoid interaction with the mother and others – the baby is indifferent to the mother and therefore does not seek proximity. Separation anxiety tends not to be an issue, and the baby shows little emotional response towards the mother's presence or absence. *Stranger anxiety is also not an issue* - the baby does not treat unfamiliar people much differently from the mother, and thus *can be comforted by a stranger*. However, distress is caused by being alone.

- **Type C: insecure-resistant (10%):** A baby with this type of insecure attachment tends to display a degree of anxiousness. The mother is *not seen as a secure base*, the baby *lacks confidence in exploring* and remains very close, often displaying *clingy behaviour*. When separated from the mother, the baby shows *high levels of separation anxiety* demonstrated by distressed and anxious behaviour. The *baby is not easily comforted* upon the mother's return, displaying mixed emotions, seeking comfort, yet showing resentment and resistance towards the mother when she initiates comfort. The baby will also become distressed by unfamiliar people, even when the mother is present, exhibiting high levels of *stranger anxiety*.

◆ Evaluation

Strengths

✔ **Reliable.** A strength of the Strange Situation test other researchers can easily repeat it using the same controlled experimental conditions. This allows them to see if the findings into attachment types are the same as the original. In fact, this study has been repeated numerous times and gained consistent results in the USA, indicating test-retest reliability. For example, Wartner et al. (1994) tested the reliability of the Strange Situation in Germany and found that 78% of the children were classified in the same way at the age of one, and later at six years of age. This provides credible support for the Strange Situation as a measuring technique for assessing attachment types, which means generalisations can be made about the different types of attachments.

✔ **Ainsworth's research has real-life usage.** A strength of this research is its real-world importance. Ainsworth's research led her to explain that 'maternal sensitivity' underlies secure attachment. Mothers who show sensitive and responsive parenting to their infant's needs tend to have infants with secure attachments. We can use these findings to improve children's lives. In situations where insecure attachment develops, intervention strategies can be put in place to help the mother. These strategies teach mothers to be more responsive to their infant's needs and results show that this has changed infants' attachment types for the better. However, Ravel et al. (2001) found low correlations between measures of maternal sensitivity and the strength of attachment. Slade et al. (2005) found that the ability to understand what someone else is thinking and feeling, rather than maternal sensitivity, may be the central mechanism in establishing attachment type.

Weaknesses

✗ **Low in internal validity.** A weakness of the Strange Situation procedure is that it is low in internal validity. Main and Weston (1981) found children behave differently depending on which parent they are with. This is an issue because the infant may be securely attached to their mother, but insecurely attached to their father. As a result, the Strange Situation may not be measuring what it intends to measure – the attachment type of the infant itself. It may be measuring the quality of the relationship with a particular carer. This finding reduces the validity of the Strange Situation as a measure of the infant's attachment type.

✗ **Third variable.** Another limitation is that an infant's temperament may be a confounding variable. Ainsworth assumed that the main influence on separation and stranger anxiety was the quality of the attachment between the infant and the mother. However, Kagan (1984) suggested that a child's temperament (their genetically influenced personality) is a more important influence on behaviour in the Strange Situation. For example, some infants show more friendly behaviour than others which makes it easier to demonstrate secure attachment with the mother. Other infants do not require their mother's maternal interest (not so friendly) and may be classified as having an insecure attachment. This challenges the validity of the Strange Situation because this technique intends to measure the quality of attachment, not the temperament of the child.

✗ **Culturally biased.** The Strange Situation test has been criticised for being culturally biased (ethnocentric). It was designed to investigate attachment behaviours in American babies and such a test may not be appropriate to apply to other cultures. For example, behaviour classified as having an insecure-attachment type under the Strange Situation test may not be universal. In some cultures, mothers hardly ever leave their baby alone, so the experience of being separated during the test will be highly distressing to the baby. This suggests that it is the unfamiliarity of the Strange Situation rather than demonstrating an insecure relationship with the mother, which influences the baby's behaviour.

✗ **Ethical issue.** The Strange Situation technique has been criticised for causing psychological harm. Psychologists have argued that it is unacceptable to place babies and their mothers in a situation that will cause mild or extreme stress just to test their attachment type. On the other hand, others have argued that the distress is short-term and the benefits outweigh this, such as enriching our understanding of the potential harm of children being hospitalised, orphaned, or left in daycare.

Practice exam questions

1. Outline two characteristic behaviours displayed by a 'secure' baby. **[2 marks]**

2. Outline two characteristic behaviours displayed by a 'insecure-resistant' baby. **[2 marks]**

3. Outline two characteristic behaviours displayed by a 'insecure-avoidant' baby. **[2 marks]**

4. Describe Ainsworth's research study into the different types of attachment. **[6 marks]**

5. Explain why Ainsworth's 'Strange Situation' study may be lacking in validity. **[3 marks]**

6. Outline two criticisms of Ainsworth's 'Strange Situation' study. **[2 marks + 2 marks]**

7. Describe and evaluate Ainsworth's 'Strange Situation' study. **[12 marks AS, 16 marks A-level]**

AQA specification for Topic 3: Attachment

- Cultural variations in attachment, including van Ijzendoorn.

◆ Key term

- **Cultural variations** in attachment are the variety of attachment types (secure, insecure-avoidant, insecure-resistant) that exist across different cultures. Research has shown the types of attachments that exist between the mother and baby are often due to different cultural child-rearing practices.

◆ Introduction

Many of the studies into attachment types, such Ainsworth's study, have been criticised for being culturally specific, because they have mainly based their research evidence on babies that have been raised in the American culture. In order to counter this criticism, psychologists have applied the Strange Situation experiment to a variety of different cultures in order to see if Ainsworth's explanations into attachment types can be applied universally.

AN 'EYE' ON THE STUDY

Cultural studies of attachment
(Van Ijzendoorn and Kroonenberg, 1988)

Aim

- Van Ijzendoorn and Kroonenberg investigated cross-cultural variation, in order to find out if Ainsworth's classification of attachment types can be applied across other cultures, or whether it is culturally specific.

Procedure

- They carried out a meta-analysis on 32 studies that had used the Strange Situation technique to test the attachment type between the mother and the infant.

- This involved over 2000 children from eight different countries, five Western countries (USA, Great Britain, Netherlands, Sweden, West Germany) and three non-Western countries (Israel, Japan and China).

Findings and conclusions

Results – see Table 1 (below)

- *Consistency across cultures:* The overall pattern of attachment types was similar to Ainsworth's findings across all cultures. Secure attachment (Type B) was the most common in all eight countries. The lowest percentage of secure attachment was shown in China and the highest in Great Britain.

- *Difference in insecure-avoidant attachments:* There were significant differences between cultures with regards to insecure attachments. Insecure-avoidant attachment (Type A) was more common in Western cultures, with the highest percentage in West Germany; and lowest in non-Western cultures, e.g. Israel and Japan, where it was rare.

- *Difference in insecure-resistant attachments:* In the non-Western cultures (China, Japan and Israel), the results showed a high proportion of insecure-resistant attachment (Type C), in comparison to Western cultures. China was the only exception; the percentage of avoidant and resistant types was the same.

→

- *Variation within the same country:* Another key finding was that there was 1.5 times greater variation within the same cultures (countries) than between different cultures. For example, in the three separate sample studies from West Germany, the researchers found very different attachment types. In the only two samples taken from Japan, one study found that none of the babies showed Type A attachment, whereas the other study showed Type A to be approximately 20%, which is close to the results for Ainsworth's (1988) original study carried out in America.

Country	Number of studies	(Type B) % Secure	(Type A) % Insecure-avoidant	(Type C) % Insecure-resistant
Great Britain	1	75%	22%	3%
USA	18	65%	21%	14%
Sweden	1	74%	22%	4%
Netherlands	4	67%	26%	7%
West Germany	3	57%	35%	8%
Japan	2	68%	5%	27%
China	1	50%	25%	25%
Israel	2	64%	7%	29%
Total studies	32			
Overall average		65%	21%	14%

Conclusions

- The overall universal global pattern in attachment types seems to be similar to that found in the USA, suggesting the secure attachment type is also the norm in other cultures.

- There are significant cultural variations in attachment types, especially in terms of avoidant and resistant insecure attachments.

- There are greater intra-cultural variations (within) than inter-cultural variations (between) in attachment types between the mother and the infant.

AN 'EYE' ON THE STUDY

Japanese infants
(Takahashi, 1990)

- Van Ijzendoorn and Kroonenberg's findings showed that a high proportion of Japanese babies (27%) were classified as Type C (insecure resistant) in comparison to other countries. This was supported by a later study by Takahashi (1990), who investigated 60 middle-class Japanese infants using the Strange Situation test. He found that a relatively high proportion of attachments in Japanese infants were classified Type C (32%). One explanation is that Japanese mothers tend to keep much closer body contact throughout the day with their infants. Japanese infants are rarely separated from their mothers, left alone, or left with a stranger at such an early age. Therefore, a Japanese infant would have found some parts of the Strange Situation technique (separation from mother or being with a stranger) extremely distressing because of the unusualness of such an experience. The Japanese infants' response of displaying high levels of separation anxiety appeared to demonstrate an insecure attachment, but may, in fact, have been due to the unfamiliarity of the experience.

AN 'EYE' ON THE STUDY

German infants
(Grossman and Grossman, 1991)

- Van Ijzendoorn and Kroonenberg's findings showed that the German infants had the highest Type A (insecure-avoidant attachment) classification (35%) in comparison to the other countries. This is further supported by an earlier study by Grossman and Grossman (1991), who studied German infants using the Strange Situation test and found that 52% were insecure-avoidant, whereas 35% were securely attached (compared with around 65% in the USA). The high percentage of German infants showing insecure-avoidant attachment can be explained in the different approach to child-rearing practices. German child-rearing practices emphasise interpersonal distance between the parent and the infant. German mothers encourage their children to be more independent and encourage non-clinging behaviour from early on, more so than other cultures. This may explain why most German babies were less affected by the mother's absence; they were less inclined to display proximity-seeking behaviour or separation anxiety when the mother left the room in the 'Strange Situation' experiment.

◆ Explaining the differences for cultural variations for types of attachments

- At face value, Van Ijzendoorn and Kroonenberg's cultural research showed a high proportion of infants from Japan, China, Israel and West Germany as having an insecure attachment (Type A or C). It would be wrong to assume that infants in such cultures are less securely attached to their mothers than in other cultures, demonstrating that replicating the Strange Situation test in other cultures is inappropriate. Explanations for cultural variation in attachment types point to another reason – cultural differences in child-rearing practices and attitudes.

◆ Evaluation

Strengths

✔ **Population validity.** A strength of Van Ijzendoorn's (1988) study is that it has high population validity. This is because it involved studying a large sample size of over 2000 children, from within different cultures and between different cultures. This means we can make general statements about attachment types within and between cultures, both for collectivist and individualistic cultures. For instance, secure attachments are the most common across all types of cultures. Therefore, the findings have high external validity.

✔ **Study was ethical.** Another strength of Van Ijzendoorn's (1988) study is that it did not raise any ethical issues. This is because the researchers analysed secondary data (meta-analysis) to investigate the findings of studies using the Strange Situation test in different cultures. This means the researchers were free from potentially causing psychological harm, as would occur if the researchers conducted the Strange Situation test themselves. Psychologists have argued it is unacceptable to place babies and their mothers in stressful situations just to test the infants' attachment type. Therefore, Van Ijzendoorn's meta-analysis study is an appropriate method to use when investigating cross-cultural differences in attachment behaviour.

Weaknesses

✗ **Uneven sample.** Van Ijzendoorn and Kroonenberg's meta-analysis has been criticised because of the limited number of studies in some countries. Although the meta-analysis was carried out in eight countries, the range in sample size between Western and non-Western cultures was not evenly distributed because there was a very limited sample coming from non-Western countries. For example, 27 of the studies were from Western countries and the remaining five were from non-Western countries. Only one was from China, two from Japan, and two from Israel. This means that there is a problem of generalisation from a limited sample about cultural variation in attachment types.

✗ **Cross-cultural studies suffer from imposed etic.** Van Ijzendoorn and Kroonenberg's research on cross-cultural variation has been criticised for suffering from an **imposed etic**. This is where a culturally specific idea is wrongly imposed on another culture. This is because the Strange Situation technique was developed in America, to test attachment behaviours based on American cultural norms, and is not be appropriate for making cross-cultural comparisons of attachment types. For instance, Ainsworth, an American, assumed that the mild 'separation anxiety' was an indication of secure attachment. However, Takahashi (1990) suggested that in non-Western countries (collectivist cultures) such as Japan and China, infants are rarely left alone or with a stranger. Therefore, this unusual experience would account for the extreme distress response it caused in the Strange Situation test. This does not mean the Japanese infants had an insecure attachment with their mother but shows different child-rearing practices. This means the Strange Situation technique may be low in ecological validity because the findings might not give a true reflection of cultural variations in attachment and as a result, van Ijzendoorn and Kroonenberg's meta-analysis study may be inherently flawed.

✗ **Internal validity questioned.** Van Ijzendoorn and Kroonenberg's meta-analysis research in cross-cultural variation has been criticised for possibly having low internal validity. This is because the Strange Situation test may not be an accurate 'measuring tool' to determine mother-infant attachment types. Although the infant-mother relationship has a strong influence on attachment types, there are other factors that can affect attachment relationships. Kagan (1984) argued that the baby's temperament (personality) can also determine this. Some babies do not require the mother's maternal interest, which makes it difficult to establish an attachment bond and this will affect how the mother responds to the infant. Also, children who have been in daycare may display 'insecurely-avoidant' behaviour because they are used to being separated from their mother, and not 'insecure-avoidant'. This means that Van Ijzendoorn and Kroonenberg's findings may be flawed, because the Strange Situation test may actually be measuring the difference in temperament between cultures, rather than infant-mother parenting style.

1. In van Ijzendoorn's cross-cultural investigations of attachment, which one of the following countries was found to have the highest percentage of anxious-avoidant children?

   Circle **one** letter only.

   A. China

   B. Germany

   C. Great Britain

   D. Japan   **[1 mark]**

2. Explain what is meant by the term 'cultural variations'.   **[2 marks]**

3. Describe the procedure of one study into cultural variations in attachments.   **[4 marks]**

4. Explain one criticism of research into cultural variations in attachments.   **[3 marks]**

5. Describe one or more studies that have investigated cultural variations in attachments.   **[6 marks]**

6. Discuss research into cultural variations in attachments.   **[12 marks AS, 16 marks A-level]**

AQA specification for Topic 3: Attachment

- Bowlby's theory of maternal deprivation.

◆ Key term

- Deprivation: Psychologists see deprivation as the loss of attachment between the caregiver and infant through separation. This can be short term, for example when a child goes into hospital, or long term, as in a divorce or death.

◆ Bowlby's maternal deprivation theory

- John Bowlby's (1951) maternal deprivation theory suggested that if the mother-infant attachment is disrupted (for a long time) or lost, or no attachment is formed during the critical period (before age 2½ years); this can have negative effects on the child's intellectual, social and emotional development e.g. affectionless psychopathy, delinquency, or low IQ. According to Bowlby, these effects will be permanent and irreversible. Bowlby also proposed the continuity hypothesis, which states that if there are prolonged separations between the infant and their mother, the negative psychological effects will continue into adulthood.

- Bowlby did believe that the negative psychological effects could be minimised if a mother substitute took on the role of the absent mother and was able to provide emotional care (sensitive parenting) to the infant.

- Bowlby suggested that a child develops a mental representation of their first attachment (with the primary caregiver), which will then profoundly affect all future relationships and their own success as a parent. This is called the internal working model. So, if an infant experiences an insecure attachment with the mother, this can lead to the inability to be a good parent themselves to their children. A study by Bailey (2007) questioned 99 teenage mothers with one-year old babies about their attachment to their own mothers. They also observed the teenage mothers with their own babies. They found that those teenage mothers who reported insecure attachments to their own parents were much more likely to have children whose behaviour implied insecure attachment. This suggests that, as Bowlby proposed, a pattern of insecure attachment was being passed from one generation to the next.

- According to Bowlby, the psychological consequences of maternal deprivation include:

  - An inability to form attachments in the future
  - Affectionless psychopathy (inability to feel remorse and feelings for others)
  - Delinquency (behavioural problems in adolescence)
  - Problems with cognitive development (low IQ).

👁 AN 'EYE' ON THE STUDY

Supporting evidence for the maternal deprivation theory
A study of 44 juvenile thieves

John Bowlby carried out a study on 44 juvenile thieves to show the link between maternal deprivation and affectionless psychopathy.

Aim

- The aim was to see the effects of long-term maternal deprivation on a child's emotional development.

→

Procedure

- Bowlby (1944) carried out a case study over a number of years to investigate the effects of long-term bond disruption. The study was based on a sample of 88 children (aged 5–16 years) who were selected from the London Child Guidance Clinic where Bowlby worked. All the children that attended the clinic were emotionally maladjusted. A group of 44 juvenile 'thieves' (referred for stealing) was compared with a control group of 44 children, the 'non-thieves'. All the 88 children were given a variety of psychological assessments for signs of affectionless psychopathy; lack of affection to others, lack of guilt or shame at their actions, or a lack of empathy for their victims. Bowlby interviewed the children and mothers separately to establish any prolonged separations from mothers in their first two years of life.

Findings

- Bowlby found that 32% (14 of the 44) of the thieves were diagnosed with affectionless psychopathy, whereas none of the children in the control group was diagnosed with affectionless psychopathy.

- Next, he found that, of those thieves diagnosed with affectionless psychopathy, a high number had experienced early and long periods of separation from their mothers (86% or 12 of the 14 thieves with affectionless psychopathy). Only five of the 30 (17%) thieves not classified as affectionless psychopaths had experienced early separations.

- Bowlby also found that 39% (17 of the 44) of thieves had experienced early and long periods of separation from their mothers, whereas only 4% (two of the 44) of the control group had experienced long periods of separation.

Conclusion

- These findings support the maternal deprivation theory because they demonstrate a link between early separation and later social and emotional maladjustment. In the most severe form, maternal deprivation appears to lead to affectionless psychopathy. In the less severe form, it leads to antisocial behaviour (stealing).

Strengths

✔ **Depressed children.** Spitz and Wolf studied 100 children who showed symptoms of depression (sad facial expression, crying, withdrawal, loss of appetite, mental deterioration) after staying in hospital. If the separation from the mother lasted less than three months, recovery from depression was very good, suggesting the effects are reversible. However, if the mother and the child were reunited after three months, full recovery was unlikely, and the emotional effects of long-term separation could often be permanent.

✔ **Changes towards child-rearing practices.** A further strength is that Bowlby's maternal deprivation theory has real-life application to childcare practices. Before Bowlby's research, children were separated from their parents when they spent time in hospital and visiting was discouraged. However, Bowlby's research led to major social changes in the way children were cared for in hospitals, such as changing hospital visiting times and allowing parents to stay in the hospital, in order not to disrupt the bond between child and caregiver. This shows that his theory has made an invaluable contribution to childhood development by helping society to change practices and policies in order to ensure a positive attachment experience.

◆ Evaluation

✗ **Damaged caused by privation and deprivation?** Rutter (1972) criticised Bowlby's concept of maternal deprivation for being too general, as it did not account for the different types of early attachment experience (separations). These experiences can have quite different psychological effects on the child's development. Rutter (1981) argued that Bowlby's maternal deprivation theory did not distinguish between deprivation and privation experiences. Privation refers to the absence of any attachment figure, whereas deprivation means an attachment had been established and then lost. Rutter claimed that the distinction is important because the two can have different effects. It may be privation, and not deprivation, that has far more serious and permanent negative consequences for the child than the loss of an attachment bond. Case studies of privation such as Curtiss' 1977 study of 'Genie', support the argument that the effects of privation, are permanent and irreversible. This means there is a key distinction between the two, and a lack of clarity may affect the validity of research findings.

✗ **Based on retrospective data.** Bowlby's study of 44 juvenile thieves has also been criticised because the data collected was retrospective. The study relied on the parents and the children looking back and recalling past events (over 14 years), of when they had become separated from their children. As a result, their memory recall may have been inaccurate, or they may have distorted the information to avoid embarrassment or criticism. This means that findings could be low in reliability and validity, which weakens the credibility of the maternal deprivation theory.

✗ **Correlational evidence.** Another weakness is that, although Bowlby's maternal deprivation theory showed a link between frequent separation and emotional maladjustment (affectionless psychopathy), we cannot be certain that frequent separation actually caused affectionless psychopathy. This is because this was not a true experimental study, so it is possible that a 'third' variable caused the affectionless psychopathy, not separation from the mother. For example, children from an unhappy home (abuse/neglect) are more prone to anti-social behaviour, which also leads to emotional maladjustment. In this case, it would be an unhappy home that caused the emotional problems and not the separations. This suggests that the research findings may be low in validity because we cannot be certain of a cause-and-effect relationship between the two variables.

✗ **Family discord (conflict).** Rutter (1981) raised additional issues with Bowlby's theory, when he studied a large number of boys aged 9 – 12, who had all been separated from their mother for some time during early childhood. He found that the majority did not become delinquent, but for those who did, the separation usually involved stressful factors, such as a parent in prison or with a mental health problem, or difficult divorce. Rutter concluded that was the difficulties that often follow separation that caused the problem, and not simply the separation. This suggests that discord, rather than separation on its own, causes delinquency and emotional maladjustment. As a consequence, this reduces the credibility of Bowlby's '44 thieves' study and also the explanatory power of the maternal deprivation theory.

✘ **Critical period is a sensitive period.** One weakness of Bowlby's maternal deprivation theory is that there is evidence to suggest that deprivation in the critical period is not inevitably damaging. There are cases of maternal deprivation where children have still developed normally if given proper aftercare. For example, Koluchova (1976) reported a case of twin boys from Czechoslovakia who were isolated from 18 months until they were seven years old. They were later adopted by two loving sisters and appeared to make a full recovery. This study weakens the maternal deprivation theory because it shows that the critical period identified by Bowlby may be more of a 'sensitive' period and with good quality care, a child can recover fully from the deprivation. As a result, this reduces the validity of Bowlby's theory of deprivation.

Practice exam questions

1. Explain what is meant by the term 'critical period' in relation to attachment. **[2 marks]**

2. Explain what is meant by the term 'internal working model' in relation to attachment. **[3 marks]**

3. Explain what is meant by the term 'monotropic' in relation to attachment. **[2 marks]**

4. Explain two criticisms of Bowlby's monotropic theory of attachment. **[3 marks + 3 marks]**

5. Briefly outline one research study that supports Bowlby's monotropic theory of attachment. **[3 marks]**

6. Abi had a happy, secure childhood with parents who loved her very much. She now has two children of her own and loves them very much too. The two children make friends easily and are confident and trusting.

   Referring to Abi and her family, explain what psychologists have discovered about the internal working model. **[Total 6 marks]**

7. Discuss Bowlby's monotropic theory of attachment. **[12 marks AS, 16 marks A-level]**

AQA specification for Topic 3: Attachment

- Romanian orphan studies: effects of institutionalisation.

◆ Key term

- **Institutional care and institutionalisation:** Institutional care is where a child is raised in an institution (e.g. orphanage or children's home). Institutionalisation is the negative effect (in this case on a child's development) of being raised in an institution.

◆ Introduction

- Bowlby's material deprivation hypothesis was largely based on studies in the 1940s of children raised in institutional care. One method for seeing the effects of deprivation is to look at orphan studies. In the 1990s, the media revealed the horrific conditions of children brought up in Romanian orphanages. This sad discovery gave psychologists the opportunity to study the effects of institutional care on children in detail.

AN 'EYE' ON THE STUDY

Rutter's English and Romanian Adoptee (ERA) study
(Rutter, 1998)

Aim

- The aim was to assess whether good quality care (demonstrating love and nurturing) could overturn the effects of poor early experiences of children in Romanian orphanages.

Procedure

- Michael Rutter et al. carried out a longitudinal study (beginning in 1998) using a natural experiment involving 165 Romanian orphans adopted in Britain, and assessed them at four, six, 11 and 15 years of age. A group of 52 British children adopted around the same time served as the control group, so the independent variable (IV) was the age of adoption. The experiment had three conditions:

Condition 1: Children adopted before the age of 6 months.

Condition 2: Children adopted between 6 months and two years.

Condition 3: Children adopted after the age of two years.

When the Romanian children first arrived, half of them showed deficient cognitive functioning e.g. intellectual disability, and many were malnourished (underweight). When the children were 11, the researchers compared the rate of recovery according to what age they were adopted (the earlier the better).

In term of the mean IQ score, the researchers found that:

- - in those adopted before six months, the mean IQ was 102

→

- - in those adopted between six months and two years, the mean IQ was 86

- - in those adopted after two years, the mean IQ was 77.

These differences remained at age 16.

In terms of attachment behaviour, they found that those adopted:

- before six months had fairly healthy attachments

- after six months displayed disinhibited attachment (attention-seeking, clinginess and social behaviour directed indiscriminately towards all adults regardless if they were familiar or not) and had problems with peer relationships.

Conclusion

- These findings support the view that there is a sensitive period in the development of attachments. A failure to form an attachment before the age of six months appears to have long-lasting effects. In those children adopted earlier from institutions (before 6 months), the chances of a full recovery are much better.

AN 'EYE' ON THE STUDY

The Bucharest Early Intervention Project (BEIP)
(Zeanah et al., 2005)

Another well-known Romanian orphan study is known as the Bucharest Early Intervention Project (BEIP).

Aim

- The aim of the study by Charles Zeanah and others (2005) was to examine the effect that institutionalisation has on the behavioural development of young children.

Procedure

- Using the Bucharest Early Intervention Project, Zeanah assessed attachment in 95 children aged 12-31 months, who had spent most of their lives in institutional care. The researchers compared the children to a control group of 50 children who had never lived in an institution. They measured the children's attachment types using the Strange Situation technique. Carers were also asked about unusual social behaviour including clingy, attention-seeking behaviour directed inappropriately at all adults (disinhibited attachment).

Findings

- 74% of the control group were categorised as securely attached (Type B) after the Strange Situation test but 19% of the institutionalised group were securely attached.

- 65% of institutionalised infants were classified as showing disorganised attachment (lack of consistent or predictable social behaviour towards others).

- 44% of institutionalised infants were classified as showing disinhibited attachment with only 20% of the non-institutionalised children demonstrating this.

.Conclusion

- Institutionalisation can have a negative impact on the child's ability to form a secure attachment and these children are more likely to be classified as having a disorganised attachment type.

◆ Possible effects of institutional care

Research (by Goldfarb, Spitz, Rutter, etc.) into children in institutional care, not just in Romanian orphanages, has found these possible effects in childhood and adulthood:

- **Delayed intellectual development** (e.g. low IQ/problems with concentration)
- **Delayed physical growth** (e.g. restricted growth, such as dwarfism)
- **Impaired language** (e.g. spoken and written)
- **Disinhibited attachment** (e.g. cannot discriminate between different people or shows inappropriate behaviour towards strangers, such as being over-friendly, clingy or attention-seeking)
- **Disorganised attachment** (e.g. inconsistent emotional behaviour towards others)
- **Emotional issues** (e.g.temper tantrums, etc.)
- **Lack of internal working model** (e.g. shows difficulty interacting with peers, forming close relationships, etc.)
- **Quasi-autism** (e.g. has difficulties understanding social situations or interaction)
- **Affectionless psychopathology** (e.g. shows a lack of remorse/guilt).

◆ Evaluation

Weaknesses

✗ **Cause and effect cannot be established.** One problem with Rutter's (1998) natural experiments is we cannot conclude, with certainty, of a that there is a cause-and-effect relationship between the experiences children have in institutional care and the damaging psychological effects children experienced. This is because children were not randomly assigned to either the adoption groups or control group as the researchers did not interfere with the adoption processes (being a natural experiment). This is a problem because it may be that those orphans adopted before they were six months old were more sociable, and of higher intelligence than those who were adopted later. This means the lack of random assignment can be a potential confounding variable that casts doubt over the internal validity of the findings on the effects of institutionalisation on children.

✗ **Problems of generalising.** Another issue with research into seeing the effects of Romanian orphanages is that such orphanages are not typical. This is a problem because the conditions in the Romanian orphanges were so poor that we cannot generalise the findings to understand the impact of institutional care, especially in better-quality orphanges in other countries. Romanian orphanages had very low standards of physical care and intellectual stimulation, which would not allowed to occur in other, more developed, countries then, and would not be permitted today. As a result, this casts doubt over the credibility of the effects institutional care has on child development.

Strengths

✔ **Real-life applications.** A strength of the research findings into the effect of institutionalisation, is that it has led to improvements in the way children are cared for in institutions. For example, orphanages and children's homes now avoid having large numbers of caregivers for each child. Instead, they now ensure that a smaller number of people play a central role for the child, often assigning each child a maximum of two caregivers. Having two key workers means that children have the chance to develop normal attachments and helps avoid disinhibited attachment occurring, which is immensely valuable in practical terms.

✔ **Evidence points to long-term effects.** It is too early to be certain say whether these Romanian children have suffered short-term or long-term effects. However, according to Edmund Sonuga-Barke (2017), regardless of the age adopted, emotional, social and cognitive issues still occur in adulthood such as difficulty engaging with other people or forming relationships, and problems with concentration and attention levels. For example, even those Romanian orphans that were adopted before six months were three to four times more likely to experience emotional problems as adults, with more than 40% having contact with mental health services, compared to non-institutionalised infants. However, it is clear that the earlier children are adopted and given good quality and consistent aftercare, the more likely this will minimise or overcome some of the effects of being raised in institutional care.

Weaknesses

✘ **Emotional deprivation may not be the single cause.** Some researchers have criticised the findings from Rutter's study as having low ecological validity. This is because we cannot be sure whether emotional deprivation (e.g. Bowlby's maternal deprivation theory) caused the physical and psychological effects on the children or whether they were due to the horrendous conditions. The Romanian orphans experienced appalling physical conditions that affected their health, and a lack of cognitive stimulation that affected their intellectual development; as well as emotional deprivation. As a result, we should be cautious when interpreting the effects of Romanian orphan studies as emotional deprivation may not be the single cause as suggested by Bowlby, but a number of factors may play a role.

Practise exam questions

1. Explain what is meant by the term 'institutional care' in terms of attachment. **[2 marks]**

2. Using an example of an attachment research study, explain what is meant by 'institutionalisation'. **[4 marks]**

3. Describe the procedure of one Romanian orphan study. **[4 marks]**

4. Describe one study of Romanian orphans. Include details of what the researcher(s) did and what they found. **[6 marks]**

5. Outline the effects of institutionalisation on the development of attachment. **[2 marks]**

6. Anca is an orphan who has recently been adopted by a British couple. Before being adopted, Anca lived in an institution with lots of other children in very poor conditions. Her new parents are understandably concerned about how Anca's early experiences may affect her in the future.

   Use your knowledge of the effects of institutionalisation to advise Anca's new parents about what to expect. **[5 marks]**

7. Discuss the effects of institutionalisation. Refer to the studies of Romanian orphans in your answer. **[12 marks AS, 16 marks A-level]**

AQA specification for Topic 3: Attachment

- The influence of early attachment on childhood and adult relationships, including the role of an internal working model.

◆ Introduction

Psychologists have been interested in seeing whether attachments made in infancy have an effect on relationships later on in life, such as relationships in childhood (including adolescence) and as adults.

◆ Internal working model

- John Bowlby (1969) argued that the type of relationship the baby experiences with the primary attachment figure will form a mental representation of this relationship. This will act as a template for what attachments/relationships are like, which Bowlby referred to as the internal working model. For example, a child who experiences a loving relationship with their mother will tend to form an expectation that all relationships are like this. As a result, the child's internal working model will influence later relationships in childhood and adulthood. This known as the continuity hypothesis, in other words, the attachment style that the infant experienced with their mother will continue to guide their relationship behaviour.

Childhood relationships

- Research indicates there is a continuity between early attachment styles and the quality of peer relationships in childhood. Kerns (1994) found that securely attached infants tend to form good childhood friendships, whereas insecurely attached infants have problems forming friendship later on, supporting the idea of continuity from early attachment and the internal working model. Myron-Wilson and Smith (1998) assessed attachment type and bullying involvement. They found that secure children were very unlikely to be involved in bullying. Insecure-avoidant children were the most likely to be victims and insecure-resistant children were most likely to be bullies

Adult relationships

- Research suggests that infant attachment style affects the quality of adult relationships. One of the most influential studies was conducted by Hazen and Shaver (1987). They suggested that there were similarities between infant and caregiver relationships and the relationship between adult romantic partners. Notably, they argued that the pattern of attachment described in Ainsworth's research was similar to what they called adult 'love styles' (see study below).

AN 'EYE' ON THE STUDY

Romantic relationships study
(Hazen and Shaver, 1987)

Aim

- Cindy Hazen and Philip Shaver (1987) conducted a study to see if the type of attachment style during infancy would be reflected in their adult romantic relationship.

→

Procedure

- Hazen and Shaver carried out a survey using a questionnaire. The questionnaire was printed as a 'love quiz' in a local American newspaper. There were 620 adults who replied to the advert for the 'love quiz' (self-selecting sample); they were all between 14 and 82 years old, 205 were men, and 415 were women. The average age of the respondents was 36 years. The quiz had three sections, all containing multiple-choice statements. The three sections assessed:

  - Section 1: Current or most important relationship

  - Section 2: General romantic experiences

  - Section 3: Type of relationship with parents (i.e. attachment type/internal working model).

Findings

- The psychologists analysed the questionnaire and found that:

  - *56% of respondents were identified as securely attached.* These respondents described their love experiences as happy and trusting, and did not fear intimacy. They were also comfortable being dependent on the partner and felt confident they were lovable. They were most likely to have a longer-lasting relationship and, if they were married, least likely to get a divorce.

  - *25% of respondents were identified as insecure–avoidant.* They described themselves as being uncomfortable with getting close with their partner (fear of intimacy), less trusting, and felt they would be fine if they were not in a relationship. The average relationship length was approximately 6 years.

  - *19% of respondents were identified as insecure–resistant.* They describe themselves as being preoccupied with obsessive love (e.g. jealously, possessiveness) and felt insecure when in a relationship (about whether a partner would stay or abandon them). These people were the most likely to be divorced. The reported average relationship length was about 5 years.

Conclusion

- The findings suggest that early attachments do affect later, romantic attachments. Notably, there is a relationship between individuals' perception of love and their attachment type, with securely attached individuals tending to have a positive internal working model.

Adult relationships as a parent

- Bowlby's idea of the internal working model predicts that patterns of attachment will be passed on from one generation to the next. Bailey et al. (2007) tested this idea. They questioned 99 teenage mothers with one-year old babies about their attachment to their own mothers, using interviews. They also observed the participants with their own young children in the Strange Situation test. They found that those mothers who reported insecure attachments to their own parents were much more likely to have children whose behaviour implied insecure attachment. This supports the idea that a pattern of insecure attachment was being passed from one generation to the next, supporting Bowlby's internal working model concept.

Weaknesses

✘ **A study against the internal working model.** An issue with Bowlby's idea that the internal working model affects later adult relationships is that the evidence to support this is mixed. A study by Zimmerman (2000) assessed infant attachment types and then later their adolescent attachment to their parents. They found very little relationship between the quality of infant and adolescent attachment. This is criticism because it does not support the view that the internal working model is important in the development of relationships. As a result, this reduces the validity of Bowlby's theory of the internal working model.

✘ **Cannot establish cause and effect.** Another issue with the research into the influence of early attachment on later adult relationships is that we cannot establish, with certainty, that there is a cause-and-effect link between the internal working model and later relationships. Many of the studies relied on non- experimental methods (questionnaires), which means other factors could have influenced adult attachment style. For example, a child's temperament (their personality traits) may influence both infant attachment and the quality of later relationships. As a result, we need to be cautious in drawing causal relationships from such research evidence.

✘ **Love questionnaire prone to social desirability.** An issue with Hazen and Shaver's research is that the evidence was based on a questionnaire and this method is prone to social desirability, for example, respondents may have lied and given inaccurate answers. This is because asking people about their intimate relationships and their upbringing is sensitive, so they may lie, exaggerate, or cover up their relationships through embarrassment. Furthermore, the questionnaires relied on retrospective data: people reporting about childhood memories, which may be prone to inaccuracies. As a result, Hazen and Shaver may not have measured what they set out to measure (whether attachment types affect the type of relationship in adulthood). This means the internal validity of the study can be questioned.

✘ **Too pessimistic.** Some psychologists argue that the influence of infant attachment on future relationships is exaggerated. Feeney (1999) argued that adult attachment patterns may be the result of the relationship, not the individual. For example, it may be that having a secure/insecure adult relationship has caused the adult attachment type. Furthermore, Clarke and Clarke (1998) suggested that the influence of infant attachment on later relationships is based on probability. People are not definitely doomed to always have bad relationships because they had attachment problems - they just have a greater risk of problems. By over-emphasising this risk, we become too pessimistic about people's futures. People can mentally work through their negative internal working model (poor experiences) and alter them to a more positive one.

✘ **Deterministic.** Another issue with the continuity hypothesis is that critics have accused it of being deterministic. For example, it suggests that children who are insecurely attached are destined to have insecure relationships later in life. This view is deterministic because it assumes that individuals do not have the choice or free will to do something about it and the outcome is inevitable. This assumption is false, as individuals do experience positive adult relationships despite being insecurely attached in childhood. Furthermore, individuals can change how they view relationships or seek professional help, which shows that choice (free will) allows individuals to develop and work towards more positive healthy relationships, instead of their fate being determined by their childhood environment.

116 Topic: Attachment   www.psychologyzone.co.uk

1. Bowlby proposed that infants develop mental representations of attachment relationships that form the basis for expectations for future relationships. He referred to this as:

   Circle one letter only.   **[1 mark]**

   A. Biological model

   B. Hypothetical working model

   C. Internal working model

   D. Maternal deprivation model

5. Explain what is meant by the 'internal working model'.   **[2 marks]**

6. Explain the role of the internal working model in the development of later relationships.   **[6 marks]**

7. Describe one study into the influence of early attachment on childhood and adult relationships.   **[6 marks]**

8. Discuss the influence of early attachment on later relationships.   **[12 marks AS, 16 marks A-level]**

Topic 4

Approaches in Psychology

AQA specification for Topic 4: Approaches

AS and A-level:

Origins of Psychology: Wundt, introspection, and the emergence of Psychology as a science.

The basic assumptions of the following approaches:

- Learning approaches: i) the behaviourist approach, including classical conditioning and Pavlov's research, operant conditioning, types of reinforcement and Skinner's research; ii) social learning theory including imitation, identification, modelling, vicarious reinforcement, the role of mediational processes and Bandura's research.

- The cognitive approach: the study of internal mental processes, the role of schema, the use of theoretical and computer models to explain and make inferences about mental processes. The emergence of cognitive neuroscience.

- The biological approach: the influence of genes, biological structures and neurochemistry on behaviour. Genotype and phenotype, the genetic basis of behaviour, evolution and behaviour.

A-level only:

- The psychodynamic approach: the role of the unconscious, the structure of personality, that is: Id, Ego and Superego, defence mechanisms including repression, denial, and displacement, psychosexual stages.

- Humanistic Psychology: free will, self-actualisation and Maslow's hierarchy of needs, focus on the self, congruence, the role of conditions of worth. The influence on counselling Psychology.

- Comparison of approaches.

AQA specification for Topic 4: Approaches in Psychology

- Origins of Psychology: Wundt, introspection and the emergence of Psychology as a science.

◆ Introduction

The term 'psychology' comes from the Greek words 'psyche', meaning 'soul' or 'mind' and 'ology' meaning 'study'. No one really knows where and when the study of Psychology began, as it is difficult to establish exactly what psychology is. Certainly, discussion about the 'mind' in terms of the 'soul' and 'spiritualism' can be traced back to early religious times (Babylonians and Buddhists). However, psychology as a 'loose, general' subject can trace its roots back to Ancient Greece (around 400-300 BC), to the Greek philosophers Plato (428-348 BC) and Aristotle (384-322 BC). Psychology had its roots within philosophy (study of knowledge, reality, and our existence). Topics on the 'psyche' such as mind-body dualism, reasoning, impulses, free will versus determinism, and nature versus nurture were debated and this set foundations for the study of human behaviour i.e. psychology.

◆ Wundt

- Psychology did not emerge as a separate discipline until approximately 155 years ago! It was the work of Wilhelm Wundt (pronounced as 'Vill-helm Voont') in 1879 in Germany that can be attributed to moving psychology away from its philosophical roots. After studying medicine, Wundt worked as a physiologist at Heidelberg University and later at Leipzig University. While at Heidelberg, he delivered the first university course on scientific psychology and went on to write the first textbook on psychology, *'Principles of Physiological Psychology'* (Wundt, 1873-4). In 1879, at Leipzig University, he set up the first psychology laboratory, dedicated to experimental psychology. He later founded the *Institute of Experimental Psychology* in order to study internal mental processes by using controlled experimental methods. He became the first person to be called a 'psychologist' and was the founding father of 'experimental psychology'.

◆ Introspection

- Wundt argued that the structure and content of conscious mental processes (the mind) can be studied scientifically using a method called introspection to gather data. Introspection comes from the Latin word 'looking into' and refers to the process of observing and examining your own conscious thoughts and emotions. *(If you stop right now and examine your own thoughts or feelings, you will be carrying out introspection.)* Wundt's researchers were trained to analyse their own personal consciousness through thoughts and emotions. The experiment was carried out in Wundt's room in a controlled environment. For example, the researchers would be exposed to different various stimuli (e.g. a light, object, image, or the sound of a metronome) and asked to report the conscious thoughts they were experiencing. The researchers would then report back to Wundt what they had experienced.

- The aim was to break down and analyse the conscious mind into different structural parts (e.g. thoughts, sensations, perception, actions) and develop a theory of human consciousness. Breaking down consciousness into different structures in order develop a theory of how the mind works is known as structuralism in psychology. Wundt is seen as the father of 'structuralism'.

Wundt's experimental method

- Most of the experiments conducted by Wundt's laboratory involved studying the behaviour of a single individual in detail. However, Wundt attempted to study human consciousness scientifically by using controlled laboratory experiments. This meant that the study was:

    - Systematic. The experiment followed a set of procedures in an orderly way, e.g. how the stimuli were presented to the participants, recorded and measured.

- In a controlled environment. For example, the participants were given a variety of stimuli and the reaction time taken to respond to each different stimulus was measured. Different reaction times suggested that different parts of the mind were being used.

- Objective. Wundt trained his researchers to analyse the content of their own thoughts objectively (rather than subjectively). Once the stimuli were presented, they carefully recorded only what they directly observed in their mind's eye but avoided reporting the *meaning* of the stimuli observed. For example, when presented with a golf ball they might say, "I am aware of roundness, hardness and whiteness" (the elements in the mind's eye), rather than giving an interpretation of the image as a golf ball (subjective interpretation).

◆ The emergence of psychology as a science

- **Psychology as science started with Wundt.** The emergence of psychology as a scientific discipline arguably came about in 1879, when Wilhelm Wundt established the *Institute of Experimental Psychology*, where he carried out his controlled experimental research to investigate conscious thoughts. As noted above, this was the point when psychology became a distinct scientific discipline away from philosophy and biology.

- **Behaviourists are critical of Wundt's introspection.** However, others argue the emergence of psychology as a science happened when behaviourism arrived in the early 20th century (1920s). The behavioural psychologist John Watson (1878-1958) played a key role in this change. Watson questioned the scientific credibility and value of Wundt's introspection because:

  - Only observable behaviour is acceptable. Watson believed that scientific research (which the behaviourist approach adopted), should concern itself only with *observable behaviour* of people and animals and not with the *unobservable* mental processes (e.g. thoughts, perception, emotions) that Wundt's introspection relied upon. Watson believed psychology to be a science and therefore the psychological theories it develops must be based on scientific empirical evidence (through observation and experimentation) rather than making inferences (infer) from what is not observable.

  - Evidence must be objective, not subjective. Another criticism of introspection by Watson was that it produced data that was *subjective*. This means that it was based on someone's personal interpretation of their mental processes, and this can vary greatly from person to person. This means that is no way to verify the accuracy of introspection and this makes the study *unreliable* as others cannot check the results. Watson believed only observable behaviour should be studied, as the data can be measured and recorded *objectively* (no interpretation is required), because this prevents individual biases (values/opinion) and expectations from influencing the measuring and recording of the behaviour.

  - Different scientific approach. Based on the criticism above, behaviourists such as Watson (1913) and later Skinner (1953) brought new principles that 'tightened' the scientific research methods in studying behaviour. They felt that the study of human behaviour should use experimental methods like the natural sciences and only study *observable* behaviour *objectively*, with the goal to predict and control human behaviour. For example, Bowlby *predicted* that insecure attachment causes emotional problems. By *controlling* or manipulating certain conditions, we can influence behaviour in order to bring the desired outcome, e.g. we can 'intervene' by offering parenting intervention programmes to improve infant-mother attachment. This meant there was a gradual move away from introspection towards a more scientific method.

Scientific method used in psychology now

- The behaviourists laid the foundations for a more scientific method. In order to develop knowledge that is scientifically sound, psychologists need to use the scientific research method when conducting research (just like in the natural sciences). The scientific method requires the research study to be objective, systematic and replicable, and the results to be based on empirical evidence.

Below are some of the key features of carrying out the scientific method:

- *Empiricism.* An important and fundamental feature of the scientific method is empiricism (or empirical evidence). This means all evidence, data, results, or knowledge gathered can only be obtained from what is directly observable through our senses – either through *observations* or *experimentation* (introspection, opinion, intuition, reasoning, and belief are excluded as unscientific).

- Objective. The scientific method requires the study to be *objective*. This means the researchers do not let their own biases (values/opinions) and expectations influence the measuring and recording of the data. The researcher must also consider and control possible influences throughout the research process that may affect the results obtained (e.g. demand characteristic, investigator effect and so on).

- Systematic. The research must be *systematic*. This means the observations or experiments follow a set of procedures, and steps, measurements and recordings are carried out in a standardised (orderly) way.

- Replication. Another key feature of the scientific research method is *replication*. Can the observations or experiment be repeated by other researchers to determine whether similar results are obtained, and, if so, are the results consistent? If results are not replicable, then they are not reliable (inconsistent), and the results cannot be accepted as being universally true.

Laboratory experiments

- Laboratory experiments are the most scientific methods and are commonly used in psychology. This is because they allow the researchers to precisely control variables, conditions and measurements in which learning happens to see the effects. The high control found in laboratory experiments means the same standardised instructions and procedures are given to all participants, allowing the study to be repeated (replicability) by others to test if the results are reliable. The great majority of experiments involve comparing the performances of two groups of people. The advantage of this approach over Wundt's method (i.e. using just single individuals) is that we can be confident that the findings can be generalised to the wider population.

- The research process often begins with the development of scientific theories/hypotheses and the constant testing and modifying or refining of these theories through controlled observation and experimentation completes the scientific cycle of good science.

◆ The origins of psychology

Below is a basic timeline of the emergence of the different major psychological approaches.

| 300 BC - 19th century | Non-scientific approach |

Philosophy

Psychology was not a separate discipline but was rooted within philosophy dating back to the ancient Greeks. Concepts such as mind-body dualism and free will were often discussed by philosophers such as Plato (428-348) and Aristotle (384-322 BC), who used logic and reason as evidence (rather than scientific methods).

| 1879 | Scientific approach |

Introspection

Wilhelm Wundt establishes the first experimental psychology lab in Germany in 1879. Wundt was the founder of the method of introspection - examination of one's own mental or emotional processes in a controlled and objective way. The event is considered the starting point of psychology as a separate science.

1900s   Scientific approach

Psychodynamic

Sigmund Freud establishes the psychodynamic approach, which focuses on the role of our unconscious thoughts, feelings, and memories and our early childhood experiences in determining behaviour. He developed a therapy called psychoanalysis.

1879   Scientific approach

Behaviourism

J.B. Watson and B.F. Skinner introduce the behaviourist approach. They were critical of Wundt and psychodynamic approach as they believed it was not possible to study the mind (e.g. cognition, emotions) in an objective scientific manner because it is 'unobservable'. Behaviourists believe that our responses to environmental stimuli shape our actions (via conditioning). Therefore, behavioural psychologists study behaviour that is observable and measurable using laboratory experiments.

1950s   Non-scientific approach

Humanistic approach

Carl Rogers and Abraham Maslow develop the humanistic approach. They rejected both the scientific approach of the behaviourists and psychodynamics as over-reliant on past experiences and the destructive forces of the unconscious. The humanistic approach emphasises the importance of free will in shaping our behaviour and the importance of personal growth (self-actualisation).

1956   Scientific approach

Cognitive approach

The cognitive approach emerged in the mid 1950s, when psychologists began studying the mind's mental processes (e.g. perception, thinking, memory). Cognitive psychologists believe that we can make inferences (infer) how the mind works based on results from laboratory experiments. George A. Miller's (1956) article "The Magical Number Seven, Plus or Minus Two" on information processing is an early application of the cognitive approach.

1960s   Scientific approach

Social learning approach

Around the same time as the emergence of the cognitive approach, Albert Bandura establishes the social learning approach. Bandura agreed with the behaviourist approach - that our responses to environmental stimuli shape our actions. However, he believed new behaviours can also occur through observing others (observation learning) and therefore the role of mental processes (cognitive factors) is required e.g. attention and memory.

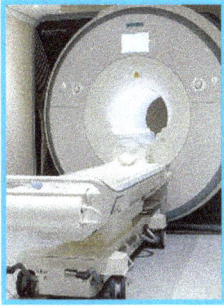

1980s Scientific approach

Biological approach

The biological (biopsychology) approach established itself recently due to the advancement in technology for examining the brain. This has allowed psychologists to have an increased understanding of the functioning human brain. The biological approach (including cognitive neuroscience) is now the dominant approach in psychology.

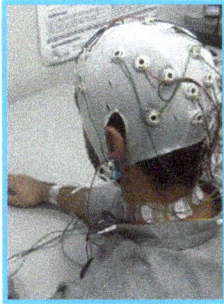

2000s Scientific approach

Cognitive neuroscience

The most recent development in psychology is cognitive neuroscience. This approach brings together the biological and cognitive approaches. This approach investigates how biological structures and processes influence mental states and behaviour.

◆ Evaluation

Strengths

✔ **Wundt method still classified as scientific.** A strength of Wundt's introspection experimental method is that it would be still classified as a scientific method today. Although this approach relied primarily on 'non-observable' responses (memory, perception), he still investigated introspection in a controlled laboratory setting. For example, the study was conducted in a systematic way and the experiment followed a set of standardised procedures, so all participants received the same instructions. The same stimuli were presented to the participants and they were tested and measured in the same way. The participants attempted to analyse the content of their own thoughts objectively rather than subjectively (see above - golf ball example). However, some critics argue that the participants' subjective experience of mental thought processes made it difficult to check for reliability, as they were based on interpretations (prone to bias/distortion). Replication is a key feature of the scientific method.

✔ **Empirical method now main method in psychology.** A strength of the empirical method is that this has become the main method used in psychology now. Many modern psychologists and approaches continue to rely on this type of experimental method as part of their research and practices. For example, the biological approach uses experimental methods to study physiological processes. Biopsychologists can test and measure chemical brain activity objectively using scanning technologies (e.g. magnetic resonance imaging (MRI) and electroencephalograms (EEG)), to see the effect drugs have on a neurotransmitter and to measure any changes in behaviour that occurs. The scientific method has widened considerably since the behaviourists. For example, the cognitive approach of mental processes is now seen as a legitimate and highly scientific area within psychology. Although mental processes remain 'private' (unobservable), cognitive psychologists can still make inferences about how they work based on well-controlled laboratory experiments.

Weaknesses

✗ **Not all approaches use scientific methods.** The humanistic approach believes that the scientific method is not suitable for studying people. This is because each person's subjective experiences are unique and trying to generalise from one individual to another (i.e. to formulate general laws of behaviour) is inappropriate. Similarly, the psychodynamic approach favours case studies and interviews to study human behaviour and therefore its approach tends to be non-scientific. This is because the information collected from such methods tends to focus on single individuals, so the information is subjective and therefore open to biases/distortion, and unrepresentative of the population. This means not all approaches see the scientific approach as possible or desirable.

✗ **The limitation of the scientific approach.** Several criticisms have been levied towards the scientific approach. The first one is that studying humans in a controlled environment (e.g. laboratory) is seen as artificial and does not tell us how humans behave in a real-life environment (lacks ecological validity), and as such, some approaches do not favour scientific methods (e.g. psychodynamic/humanistic approach). Furthermore, much of the subject matter in psychology is not directly observable and is invisible to our senses. This is because many studies involve investigating the mind (e.g. attitudes, memory, cognitive perception, and emotions) rather than actual behaviour. In these studies, psychologists frequently use inference (inferring) when developing theories (e.g. multi-store model) and this approach is prone to inaccuracies and bias. This would suggest that much psychological research does not meet the criteria of being scientific as it fails to provide hard empirical evidence, as claimed by the behaviourists.

Practice exam questions

1. Explain what is meant by 'introspection'.   **[2marks]**

2. Discuss Wundt's role in the development of psychology.   **[6 marks]**

3. Outline two criticisms of introspection as a method of investigation.   **[2 marks + 2 marks]**

4. Outline and evaluate the work of Wundt.   **[12 marks AS, 16 marks A-level]**

5. Discuss the emergence of psychology as a science.   **[12 marks AS, 16 marks A-level]**

AQA specification for Topic 4: Approaches in Psychology

- Learning approaches: the behaviourist approach, including classical conditioning and Pavlov's research, operant conditioning, types of reinforcement and Skinner's research.

◆ Basic assumption of the behavioural approach

- **Critical of introspection.** Behaviourism arose because there was dissatisfaction with other approaches in psychology that involved 'unscientific', techniques such as *introspection*, which dealt with vague concepts that were unmeasurable aspects of behaviour, such as the role of the unconscious mind (e.g. psychodynamic theory of Sigmund Freud.).

- **"Behaviourists have a basic view of behaviour"** In contrast to the above, early behaviourist researchers like Ivan Pavlov and John B. Watson began to develop a framework that emphasised observable processes (environmental 'stimuli' and behavioural 'responses'). By this, we mean that they were interested primarily by experiences within the environment and how these influenced behaviour. They refer to this as the stimulus-response link – the association between an *observed stimulus* and *observed response*.

- **Scientific approach.** Behaviourists try to explain the causes of behaviour by studying only those behaviours that can be *observed* and *measured* from our environment. As a result, they prefer using a *scientific approach* to studying human behaviour, because external events (environmental) which influence our behaviour can be observed and measured in an objective way (unbiased way), using laboratory experiments that allow more control and objectivity. Behaviourists suggest that the basic processes that govern learning are the same in all species, so they use animals as experimental subjects and generalise their findings to human beings. Subsequently, behaviourists believe you can make general laws about how humans behave (prediction, patterns, etc.).

- **Learning processes:** The behaviourist approach describes two types of learning processes from our experiences within the environment that shape our behaviour. They are *classical conditioning* and *operant conditioning*. Therefore, according to strict radical behaviourism, mental thought processes have no place in psychology, nor do the principles of inheitance fully explain our behaviour.

◆ Classical conditioning

- **Classical conditioning** is the view that learning is done by **association**. This was the first type of learning to be discovered and studied within the behaviourist tradition (hence the name 'classical').

- A Russian physiologist called Ivan Pavlov studied salivation in dogs as part of his research programme. Normally, dogs will salivate simply when food is presented, but Pavlov was interested in why the dogs had started to salivate simply when they saw the people that usually fed them (they also responded to the sound of the dishes being used for their meals).

- Pavlov set up an experiment to find out if the dogs could be trained to salivate at other stimuli such as the sound of a bell or a light. At feeding times, Pavlov would ring a bell and the amount of saliva produced by the dog was measured. After several 'trials', Pavlov rang the bell without presenting the food and found that the dogs salivated in the same way as if the food was being presented.

  - So, Pavlov was able to show how a *neutral stimulus* (e.g. the bell) can come to elicit a new response (*conditioned response*) through association.

How did the classical conditioning procedure work?

1. First, Pavlov presented the food to the dog. The food is the **unconditioned stimulus** (UCS), which means that it stimulates a response that occurs involuntarily (i.e. you cannot control it).

2. Next, the dog salivated when it saw the food. This is known as the unconditioned response, which means that it is a response that occurs involuntarily.

3. Pavlov also tried introducing a bell sound without the food. The bell sound was a neutral stimulus (NS) because it did not elicit any type of response from the dog, when it was presented on its own.

4. Next, Pavlov began the *conditioning procedure*, where he introduced the bell sound just before giving food to the dog. The bell became a conditioned stimulus (CS) because it produced salivation, on the condition that it was presented with the food.

5. Finally, Pavlov presented the bell sound and the dog salivated, even without the presence of the food.

6. The dog had learned an association (link) between the bell and the food and also learned a new behaviour. The bell sound (originally a neutral stimulus) was now the conditioned stimulus (CS), which elicited a learned response from the dog (i.e. to salivate), otherwise known as a conditioned response (CR).

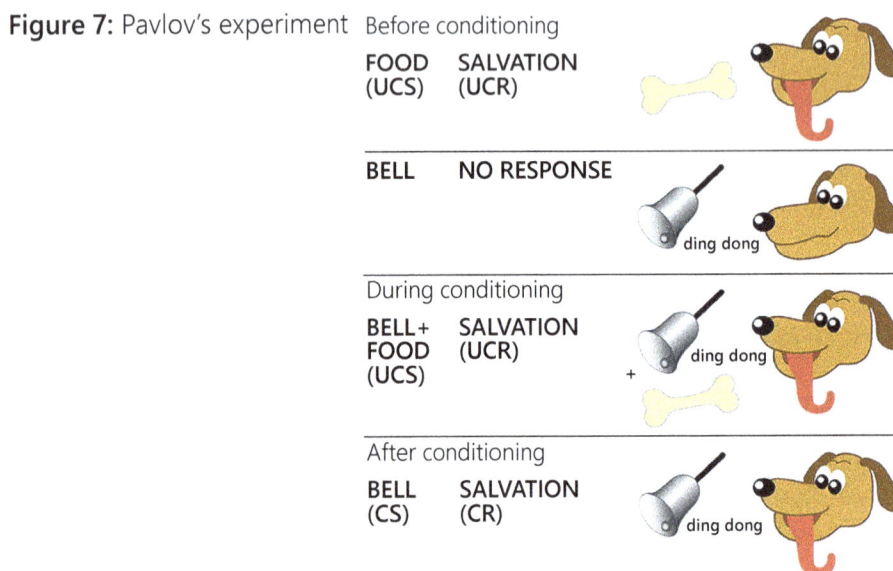

Figure 7: Pavlov's experiment

Before conditioning

FOOD (UCS)   SALVATION (UCR)

BELL   NO RESPONSE

ding dong

During conditioning

BELL+ FOOD (UCS)   SALVATION (UCR)

ding dong +

After conditioning

BELL (CS)   SALVATION (CR)

ding dong

Principles of classical conditioning

Here are some of the important principles of classical conditioning which can help shape behaviour:

- *Forward conditioning.* Classical conditioning becomes more effective when the NS appears about 30 or so seconds before the UCS is presented and remains during the UCS, this is called forward conditioning

- *Extinction.* This is when a conditioned stimulus is repeatedly presented without the unconditioned stimulus, which means that the conditioned response will disappear. This is known as extinction. If a dog learns to associate the sound of a bell with food and then the bell is rung repeatedly, but no food is presented, the dog will soon stop salivating at the sound of the bell.

- *Stimulus generalisation.* This is the extension of the conditioned response (CR) from the original stimulus to similar stimuli. For example, a dog that has been conditioned to salivate to the sound of a bell of one tone may well salivate to a similar-sounding bell or a general buzzer.

- *Discrimination.* An animal or person can be taught to discriminate between different stimuli. For example, if a dog is shown a red circle every time he is fed, then he will salivate at the sight of the red circle alone. But initially, the dog may generalise and salivate at circles of any colour. If the dog is only fed when the red circle is presented and not when other colours are shown, he will learn to discriminate between red and the other colours.

- *One trial learning.* Learning usually takes place over many repeated trials, but in some cases or instances (as being stung by a bee) one incident is enough to create a lasting CR. This is known as one trial learning.

◆ Operant conditioning

- Operant behaviour is mainly based on the work of Skinner (1904-1990) and is another principle of the behaviourist approach to learning. Operant conditioning works on the principle that how we behave is based on the *consequences* after our action has been performed. Whether such behaviour is rewarded or punished will determine if we repeat that behaviour.

The Skinner Box

- B.F. Skinner proposed his theory on operant conditioning by conducting various experiments on animals. He used a special box known as the "Skinner Box" for his experiment on rats. As the first step to his experiment, he placed a hungry rat inside the Skinner Box. When the rat pressed the lever in the box, it was rewarded by a food pellet. After eating enough, the rat would explore the box, pressing the lever again as it grew hungry. From then on, the rat would press the lever whenever they were hungry. The experiment showed how we can get an animal to perform the desired behaviour (teaching it to press a lever), by rewarding such behaviour. Skinner carried out further experiments and found that there are three main ways in which this operant conditioning can occur:

  - *Positive reinforcement.* If the consequences of the actions are rewarded, the action of the behaviour is more likely to be reinforced and thus repeated again. For example, giving a child sweets for good behaviour after completing house chores means they are more likely to repeat that behaviour. The child starts linking chores with sweets, and as a result, they complete their chores more reliably and enthusiastically in the hopes of earning more sweets.

  - *Negative reinforcement.* The term negative reinforcement is misunderstood and does not mean punishment. The word 'negative' does not refer to something bad but rather the *removal/ending* of an unpleasant stimulus to bring about the desired behaviour and increase the likelihood of behaviour occurring again. An example of negative reinforcement is an overprotective parent who gives less strict attention when the child receives good grades. The teenager begins to associate academic success with the parent's reduced strictness and continues to study hard so as to enjoy their freedom. Another example is cleaning your room to avoid moaning parents, the behaviour is reinforced - you are more likely to repeat it to avoid your parents being frustrated.

  - *Punishment.* This is when a consequence for a certain behaviour is punished e.g. being shouted at by a teacher for talking in a lesson. Therefore, if the action of the behaviour is punished, it is less likely to be repeated. This makes NOT talking in class more likely.

- Positive and negative reinforcement increase the likelihood that behaviour will be repeated. Punishment decreases the likelihood that behaviour will be repeated. Operant conditioning is used widely in society in schools, prisons, and homes.

Schedules of reinforcement

- There are various ways of giving reinforcements. The frequency and ways in which reinforcement is administered can affect the likelihood of it affecting our behaviour. For example, schedule reinforcement is a *continuous reward* given every time a response is made. This schedule is best used during the initial stages of learning to create a strong association between the behaviour and response. Partial schedule reinforcement is when rewards are given intermittently, at different times and/or frequency. For example, a fixed interval means that a reward will occur after a fixed amount of time such as every five minutes. This means the response rate speeds up as the next reinforcement becomes available. For example, if a child knows she gets her allowance on Sunday as long as her bedroom is clean, she probably won't clean up her room until Saturday night. By controlling rewards (and punishments), you can shape the specific behaviour in animals and humans.

- Pavlov also introduced another behavioural principle known as the law of extinction, which states that a behavioural response that is not followed by a reinforcement stimulus (reward) is weakened and therefore less likely to occur again. This process is also called extinguished behaviour.

◆ Evaluation

Strengths

✔ **Scientific credibility.** A strength of the behaviourist approach is that it has high scientific credibility. This is because behaviourism adopts a scientific approach that can easily be tested. The use of experimental methods in the laboratory allows the independent variables (IV) and dependent variables (DV) to be operationalised and observed and measured objectively (e.g. Pavlov's dogs and Skinner's rats). This is a strength because it emphasises the importance of scientific processes such as objectivity and replication, which are key features when defining the scientific method. As a result, the credibility and status of the behaviourist approach are increased.

✔ **Real-life application.** A strength of the behaviourist approach is that it has practical applications in many areas of human life. For example, operant conditioning has been used to develop token economy systems in prisons and psychiatric wards, where patients or prisoners are rewarded with tokens when they behave in the desired way, which they can exchange for goods. Classical conditioning has been used in psychological therapy such as the treatment of phobias. For example, systematic desensitisation is a technique where patients learn to associate feeling calm when faced with their phobia. This is a strength because it shows that the behaviourist approach is accurate in its assumptions about human behaviour and that we can use these understandings to better the existence of humans, i.e. to enable better lifestyles and treatments of potentially debilitating disorders. As a result, the credibility of the behaviourist approach is increased.

Weaknesses

✗ **Mechanistic view of behaviour.** A weakness of the behaviourist approach is that it is reductionist. This means it reduces the complexity of human behaviour to a stimulus-response link. It considers animals, including humans, to be passive and machine-like responders to the environment, with little to no conscious insight into their behaviour. This is a weakness because it fails to consider the complexities of human behaviour. Other approaches such as the social learning theory or the cognitive approach have emphasised the importance of mental events during learning. These processes, which mediate between stimulus and response, indicate that people may play a much more active role in their own learning. This means that behaviourist learning theory may apply less to human than to animal behaviour. Consequently, the credibility of the behaviourist approach is reduced.

✗ **Deterministic approach.** A further weakness of the behaviourist approach to reducing human behaviours to a stimulus-response response is that it implies humans have no control over their behaviour, i.e. ignores that humans have free will. There are serious moral and legal implication if we take a deterministic position on human behaviour. If one assumes that individuals do not have free will, then they are not morally responsible for their actions. This raises the question of whether it is moral to punish human beings, as it could be argued that they did not act freely and thus should not be punished, for even the most horrific crimes, an idea which most people would find problematic.

✗ **Problems of research on non-humans.** A weakness of these findings is that most of the research carried out by the behaviourists have been on animals in laboratory experiments. This raises an ethical issue as many would see this as unjustified. Furthermore, human behaviour is far more complex than that of animals such as rats; humans have a high level of consciousness, with the ability to be reflective in thought and/or in emotions and this affects how humans think and behave. This suggests that findings from animal research may be inappropriate for explaining the complex and diverse behaviour of humans.

Practice exam questions

1. Explain what is meant by 'classical conditioning'. **[4 marks]**.

2. Outline Skinner's research into operant conditioning. **[4 marks]**

3. Explain two criticism of the behaviourist approach. **[2 marks + 2 marks]**

4. A psychology student made the following observation to his teacher.

   'The behaviourist approach has been presented to us as helpful in understanding human behaviour. However, most of the data have been obtained from research using animals.'

   Discuss the value of behaviourism in helping us to understand human behaviour. **[5 marks]**

5. Outline and evaluate the behaviourist approach in psychology. **[12 marks AS, 16 marks A-level]**

6. Outline the behaviourist approach. Compare the behaviourist approach with the biological approach. **[12 marks, 16 marks A-level]**

AQA specification for Topic 4: Approaches in Psychology

- Learning approaches: social learning theory, including imitation, identification, modelling, vicarious reinforcement, the role of mediational processes and Bandura's research.

◆ Basic assumptions of the social learning theory

- **Assumptions.** Social learning theory (SLT) holds the belief that people are shaped in fundamental ways by their environment through learning processes. Social learning theory shares many assumptions with the behaviourist approach – that behaviour is learnt through classical and operant conditioning. However, SLT adds 'learning processes' to the behavioural approach: observational learning. Social learning theorists believe people learn by observing others and therefore that other people (the social environment) are particularly important as an influence on behaviour. With the emphasis on observational learning comes a belief that it is impossible to explain human behaviour, without considering the role of internal, mental processes in human behaviour, which is something that behaviourists reject.

- **Scientific methods.** Social learning theorists share with behaviourists a commitment to the *scientific method*. They favour objective, *quantitative* approaches to research and use the experimental method if possible. Unlike behaviourists, they do not study animal learning. They conduct research in any context in which learning occurs, particularly favouring research using children, whose behaviour is more obviously influenced by the people around them than adults (although adults also learn through observation). Social learning research therefore may include observation of children and adults in school and family settings. However, the *laboratory* setting is favoured by many researchers because of the opportunities it gives to isolate and examine the causal effects of different influences on observational learning.

Vicarious reinforcement

- According to the social learning theory, behaviour is learnt primarily through indirect observation, watching the behaviour of others. Imitation is more likely to occur if the behaviour is rewarded (i.e. reinforced) rather than punished. Behaviour can also be learnt by vicarious reinforcement, watching others being rewarded for their behaviour. For example, a brother may see his sister getting what she wants when she starts crying, so the brother may imitate the behaviour in a similar situation.

The role of mediational processes

- The social learning theory proposes a number of mental (cognitive) processes that are involved in learning. Mediational processes refer to mental factors (e.g. attention, memory, motivation) that are required for learning new behaviours. These mental factors intervene in the learning process between the behaviour observed and whether the person imitates the behaviour or not. Bandura (1961) identified four mediational processes:

  - *Attention* – In order to learn the behaviour of another, the person must first pay *attention* to what the another person (called a model) is doing – they must notice the behaviour.

  - *Retention* – This refers to how well the behaviour is remembered. The observer must then *encode* and form a memory of the behaviour the model performs. At a later time, this memory must be translated back into a behaviour, so that the observer may *imitate* it.

  - *Motor reproduction* – This refers to the ability of an observer to perform the behaviour. In order to imitate the behaviour effectively, the observer may need to *practise it*.

  - *Motivation* – Whether or not the observer actually makes use of the behaviour they have learned, depends on whether they are motivated to do so. The observer's *motivation* may be affected by several factors: whether they believe that *reinforcement* is available if they *imitate*, for example, or whether their behaviour rewarded or punished in the past. Conversely, in terms of *vicarious reinforcement,* if the model was observed to be punished then imitation becomes less likely.

Identification

- People (especially children) are much more likely to imitate the behaviour of people with whom they identify i.e. role models. This process is called modelling. A person becomes a role model if they possess similar characteristics to the observer (e.g. age, gender) and/or are attractive and have high status. Role models may not necessarily be physically present in the environment. This has led to implications for the influence of the media on behaviour e.g. being influenced by violence seen on TV and in video games, etc.

◆ Evaluation

Strengths

✔ **The importance of cognitive factors in learning.** A strength of social learning theory (SLT) is that it offers a more adequate account of learning than behaviourist perspectives. For example, it considers that humans and other animals do store information about the behaviour of others (by observing) and then use this to make their own judgements, about when it is appropriate to perform certain actions (imitation). This is a strength because SLT provides a more comprehensive explanation of learning by recognising these mediational processes. Neither classical nor operant conditioning can offer an adequate account of learning on their own. Consequently, this strengthens the credibility of SLT as an explanation for the learning behaviour of humans and animals.

✔ **Real-life application.** A strength of the social learning theory is that this theory can be used to explain behaviour in real life. For example, it has contributed significantly to our understanding of processes like aggression and gender development and has also formed the basis of a range of treatments for problems like phobias (e.g. CBT). Furthermore, the theory is often used to offer an effective explanation for the development of different types of behaviour, especially when such behaviours feature constantly in the media, notably the influence of role models (e.g. supermodels, YouTube influencers, Kim Kardashian, rappers, etc.). This may also account for cultural differences in behaviour in different countries, for example, why some behaviours are more prevalent than others.

✔ **Experimental research support.** A strength of this theory is that there is reliable experimental research that supports the social learning approach to the acquisition of learnt behaviour. For example, Albert Bandura (1965) has shown that aggression is learnt through observation. Bandura showed children a film of an adult behaving aggressively towards an inflatable toy called a Bobo doll. Some children saw the aggressive adult being reinforced by another adult, others saw them being punished. Afterwards, the children were given the opportunity to play with a range of toys including a Bobo doll. It was found that the children were more likely to imitate if the model was rewarded. Those children who had seen the model getting punished were much less likely to imitate the aggressive actions, showing the influence of vicarious punishment on imitation. As demonstrated by Bandura's Bobo doll study, behaviour is influenced by watching others.

Weaknesses

✗ **Over-reliance on evidence from laboratory studies.** One weakness of research used to support social learning theory is that it has low ecological validity. For example, Bandura's Bobo doll study was conducted in a highly controlled lab setting, which did not mirror a real-life setting. This is an issue because if lab studies are not reflective of real-life settings, then demand characteristics may occur. For example, in the Bobo doll study, because the main purpose of the doll is to strike it, the children were simply behaving in a way that they thought was expected. This, therefore, tells us very little about how children may actually learn behaviours in everyday life. Because the research into SLT has low ecological validity, the credibility of SLT as a theory for how humans learn behaviour is weakened.

✗ **Reductionism.** One issue with social learning theory as an explanation for human behaviour is that it is reductionist. SLT states that we simply learn all behaviours from observation of others and then imitating this behaviour in the appropriate social setting. This is an issue because Bandura makes little reference to the impact of biological factors on social learning. One consistent finding in the Bobo doll experiment was that the boys were often more aggressive than girls regardless of the experimental situation. This may be explained by biological, specifically hormonal, factors. Biologically, boys have higher levels of testosterone than girls, which is linked to more aggressive behaviour. This biological factor is completely ignored in SLT. Therefore, the credibility of SLT as an explanation for the learning behaviour of humans is reduced.

✗ **Underplays biological influences.** A further criticism of social learning theory is the over-emphasis on the environmental experiences, as the main influence on our behaviour, and the tendency to under-play biological factors. For example, there are several gender differences that appear to be universal, such as preferences for particular characteristics in a potential heterosexual partner (men prioritise youth and fertility, women prioritise status and resources) and differences in the thinking patterns of boys and girls (boys tend to be more rigid) that social learning theory cannot account for. It may be that differences like these reflect *genetic influences* on behaviour that social learning theory cannot account for.

Practice exam questions

1. What do social learning theorists mean by 'imitation'? **[2 marks]**

2. What do social learning theorists mean by 'identification'? **[2 marks]**

3. What do social learning theorists mean by 'modelling'? **[2 marks]**

4. What do social learning theorists mean by 'vicarious learning'? **[2 marks]**

5. What do social learning theorists mean by 'mediational processes'? **[2 marks]**

6. Discuss two limitations of social learning theory. **[6 marks]**

7. Describe and evaluate social learning theory in psychology. **[12 marks AS, 16 marks A-level]**

8. Outline and evaluate social learning theory. In your answer, make comparisons with at least one other approach in psychology. **[16 marks A-level]**

AQA specification for Topic 4: Approaches in Psychology

- The cognitive approach: the study of internal mental processes, the role of schema, the use of theoretical and computer models to explain and make inferences about mental processes. The emergence of cognitive neuroscience.

◆ Internal mental processes

- The cognitive approach is a relatively modern approach, developed in the 1960s. Unlike behaviourism or psychoanalysis, there isn't one major theorist who has dominated this approach. Cognitive psychologists believe *behaviour* is the result of *how we process information*, which they call the internal mental processes. The cognitive approach has been used to explain a wide range of topics in psychology including memory, perception, intelligence, social behaviour, and emotional and psychological disorders.

◆ The use of theoretical and computer models

- Cognitive psychologists explain our mental process by using a computer metaphor which makes the comparison between our mind and computers, the idea that human information processing works in a similar fashion to computers. This is because minds and computers have some similarities: both have inputs, outputs, memory stores and retrieval systems, and a limited capacity for how much information they can process at any one time. The way a computer works is a three-stage information processing step: *input—processing—output*, and cognitive psychologists believe that human behaviour can be explained in the same way.

Computers

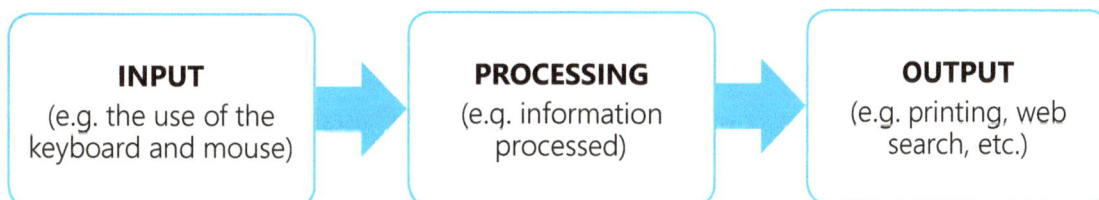

| INPUT (e.g. the use of the keyboard and mouse) | → | PROCESSING (e.g. information processed) | → | OUTPUT (e.g. printing, web search, etc.) |

Humans

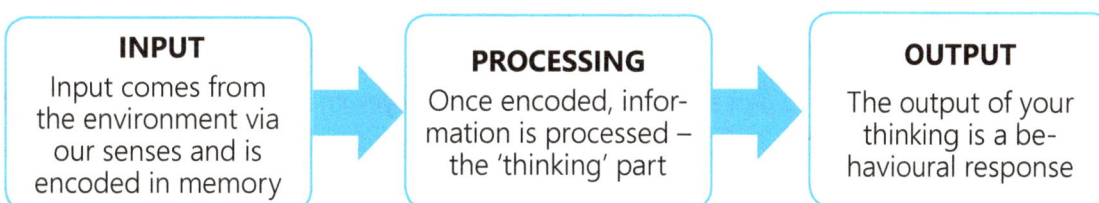

| INPUT Input comes from the environment via our senses and is encoded in memory | → | PROCESSING Once encoded, information is processed – the 'thinking' part | → | OUTPUT The output of your thinking is a behavioural response |

Example of an information-processing approach

- For example, Ben sees an old lady in a supermarket struggling to reach the top shelf for a packet of biscuits. He offers to get them down for her and reaches up for them. In terms of the information-processing approach, Ben sees the old lady struggling to reach the biscuits and encodes this information. Ben then will make the decision from his processing and understanding of the information, that she needs help and that he can help her. As a result of his thinking, he asks the lady if she would like him to get the biscuits down for her and then reaches up for the biscuits and gives them to her.

Abnormality is faulty thinking

Internal mental processes can sometimes go wrong and result in abnormal behaviour. For example, in an attempt to explain atypical behaviours like phobias, a cognitive psychologist would start from the assumption that the atypical feelings (anxiety) and behaviour (avoidance) reflect faulty processing of information about threats. A person with arachnophobia, in this view, processes information about spiders as threatening, even when they pose no threat.

◆ The role of schemas

- A central role of internal mental processes is the ability to make sense of the incoming information. People make sense of their environment by imposing meaning on the things they encounter and, as a result, determine how they behave. According to cognitive psychologists, we use schemas to make sense of the world around us. Schemas are a collection of mental concepts (or mental frameworks) that are stored in memory. Our brains create and use schemas to help make sense of the world by interpreting the incoming information (objects, situations, expectations, people, etc.). Schemas are created through experiences from very early on in life.

- For example, an infant will create a schema for a 'dog' – an animal with four legs. When they next see a dog, they will search through their existing memory store to see if the object matches any existing schema and will be able to identify that object as a dog. When a child then sees a 'cat', they may mistakenly assume this to be a dog (as they have created a schema of an animal with four legs and not one for a cat). After learning the difference, the child will create a new schema for a cat and so on, and this is how schemas develop. As we get older our schemas become more detailed and sophisticated. Schemas influence behaviours in a wide range of environments. For instance, if Joe is employed as a surgeon in a hospital, he displays his professional role in the hospital but probably behaves differently when on vacation with his family. As observers, our expectations about how we should act differ depending on the social situation.

Therefore, cognitive psychologists see schemas as being useful because they help us to:

- *Predict.* Schema help us predict what will happen in our world based on our experiences.

- *Rapidly process.* Schemas enable us to process vast amounts of information rapidly.

- *Avoid being overwhelmed.* Schemas prevent us from becoming overwhelmed by environmental stimuli.

Schemas might not be useful when processing information from the world around us because they can cause:

- *Distortion.* Schemas can distort our interpretation of sensory information.

- *Inaccuracy.* Schemas lead to perceptual errors or inaccurate eyewitness testimony (EWT)/memories.

- *Bias.* Schemas can cause biased recall e.g. we see what we expect.

- *Mental disorder.* Negative/faulty schemas may have a negative impact on mental health.

◆ The emergence of cognitive neuroscience

- The aim of cognitive neuroscience is to identify and explain mental processes and how behaviour relates to brain mechanisms. Cognitive neuroscience looks at how neural mechanisms (which are neurons, neural circuits and regions of the brain) associate with certain cognitive processes. In the last 20 years, with advances in brain-imaging techniques such as functional magnetic resonance imaging (fMRI) and positron emission tomography (PET) scans, scientists have been able to systematically identify neurological activity and structures within the brain and relate these to certain cognitive processes.

- Functional neuro-imaging has enabled us to link brain activity with particular tasks. In research involving tasks that require the use of episodic and semantic memory, Tulving et al. were able to show how these different types of long-term memory may be located on opposite sides of the prefrontal cortex.

Possible practical applications in the use of cognitive neuroscience

Psychologists take the view that knowledge about the brain and nervous system can lead to a deeper understanding of complex mental functions such as memory, language, emotion, perception, attention and consciousness. Some useful applications of cognitive neuroscience are:

- The use of imaging of the brain to locate different types of memory in different areas of the brain, which can lead to treatment for memory problems.

- The use of imaging techniques to study mental processing in patients with depression or obsessive-compulsive disorder (OCD), in children with autism or dyslexia.

- The use of imaging techniques and angiography to study the effects of normal ageing on the brain or to observe the effects of stroke on the brain.

◆ How do cognitive psychologists study human behaviour?

- Cognitive psychologists follow the example of behaviourists in preferring objective, controlled, scientific methods such as experiments for investigating behaviour. Although we cannot see what is going on in our brains, as they cannot be observed directly, we can study them indirectly and make inferences about what is going on in people's minds based on how they behave. Therefore, cognitive psychologists use experimental results of their investigations as the basis for making inferences about mental processes.

- One strand of cognitive research involves conducting case studies of people with brain damage. Comparing their performance on mental tasks with that of uninjured people can help psychologists understand which parts of the brain are used to process which sorts of information.

◆ Evaluation

Strengths

✔ **Better understanding.** A strength of the cognitive approach is that it addresses some of the shortcomings of the behaviourist and social learning approaches by offering a more developed account of the internal processes that shape behaviour. For example, the cognitive approach focuses on the important part of the 'processes' that occur between stimulus and response, whereas behaviourists do not attempt to investigate what goes on inside the 'black box'. Additionally, can explain how two people can react differently to the same stimulus (because they perceive the stimulus differently), something that behaviourism fails to do.

✔ **Real-life application.** Another strength is that the cognitive psychology approach can be applied in everyday life. The cognitive approach has led to the development of useful ways of understanding and treating psychological disorders. For example, cognitive therapies are amongst the most effective ways of treating problems like depression and avoid many drawbacks of other therapies, being relatively fast-acting and free from side effects. Also, the cognitive approach has led cognitive psychologists to look at ways of improving people's memories using retrieval cues such as the Method of Loci.

✔ **Cognitive psychologists use scientific methods.** A strength of the cognitive approach is that it uses scientific methods to investigate human memory. Researchers can test theories of 'thinking processes' by making clear predictions about what will happen when people are exposed to certain stimuli. These theories can then be tested to demonstrate if they are true or not. Psychologists can do this by using experiments as they are able to control as many variables are possible, so we can truly see if there is any kind of causal relationship. For example, Bugelsky and Alampay (1962) conducted their rat-man experiment in a lab. Two groups of participants were shown either a sequence of faces or animals before all being shown the same figure. They found that participants who saw the sequence of faces were more likely to see the final figure as a man, and those shown a sequence of animals were more likely to see the figure as a rat.

Weaknesses

✗ **Machine reductionism.** A weakness of the cognitive approach is that it suffers from machine reductionism – it portrays human behaviour as that of a machine. For example, the over-reliance of the cognitive approach on the computer metaphor to compare the human mind to the operations of a computer (similarities between the two e.g. inputs and outputs, storage systems, the use of a central processor), has led cognitive psychologists to neglect the influence of emotions on our thinking and behaviour, as well as failing to include things we know about brain functioning and the influence of genes on cognition (e.g. intelligence). For instance, research has found that human memory may be affected by emotional factors, such as the influence of anxiety on eyewitness testimony. As a result, the credibility of the cognitive approach is reduced.

✗ **Lacks mundane realism.** A criticism of the cognitive approach is that research into the cognitive approach lacks mundane realism. For example, some would question the value of the experimental research, which often makes use of very contrived and unrealistic tasks and measures (such as tests of memory involving word lists). These tests may not adequately reflect real-world psychological and behavioural processes and therefore lack mundane realism. This is an issue because cognitive psychologists can only make inferences about mental processes from the behaviour they observe in their research. This means that cognitive psychology may be too abstract and theoretical in nature and may not be an accurate explanation of behaviours. As a consequence, the internal validity of the research is reduced, which in turn reduces the credibility of the cognitive approach.

Practice exam questions

1. Explain what is meant by 'internal mental processes'. **[2 marks]**

2. Explain what is meant by the 'theoretical model'. **[3 marks]**

3. Explain what is meant by 'computer model'. **[2 marks]**

4. Explain what is meant by 'cognitive neuroscience'. **[2 marks]**

5. Explain what is meant by 'inference' in the context of mental processes. **[2 marks]**

6. Outline what is meant by 'cognitive neuroscience' and describe one practical application of cognitive neuroscience. **[6 marks]**

7. Evaluate the research methods used by cognitive psychologists. **[6 marks]**

8. Outline and evaluate the cognitive approach. **[12 marks AS, 16 marks A-level]**

AQA specification for Topic 4: Approaches in Psychology

- The biological approach: the influence of genes, biological structures and neurochemistry on behaviour. Genotype and phenotype, the genetic basis of behaviour, evolution and behaviour

◆ Basic assumptions of the biological approach

Psychologists who take a biological approach (biopsychologists) assume that behaviour and experiences are caused by biological factors. This means that the influence of genes, neurochemistry (neurotransmitters, hormones) and the nervous system on the body determines our behaviour. In other words, things that people think and feel, say and do, are caused, one way or another, by the *brain structure* and *electrochemical events*, occurring within and between the neurones that make up the nervous system, particularly those in the brain. Furthermore, because the genes we inherit are the result of evolution, many biopsychologists think that behavioural and psychological characteristics may have evolutionary explanations.

◆ Genetic basis of behaviour

- Many biopsychologists believe that thoughts, feelings, and behaviours are influenced by the genes (carried in the DNA of the chromosomes in the nucleus of each cell) that we have inherited. Our genetic make-up (or genetic code) that we carry around inside us determines how the physical characteristics will develop and is known as the genotype. The phenotype of an individual is what happens when the genotype interacts with the environment and the results affect how the genotype gene is expressed. Therefore, the influence of the environment modifies the role that the genes play to a certain extent. For example, with a physical characteristic such as height, the genotype will dictate the maximum height an individual can reach but environmental factors such as nutrition will affect how likely the person can reach their full potential. Biopsychologists would accept that that much human behaviour depends upon the interaction between inherited factors (nature) and environmental factors (nurture).

- Genotype and phenotype on behaviour. Genotype and phenotype and behaviour are all linked together. For example, genes help determine the structure and function of the brain, but the environment plays a role in the final product, hence how we behave. Biopsychologists have used *twin*, *family history* and *adoption studies* to see genetic influences on behaviour. All of these involve comparing people with different degrees of genetic relatedness (e.g. parents/siblings, monozygotic and dizygotic twins) to see if a trait or behaviour runs in families. For instance, studies of patients with schizophrenia (a psychological disorder) and their families have shown that the more closely a person is blood-related to a schizophrenia patient, the greater their own risk of developing the disorder, which supports a role for genes in the disorder. A study by Gottesman (1991) into schizophrenia looked at identical twins (known as monozygotic (MZ) twins as they share 100% of their genes) that were reared apart, i.e. in different environments. He found 48% concordance rates between the pairs of twins, that is, the extent to which both twins develop schizophrenia, pointing to strong genetic influence. However, if the result was entirely due to genetic influence, the concordance rate should have been 100% as they are genetically 100% similar. The fact that only half of the time both twins developed schizophrenia demonstrates the influence of the environment (e.g. stress, family relationships, nutrients, toxins). This shows genotype, phenotype and behaviour are all linked together – behaviours could be a mixture of both genetic and environmental influences.

◆ Influence of neurochemistry on behaviour

- Biopsychologists believe that chemical processes in the brain can be an important influence on behaviour. The brain relies on a large number of chemicals (called neurotransmitters and hormones) to send signals between neurones. Too much or too little of any of these chemicals can result in over-or under-activity in various parts of the brain, which results in changes to thinking, feeling, and behaviour. For example, some researchers have shown how behaviour can be affected by altered levels of sex hormones. Increased testosterone leads to increased risk-taking, whereas increased oxytocin leads to increased nurturing and social responsiveness. In terms of psychological disorders, a high level of a neurotransmitter called dopamine has been linked to schizophrenia.

◆ Evolution and behaviour

- According to the biological approach, the genes we inherit are the result of evolution. Charles Darwin's natural selection theory of evolution is used by biopsychologists to explain many behavioural and psychological characteristics. The theory suggests that our hunter-gatherer ancestors were confronted with problems in the environment. Those who had certain behavioural characteristics or traits (e.g. intelligence) developed ways of solving the problems, giving them an advantage over others and increasing their chance of survival. A higher chance of survival means you are more likely to pass on your genes, thus this trait becomes adaptive through natural selection. Consequently, these characteristics or traits will become more common in the population whereas traits that do not enhance survival will gradually disappear.

- Therefore, according to biopsychologists, certain mental and psychological traits are explained in terms of evolutionary principles, i.e. intelligence and aggression were once adaptive. Another example is Bowlby's theory of attachment, where a newborn baby's attachment behaviour promotes survival by displaying certain behaviour (social releasers) towards the mother to elicit an emotional response (see the previous topic on Attachments, specifically *Bowlby's theory of attachment*). Such behaviours are adaptive and naturally selected.

◆ How do biopsychologists study human behaviour?

- The role of biological processes in behaviour can be studied in many ways, but researchers favour scientific methods as they are objective and well-controlled (e.g. experiments) and they are the most likely methods to produce valid scientific evidence.

- Various types of brain-scanning technology including positron emission tomography (PET) and functional magnetic resonance imaging (fMRI) can be used to study the structure and functioning of the brain. The nervous system can also be studied by manipulating the brain surgically. This might be done with animals, as biopsychologists view the human nervous system as having a lot in common with those of other mammals. Alternately, researchers might investigate the effects of brain injury or brain surgery in people who have had an operation in order to remove a tumour or an epileptic focus.

◆ Evaluation

Strengths

✔ **Scientific methods.** One strength of the biological approach is that it uses scientific methods of investigating human behaviour. Scientific methods use experiments, medical techniques and instruments to carry out research in a well-controlled and objective manner, focusing on observable rather than subjective experiences. This allows psychologists to understand how things work and it is easier to establish a causal relationship. For example, we can gather information about a person using fMRI scanning techniques to identify neural activity and functions related to certain tasks, disorders and operations. This is a strength because the techniques are highly precise and can be repeated successfully, increasing the validity and reliability of studies and techniques (such as fMRI). As a result, the credibility of the biological approach in explaining human behaviour is increased.

✔ **Real-life application**. A strength of the biological approach is that it has real-life application. For example, the increased understanding of biochemical processes in the brain has led to the development of psychoactive drugs that treat serious mental illnesses, such as depression and schizophrenia. This is a strength for the biological approach because it means that sufferers are able to manage their condition and live a relatively normal life, rather than remain in hospital. Although these drugs are not effective for all patients, they have revolutionised treatment for many. Consequently, the credibility of the biological approach in explaining human behaviour has increased.

Weaknesses

✗ **Deterministic approach.** A weakness of the biological approach is that it is deterministic on the outlook of human behaviour. For example, it states that human behaviour is governed by internal, biological causes (such as genes) that we have little control over. This approach could encourage people diagnosed with 'diminished responsibility' not to take responsibility for their own actions and blame their genetic makeup for all sorts of behaviours, such as low IQ, sexually deviant behaviours, mental disorders (e.g. depression), aggressive behaviour and different personality types. This is an issue as it ignores the ability of people to make choices (free will) and alter their course of behaviour such as not to commit a criminal act. As a result, the credibility of the biological approach is explaining human behaviour is reduced.

✗ **Reductionistic approach.** The biological approach has been criticised for reducing complex behaviours down to simple biological ones i.e. a reductionist approach. Critics say this is an issue, as by excluding the consideration of environmental and cognitive factors explaining human behaviour means it is difficult to fully explain or understand human behaviour, without reference to environmental/social influences, as it does not provide a complete picture. For example, obesity can be the result of both the genetic predisposition to gain weight (a biological factor) and the learning of bad habits (psychological factors). The biologist seeks to reduce the explanation to a genetic level, but it is still up to the psychologist to understand the current social and psychological circumstances that influence a person to increase his eating habits.

Practice exam questions

1. Explain what is meant by 'genotype'. [2 marks]

2. Explain what is meant 'phenotype'. [2 marks]

3. Describe the influence of 'genes' on behaviour. [6 marks]

4. Describe the influence of 'biological structures' and 'neurochemistry' on behaviour. [6 marks]

5. Rita and Holly are identical twins who were separated at birth. When they finally met each other at the age of 35, they were surprised at how different their personalities were. Rita is much more social and outgoing than Holly.

   Use your knowledge of genotype and phenotype to explain this difference in their personalities. [4 marks]

6. Describe and evaluate the biological approach in psychology. [12 marks AS, 16 marks A-level]

AQA specification for Topic 4: Approaches in Psychology

- The psychodynamic approach: the role of the unconscious, the structure of personality, that is: Id, Ego and Superego, defence mechanisms including repression, denial, and displacement, psychosexual stages.

◆ Introduction

The psychodynamic approach is one of the oldest and most famous approaches that was developed by Sigmund Freud (1856 – 1939). The word 'psychodynamic' is used because this approach sees the 'psyche' (the mind) being influenced by powerful active (dynamic) unconscious forces that determine our thoughts, feelings, and actions. Freud also developed a therapy called psychoanalysis designed to treat mental disorders, mainly neuroses (anxiety).

◆ The role of the unconscious

The iceberg analogy of the mind

Before we discuss the *role of the unconscious mind* it is worth explaining how Freud saw the mind to get a better understanding. Freud saw the mind as having three different levels: *'conscious', 'preconscious'* and the *'unconscious mind'*. To help you understand the unconscious mind better, consider the iceberg analogy. Everything above the water represents the conscious mind (awareness), while everything below the water represents the unconscious mind.

- The *conscious mind* is the smallest part of our mind, responsible for mental activity such as attention, perception and our thoughts e.g. what we are thinking about.

- The *preconscious mind* is just below the surface of the conscious mind, and holds our memories, thoughts and knowledge that are accessible, but not at the forefront of our thoughts. For example, if I asked what your telephone number is, you would be using the preconscious part of your mind to bring into awareness i.e. into the conscious mind.

- The *unconscious mind* is the largest part of our mind. The role of the unconscious is to keep all our negative and unacceptable experience and desires repressed so we are not aware of them. However, the unconscious mind still influences our behaviour/personality, but we are not aware of it happening (see below for full description).

Figure 8: Freud's view of the human mind: the mental iceberg

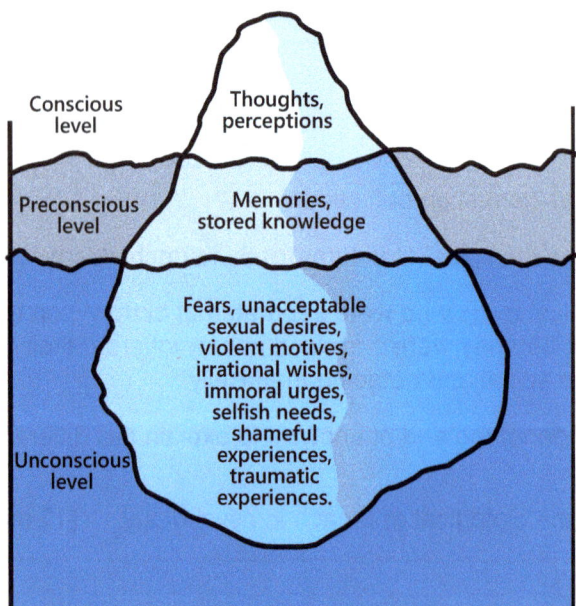

The unconscious mind

According to Freud, most of our mind is made up of the unconscious. The unconscious is a vast storage that contains all the *unacceptable* biological instincts, urges, and desires that we have (e.g. immoral urges or unacceptable sexual wishes). It also contains all the *unpleasant* memories, thoughts, feelings and emotions (e.g. anxiety, and traumas) we experienced since early childhood (e.g. anger at one's mother, memories of childhood abuse, hatred of a family member). The person is not aware of these unacceptable and unpleasant desires/memories. This is because they have been repressed from our conscious (by our ego defence mechanism – see below) to the unconscious to make them inaccessible; a person cannot access them, they are locked away and forgotten.

How the unconscious influences our behaviour

The important part to understand is that the unconscious mind continues to influence our behaviour and personality, and abnormal behaviours, even though we are unaware of these underlying influences. For example:

- In terms of unacceptable desires, the unconscious is constantly influencing our behaviour, particularly with urges to seek pleasure. Sometimes the unconscious (usually sexual in nature, but not always) may show itself through our *dreams* or through a *'slip of the tongue'* (Freud referred to these slips as 'parapraxes'), which unconsciously reveal what we really think e.g. a man accidentally calls his wife by the name of his mistress.

- In terms of unpleasant memories and emotions, Freud believed that repressed memories of early traumatic experiences would be too painful and unpleasant for us and disrupt our normal everyday life if we became consciously aware of them. But Freud argued that such experiences could appear later in adulthood in the form of depression, phobia and obsessive or compulsive behaviour, now known as OCD. Freud therefore believed that if we have problems or challenging behaviour (e.g. anxiety, phobias), then we must access the unconscious mind to sort it out.

◆ The structure of personality

- As well as believing that the brain was made up of three different levels, Freud also believed that personality is divided into three different parts. Freud described personality as made up of the id, ego and superego (these are not part of the brain but hypothetical concepts). These three parts interact with each other, and how they interact will determine our thoughts and behaviour (normal behaviour).

- The id (instinctual needs) is the primitive part of our personality. This is because the id consists of all our instinctual biological needs such as sexual instincts (called libido), aggression, food, water, etc. The id works on the pleasure principle, because these instinctual needs are driven by a strong selfish desire to seek immediate gratification. The id will not tolerate delayed gratification, regardless of the circumstances or consequences of our behaviour. There is no organisation at this level, no rationality, no morality, no sense of justice or care for social rules. The id is formed before birth and is located in the unconscious part of our mind.

  - *For example (if someone was living purely by their id part of their personality)*: If someone angers you, you kill them; if someone excites you, you have sex with them. If you need to urinate, you do it wherever you are, regardless of the consequence. Freud described babies as being just a 'bundle of id' – their continuous demand for satisfaction is a good example of living in the id mode.

- The ego (rational thinking) is the rational part of the personality, the voice of reason. The ego works on the reality principle by acting as a mediator in an attempt to negotiate a compromise (balance) between the unacceptable demands of the id and the moral restrictions imposed by the superego, in order to find behaviour that is realistic and socially acceptable. The ego is formed between 18 months – 3 years and is located in the conscious part of our mind.

- The superego (moral standards) is the morality aspect of the personality. It works on the moral principle, by acting as a moral guide and judge of what behaviours are right or wrong. It punishes the ego, making us feel guilt and shame when our behaviour is inappropriate. One of its main functions is to try and moralise the action of the id to more appropriate or acceptable action. The superego is formed between 3-6 years and is located in the unconscious part of our mind.

How the structure of the personality influences our behaviour

According to Freud, the id, ego, and superego are in constant dynamic conflict with each other to dominate our behaviour and thoughts. In other words, how you act in certain situations may be influenced by the three parts of the personality.

The id, the ego and the superego all function on different levels of consciousness and these three have to work harmoniously, in order to produce a healthy mental state. Abnormal behaviour occurs when there is an imbalance between the three.

Normal behaviour

If you found a wallet full of money in a restaurant, the id part of your personality would influence you to keep the money for yourself. However, your superego acting on the morality principle would push you to hand the wallet to the restaurant manager. If you satisfy the demands of the id and keep the wallet, you risk feeling guilty and shameful as the conscience within the superego punishes you for acting immorally. The decision you make is down to the ego, which tries to balance the demands of the selfish id and the moral superego. You may do the right thing by handling in the purse but selfishly hope to get praise or a reward for doing so, thus satisfying both the moral and pleasure-seeking sides of your personality.

Abnormality

According to the psychodynamic approach, psychological disorders/abnormal behaviours are due to an imbalance between the three parts of the personality. This usually occurs when the ego is weak (e.g. due to a life crisis such as loss or separation) and is overcome by the id or the superego, which then dominate our personality (behaviour and thoughts). For example:

- *Deviant behaviour.* If the superego is weak and is overpowered by the id, this may express itself in abnormal, immoral and destructive behaviour (e.g. deviant sexual or criminal behaviour).

- *Anxiety.* If the superego is strong and the id is weak, this can lead to unrealistic standards of behaviour and as a result, we experience high levels of shame and guilt that can lead to moral anxiety and anxiety disorders (e.g. phobias and obsessive-compulsive disorders).

◆ Defence mechanisms

Freud argued that when the ego cannot remove or reduce anxiety, the ego will use irrational methods called a defence mechanism, to protect us from anxiety and unwelcome ideas and to keep the ego strong in order to mediate. It is important note that when the ego uses a defence mechanism, this is an unconscious process, the person is unaware they are using them. Also, the ego's defence mechanisms falsify and distort reality. There are several ego defence mechanisms, the ones you need to know for the AQA examination are *repression, denial* and *displacement* (although we have also explained some others below).

- Repression. Repression is when unacceptable memories, emotions, desires or traumatic experiences are pushed into the unconscious and thus we are prevented from becoming conscious of them. This means we cannot recall the event or situation ever happening and thus prevents anxiety. Although they remain in the unconscious, they can still influence our behaviour, although we are not aware of this. For example, someone who was abused by a parent as a child may have no recollection of these events, but has trouble forming relationships.

- Denial. Denial is the refusal to accept the reality of a situation in order to avoid having to deal with any painful feelings that might be associated with an event. For example, an alcoholic will often deny that they have a drinking problem, even though they are heavily dependent on alcohol.

- **Displacement.** Displacement is when a person has strong thoughts and feelings towards a person or situation but is unable to express them in the presence of the person, so such feelings are redirected onto a neutral person or object. This gives hostile feelings a route for expression, even though they are misapplied. For example, anger at one's partner that may cause a lot of damage to the relationship, if expressed directly, is taken out on the dog, and thus reduces anxiety by allowing the expression of emotions on an alternative object.

- **Projection.** This is when an individual has undesirable characteristics or desires that are attributed to someone else, for example, accusing someone of 'being a gossip' when actually you're the one being a 'gossip'. Therefore, anxiety is reduced by projecting your emotions onto someone else.

- **Reaction formation.** This is when an individual takes up the opposite feeling, impulse, or behaviour of what they really believe. An example of reaction formation would be treating someone you strongly dislike in an excessively friendly manner, in order to hide your true feelings. Reaction formation reduces anxiety by turning emotions/desires into their opposite.

◆ Psychosexual stages of development

One of Freud's key assumption was that early childhood experiences have a powerful influence on our adult personality (and thus on our behaviour). He also believed that abnormal behaviour later on in life, derives from early childhood experiences. Freud believed that all children go through the five psychosexual stages and how the child experiences these five stages will shape their personality in adult life.

At each psychosexual stage (apart from latency stage), the libido, the pleasure-seeking sexual energy of the id, becomes focused on certain erogenous areas of our body as this brings the greatest source of pleasure and gratification. To make a smooth transition from one psychosexual stage to the next, the child must not experience frustration (being 'under-gratified') or experience being satisfied too often and too easily (being 'over-gratified'). Both experiences will cause the child to become fixated, which means the child's libido becomes stuck at this stage and as a result of this fixation, will carry certain behaviours associated with that stage through to adult life – it will form part of their adult personality. Freud stated that any fixations occuring in the first three stages are the most important and have an enduring effect on the adult personality.

- **Oral stage** (0 mths -1½ years). The child's libido (sexual energy) is centred around the mouth. The mouth is the focal point of pleasure from oral stimulation through gratifying activities such as sucking (breastfeeding) and biting. Conflict can arise during weaning. If a child is breastfed too early, too much, too late, or feeding patterns are erratic, it is argued that that the child will become fixated at the oral stage. For example, if a child is over-fed, this will have an unconscious effect on their personality. In adulthood, this fixation might mean they are dependent, very passive and gullible (believe anything you say). Or if a mother consistently fails to comfort and breastfeed her child, failing to satisfy the child's oral needs, fixation will occur, making the baby feel insecure. This can lead to displaying a personality in adult life that reflects this fixation, such as the mistrust for others or extreme dependency on others known as a *dependent personality disorder*.

- **Anal stage** (1½ -3 years). After the oral stage, the dominant pleasure of the libido becomes the anus-bowel movements. The pleasure of the id is derived from the child either retaining or expelling faeces. However, this is also the age at which the child is being potty trained, where the child *must learn to control its impulses*. Conflicts can occur when parental training has been inappropriate or poor. For example, if parents are too relaxed, or lenient with potty training, or the child is overly keen and loves to use the potty, this will have an unconscious effect on their personality. In an adult, this fixation translates to a generous person, messy, wasteful, who is demonstrative with their emotions (known anal-expulsive personality). If parents are too strict with potty training, too early, the child will become anxious about using the potty and try to hold onto the faeces rather than use the potty. An adult with an unconscious fixation at this stage will display personality characteristics such as being controlling, organised, very neat and reluctant to spend their money (known anal-retentive personality).

- Phallic stage (3-5 years). The libido's pleasure is now focused on the genitals. At this age, children have a fascination with their own genitals and those of others. They begin to discover the differences between males and females and they also become sexually interested in the opposite sex. Freud believed that boys in the phallic stage will experience the Oedipus complex and girls will experience the Electra complex.

    - The Oedipus complex. The Oedipus complex is when the male child *unconsciously* wishes to possess - experience an intense sexual feeling for - their mother. His father is then seen by the small boy to be a rival and therefore the boy wants to get rid of him so that the mother can focus on the child. As a result of this desire, the child feels threatened by the father (being bigger and stronger) and he fears that he will be punished by the father for seeing him as a rival. Because of this fear, the boy will experience castration anxiety – the father will punish the boy by removing his penis. In order to reduce the anxiety, the boy befriends his father by acting similarly to the father, he sees him as an ally rather than a rival for his mother's affections. This process of the boy identifying with the father is called identification. By identifying with the father, the son internalises (adopts) his *moral values* as his own, (and thus the superego is now fully developed), *attitudes, characteristics* that his father holds (e.g. personality, gender role, masculine behaviours, etc.). If the Oedipus complex is not resolved, this can lead to boys becoming fixated on their mothers, causing them to choose romantic partners that resemble their opposite-sex parent as adults.

    - The Electra complex. The Electra complex is a term used to describe the female version of the Oedipus complex, which girls experience between 3-6 years of age. The Electra complex is when the female child realises that they do not have a penis which they think is very important, and they think that their mother has removed it from them. This causes the child to resent her mother for 'castrating' her and subsequently the girl develops penis envy – longs to have a penis of her own. Because of this envy to have a penis, she develops an unconscious sexual feeling for the father, who has this 'valued organ' she wants to share and at the same time get rid of her mother. However, when the desire to be with her father is not fulfilled, she realises she doesn't want to lose her mother's love, she represses her feelings in order to remove the tension, and instead, the little girl identifies with her mother. By identifying with the mother, she internalises the mother's moral values as her own, as well as attitudes, characteristics that her mother holds (e.g. personality, gender role, feminine behaviours, etc.). Fixation occurs when the Electra complex is not resolved, which can continue to affect behaviour into adulthood, and, according to Freud, the girl marrying someone like her father.

- Latency stage (6 years to puberty). At this stage, the child enters a latent stage, an inactive period. The libido is dormant, there is no main area of the body for sexual pleasure.

- Genital stage (from puberty onwards). This is the final stage of development and begins at puberty. The libido once again is focused on the genitals at this stage, where pleasure derives from having sexual relationships, and this is where it stays for the rest of the life. Everyone reaches this stage and from here the child becomes an adult.

◆ Evaluation

Strengths

- ✔ **Positive contribution of psychodynamic approach.** The psychodynamic approach has provided valuable contributions to psychology. For example, Freud and other psychologists were the first to demonstrate the potential of psychological factors as the cause of mental disorders, rather than biological factors, and subsequently developed psychological forms of treatment for mental disorders, such as depression and anxiety (e.g. phobias). Before Freud, most explanations of mental illness were based on physical causes or ideas (e.g. possession of evil spirits). This is a strength of the psychodynamic approach because this approach changed how mental illness was viewed, which led to the development of many psychotherapies for the treatment of psychological disorders.

✔ **Supporting research evidence.** A further strength of the psychodynamic approach is that this approach has led to successful treatment. For example, Maat et al.'s (2009) large-scale review of psychotherapy studies concluded that psychoanalysis (therapy) produced significant improvement in symptoms for many years after treatment. However, other psychologists have questioned how effective psychodynamic therapies are. For example, Eysenck (1952) carried out a review of data from 24 studies that investigated the effectiveness of psychoanalysis. He found that approximately 44% of neurotic patients who received psychoanalysis had improved, compared to 66% of neurotic patients who received no therapy but still improved (were on a waiting list and unexpectedly got better - known as spontaneous remission). According to Eysenck, this demonstrates that psychoanalysis is not an effective treatment as people can get better without the needs for such therapy.

✔ **Research evidence for defence mechanisms.** There is research evidence to support the use of repression as a defence mechanism. There are patients that have experienced child abuse and do not remember, but subsequently, such memories are recovered in a therapeutic setting. However, some critics have questioned the validity of recovered repressed memories as often being false and are often due to the therapist's suggestion that such events occurred (Geraerts et al., 2007).

Weaknesses

✘ **Unscientific.** A criticism of Freud's theory is that many of his concepts are untestable, which make them unscientific. For example, Karl Popper argued that for a theory to be scientific it must be tested empirically, through experiments or observations to see if it is true or false. This is a criticism of Freud's theories because many of his concepts such as the id, superego, fixation, Oedipus complex, and defence mechanisms are said to occur at an unconscious level, which makes the concepts impossible to test empirically to see if they are true, which makes his theories unscientific. Consequently, the difficulty of testing such concepts has meant supporting research evidence from studies for his theory have been very few. Furthermore, many of Freud's theories cannot be falsified – cannot be tested to see if they are true or not. For example, the psychodynamic approach may predict that children who experience harsh potty training will grow up to be over-tidy with a tendency for perfectionism. Even if this does not happen, this does not show his theory is wrong, but another explanation may be offered, that is, the person is displaying reaction formation (showing the opposite behaviour). For Popper, this is unscientific as Freud's theory can never be proven wrong. As a result, the credibility of the psychodynamic approach is reduced.

✘ **Based on case studies.** Another weakness of the psychodynamic approach was its reliance on the use of case studies. For example, Freud came up with the concept of the Oedipus complex through a single case study. Little Hans was a five-year-old boy who developed a phobia of horses after seeing one collapse in the street. Freud suggested Hans' phobia was a form of displacement in which his repressed fear of his father was displaced onto horses. Thus, horses were merely a symbolic representation of Hans real unconscious fear of castration experienced during the Oedipus complex. Furthermore, his case studies were culturally specific; his patients belonged to a distinct cultural group of mainly Jewish, white, middle-class Viennese women, who were suffering from neurotic disorders and at a particular historical period (i.e. between the 1880s and the 1920s). This is a weakness of the psychodynamic approach and Freud's theory because his case studies lack reliability and cannot be generalised to the general population, which makes it difficult to apply his theory universally. Therefore, this reduces the credibility of the psychodynamic approach in explaining human behaviour.

✗ **Too deterministic.** A further criticism of the approach is that it is based on psychic determinism. The psychodynamic approach explains all behaviour as determined by unconscious forces and early childhood experiences, suggesting there is little you can do about changing this. Even something as apparently random as a 'slip of the tongue' is driven by unconscious forces and has deep symbolic meaning. Critics argue this is an extreme determinist stance to take and underestimates the control that we have over own behaviour (free will). As a result, the psychodynamic approach raises ethical concerns because the approach implies that others may be to 'blame' for the cause of the person's mental disorders. The suggestion that the parent may be partly to blame can bring about more distress to the individual and to the parents (e.g. guilt).

Practice exam questions

1. Using an example, explain the role of the unconscious in behaviour. **[5 marks]**

2. Outline the structure of personality according to the psychodynamic approach. **[5 marks]**

3. Explain what is meant by the term id, ego and superego. **[2 marks each]**

4. Explain the defence mechanisms of 'repression' 'denial' and 'displacement'. **[2 marks each]**

5. Name and explain three of Freud's psychosexual stages of development. **[2 marks each]**

6. Briefly evaluate defence mechanisms as a way of explaining human behaviour and experience. **[4 marks]**

7. Describe and evaluate the psychodynamic approach to psychology. **[16 marks]**

AQA specification for Topic 4: Approaches in Psychology

- Humanistic Psychology: free will, self-actualisation and Maslow's hierarchy of needs, focus on the self, congruence, the role of conditions of worth. The influence on counselling Psychology.

◆ Introduction

Humanism arose in the late 1950s in psychology, primarily in response to dissatisfaction with the behaviourist and psychodynamic approaches for their treatment of human behaviour (people) in very deterministic and scientific ways (emphasis on the mechanistic stimulus-response to determine behaviour and evidence heavily dependent on experimental animal research). Humanistic psychology rejected the psychodynamic approach for its unhealthy negative view of human behaviour such as focusing on past experiences and the destructive unconscious forces that shape human behaviour. Humanists see all individuals as naturally good, with personal growth and fulfilment in life as a basic human motive. The humanistic approach is thus often called the 'third force' in psychology after behaviourism ('second force'), and psychoanalysis ('first force') (Forces are specific ideological movements in the history of psychology.)

◆ Key assumptions of the humanistic approach

The uniqueness of humans

- Humanistic psychologists start from the assumption that every person is different, they differ in the way they perceive and understand the world and the things they do only make sense in this light. Every person is different because we have all had different subjective experiences in life, which make us all unique. Therefore, humanistic psychologists do not believe you can make generalisations about human behaviour, and thus reject the *nomothetic approach* (an approach in psychology that seeks to establish general laws on human behaviour) and favour the idiographic approach (which views people as unique individuals). Therefore, the aim of this approach is the study of the subjective experience of the individual rather than to establish general laws. This approach is often referred to as a person-centred approach in psychology.

Free will

- A core assumption of the humanistic approach is that we have free will. This means we have the ability to choose how to behave without being influenced by external forces - we are in control of our behaviour. This also means that we are in charge of how we develop and progress through life. However, humanistic psychologists do accept there are restrictions to people's choices (free will), due to social rules, morals, and laws, although these only reduce the number of choices available. These choices are driven by the need to self-actualise (i.e. develop potential to the fullest). The belief that human behaviour is governed by free will go against all the other approaches, which believed thoughts and behaviours were determined and that we do not have choices or control. This is another reason that humanistic psychologists such as Rogers and Maslow, reject scientific models that attempt to establish general principles of human behaviour.

Self-actualisation and Maslow's hierarchy of needs

- Abraham Maslow, a humanist psychologist, proposed the 'motivational theory' in which he believed that a human is motivated towards personal growth and achievement of their full potential, to become the best they can possibly be. This achievement of that full potential is a human state called self-actualisation. Maslow created a 'hierarchy of needs' (see figure 9 below) before a person can become self-actualised. He arranged these in the form of a pyramid, where the basic needs are the four lower levels of the hierarchy. Maslow proposed that motivation is required in order to achieve certain needs. Maslow believed that those who satisfied all their needs might become self-actualised. However, Maslow thought that not everyone will manage this, he believed that there are important psychological barriers that may prevent a person from become motivated and become 'stuck' (for some time) at a level, which prevent them from reaching their potential (e.g. having low self-esteem, poverty, death).

Figure 9: Maslow's hierarchy of needs

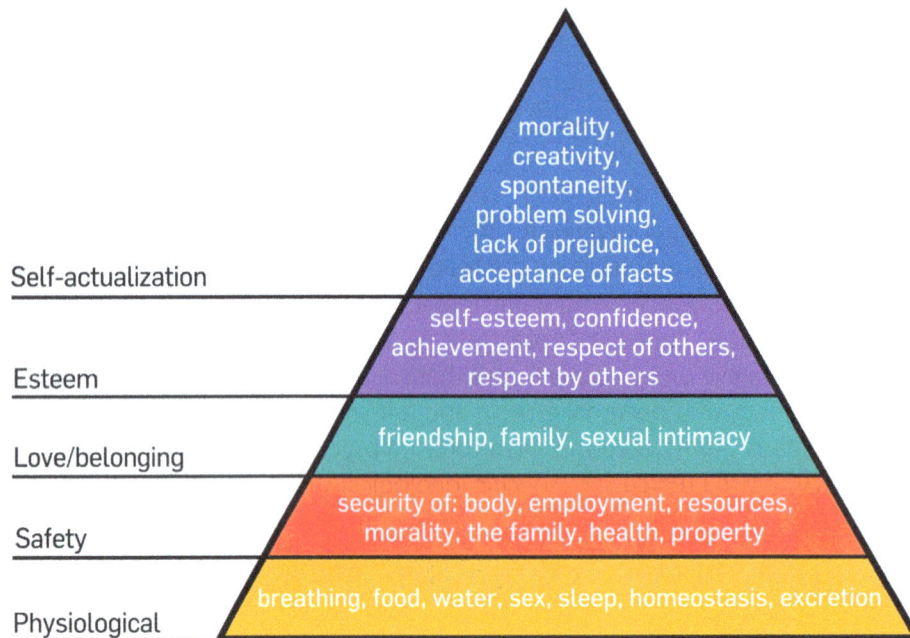

The self, congruence and conditions of worth

- One of the leading psychologists in the development of the humanistic approach was Carl Rogers. Like Maslow, Rogers believed humans have a drive for personal growth (to be 'self-actualised'). He argued that the achievement of personal growth will depend on a person's own self-concept (the way they see themselves e.g. how we think, feel, behave and look), also referred to as the real-self. He also believed we hold an ideal-self (the person we wish to be like). According to Rogers, a healthy individual tends to see a congruence (similarity) between the real-self and the ideal-self, this leads to a positive self-regard. Therefore, according to Rogers, to achieve self-actualisation it is necessary for a person to be congruent. When there is a mismatch, a difference between the real-self and ideal-self, the person will experience a state of incongruence, which leads to negative feelings of self-worth (unhappiness), and poor mental health, meaning self-actualisation will not be possible. The greater the difference between the real-self and ideal-self, the more likely the person is to suffer from poor mental health.

- Rogers believed that an important part of achieving congruence (and thus having a positive self-regard) and reaching your full potential, is if the person has unconditional positive regard from others. That is, if they feel that they are valued and respected for who they are without reservation or condition by those around them, e.g. parents, family members, friend, partner or therapist! However, Rogers felt that it was rare for a complete state of congruence to exist and that all people experience a certain amount of incongruence.

- According to Rogers, whether we become self-actualised often has its roots in childhood experiences. He argued that it is important that children receive unconditional positive regard from significant others (e.g. parents, family members). However, the problem that most people have, as Rogers saw it, was that most children don't perceive the positive regard of others as being unconditional – they often experience conditional regard. Rather, they think they will only be loved and valued if they meet certain conditions of worth (e.g. behaving well, passing exams, etc). The problem with conditional regard is that it inhibits personal growth, preventing self-actualisation from occuring.

The influence on counselling psychology

- **Types of psychological issues.** The humanistic approach has had major influences on counselling psychology. In 1942, Rogers, based on his humanistic approach, developed client-centred therapy (also known as client-centred counselling). It deals with many issues such as relationship problems, depression, anxiety, bereavement, addictions, sexuality, anger, and transitions in life.

- **Aim of client-centred therapy.** Rogers believed that a person's psychological problems were a direct result of their conditions of worth and the conditional positive regard they receive from other people, most notably their parents. This leads to incongruence between the real-self and the ideal-self, which can lead to disorders such as depression and low-esteem. The aim of client-centred therapy is to increase the feelings of self-worth and reduce the incongruence between the real-self and the ideal-self of the client.

- **Client led.** Client-centred therapy, as the name suggests, is led more by the client and less by the therapist and clients see themselves as facilitators, helping people to understand themselves and find ways to enable their potential for self-actualisation.

- **Three important elements.** In Roger's client-centred therapy, there are three important elements that counsellors must ensure for the therapy to be effective:

  - *Genuineness.* The therapist needs to share her/his feelings, in a genuine way.

  - *Empathy.* The therapist must strive to understand the client's feelings and thoughts, in a compassionate way.

  - *Unconditional positive regard.* The therapist must allow the client to express his or her true emotions, without fear of rejection or judgment by the therapist.

- **Outcome of the therapy.** For effective counselling, the therapy must entail the three elements above. The therapist must show empathy and unconditional positive regard, expressing their acceptance and understanding of what the client says. By doing this, the therapist is able to offer a supportive and comfortable environment to help increase the client's feeling of self-worth, thus reducing the incongruence between the client's real-self and the ideal-self.

◆ Evaluation

Strengths

✔ **Optimistic view of human nature.** A strength of this approach is it portrays a positive image of humans having free will, allowing them to be in control of their lives and motivated towards growth in order to better themselves. However, critics argue humans do not have a positive nature or are growth-oriented as humanistic theories suggest. The approach does not adequately recognise people's capacity for pessimism and self-destructive behaviour (as Freud's theory does). Freud's theory and the biological approach view human beings as slaves to their past or determined by internal physiological make-up (genetic or chemical imbalances), which reduce their ability to control our behaviour. Therefore, the assumption that all problems arise from 'incongruence' is an oversimplification, so encouraging people to focus on their own self-development, rather than on the situation, may not be appropriate.

✔ **Holistic approach.** A strength of the humanistic approach is that it adopts a holistic approach to understanding human behaviour. This means that a person's subjective experience can only be understood when you consider the person as a whole (family relationships, past experiences, childhood, etc). This contrasts with other approaches that take a reductionistic approach and understand human behaviour, by breaking up behaviour and experience into small isolated components. For example, the biological approach sees humans purely as biological organisms made up of physiological processes, which humanists reject as this does not provide a valid and meaningful understanding of human behaviour. This approach may have more validity than its alternatives by considering meaningful human behaviour within its real-life context.

✔ **Real-world application.** A strength of the humanistic approach is the development of client-centred therapy, which has proved to be effective. For example, Grave et al. (1990) compared person-centred therapy with three forms of behavioural therapy in clients having interpersonal problems. They found that all four forms of therapy were moderately and comparatively effective (similar in result). However, the clients who did the best with personal-centred therapy had a relatively high level of social skills and assertiveness, suggesting therapy was successful for certain people. However, this result can be questioned as the measures were subjective (opinion based on the client), so it could have been biased. Furthermore, Roger's client-centred approach is not suitable for treating serious mental disorders, such as schizophrenia or depression, so it has limited use.

Weaknesses

✗ **Untestable concepts.** A criticism of the humanist approach is that the over-reliance on the individual's subjective experiences means the concepts are not tested objectively, under scientific conditions. This is because a number of humanistic concepts are vague and abstract such as 'self- actualisation' and 'congruence', which makes them difficult to test. For example, 'self-actualisation' cannot be objectively measured, due to individual differences and a lack of a universal objective measuring scale. The impact of this means that client-centred therapy cannot be tested under controlled experimental conditions and therefore we cannot know for sure if changes in 'congruence' or 'increase in self-worth' were the result of humanistic therapy or other factors outside counselling. This means that it is difficult to evaluate the humanistic approach, and its therapy, scientifically. Rogers did attempt to introduce more rigour into his work by developing an objective measure of progress in therapy, however, critics argue that this is still subjective, as it is reliant on the client's interpretation, which is open to bias.

✗ **Cultural bias.** A weakness of humanistic psychology is that it may be biased towards Western cultures. For example, key humanistic concepts such as Maslow's ideas of self-actualisation, personal growth, and congruence are typical values of Western, individualistic cultures (including the United States). However, in collectivist cultures, such as Asian countries (e.g. Japan, India), emphasis is on the needs of the family group, community, and inter-dependence (extended family). This potential cultural bias is a weakness for the humanistic approach, because non-Western cultures may not identify with the ideals and values of humanistic psychology. This means this approach may not be appropriate for other cultures where a desire for personal growth may be seen as a selfish act, which does not consider that the needs of the group are more important than that of the individual.

Practice exam questions

1. Explain what is meant by the term 'free will'. **[2 marks]**
2. Explain what is meant by the term 'self-actualisation'. **[2 marks]**
3. Explain what is meant by the term 'congruence'. **[2 marks]**
4. Explain what is meant by the term 'conditions of worth'. **[2 marks]**
5. Outline Maslow's 'hierarchy of needs'. **[4 marks]**
6. Explain the influence of humanistic psychology on counselling psychology. **[4 marks]**
7. Referring to two assumptions of the humanistic approach, explain why humanistic psychologists have rejected the scientific method **[4 marks]**
8. Describe and evaluate the humanistic approach to psychology. **[16 marks]**

AQA specification for Topic 4: Approaches in Psychology

- Comparison of approaches.

◆ Introduction

You will have realised by now that the six approaches we have described all have different ways to explain behaviour. Although there are disagreements between approaches, there are similarities in the assumptions they make about human behaviour. For the exam, you need to compare the approaches, that is, be able to explain ways in which they are *similar* and *different*. You can do this by examining where the approaches stand on central issues in psychology. These central issues are (1) cause of behaviour; (2) determinism/free will; (3) nature vs. nurture; reductionism/holism; (4) research methods.

◆ Causes of behaviour

This section is an overview of comparing the different approaches on what influences our behaviour.

Approach	Cause of behaviour
Behaviourist	*Behaviour:* External forces in the environment shape our behaviour. We are born as a 'blank slate' and all behaviour is learned through a stimulus-response process, through classical and operant conditioning. *Abnormal behaviour:* arises from maladaptive or faulty learning (i.e. a person has associated fear with an object or situation). Behavioural therapies take a symptom-based approach to the unlearning of behaviour. *Therapy:* Aversion therapy and systematic desensitisation to unlearn the association.
Social learning	*Behaviour:* is learned as a result of the observation of others e.g. through the process of identifying and imitating others by modelling their behaviour, vicarious reinforcement, and the role of mediational processes. *Abnormal behaviour:* arises through modelling (watching others) and has been used to explain the development of aggression, eating disorder, and phobias. *Therapy:* Modelling therapy (as well as behaviour therapy) helps people change their behaviour by simply watching models of other people successfully coping with the problems they face.
Cognitive	*Behaviour:* is the result of internal processes of the mind. The mind consciously processes information in a similar fashion to computers 'input—processing—output'. A central role of mental processes is the development of schemas that help us to interpret and make sense of the world around us. *Abnormal behaviour:* Faulty cognition such as negative thoughts process and errors in logic, leading to abnormal behaviour. *Therapy:* Cognitive behavioural therapy (CBT) aims to change negative irrational thoughts into positive rational thoughts leading to a change in behaviour.
Biological	*Behaviour:* is the result of internal influences, inherited genes, and/or physiological factors (neurotransmitters/hormones), and the nervous system of the body, which all determine our behaviour. *Abnormal behaviour:* is affected by damage to brain structures, genetic abnormalities and changes in levels of neurochemicals. *Therapy:* Drugs and psychosurgery are used to target physical abnormalities and re-balance neurotransmitters in the brain to treat mental disorders.
Psychodynamic	*Behaviour:* is shaped by internal influences such as our unconscious mind (e.g. the id), which affect our behaviour without us being consciously aware it is occurring. Childhood experiences (psychosexual stages) affect the development of the personality. *Abnormal behaviour:* A lack of balance between id, ego and superego, unresolved fixations during psychosexual development, or repression of painful memories or traumatic experiences all emerge from the unconscious leading to abnormal behaviour e.g. anxiety disorders. *Therapy:* Psychoanalysis (dream analysis, projective test, free association) can help alleviate these disorders by unlocking and resolving unconscious thoughts/conflicts.

Humanistic	*Behaviour:* is shaped by each person's subjective experience in life, which is unique. This is because humans are born with free will, so our behaviour is under our control. Humanists believe we have an inborn drive to self-actualise, a drive to develop our potential to the fullest – we become the best we can be. *Abnormal behaviour:* Poor mental health and unhappiness (e.g. depression) when a person experiences incongruence (difference between ideal-self and real-self) mean that self-actualisation (personal growth) will be blocked – you cannot grow. *Therapy:* Person-centred therapy (counselling) is a non-directive approach, as it respects an individual's ability to solve their problems. Therefore, it aims to provide a supportive environment, where clients can discover their own solution, and to help reduce incongruence and stimulate personal growth.

◆ Determinism and free will

This section compares the different approaches towards the determinism and free will debate. Free will is the idea that what we do is voluntary and based on our own choices about thoughts and behaviour. Determinism is the opposite of this: the belief that an individual's behaviour choices and thoughts are determined by forces other than the individual's will to do something. These forces can be internal (inside our body) or external factors (the environment). As often the answer usually lies somewhere in between, our behaviour is probably a mixture of the two extremes.

Approach	Determinism and free-will
Behaviourist	Behaviourists see behaviour as being deterministic – it is environmentally determined by external forces that we cannot control. For example, Skinner saw behaviour as determined by the consequences (e.g. rewards and punishment) of our actions, which influence the likelihood of a behaviour reoccurring. Behaviourists argue that we feel like we have a choice when there is no threat of punishment, but even in those circumstances we are driven to choose whatever gave us pleasure in the past (i.e. our enforcement history).
Social learning	The social learning approach argues for a level of choice in our behaviour because we can choose who we want to observe and imitate or not. However, learning by observing others (vicarious learning) is still determined by our experiences, and therefore not our choice. Bandura advocated reciprocal determinism. That is, an individual's behaviour can influence their environment (e.g. being horrible at work) and is also influenced by the environment (others being horrible in return).
Cognitive	The cognitive approach believes the way we process information from the environment is determined by our experiences (schemas), which in turn determine our behaviour. However, not all thought processes are based on past experiences or acted upon, which suggests that individuals have some degree of control over their behaviour (free will). For example, cognitive therapy requires the individual to change their thoughts. Therefore, the cognitive approach adopts a soft-determinism view.
Biological	The biological approach is strongly deterministic as it believes our behaviour is determined by physiological (e.g. neurochemical and hormonal) factors and/or inherited gene factors (genetic determinism) and both are outside our conscious control.
Psychodynamic	The psychodynamic approach assumes that many of our behaviours and thoughts are influenced by the unconscious mind. As the unconscious mind is largely unknown to us and we have no control over it, we can argue that the approach is strongly deterministic (known as psychic determinism). Freud believed that even trivial phenomena such as Freudian slips, e.g. calling someone by the wrong name, are caused by unconscious factors.
Humanistic	The humanistic approach is the only approach to fully advocate the existence of free will and the idea that we can choose our path in life. Humanist psychologists such as Abraham Maslow and Carl Rogers believed that people exercise choice in their behaviour, rather than being at the mercy of outside forces, such as biological predispositions or reinforcement history.

◆ Nature versus nurture

This section compares the different approaches towards the nature-nurture debate, which examines whether human behaviour is the product of a person's genetic make-up (nature) or what they experience as a result of interacting with their environment (nurture).

In fact, the different approaches are usually more concerned with how nature or nurture interact.

Approach	Nature vs. nurture
Behaviourist	Behaviourist explanations emphasise the role of *nurture* more than nature in shaping our behaviour. They believe we are born as 'blank slates' at birth and it is the interaction with our environment that forms and shapes our behaviour through learned associations (stimulus-response link) and the consequence of our behaviour (positive/negative reinforcements). For this reason, behaviourists take an extreme nurture position.
Social learning	Social learning explanations emphasise the role of *nurture* more than *nature* in shaping our behaviour. They argue that the origin of behaviour is primarily *nurture* in that behaviour is learned from observing others in the environment. There is no acknowledgement of the innate and inherited capacities of the individual. However, it is generally assumed that the capacity to learn from observation of others has some adaptive value, therefore, this capacity is likely to be innate (*nature*).
Cognitive	Cognitive approach accepts both sides of the debate – behaviour is influenced by both *nature* and *nurture*. On the one hand, it acknowledges that we all share the information-processing mechanism that is important for the development of thought and language, and this mechanism is innate (nature). However, this theory also recognises the role of our environment (experiences) in constantly shaping our thought processes, e.g. people develop irrational thoughts and beliefs as a result of their experiences, (nurture), and therefore this approach also accepts the nurture side of the debate.
Biological	Biological explanations of behaviour emphasise the role of *nature* more than nurture in shaping our behaviour. This is because one core assumption of the biological approach is that our behaviour can be passed on through genetic inheritance (genotype). However, biopsychologists acknowledge that the environment can modify our genetic makeup, and this is illustrated by the phenotype of the individual. Maguire al.'s (2000) study of London taxi drivers found structural changes in the drivers' brains, as a result of them learning to navigate London's complex road layout.
Psychodynamic	Psychodynamic explanations of behaviour emphasise the roles of both *nature* and *nurture* in shaping our behaviour. The approach focuses on the *nature* side of human behaviour, as they see much of our behaviour and personality is driven by innate biological drives and needs, which stem from the unconscious mind (e.g. the demands of the id). However, they believe that the outcome of our personality and behaviour is ultimately shaped by interaction and experiences with our parents during childhood, therefore *nurture* plays a role too.
Humanistic	Humanistic explanations of behaviour emphasise the role of *nature* and *nurture* in shaping our behaviour. The approach assumes we have an innate drive to be the best we can be – to 'self-actualise' (*nature*) However, it also acknowledges that the environment can inhibit or help the process of self-actualisation (*nurture*). The problems in achieving self-actualisation may arise from our experiences and upbringing, e.g. our experience of conditional positive regard and conditions of worth (*nurture*). This approach seems to take an interactionist stance – both nature and nurture interact with each other.

◆ Reductionism and holism

For any single behaviour, there are different levels of explanations from the social context to the neural level. Reductionism can be defined as the attempt to explain any act by reducing it to a simpler level. Holism is when the explanation takes into account the interaction of all or many different factors affecting the behaviour – it looks at the whole picture, rather than one specific part.

Approach	Reductionism and holism
Behaviourist	The behavioural approach applies environmental reductionism to explain human behaviour. This is because behaviourists break up behaviour into isolated elements and explain such elements through a simple stimulus-response link (e.g. through 'association' and/or 'positive/negative reinforcement'). Such behaviour can be tested and measured under laboratory conditions and thus accepted as experimental reductionism.
Social learning	The social learning approach takes a reductionistic approach to explain behaviour, that is, applying environmental reductionism. This is because most complex things that people do (behaviour/thoughts) can be explained by breaking them down to observational processes and reinforcement. This approach also recognises how cognitive factors (processes of learning, e.g. the role of mediational processes) interact with the external environment, and explains this as machine reductionism.
Cognitive	Cognitive psychology supports machine reductionism. They use a computer analogy to explain information-processing (that governs our thoughts and behaviour), which ignores human emotions. This is reductionist because it suggests that human cognition can be represented in the same way as a machine function, e.g. the multi-store model of memory as a series of inputs, outputs and processes.
Biological	The biological approach is associated with reductionism. The approach attempts to explain behaviour through applying biological reductionism, which reduces explanations of human behaviour to the level of the gene or neuron (chemical level).
Psychodynamic	The psychodynamic approach mainly takes a holistic view to explain human behaviour. For example, the approach views personality as a dynamic holistic interaction (e.g. psyche (ego, id, superego) interacting with environment and shaping our behaviour). However, to say this approach is purely holistic would be a mistake, because the approach also takes a reductionist view to explain elements of our behaviour (e.g. biological drives and instincts underpin our behaviour and thoughts). However, it is widely considered that the psychodynamic approach is more holistic than reductionist.
Humanistic	The humanistic approach is holistic. It does not believe in reducing behaviour to specific elements and believes that individuals should be regarded as a whole. Humanists also reject using the scientific method to investigate behaviour, as this approach does not have any elements of experimental reductionism.

◆ Research methods

Psychology is often defined as the scientific study of behaviour. This is because psychologists have adopted scientific methods as the most appropriate way of studying human behaviour. However, some approaches are more scientific than others. Below we examine whether an approach is more focused on the uniqueness of an individual (idiographic) or whether it is trying to establish universal rules (nomothetic).

Approach	Research methods
Behaviourist	The behavioural approach uses scientific methods to investigate human behaviour. For example, behaviourists use well-controlled experiments to test and measure people's responses (stimulus-response link), which can be measured objectively (not based on subjective interpretation). This also allows for a high degree of replication, which is an important part of the scientific process. The behavioural approach takes a nomothetic outlook as it believes we share the same process for learning behaviour, which means we can establish general laws on behaviour and therefore seeks to generalise to all.
Social learning	The research methods used by the social learning approach tend to be scientific. They accept the 'behavioural elements' can be observed using controlled, objective methods such as experiments (e.g. Bandura Bobo doll study), allowing for cause and effect to be established. The 'cognitive element' (studying mental processes such as the multi-store model) of the social learning theory is not directly observable, so it is more susceptible to bias and therefore seen as less scientific. The social learning approach takes a nomothetic outlook as it believes we share the same process for learning behaviour, which means we can establish general laws on behaviour and therefore seeks to generalise to all.

Cognitive	The cognitive approach uses scientific methods to investigate cognitive processing. Well-controlled laboratory experiments mean that the data from cognitive experimentation is reliable and therefore more scientific. However, because thoughts are not directly observable a great deal of inference is necessary to develop models of cognitive processing (e.g. multi-store model) so they can be argued to be biased. This means that the approach is not as scientific in its methodology as the biological approach. Because the cognitive approach focuses on the scientific study of cognitive processing in groups of people together, this means this approach is nomothetic as it recognises that although individuals have vastly differing thoughts, the processes underlying these are the same and can be generalised to all humans.
Biological	The research methods used by the biological approach favour a scientific approach towards studying behaviour. This because it can apply the use of experimental methods to study physiological processes. For example, bio-psychologists can test and measure chemical brain activity using scanning technologies and physical measures to see the effect drugs have on a particular neurotransmitter in the brain and then measuring any changes in the behaviour that occurs. As it adopts a scientific approach, it is nomological (nomothetic) in its outlook as it is working on the idea that we share a common physiological and biochemistry.
Psychodynamic	The psychodynamic approach favours qualitative research methods (e.g. case studies, interviews) to study human behaviour and therefore its approach tends to be non-scientific (e.g. unconscious mind cannot be tested and measured scientifically). Although, 'projective test' and 'dream analysis' are techniques used to access the 'unconscious mind', it can never be proven that the techniques are actually accessing the unconscious mind. Furthermore, results are subjective as they require interpretation. The psychodynamic approach has elements of being both ideographic and nomothetic. It focuses on the unique childhood of each individual, using case studies, (ideographic), but it does generalise to all humans the innate drives in the unconscious mind we act upon (nomothetic).
Humanistic	The humanistic approach believes that scientific methods are not suited for studying humans. This is because complexities of human consciousness and unique individual experiences cannot be tested by artificial and limited methods. As the humanistic approach focuses on the uniqueness of individuals, that establishes this approach as firmly ideographic and would see no merit in trying to generalise from one individual to another. However, it could be argued that there are nomothetic elements, such as the hierarchy of needs, as this is seen as innate to all humans.

Practice exam questions

1. Outline and evaluate social learning theory. In your answer, make comparisons with at least one other approach in psychology. **[16 marks]**

2. Outline the psychodynamic approach. Refer to other approaches in your answer. **[16 marks]**

3. Outline and evaluate the humanistic approach in psychology. Refer to at least one other approach in your answer. **[16 marks]**

4. Outline the cognitive approach in psychology. Compare the cognitive approach with the psychodynamic approach. **[16 marks]**

5. Outline the behaviourist approach. Compare the behaviourist approach with the biological approach. **[16 marks]**

Topic 5

Biopsychology

AQA specification for Topic 5: Biopsychology

AS and A-level:

- The divisions of the nervous system: central and peripheral (somatic and autonomic).

- The structure and function of sensory, relay, and motor neurons. The process of synaptic transmission, including reference to neurotransmitters, excitation, and inhibition. The effect of endogenous pacemakers and exogenous zeitgebers on the sleep/wake cycle.

- The function of the endocrine system: glands and hormones.

- The fight or flight response including the role of adrenaline.

A-level only:

- Localisation of function in the brain and hemispheric lateralisation: motor, somatosensory, visual, auditory, and language centres; Broca's and Wernicke's areas, split-brain research. Plasticity and functional recovery of the brain after trauma.

- Ways of studying the brain: scanning techniques, including functional magnetic resonance imaging (fMRI); electroencephalogram (EEG) and event-related potentials (ERPs); post-mortem examinations.

- Biological rhythms: circadian, infradian, and ultradian and the difference between these rhythms. The effect of endogenous pacemakers and exogenous zeitgebers on the sleep/wake cycle.

AQA specification for Topic 5: Biopsychology

- The divisions of the nervous system: central and peripheral (somatic and autonomic).

◆ Introduction

There are close links between biology and psychology. Biology can influence our behaviour. For example, changes in our brain chemicals influence our moods and emotions (think of serotonin and dopamine) and can also influence our biology. For example, certain stressors in life (e.g. work, deadlines, social relationships) have been shown to influence our immune system. So, the term biopsychology is concerned with the ways in which biological factors influence our emotions, behaviours, and mental processes.

◆ Nervous system

All humans are made up of cells. Neurons (nerves) are specialist cells that make up the nervous system. The nervous system is made of trillions of neurons (or nerve cells) whose purpose is to carry messages passed by neurotransmitters as part of electrical and chemical (electrochemical) processes. The nervous system is divided into two subsystems: the *central nervous system* (CNS) and *peripheral nervous system* (PNS). The CNS comprises the brain and spinal cord, which carry sensory information from the arms, legs and body to the brain. The two main roles of the CNS are: 1) To control our behaviour by processing and responding to information from the environment, and 2) To regulate and co-ordinate the working of different physiological processes (e.g. organs and cells) in the body. To do this, the brain receives information from the sensory receptors (e.g. eyes and skin) about the social environment and sends messages to the body's muscles and glands. These messages are sent through the spinal cord, a collection of nerve cells that are attached to the brain and run the length of the spinal column.

◆ The central nervous system (CNS)

As mentioned above, the brain and the spinal cord make up the central nervous system (CNS). The nerves that spread out from the CNS make up the peripheral nervous system. The PNS is connected to all our body parts such as our internal organs, muscles and glands. The CNS does not have any direct communication with the outside world. It is the PNS that conveys the information about the outside world to and from the CNS. The spinal cord is vital for the processing and transferring of information, which takes place via neurons. The main job of the CNS is to process the information and regulate physiological processes, to ensure that life is maintained!

The brain

The brain is divided into four main areas:

- Cerebrum: the largest part, which is responsible for many functions such as speech production and processing visual images.

- Cerebellum: the part that controls motor skills and balance.

- Diencephalon: the part that contains the thalamus which acts as a relay station for nerve impulses coming from the senses, and the hypothalamus which is responsible for the regulation of body temperature among other things. The hypothalamus also triggers hormones to be released from the pituitary gland.

- Brain stem: the part that regulates functions essential for life such as heartbeat, swallowing and breathing.

The spinal cord:

- Relays information between the brain and the rest of the body.

- Is connected to different parts of the body by spinal nerves that connect to specific muscles and glands.

- Contains circuits of nerves that perform simple reflexes without the direct involvement of the brain, such as pulling your hand away from a hot plate.

◆ Peripheral nervous system (PNS)

- Nerves that come off from the central nervous system are called the peripheral nervous system (PNS). The PNS can be further divided into two sections the somatic nervous system and the autonomic nervous system.

The somatic nervous system

- Somatic nervous system (SNS) is responsible for transmitting sensory information via the central nervous system (CNS) to other areas of the body. The SNS does this by carrying sensory information about the environment (e.g. from the eyes, sound, skin) using sensory neurons to the CNS (spinal cord and brain), which then sends the information from CNS to other areas of the body (e.g. skeletal muscles), using motor neurons. The SNS is also involved in reflex actions without the involvement of the central nervous system, which allows the reflex to occur very quickly. So, in a nutshell, the SNS:

  - is under our conscious control whereas the ANS (below) is involuntary (not under our control).

  - is made up of nerves coming from the brain and the spinal cord.

  - contains both sensory and motor neurons.

    » Sensory neurons relay messages *to* the CNS (spinal cord + brain).

    » Motor neurons relay messages *from* the CNS (spinal cord + brain).

The autonomic nervous system

- The role of the autonomic nervous system (ANS) is to regulate the involuntary actions of internal body organs, such as heartbeat, glands, digestion, breathing, and temperature, without us being consciously aware of these happening. It is called autonomic (automatic) because we have no control over it, it happens involuntarily. The ANS is necessary because things like heartbeat and digestion would not work so efficiently if we had to think about them. The ANS can be further divided into two parts, the *sympathetic* and *parasympathetic*. These work on the same organs but have opposite effects. One increases the activity, the other decreases the activity.

  - The sympathetic nervous system (SNS) is primarily involved in increasing body responses that respond to a perceived threat, danger or emergency. It produces physiological changes such as increased heart rate, breathing and blood pressure and also prepares the body for fight or flight.

  - The parasympathetic nervous system (PNS) is involved with energy conservation and slows down physiological activity (such as heart rate), decreases blood pressure, stimulates the digestive system, and stores energy for future use, when the threat has passed.

Figure 10:

```
                          ┌─────────────────────────┐
                          │  Human nervous system   │
                          └────────────┬────────────┘
            ┌──────────────┬───────────┴───────────┬──────────────────┐
    ┌───────┴──────┐ ┌─────┴──────┐ ┌───────────────┴─────┐ ┌──────────┴──────────┐
    │    Brain     │ │ Spinal cord│ │ Autonomic nervous   │ │ Somatic nervous     │
    └──────────────┘ └────────────┘ │    system (ANS)     │ │    system (SNS)     │
                                     └──────────┬──────────┘ └─────────────────────┘
                                       ┌────────┴─────────┐
                              ┌────────┴────────┐ ┌───────┴─────────┐
                              │   Sympathetic   │ │  Parasympathetic│
                              │     system      │ │     system      │
                              └─────────────────┘ └─────────────────┘
```

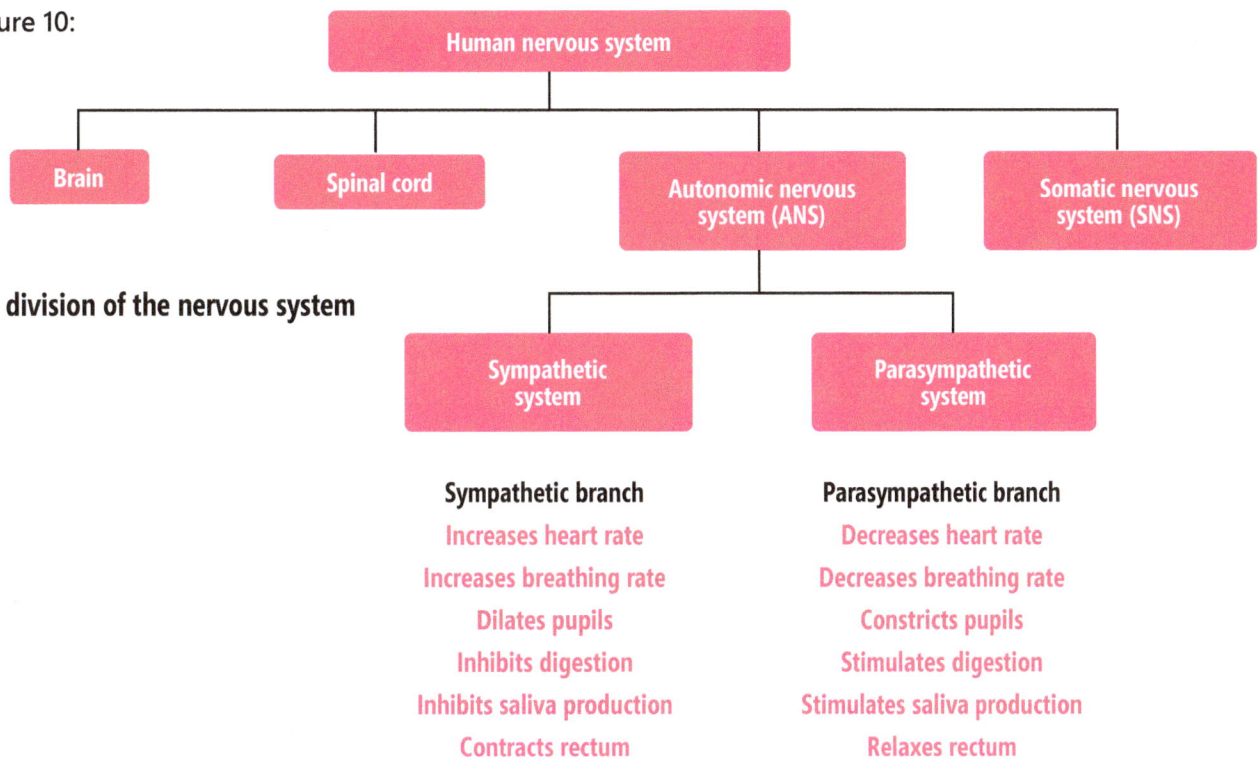

The division of the nervous system

Sympathetic branch	**Parasympathetic branch**
Increases heart rate	Decreases heart rate
Increases breathing rate	Decreases breathing rate
Dilates pupils	Constricts pupils
Inhibits digestion	Stimulates digestion
Inhibits saliva production	Stimulates saliva production
Contracts rectum	Relaxes rectum

Practice exam questions

1. Complete the following sentence.   [1 mark]
   Circle one letter only.
   Motor neurons carry information:
   A. away from the brain.
   B. both to and from the brain.
   C. towards the brain.
   D. within the brain.

2. Complete the following sentence.   [1 mark]
   Circle one letter only.
   The somatic nervous system:
   A. comprises of two sub-systems.
   B. connects the central nervous system and the senses.
   C. consists of the brain and spinal cord.
   D. controls involuntary responses.

3. Identify two components of the central nervous system.   [2 marks]

4. Outline the role of the central nervous system.   [4 marks]

5. Identify two divisions of the autonomic nervous system.   [2 marks]

6. Outline the role of the somatic nervous system.   [4 marks]

7. Outline the role of the autonomic nervous system.   [4 marks]

AQA specification for Topic 5: Biopsychology

- The structure and function of sensory, relay, and motor neurons. The process of synaptic transmission, including reference to neurotransmitters, excitation and inhibition.

◆ Introduction

The nervous system is made up of neurons. These are specialist cells that carry electrical impulses. Their function is to receive information and transmit this to the brain, as well as to other neurons throughout the body. There are thought to be around 100 billion neurons in the brain and one billion neurons in the spinal cord.

◆ The structure and function of the neuron

Neurons are responsible for everything we do – our thoughts, memories, emotions, physical sensations and the co-ordination of all the physical functions of the body. The nervous system (including the brain) has three main types of neurons - *sensory neurons*, *relay neurons* and *motor neurons*, and they perform different functions.

Functions

- Sensory neurons (the 'sensing' neurons) respond to stimulation from our five senses, i.e. vision, smell, taste, touch and hearing. These neurons are located in the peripheral nervous system (PNS) and are found all over the body. They receive information from the sensory receptors (e.g. in the skin, tongue and eyes) and convert this information into electrical impulses. When these impulses reach our brain, they are translated into sensations such as pain, sight or heat. Not all sensory information travels to the brain, however. Some neurons terminate in the spinal cord. This allows reflex actions to occur quickly without the delay of sending impulses to the brain. So *sensory neurons carry signals <u>towards</u> the CNS (spinal cord and brain)*.

- Motor neurons (the 'moving' neurons) are located in the central nervous system (CNS), from the brain stem nerves to the muscles of the face and head, and from the spinal cord nerves to the muscles and glands. Motor neurons help both glands and muscles to function; for example, they make muscles contract and keep the heart beating. So *motor neurons carrying information <u>away from</u> the CNS*

- Relay neurons (the 'connecting' neurons) connect motor neurons and sensory neurons, allowing them to communicate by passing signals to one another, that is, they transmit messages from one neuron to another neuron. They can also receive signals from other relay neurons. In fact, *most* relay neurons are found in the CNS. These neurons help the brain to process information from the environment.

Figure 11: Structure of typical neurons

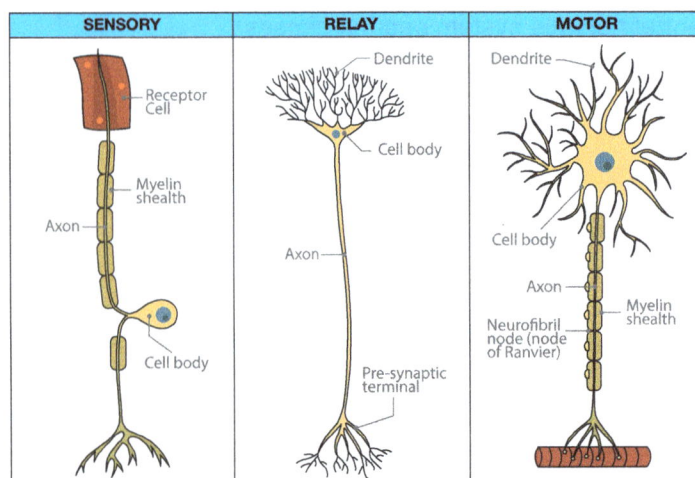

The structure of neurons

- All three types of neurons have the same components (dendrites, cell body, axon, etc.) but they differ in their shapes, locations and the roles they play.

How information is passed within a neuron

- All three neurons have what is known as dendrites (receptors at one end of the neuron). The dendrites receive information from sensory receptors or other neurons. The dendrites then pass the information to the cell body and then on to the axon and the axon terminals at the other end of the neuron. Information travels down the neuron as an electrical signal, ready to be passed onto the next neuron. The myelin sheath is an insulating layer that forms around the axon. This helps the signal to be transmitted more rapidly. If this sheath is damaged, the signals slow down.

◆ Synaptic transmission

How messages are transferred from one neuron to the next

Synaptic transmission is the sending of messages from one neuron to the next neuron or to body tissue (e.g. muscle). Once an electrical signal has arrived at the axon terminal, it needs to be transferred to another neuron. Here's how it works:

1. Initially, the signal (electrical impulse) travels down the neuron where it reaches the presynaptic terminal (which is at the very end of the axon terminal). Each neuron is separated from the next neuron by a tiny *gap* called a synapse (or synaptic fluid or synapse cleft).

2. When an electrical impulse reaches the end of the neuron, this activates the presynaptic terminal to release chemicals (neurotransmitters) from tiny sacs known as vesicles. The vesicles are found at the end of the axon, and cluster near the axon terminal. These sacs spill the neurotransmitters into the synaptic fluid/cleft.

3. These chemicals diffuse across the gap and are taken up by the adjacent neuron receptors on the dendrites of the next neuron. The postsynaptic neuron then converts these chemicals back into an electrical impulse to travel down the neuron to the next presynaptic terminal. *So, signals in the synapse are transmitted chemically.* In this way, the electrical impulse continues to be transmitted to the next neuron. This is how information travels.

During the transmission from one neuron to another, different receptors respond to different neurotransmitter molecules. Each neurotransmitter has a specific molecular structure that fits perfectly into a postsynaptic receptor site. The neurotransmitter will attach itself to the receiving postsynaptic receptor that recognises it. This is a 'lock and key' effect. Different receptors will only accept specific neurotransmitter molecules. The whole process takes a fraction of a second. After the neurotransmitters are received, the presynaptic neuron *re-absorbs* whatever is left in the synapse and stores it to be used again later. This re-absorption (cleaning up-process) is known as re-uptake. It refers to the process in the brain of neurons retrieving chemicals that were not received by the next neuron.

◆ Excitatory and inhibitory neurotransmitters

Neurotransmitters are chemical messengers that are released from vesicles on the presynaptic neuron. They carry signals from the presynaptic neuron to the postsynaptic neuron. After release, the neurotransmitter crosses the synaptic gap and attaches to the receptor site on the other neuron, either 'exciting' or 'inhibiting' the receiving neuron, depending on the type of neurotransmitter. So, neurotransmitters can be classified either as excitatory or as inhibitory in their action (some neurotransmitters can be both). How the receiving neuron will act depends on what kind of neurotransmitter it is.

- **Excitatory neurotransmitters** (e.g. acetylcholine or noradrenaline) increase the likelihood that an 'excitatory signal' is sent to the postsynaptic cell. This means the receiving postsynaptic neuron is more likely to fire and generate an electrical impulse.

- **Inhibitory neurotransmitters**. If an inhibitory neurotransmitter (e.g. GABA or serotonin) is sent, this decreases the likelihood of the receiving postsynaptic neuron firing and generating an electrical impulse.

Figure 12: Synaptic transmission

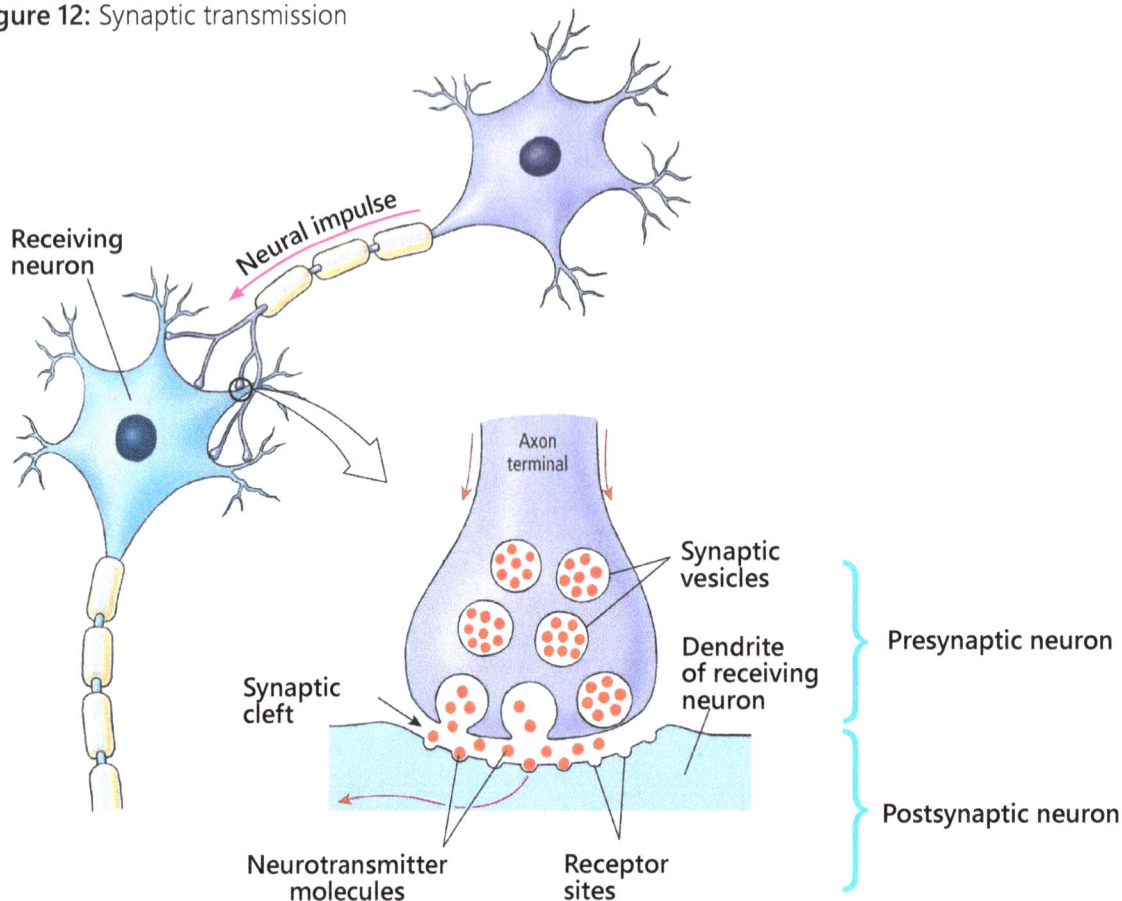

Practice exam questions

1. Explain the difference between a motor neuron and a relay neuron. **[2 marks]**

2. Briefly outline the process of synaptic transmission. **[2 marks]**

3. Briefly describe the structure of a neuron. **[3 marks]**

4. With reference to neurotransmitters, explain what is meant by 'excitation' and 'inhibition'. **[3 marks]**

5. Explain why neurons can only transmit information in one direction at a synapse. **[3 marks]**

6. Explain the process of synaptic transmission. **[5 marks]**

7. You are walking in the park, when a dog suddenly jumps forward and tries to attack you. The owner manages to control the dog and they walk away. Your breathing quickens, your mouth is dry and you have a feeling of 'butterflies' in your stomach. After a few minutes, these physical changes start to disappear. Using your knowledge of the body's response to stress, explain what you are likely to have experienced

   A. The changes that occurred in the first 30 seconds;

   B. The changes that occurred after a few minutes. **[2 + 2 marks]**

AQA specification for Topic 5: Biopsychology

- The function of the endocrine system: glands and hormones.

◆ Introduction

The endocrine system works alongside the nervous system to regulate the human body. Instead of using nerves (sensory and motor neurons) to transmit information, the endocrine system uses hormones (chemical messengers) transmitted via the bloodstream. Hormones can have a drastic effect on our behaviour and emotions. Most hormones are slow-acting because they are carried around the body fairly slowly by the blood-stream.

◆ The endocrine system

- The endocrine system is a network of glands throughout the body. These glands manufacture and secrete hormones into the blood. Hormones are chemical messengers that regulate the physiological process of the body. So the main function of the endocrine system is to:

  - secrete hormones via the blood-stream in order to communicate (like neurons) messages to certain targeted organs of the body.

  - secrete hormones to regulate many bodily functions, for example, the activities of organs and cells.

  Major glands in the body are the *pituitary gland*, the *adrenal gland* and the glands of the *reproductive organs* (ovaries and testes). The various glands produce different hormones that regulate organ and tissue activity in the body. Most of the endocrine system is controlled by the hypothalamus (a small region of the brain just above the pituitary gland). The hypothalamus controls the important pituitary gland, known as the 'master gland'. This gland produces hormones whose main function is to influence the release of hormones from other glands. The hypothalamus receives information from many sources about the functioning of the body and uses this information to regulate these functions.

- Feedback loop system. The endocrine system is regulated by a feedback loop system. For example, a 'releasing' hormone is sent from the hypothalamus to the pituitary gland. This causes the pituitary gland to secrete a 'stimulating' hormone into the bloodstream. This hormone then stimulates another targeted gland (such as the adrenal gland) to secrete its own hormone (e.g. adrenaline). As levels of hormones rise in the bloodstream, the hypothalamus shuts down the secretion of the 'releasing' hormone, and the pituitary gland shuts down the 'secreting' hormone. This slows down the secretion of hormones from the targeted glands. As a result, a stable concentration of hormones circulates in the bloodstream. This is called the feedback loop system, and it prevents hormone levels from becoming too high.

◆ Types of endocrine glands
Pituitary gland

- The pituitary gland has two main parts - the anterior pituitary (front) and the posterior pituitary (back). These two parts release different hormones, which act on different glands or cells. For example, the *anterior pituitary* releases ACTH (adrenocorticotropic hormone), which then stimulates the adrenal cortex gland. This releases a hormone called *cortisol* into the blood-stream following a stress response. The *posterior pituitary* releases a hormone called oxytocin (often referred to as the 'love hormone'), which is responsible for contractions of the uterus during childbirth and is important for mother-infant bonding.

Adrenal gland

- The adrenal gland sits on top of the kidneys and has two parts - *adrenal medulla* and *adrenal cortex*. The adrenal cortex (the outer part of the adrenal gland) releases the *cortisol* hormone. This helps the body to produce energy by breaking down the body's stored fat reserves. It also causes the liver to release glucose into the bloodstream. This is needed to maintain high energy levels and to help the body cope with the stress while suppressing the immune system. The adrenal medulla (the inner part of the adrenal gland) is responsible for releasing *adrenaline* (which increases heart rate and blood flow to the muscles) and *noradrenaline* (which constricts blood vessels, increasing blood pressure). Both play a key role in the fight or flight response (see Exam Notes 4 for this topic).

◆ Thyroid gland

- This gland releases a hormone called thyroxine, which is responsible for regulating the body's metabolism rate. Metabolism is the speed at which the chemical processes in your body work to break down what you eat to make energy. The *thyroxine* hormone also affects how fast your heart beats. Insufficiency of the thyroxine hormone will slow down your heart rate, whereas excessive thyroxine will speed it up.

◆ Sex glands

- In males the *testes* are the glands that release androgens (male sex hormones), which include the main hormone *testosterone*. Testosterone is responsible for the development of male sex characteristics during puberty. It also promotes muscle growth. In females, the *ovaries* are the glands that release the hormone *oestrogen*. This regulates the female reproductive system, including the menstrual cycle and pregnancy.

Nervous system	Endocrine system
• Consists of nerve cells	• Consists of glands
• Acts by transmitting nerve impulses	• Acts by releasing hormones (chemical messengers)
• Acts rapidly	• Acts slowly
• Direct control	• Indirect control
• Specific localised effects of neurotransmitters	• Hormones spread around the body
• Short-lived effects	• Hormones remain in the blood for some time

Figure 13: Endocrine system

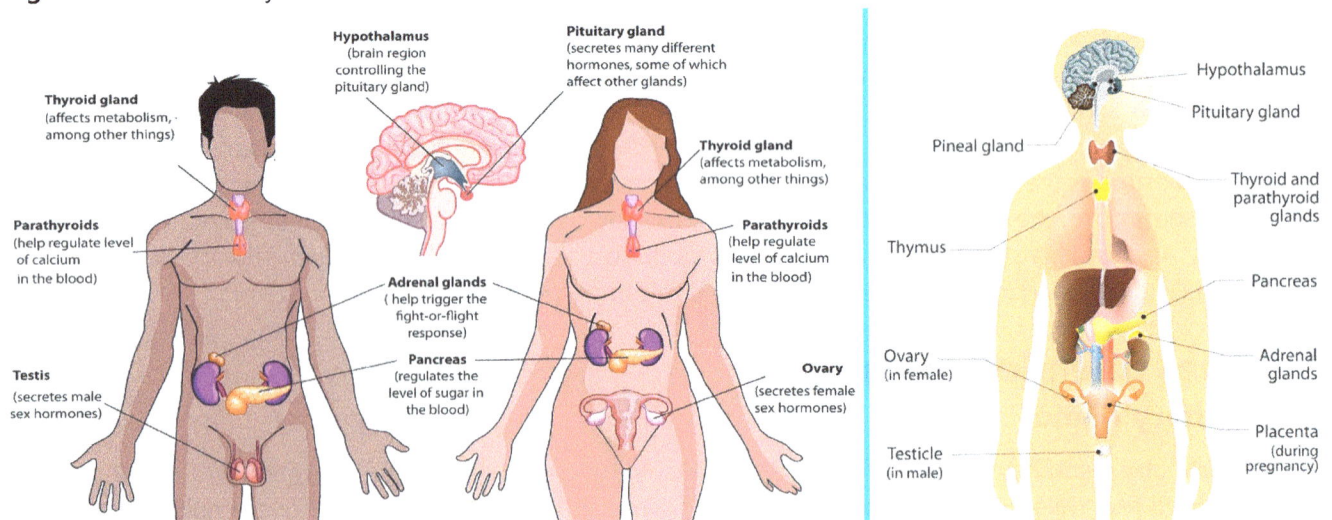

Practice exam questions

1. Identify two glands of the endocrine system and describe their function. **[4 marks]**

2. Explain the function of the endocrine system. **[4 marks]**

3. Explain one difference between the nervous system and the endocrine system. **[2 marks]**

AQA specification for Topic 5: Biopsychology

- The fight or flight response, including the role of adrenaline.

◆ Introduction

When we experience a threatening, dangerous, or stressful situation, our body reacts in specific ways. Our heart beats faster, breathing becomes more rapid and muscles tense up. These bodily reactions to threats or stressful situations are known collectively as the fight-or-flight response. Either we fight, or we flee from the situation. This response is a survival mechanism, enabling animals and human beings to react quickly to life-threatening situations and give them the best chance of survival. The bodily changes associated with fight-or-flight allow a person to fight off the threat or flee to safety. Unfortunately, the fight-or-flight response may also be activated in conditions that are not life-threatening, meaning the response is not helpful.

◆ The fight or flight response

The amygdala and hypothalamus

- The fear response (fight-or-flight) all begins in the brain. When someone is confronted with a threat/ danger, registered from the sensory information (what we see, hear, touch or smell) to the amygdala (located in the temporal lobe), the amygdala activates emotional responses to certain incoming sensory information, e.g. fear and anger. This means that if the amygdala perceives an image or sound that is threatening or stressful, it instantly sends a distress signal to the hypothalamus. This area of the brain functions like a command centre, communicating with the rest of the body through the sympathetic nervous system. The body's response to fear or stress involves two major systems - the first for acute or sudden stress (such as a personal attack) and the second for chronic or ongoing stress (e.g. marital problems).

◆ Response to acute (sudden) stressors

- The sympathetic nervous system. After the amygdala sends a distress signal (through neurons) of a threatening/stressful situation to the hypothalamus, then this, in turn, sends signals to the sympathetic nervous system (SNS) and prepares the body for action – fight or flight response. It works like this:

  - The amygdala sends a distress signal of a threatening/stressful situation to the hypothalamus.

  - The hypothalamus sends signals to the autonomic nervous system (ANS), which stimulates the adrenal medulla gland (the inner part of the adrenal gland, above the kidneys) to release the hormone adrenaline into your bloodstream.

  - The adrenaline then activates your sympathetic nervous system (SNS), which means the body changes from a resting state (the parasympathetic state) to a sympathetic state. This state brings several physiological changes, preparing the body for a fight or flight response to the threat/stressor. The physiological effects of adrenaline on the body are:

    o *Increase in heart rate* (blood is distributed more quickly around the body).

    o *Constricting blood vessels* (e.g. SNS causes the arteries and veins to narrow, increasing the rate of blood flow and blood pressure, supplying oxygen and energy to the brain, organs and skeletal muscles more quickly).

    o *Breathing rate increases* (more oxygen enters the blood, to meet the need from organs and muscles).

    o *Increase in respiration* (regulates body temperature to keep you cool).

- o *Dilation of pupils* (allows more light into the eyes, especially at night).

- o *Dry mouth* (saliva production is reduced, linked to the digestive system "shutting down").

- o *Muscles become tense* and primed for action.

- o *Glucose release.* Adrenaline also triggers the release of glucose from the liver into your bloodstream, supplying energy to all parts of your body through the bloodstream.

- o *Non-essential function.* The reduction of bloody supply to non-essential functions (e.g. skin, digestive system, kidneys).

- **The parasympathetic nervous system.** Once the threat is over, the parasympathetic nervous system (PNS) takes control and attempts to reduce your 'flight-or-fight' response, by slowing down your heart rate, decreasing your blood pressure, and bringing your body back to a 'normal' resting state. Furthermore, any functions that were previously slowed down (such as digestion) start up again.

◆ Response to chronic (ongoing) stressors

- If your brain continues to *perceive* something as threatening (chronic stressors such as job-related, financial, health or relationship worries), the initial surge of adrenaline subsides. Then the hypothalamus activates the second component of the stress response system. This is known as the HPA axis (hypothalamic-pituitary-adrenal axis).

This network consists of the hypothalamus, the pituitary gland, and the adrenal glands. What happens is that your hypothalamus releases the corticotropin-releasing hormone (CRH). This stimulates your pituitary gland, which then releases the adrenocorticotropic hormone (ACTH) into your bloodstream. This then stimulates your adrenal cortex (the outer layer of the adrenal gland) to release a hormone called cortisol into your bloodstream. This helps your body to stay 'revved up' and on high alert. Cortisol helps your body to produce energy by breaking down stored fat reserves and causing your liver to release glucose into your bloodstream. This will maintain the high energy levels you need to cope with the stressor.

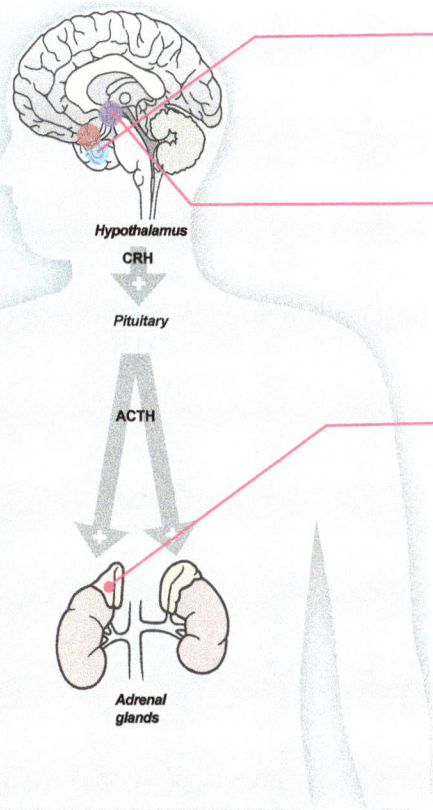

Figure 14: Fight-or-flight response

Amygdala

A person perceives a stressful/threatening situation, the amygdala sends a distress signal to the hypothalamus.

Hypothalamus

The hypothalamus activates the adrenal medulla gland to release the hormone adrenaline.

Adrenaline

Adrenaline triggers the sympathetic nervous system (SNS) to be activated.

Sympathetic nervous system

The sympathetic nervous system leads to several physiological changes (e.g. heart beats faster, breathing rate increases) and these changes prepare us for the 'fight or flight' response.

Figure 15:

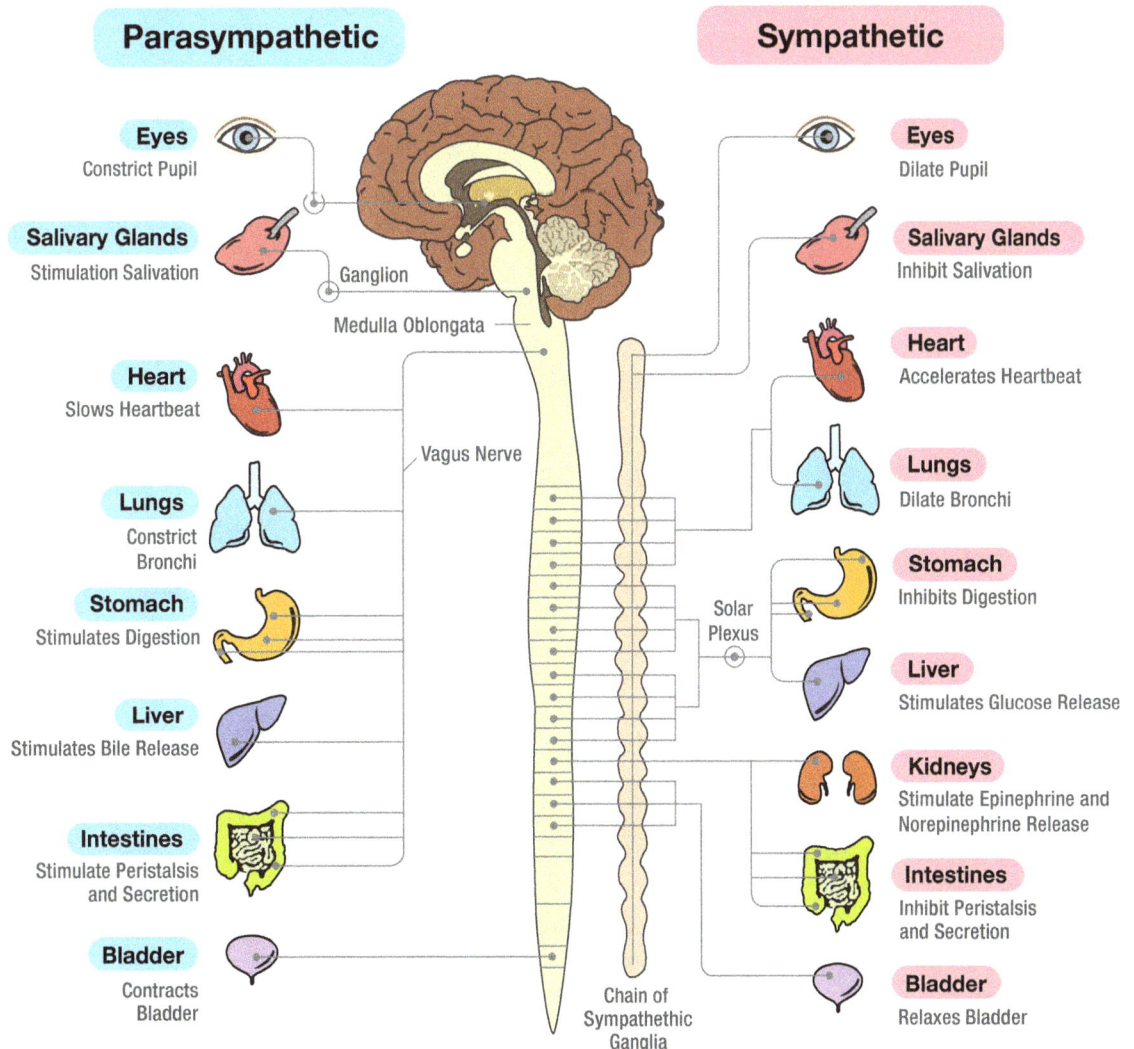

Parasympathetic

Eyes — Constrict Pupil
Salivary Glands — Stimulation Salivation
Ganglion
Medulla Oblongata
Heart — Slows Heartbeat
Vagus Nerve
Lungs — Constrict Bronchi
Stomach — Stimulates Digestion
Liver — Stimulates Bile Release
Intestines — Stimulate Peristalsis and Secretion
Bladder — Contracts Bladder

Sympathetic

Eyes — Dilate Pupil
Salivary Glands — Inhibit Salivation
Heart — Accelerates Heartbeat
Lungs — Dilate Bronchi
Stomach — Inhibits Digestion
Solar Plexus
Liver — Stimulates Glucose Release
Kidneys — Stimulate Epinephrine and Norepinephrine Release
Intestines — Inhibit Peristalsis and Secretion
Bladder — Relaxes Bladder
Chain of Sympathethic Ganglia

◆ Evaluation

✔ **The link between stress and health.** Research into the body's response has had positive implications in terms of our understanding of stress and illness. In ancestral times, the fight-or-flight response evolved as a survival mechanism to real life-threatening physical stressors (e.g. predators). In the modern world, real life-threatening situations still occur, although not in the form of predators. However, the fight-or-flight reaction is now triggered by daily social and psychological stress (e.g. relationships, finances, public speaking, etc.), in which the body still reacts as if it is facing a physical danger e.g. fighting or running away. Research has shown that this constant biological overreaction to psychological stress can lead to physical damage. In the heart it promotes the formation of artery-clogging deposits, which leads to the hardening and narrowing of the arteries, resulting in a higher risk of a heart attack. This shows there is a mismatch between the body's reaction and suggests that the fight-or-flight response is a maladaptive response in modern-day life, as it can have negative consequences on our health.

Weaknesses

✘ **Too simplistic.** A criticism of the fight-or-flight hypothesis as an explanation is too simplistic. Gray (1988) suggested that most animals, including humans, display the 'freeze response' before a fight-or-flight when faced with a threat. This is essentially a phase in which the animals are hyper-vigilant, which allows assessment of the situation before they decide to fight or flee. 'Freezing' is an adaptive response because it focuses attention and makes us look for new information in order to make the best response to a particular threat. This suggests that fight-or-flight response is not the only way animals and humans respond to a threat.

✘ **Individual differences.** Another criticism of our understanding of the fight-or-flight response is that individual differences can modify how the body responds to stress, and it is not solely a physiological response; for example, self-perception, personality, culture and gender. Research suggests that the fight-or-flight response is typically a male response to a threat and that females adopt a 'tend-and-befriend' response in threatening or stressful situations. Taylor et al. (2000) suggested that women have evolved to have a completely different system for coping with stress because they are the primary carers for children. They are more likely to protect their offspring (tend) and form alliances with other women (befriend), rather than fight or flee. Furthermore, fleeing too readily at any sign of danger would put a female's child at risk. This shows that individual differences can modify the effects of stress, which means there is no common physiological response to a threat.

✘ **Too reductionistic.** Another criticism is that the fight-or-flight explanation is reductionist (oversimplified). This is because applying physiological mechanisms to explain human behaviour means we are reducing behaviour and our thinking processes to a biological (hormonal/neurotransmitter) level. Despite the importance of biological processes in determining our behaviour, this seems too simple to explain the reaction of people to stress, as other factors may equally influence how we respond to pressures. For example, cognitive factors, such as how we perceive various threatening situations, will determine how intense and how long our response will be. This suggests that our thought processes play a big role in our fight-or-flight response, and biology may not adequately account for how people manage stress in their lives.

Practice exam questions

1. Outline the role of adrenaline in the fight or flight response.   **[4 marks]**

2. Explain what is meant by the 'fight-or-flight response'.   **[4 marks]**

3. Adrian hates flying on aeroplanes. As soon as it is time for the plane to take off, his heart starts beating really fast, and he begins to sweat. After take-off, once the plane is airborne, Adrian feels better and his heart stops beating as fast and the sweating stops.

   Using your knowledge of the body's response to stress, explain why Adrian experienced these changes and

   A. the body's reaction during take-off;

   B. the body's reaction after take-off.   **[2 marks + 2 marks]**

4. Outline and evaluate the fight-or-flight response.   **[12 marks AS, 16 marks A-level]**

AQA specification for Topic 5: Biopsychology

- Localisation of function in the brain and hemispheric lateralisation: motor, somatosensory, visual, auditory and language centres; Broca's and Wernicke's areas.

◆ Introduction

These notes deal with the localisation of function in the brain, meaning that specific areas of the brain have specific functions, such as memory, learning, and hearing. Paul Broca and Karl Wernicke discovered specific areas of the brain that were responsible for certain functions. This is often referred to as the theories of localisation. Before these discoveries (and the case of Phineas Gage), psychologists believed in a holistic theory, that every single part of the brain was responsible for all thought and action.

◆ Hemispheric lateralisation

- The human brain is split into two symmetrical halves. The left side is called the *left hemisphere* and the right side the *right hemisphere*. Each hemisphere is more dominant than the other for certain physiological and psychological functions. This is known as hemispheric lateralisation. This brain is contralateral (opposite sides) in humans. This means the right hemisphere controls the left side of the body and the left hemisphere controls the right side of the body. For example, sight from your left eye is processed in the right hemisphere of your brain.

- The cerebral cortex is made up of tightly packed neurons and is the wrinkly, outermost layer of the brain that surrounds both hemispheres. This cerebral cortex is 3mm deep and is the most developed and important part of the human brain since it is responsible for thinking, perceiving, producing and understanding language. Most information processing occurs in the cerebral cortex.

◆ The motor, somatosensory, visual, and auditory centres

The cerebral cortex is divided into four lobes (distinct structural areas): frontal lobe, parietal lobe, occipital lobe and temporal lobe, and they each have specific physiological and psychological functions. We note that these areas are most associated with certain kinds of *processing* (e.g. visual or auditory).

- The motor centre (motor cortex) is responsible for planning, controlling and carrying out fine voluntary movements such as picking up and holding a coin, pen or phone. The motor centre is located in the frontal lobe that runs across both hemispheres and it controls the opposite side of the body. The motor cortex part of the brain sends messages to the muscles via the brain stem and spinal cord. The motor cortex is particularly important for complex movement, but not basic actions such as coughing, crying or gagging. If this area were to be damaged, the sufferer might suffer a loss of control over fine movements.

- The somatosensory centre (somatosensory cortex) can be found in the parietal lobe and its role is to detect and process sensory (sensations) information arising from different parts of the body. Sensory information from receptors located under our skin are positioned throughout the body and are responsible for detecting sensations such as touch, pressure, pain, and temperature. When sensory receptors detect one of these sensations, the information is sent to the thalamus and then to the primary somatosensory cortex area in the brain.

- The visual centre (visual cortex) is found in the occipital lobe of the brain and its role is to process different types of visual information (e.g. such as colour, shape, and movement). The brain has two visual centres, one in each cerebral hemisphere. The visual centre in the right cerebral hemisphere receives its information from the left visual field (eye), while the visual centre in the left cerebral hemisphere receives its input from the right visual field. Damage to the left hemisphere can produce blindness in part of the right visual field and vice-versa.

- The auditory centre (auditory cortex) is found in the temporal lobe and its role is to process sounds. The sound vibrations entering the cochlea (in the inner ear) are converted from sound waves to electrical nerve impulses. These nerve impulses travel to the brain stem, which decodes the sounds in terms of duration, intensity, and frequency. The auditory information is then passed to the thalamus, which carries out further processing before the information is then passed to the auditory centre, where the sound is recognised and responded to if required. Damage to this area could produce hearing loss.

- The language centre deals with processing language in terms of *understanding it* and *speaking it*. The language centre is found to the left side of the hemisphere of the brain, in the frontal lobe regions known as Broca's area and Wernicke's area.

◆ Broca's area

- Broca's area is named after Paul Broca (1824-1880), a French neurosurgeon who specialised in language. He identified an area on the left side of the frontal lobe that was responsible for speech production. In 1861, Paul Broca carried out a famous case study on a patient called Louis Leborgne that he was treating. Louis lost the ability to speak at the age of 30, other than being able to say the word 'tan', a single syllable. (He came to be known as the 'Tan patient'.) Leborgne had an unusual disorder. Although he was unable to speak , he was able to understand spoken language. When he died at age 51, an autopsy confirmed that Leborgne had a lesion (tear) on his *posterior inferior frontal gyrus*, in the left frontal lobe area. Paul Broca concluded that this area was critical for speech production. Subsequently, Broca studied eight patients who all had similar difficulties in producing speech, along with lesions in their *left frontal hemisphere*. Patients with damage to these areas in the *right* hemisphere didn't have the same language problems. This led Broca to identify the existence of a language centre in the posterior portion of the frontal lobe of the left hemisphere (Broca, 1865). The term aphasia (or *Broca's aphasia*) is used today to describe patients who have difficulty in producing speech or language.

◆ Wernicke's area

- Shortly after Broca had discovered the 'speech production area' of the brain, Karl Wernicke (1848-1905), a German neurologist, discovered in 1874 another area of the brain that was involved in understanding language. This area was named Wernicke's area, the *left side* of the *frontal lobe* (the posterior portion of the left temporal lobe). Karl Wernicke carried out case studies of people who had no problem producing language but could not comprehend it. The speech produced by such people was fluent but meaningless. He later found the reason for this to be damage to what would be called Wernicke's area (*Wernicke's aphasia*). Whereas Broca's patients could understand language but couldn't speak it, patients with a lesion in Wernicke's area could use language but couldn't understand it.

Figure 16: Areas of the brain

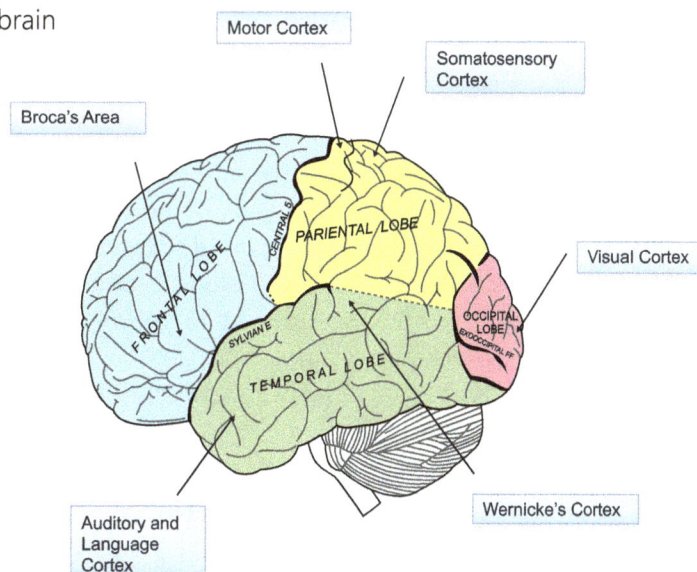

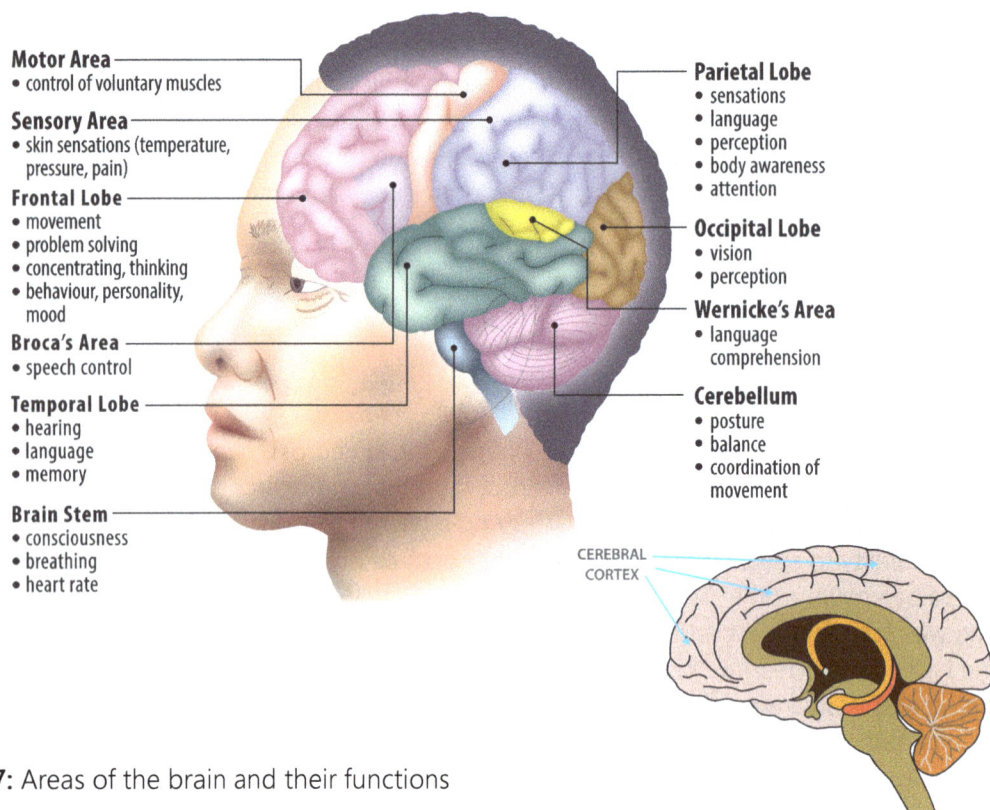

Figure 17: Areas of the brain and their functions

◆ Evaluation

Strength

✔ **Evidence from case studies supports the localisation theory.** One strength of the localisation theory is that it is supported by case studies of patients with brain damage. For instance, Phineas Gage suffered a severe brain injury, when an iron rod was driven through his entire skull, destroying much of his frontal lobe. He eventually recovered, with no apparent effect on his physiological functioning; however, psychologically he was a changed man. This injury altered his personality, turning him from a calm and reserved man before the incident, into someone who was quick-tempered, hostile, rude and vulgar, "no longer Gage." This shows that when a specific, localised area of the brain is damaged, there is a specific impact on one function. In Gage's case, only his personality changed, while the rest of his functioning recovered as normal.

Weaknesses

✗ **Experiments on rats do not support the localisation theory.** One weakness of the localisation theory is the view that brain functions may not be localised to certain regions. The holistic theory of brain function states that all psychological and physiological functions are stored all over the brain. In 1950 Karl Lashley, a neuropsychologist, removed 10 to 50% of the cortex in rats that were learning a maze circuit. After this procedure, they were still able to perform the task without any problems. He concluded that the brain did not have any specific area for memory. It appeared to be stored all over. This suggests that the idea of specific areas performing specific functions may not be completely accurate. Hence the explanatory power of the localisation theory is weakened. However, because of physiological differences, we should be cautious about generalising Lashley's findings to human beings.

✗ Other theories do not support the localisation theory. One weakness of the localisation theory is that other theories refute this. Karl Lashley (1890-1958) was a neuropsychologist who researched brain function, notably memory and learning. He claimed that not all psychological/cognitive functions were localised. He suggested that basic motor and sensory functions were possibly localised, but that higher mental functions were not. From this, he formulated the 'equipotentiality theory' which stated that if certain parts of the brain (e.g. the cerebral cortex) were damaged, other parts of the brain might take over the role of the damaged portion. According to this view, the effect of psychological or physiological damage on the brain was determined by the extent of damage to the brain rather than the location of the damage. This criticism challenges the localisation theory. It suggests that location is not important and that functions of the brain are carried out holistically.

✗ Language production may not be limited to Broca's area. Using modern brain magnetic resonance imaging (MRI), Dronker et al. (2007) examined the preserved brains of two of Broca's patients, Louis Lebornge and Lazare Lelong, to identify the extent of the damage. The MRI scans revealed that other areas besides Broca's could have contributed to the patients' reduced speech abilities. This suggests that lesions in Broca's area alone may not have caused the lack of speech production, and that language production may involve a network of regions rather than being localised to one specific area.

Practice exam questions

1. Using one example, explain what is meant by localisation of function in the brain. **[3 marks]**

2. Below is a diagram of the human brain. Identify three areas of cortical specialisation by writing A, B, C or D in each of the boxes that are provided. Use a different letter for each box. **[3 marks]**

    A. the motor centre

    B. the auditory centre

    C. the visual centre

    D. the somatosensory centre

    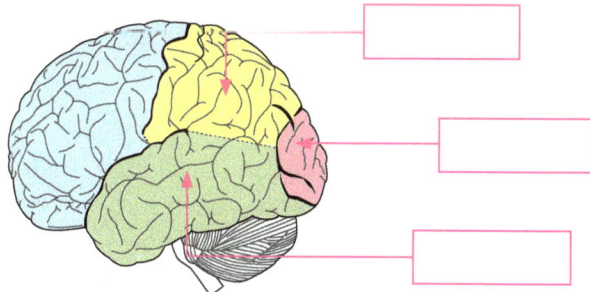

3. Describe one study in which the localisation of brain function was investigated. Include details of what the psychologists did and what was found. **[4 marks]**

4. Discuss what research has shown about localisation of function in the brain. **[8 marks]**

5. Discuss the extent to which the brain functions are localised. Refer to evidence in your answers. **[16 marks]**

AQA specification for Topic 5: Biopsychology

- Hemispheric lateralisation: split-brain research.

◆ Introduction

The brain is dived into two hemispheres. Hemispheric lateralisation is the view that the left and right parts of the brain control different physiological and psychological functions of the body. The right hemisphere controls and receives information from the left side of the body. The left hemisphere controls and receives information from the right side of the body. For instance, if a person has a stroke on the left side of their brain, their right side is affected. The two communicate with each other mainly through a bundle of nerve fibres called the corpus callosum. Split-brain is when patients have lost the connection between the two hemispheres.

◆ Hemispheric lateralisation

- As noted above, hemispheric lateralisation means that one hemisphere or the other is specialised for certain processes (visual, auditory, movement, etc) for most people. Research has found that the left hemisphere mainly controls language and speech processing (Broca's area and Wernicke's area). Research has shown that the right hemisphere is dominant for visual-motor tasking (Herve et al., 2013). It is also dominant for recognising emotions in others. Studies have shown that if a person is shown a photo of a face that has been split so that one half is smiling and the other is neutral, the emotion displayed on the left side of the picture is the emotion recognised by the participant. This is because the right hemisphere is more dominant for this task and the left visual field is processed by the right of the brain (Heller and Levy, 1981).

- It is wrong to assume, however, that specific areas in the brain are the only places to process and control certain human functions and others are not. Research tends to show that more than one region is actively working in conjunction with another region. The focus will be on the brain area that is most *dominant* with various processing tasks (e.g. auditory and visual), but other brain areas are often involved as well.

◆ Split-brain research

- The hemispheres are connected by the *corpus callosum*. There are many patients in whom the *corpus callosum* between the two hemispheres has been surgically cut, resulting in a loss of connection between the two hemispheres. The surgical procedure is known as a commissurotomy and was often performed to control epileptic seizures. Such patients are referred to as split-brain patients. Interestingly, such patients have allowed researchers to investigate the relationship between the two hemispheres and the extent to which brain functions are lateralised.

It is important to note that in split-brain individuals, the two halves of the brain still communicate with each other. They still receive sensory information, and each continues to control muscles on the other side of the body. For the most part, the individuals appear entirely normal following surgery.

Sperry and Gazzaniga's research

- Roger Sperry and Michael Gazzaniga (1967) were the first to investigate hemispheric lateralisation using split-brain patients. Their case study involved 11 epileptic patients who underwent a commissurotomy procedure in which their corpus callosum was cut to separate the two hemispheres, in order to control frequent and severe epileptic seizures. So, the main communication line between the two hemispheres in these patients was removed. Roger Sperry and his colleagues began to conduct several experiments investigating this. The collection of their findings became known as split-brain research. Below, we have described a typical experiment that was performed.

Aim: The aim of this study was to examine the effects of hemisphere disconnection and to show that each hemisphere was specialised to perform different functions independently of the other.

Procedure: They devised a way to test hemispheric lateralisation using visual and tactile (touch) tasks. This involved setting tasks separately for the two hemispheres which were isolated from each other. In the 'normal' brain, the corpus callosum would immediately share the information between both hemispheres, giving a complete picture of the visual world. In a split-brain patient, however, the information could not be conveyed from one hemisphere to the other as the corpus callosum was cut. One of the tasks was a *visual task.* A picture of an object (e.g. a dog) was presented to either the left or right visual field (eye) of a split-brain patient. They had to simply describe, in speech, what they saw.

Key findings

- Visual task. When a picture of an object (e.g. dog) was displayed to the *right visual field,* the patient could accurately describe what they had seen. This was because the visual information travelled from the right eye through the right hemisphere and then passed through the corpus callosum to the left hemisphere, where the speech centres were, so the information could be processed. This supported the idea that language was processed in the left hemisphere because in order to describe something, the region of the brain associated with speech production had to be able to communicate with areas of the brain that processed the visual information. In this instance it did.

  However, the split-brain patient could not describe the object (e.g. cat), when the *left visual field* was tested. This was because the visual information was processed in the right hemisphere and should have travelled over to the left hemisphere where the language centres were, but because it could not do so (the corpus callosum being cut), the information remained in the right hemisphere which had no language centres. That is, the visual and language centres were not able to communicate with each other.

- Tactile task. When a picture (e.g. dog) was shown to the right visual field the split-brain patient could accurately describe what they had seen. This was because the visual information was processed in the left hemisphere, the region of the brain which has the language centre and is associated with speech production.

- When a picture (e.g. cat) was presented to the left visual field, the split-brain patient could not identify or describe the image. This was because the visual information was processed in the right hemisphere. Then, it should have travelled over to the left hemisphere to the language centres, but this was not possible because the corpus callosum had been cut. This meant that the information remained in the right hemisphere, which had no language centres. In other words, the visual and language centres could not communicate with each other and the patient was unable to say they had seen the object.

◆ Evaluation

Strengths

✔ **Real-life application.** One strength of split-brain research, such as Sperry's research, is that it gives us a better understanding of hemispheric lateralisation. Such studies can show the role and extent to which the brain is lateralised, such as the left hemisphere being dominant for speech production and understanding. They show that the left hemisphere is more dominant in language processing and production, while the right is more dominant in performing spatial and music tasks, a fact previously unknown. This discovery is important because it has real-life applications in education. For example, it is suggested that those who struggle with language (words, poetry, grammar, etc.). have left-brain dominance. Educators can develop ways of presenting the information that will require pupils to use their right hemisphere. For example, presenting information in a creative, visual and audible format will help the student to understand it better.

✔ **Sperry's study had methodological strengths.** A further strength of Sperry's research is the method he used. The study involved the use of specialised equipment (the T-scope) that could objectively measure the lateralisation of function in each hemisphere. It also used standardised procedures, presenting visual information to one hemisphere at a time, to ensure only one hemisphere received it. Such a controlled study has allowed other researchers to use the same method on other split-brain patients. Thus, they can check the reliability of the findings. For example, the view that the left hemisphere is more dominant for language has been found to be consistent. This shows that Sperry's research into the split-brain has high validity.

✔ **The study has opened up the 'consciousness' debate**. One strength of the split-brain research by Sperry is that his work has ignited a theoretical and philosophical debate about the nature of consciousness. One of the controversies arising from research on split-brain patients is the question of whether we have two 'consciousnesses', one in each hemisphere of the brain. Roger Sperry claimed that these patients have two consciousnesses. Similarly, Pucetti (1977) suggested that the two hemispheres are so functionally different that in effect we all have 'two minds.' By contrast, others have argued that, far from working in isolation, the two hemispheres form a highly integrated system and are both involved in most everyday tasks. This suggests a single unity of consciousness. However, Gazzaniga (2013) argued that we have a single dominant consciousness, based in the left hemisphere. One reason why it is based there is that language is typically based there. Thus, one of the values of Sperry's work is that it has prompted a complex debate about human nature. Split-brain research has contributed scientific evidence to this debate, although it remains inconclusive.

Weaknesses

✗ **Sperry used a small sample.** One weakness of Sperry's research into split-brain patients is that it used a very small sample. For example, only 11 people took part in all variations of the basic procedure, all of whom had a history of epileptic seizures. This made the split-brain patients an unusual sample of people to test, since epilepsy may have caused the unique changes in the brain which could have influenced the findings in the study. The reason this criticism has come about is because the control group in Sperry's study were people with no history of epileptic seizures, so they could be an inappropriate group to use as a comparison. A more appropriate control group would have been people who had had a history of epilepsy but who had not had the split-brain procedure. This is a weakness in Sperry's argument because it is very difficult to generalise his findings on hemispheric lateralisation to other situations. However, as commissurotomy is a rare procedure, there are a limited amount of 'split brain' patients available for investigation, hence small sample sizes are unavoidable. All this suggests that Sperry's research into the split-brain phenomena may not be completely valid.

✗ **Difference in hemispheric function were overstated.** One weakness of Sperry's split-brain research is that he overstated the differences in hemispheric function. Modern neuroscientists suggest that the actual distinction between each hemisphere is less clear and more complex. In a 'normal' brain the two hemispheres are in constant communication when performing everyday tasks, and many of the behaviours typically associated with one hemisphere can be effectively performed by the other when the situation requires it. For example, Turk et al. (2002) showed that the right hemisphere could process and produce speech. They studied J.W, a patient who had suffered damage to the left hemisphere but eventually developed the capability to speak using the right hemisphere. This showed the brain's ability to adapt significantly following brain damage, suggesting that lateralisation is not fixed. The flexibility of the two spheres suggests that Sperry's conclusions may have been too simplistic. As a result, his research into the split-brain phenomena has been questioned.

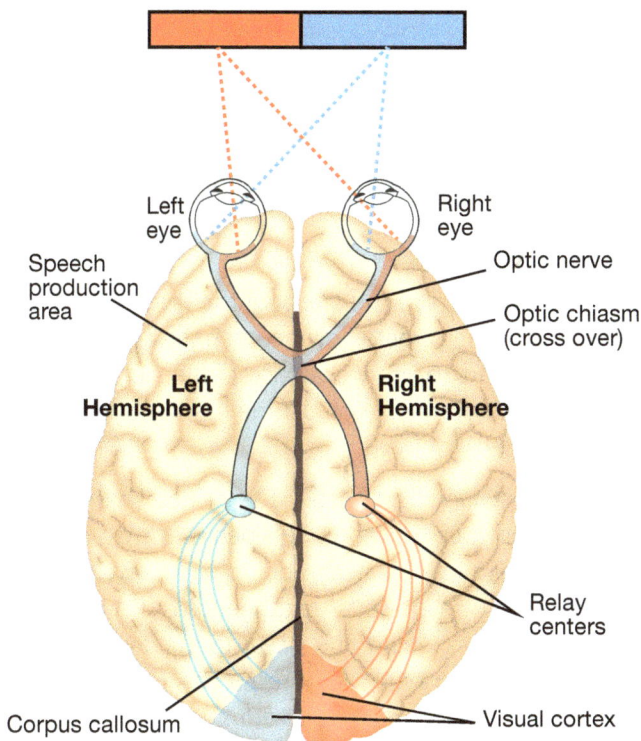

Figure 18: Sperry's split-brain research

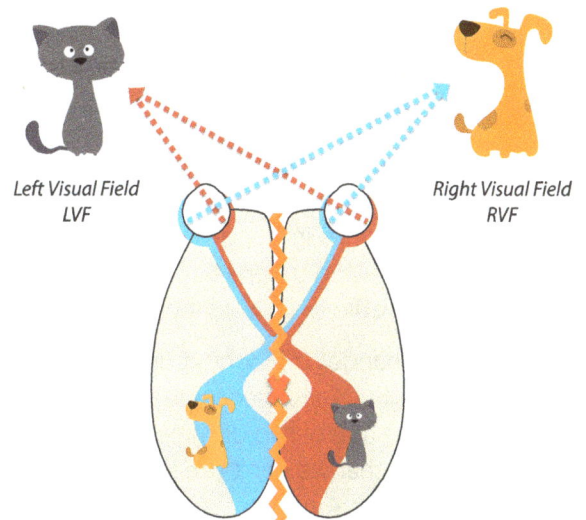

Left eye

Right eye

Speech production area

Optic nerve

Optic chiasm (cross over)

Left Hemisphere

Right Hemisphere

Relay centers

Corpus callosum

Visual cortex

Left Visual Field LVF

Right Visual Field RVF

Practice exam questions

1. Explain what is meant by 'hemispheric lateralisation'. **[3 marks]**

2. Explain what is meant by 'split-brain research'. **[3 marks]**

3. Split-brain patients show unusual behaviour when tested in experiments. Briefly explain how unusual behaviour in split-brain patients could be tested in an experiment. **[3 marks]**

4. Outline one research procedure used to investigate split-brain patients. **[3 marks]**

5. Tom has suffered a stroke to the left hemisphere, damaging Broca's area and the motor cortex. Using your knowledge of the functions of Broca's area and the motor cortex, describe the problems that Tom is likely to experience. **[4 marks]**

6. Briefly evaluate research using split-brain patients to investigate hemispheric lateralisation. **[4 marks]**

7. Discuss split-brain research. Refer to examples of such research in your answer. **[16 marks A-level]**

AQA specification for Topic 5: Biopsychology

- Plasticity and functional recovery of the brain after trauma.

◆ Brain plasticity

- The brain is not a static organ. Brain plasticity (or neuroplasticity) refers to the ability of the brain to change and adapt as a result of experiences. This means the brain continues to create new neural pathways and alter existing ones in response to experiences. Also, the brain appears to show evidence of functional recovery following trauma (injury or disease). Without this ability, any brain - not just the human one - wouldn't be able to develop from infancy to adulthood.

- The brain changes throughout one's lifetime. We develop a lot of synaptic connections as babies. During infancy, the brain experiences rapid growth in the number of synaptic connections. This peaks at around 15,000 at the age of two or three years. It's around twice as many as there are in an adult brain. As we age, connections that we don't use fade away and connections that we use a lot get strengthened. This process is known as synaptic pruning. It was once assumed that these changes would only occur to the developing brain within childhood, and that the adult brain would remain fixed. However, recent research suggests that existing neural connections can change at any time in life, beyond childhood and into adulthood. New neural connections in the brain can be formed as a result of learning and experiences from our environment.

◆ Research into plasticity

- Plasticity in London taxi drivers. Maguire et al. (2000) studied the brains of London taxi drivers and found that there was a significantly greater volume of grey matter in their posterior hippocampus than in a matched control group. This part of the brain is associated with spatial and navigational skills in humans and other animals. Part of a London taxi driver's training involves taking a test known as 'the knowledge,' which tests their ability to recall the names of streets and possible routes to them. The findings showed that drivers who had been longer on the job (more complex and ever-changing routes to learn) had a larger, more pronounced volume of grey matter in their *posterior hippocampus*. This showed a positive correlation and suggested that the new learning experience the drivers had undertaken as part of their training altered the structure of their brains. In other words, because of new experiences, new neural connections form, and human brains are capable of developing in adulthood.

- Plasticity in medical students. Draganski et al. (2006) scanned the brains of a group of German medical students three months before and three months after their final important exams. He then compared the scans to scans of students who were *not* studying for an exam. The students who were studying for an exam showed learning-induced changes in the *parietal cortex* and *posterior hippocampus*, regions known to be involved in memory retrieval and learning.

- Plasticity of video gamers. Kuhn et al. (2014) found a significant increase in grey matter in various regions of the brain after participants played video games (*Super Mario*) for 30 minutes a day, over a two-month period. Similarly, Davidson et al (2013) demonstrated the permanent change in the brain generated by prolonged meditation. Buddhist monks who meditated frequently had more active gamma waves (which co-ordinate neural activity) than students who never meditated. These studies show evidence for plasticity, the brain's ability to adapt as a result of new experiences, whether they are exams, video games, or meditation!

◆ Functional recovery of the brain after trauma

Following damage through trauma (whether caused by physical injury or illness such as a stroke), the brain appears to show evidence of functional recovery. The brain can redistribute functions usually performed by a damaged or missing area to an undamaged area. This is another example of neural plasticity.

Unaffected areas of the brain can often adapt and compensate for the areas that have been lost or damaged. Healthy brain areas may take over the functions of the areas that have been affected. Neuroscientists suggest that this process can occur quickly after the trauma, but then slow down after several weeks or months. The person may then require rehabilitative therapy to assist their recovery.

What happens to the brain during recovery?

- The brain appears to be able to recover from trauma, both structurally and functionally. It does this by forming *new* synaptic connections and creating new *neural circuits*. In this way, the brain re-wires and re-organises itself.

  - Neuronal unmasking. Existing synapses that are 'dormant' in the brain (because low neural input has made them inactive) are now activated or 'unmasked.' These once 'silent' synapses (that are now active) allow for new connections to be formed. This leads to new secondary neural pathways (new circuits) being developed to compensate for the nearby damaged region. The brain has structurally re-organised itself to enable functional recovery. This process is known as *neuronal unmasking*. Another way in which new neural pathways are created is by axonal sprouting. This is when undamaged axons cells grow new nerve endings to reconnect with neurons whose links were injured or severed. Undamaged axons can also sprout nerve endings and connect with other undamaged nerve cells, forming new neural pathways to accomplish a needed function.

  - Homologous area adaption. Further structural change in the brain can occur through homologous area adaption. This is when damage to a particular region of the brain can be compensated for by shifting its function to the opposite side of the brain, often to the homologous (similar) side to perform specific tasks. An example would be if Wernicke's area were to be damaged in the left hemisphere of the brain. The right-sided equivalent would take over the functions of the damaged area. The brain compensates for damage by reorganising and forming new connections between neurons, thus creating new neural pathways.

◆ Evaluation

Strengths

✔ **Plasticity and recovery research have real-life applications.** One strength is that research into the plasticity and functional recovery of the brain after trauma has had practical applications in real life. For example, our increased understanding in this area has contributed to the field of Neurorehabilitation, in the treatment of those who have suffered brain trauma. Techniques include the use of motor therapy and electrical stimulation of the brain to counter the reduced cognitive functions following a brain injury (e.g. a stroke.) Although the brain can fix itself to a certain extent, some intervention will likely be needed if there is to be a full recovery. Research on plasticity has shown that recovery is possible, and rehabilitation programmes based on such research have been shown to work. The cognitive functions of people suffering from brain injuries have been seen to improve. This adds strength to the theory of plasticity and functional recovery of the brain after trauma. This supporting evidence seems to validate the theory.

✔ **Age and plasticity.** The relationship between age and functional plasticity is complex making it difficult to understand. It is known that plasticity also tends to reduce with age, and this makes it less able to recover functions following a trauma. For example, Marquez de la Plata et al. (2008) found that after brain trauma, older patients (40+ years old) regained less function in treatment than younger patients. However, Bezzola et al. (2012) used functional magnetic resonance imaging (fMRI) scans to show that 40 hours of golf training increased neural representation of movement in areas of the motor cortex in middle-aged participants (40-60 years), compared to a control group (no golf training). This shows that neural plasticity does continue throughout our lifespan.

✔ **Supporting research evidence:** One strength of the theory of plasticity and functional recovery of the brain after trauma is that there is supportive research evidence. For example, a pioneering study by Hubel and Wiesel (1963) involved sewing one eye of a kitten shut and analysing the brain's cortical responses. It was found that the area of the visual cortex associated with the shut-eye was not idle but continued to process information from the other open eye. This is a strength because it shows that our brain compensates when there is trauma and that functional recovery will occur to allow for 'regular' neurological functioning. As a result, the credibility of the theory of plasticity and functional recovery of the brain after trauma is increased.

Weaknesses

✗ **Negative effects of plasticity.** One weakness of the theory of plasticity and functional recovery of the brain after trauma is that plasticity itself can sometimes have negative consequences. For example, prolonged drug use has been shown to result in poorer cognitive functioning as well as an increased risk of dementia in later life. Also, 60-80% of amputees are known to develop phantom limb syndrome (the continuing experience of sensation in the missing limb). This is an issue because although the theory has provided us with valuable understanding, plasticity itself can lead to unpleasant and painful experiences. One view is that this tends to arise from cortical reorganisation in the somatosensory cortex that results from limb loss. This shows that the theory of plasticity and functional recovery of the brain only highlights the positive aspect. It tends to overlook the negative aspects of plasticity.

✗ **Plasticity and functional recovery dependent on other variables.** One weakness of plasticity and functional recovery of the brain after trauma is that it depends on several variables. The ability of the brain to recover will vary according to the extent of the damage, the location, and the individual. For example, the more extensive the damage, the less likely is the recovery. A person's level of educational attainment will also influence how well the brain recovers after trauma. Schneider (2014) found that the more time brain-injured patients had spent in education (known as their cognitive reserve), the greater their chances of a disability-free recovery, one year after a moderate-to-severe traumatic brain injury. There is criticism because individual differences vary so much between patients, which makes it difficult to generalise. This dependency on a number of human factors thus limits the usefulness of the theory of plasticity and functional recovery of the brain.

Practice exam questions

1. Define what is meant by the 'plasticity' of the brain. **[3 marks]**

2. Briefly outline research into the functional recovery of the brain after trauma. **[6 marks]**

3. Louise is 11 years of age, and a few months ago she was involved in a serious accident and suffered head injuries that caused problems with speech and understanding language. A year later, Louise has recovered most of her language abilities.

   Using your knowledge of plasticity and functional recovery of the brain after trauma, explain Louise's recovery. **[4 marks]**

4. Discuss research into plasticity of the brain, including functional recovery. **[16 marks]**

AQA specification for Topic 5: Biopsychology

- Ways of studying the brain: scanning techniques, including functional magnetic resonance imaging (fMRI); electroencephalogram (EEG) and event-related potentials (ERPs); post-mortem examinations.

◆ Introduction

- Technological advances over the last 20 years mean that scientists now have a variety of ways to study the structures and functions of the brain. This progress has been due mainly to brain imaging techniques. These allow us to see the brain in action, giving us a deeper understanding of the relationship between brain and behaviour.

◆ Ways of studying the brain

Post-mortem examinations

- *Post-mortem* means 'after death', therefore, a post-mortem examination requires examining the brain of someone who has died. The aim of a post-mortem examination is to try to link structural abnormalities or damage in the brain, to explain certain behaviours and to establish the likely cause of a disorder the person suffered. One of the most famous post-mortem examinations was of a patient called Leborgne (see *Exam Note 5*) by a French neurosurgeon, Paul Broca. Prior to Leborgne's death, he had extreme speech problems. It was not until the post-mortem examination that Broca was able to identify a damaged region of the brain. This led him to identify a language centre in the posterior portion of the frontal lobe of the left hemisphere (named the Broca's area). Post-mortem studies have also been used to establish a link between psychological disorders such as schizophrenia and underlying brain abnormalities. For example, Harrison (2002) reviewed the research on post-mortem studies and found strong evidence of structural abnormalities in the brains of schizophrenic patients. Notably, there was a 30-40% enlargement of the lateral and third ventricles in the forebrain, and a 4% smaller volume of the cortex than in healthy control subjects.

Functional magnetic resonance imaging (fMRI)

- A functional MRI (fMRI) is a brain-imaging technique that scans the brain to provide information about the brain's functional activity, rather than looking at the 'structure' of the brain, which is what a standard MRI scan does. An fMRI detects changes in the blood flow in relation to brain activity whilst doing various tasks such as moving fingers, looking at images, reading, listening to music, or solving problems. It has been used to address a wide variety of research questions in such areas as memory, language, ageing, brain tumours, pain and psychiatric disorders. When a part of the brain is more active, neurones consume more glucose and oxygen delivered by red blood cells, and this leads to a local increase in blood flow in that particular brain area. This produces a dynamic moving picture of the brain (known as an 'activation map'), showing which parts of the brain are involved in such mental processes as reading, speaking, seeing, and hearing (among others). The picture helps us to understand localisation and function. The activity in regions of interest in the brain can be compared during a base-line task, and then during a specific task. The technique can be used to identify behavioural abnormalities that exist because of unusual activation in areas of the brain.

Electroencephalogram (EEG)

- When the brain cells (neurons) are busy processing information, they emit electrical signals. An electroencephalogram (EEG) is a machine that records the general electrical activity of brainwaves, generated by activity from neurons. A skull cap with electrodes and conductive gel is placed on a person's scalp and then plugged into a recording device. The electrodes detect neuronal activity directly below where they are placed on the scalp. Different numbers of electrodes can be used, depending on the focus of the research. The brainwaves are then picked up by the electrodes, travel to the recording device and are amplified so they can be more easily seen and examined. EEG recordings can be used to examine a variety of brain functions including sleep (the different stages of sleep) and different psychological disorders. EEG is used by clinicians as a diagnostic tool. For example, unusual arrhythmic wave patterns of brain activity may indicate abnormalities such as epilepsy, sleep disorders, and dementia.

Event-related potentials (ERPs)

- Event-related potentials (ERPs) measure brainwave activity that is the direct result of a specific stimulus task (e.g. looking at an image, doing mental arithmetic). Like EEG, this method measures brainwave activity by placing electrodes on a person's head. In an ERP, the same stimulus is presented repeatedly to see which part of the brain is active, compared to background brain activity. A computer program 'averages out' the responses, so that most common stimulus-related brain activity remains, and the irrelevant background brainwave activity is cancelled out. This leaves a clear signal - the event-related potential (ERPs) neurons that were active during the task. Clinicians use ERPs to assess sensory, cognitive, and motor function. Psychologists use ERPs to learn about how the brain processes different types of information e.g. attention, language, and memory. Remember, EEG is a recording of general brain activity usually linked to states such as sleep and arousal, while ERPs are elicited by specific stimuli presented to the participant.

◆ Evaluation

fMRI

Strengths

✔ **Non-invasive.** One strength of fMRI is that it is non-invasive. Unlike other scanning techniques, such as positron emission tomography (PET), which require potentially harmful radioactive material or involve inserting instruments directly into the brain, fMRI is virtually risk-free. This is a strength because it allows more patients to undertake fMRI scans, which could help psychologists to understand more about the functioning of the human brain. In turn, this will deepen our understanding of how the brain's functions are localised.

✔ **Whole brain activity.** Another strength of fMRI is that it can provide a moving picture of the whole brain's activity. This means that fMRI can not only capture localised brain activity (mind mapping), but can also capture the entire network of the brain areas that are engaged when subjects undertake tasks. This is something that other methods such as MRI/post-mortem examinations cannot do since they simply show the physiological structure of the brain. This is a strength because it can show which areas in the brain are actively involved in activities done by the person. However, a fMRI only tells you that a region is active during a process, not that it is necessary for a process.

Weaknesses

✗ **Does not measure neural activity.** A limitation is that fMRI can only look at blood flow activity in the brain. This means it cannot be used to actually measure the neural activity. This is because certain areas of the brain 'light up' on an fMRI screen when a particular task is carried out. This view rests on the idea that increased neural activity is linked with increased blood flow. This is a limitation of a fMRI because we cannot say that one activity causes another, as it could have been caused by other cognitive functions.

✘ **Expensive.** Another limitation of fMRI is that it is expensive. fMRI machines are expensive to buy and maintain compared to other techniques. This makes research expensive and difficult to organise. A single MRI scan can cost around £2000. The high cost of fMRI research means that sample sizes are small due to the limited availability of funding. The cost per participant is high. This negatively impacts the validity of the research and makes it difficult to generalise from.

EEG

Strengths

✔ **Valuable information.** One strength of the EEG technique is that it provides valuable information about brain activity. For example, it is a valuable tool for diagnosing certain disorders such as epilepsy as well as providing a valuable understanding of the different stages of sleep.

✔ **Cheaper.** One strength of EEGs (and ERPs) is that they are cheaper than fMRI. Since EEGs and ERPs are cheaper than other brain-scanning methods, they are more widely available to researchers, and since they are non-invasive, they present no risk to participants. This is a strength because the relatively low cost of EEGs and ERPs means larger sample sizes can be used in research and therefore we can generalise from the findings.

Weaknesses

✘ **Only superficial regions of the brain.** One limitation of EEGs is that they can only detect the activity in superficial regions of the brain but cannot reveal what is going on in the deeper regions, such as the hypothalamus or hippocampus.

✘ **Poor image display.** One limitation of EEGs (and ERPs) is their poor spatial resolution (the image display of the location). This is because the electrical neuronal activity is generated several centimetres below the recording scalp electrodes and must go through various resistive layers in the skull. This means that once the activity reaches the scalp electrodes, it provides a blurred view. This is a limitation when using EEGs and ERPs, as they cannot provide accurate information about neural activities because of the poor spatial resolution. This means we cannot use them to establish the precise brain region activities associated with the performance of any given task.

ERP

Strengths

✔ **Precise timing of brain activity.** One strength of ERPs is that they provide useful information about the precise timing of brain-processing activity in response to a stimulus. For example, psychologists can precisely measure the time response for a certain cognitive task (images or shapes) to influence speech production.

✔ **Cheaper.** See above (EEG).

Weakness

✗ **Poor image display.** One limitation of ERPs is their poor spatial resolution (the image display of the location). This means we cannot use them to establish the precise brain region associated with the performance of any given tasks and thus only allow estimations.

Post-mortem examination

Strength

✔ **Deeper understanding.** One strength of the post-mortem examination is that it has allowed a deeper understanding of the brain, by enabling us to study the brain in a detailed and precise way. For example, we now have a good understanding of certain brain abnormalities such as schizophrenia, and of the language problems identified by Broca and Wernicke. So post-mortem studies have helped to improve our medical knowledge and to generate hypotheses for further studies.

Weaknesses

✗ **Subjective interpretation.** One limitation of the post-mortem examination is the interpretation of the results. The discovery of a damaged/abnormal brain is often used to explain the associated disorder the patient was suffering from. However, this may not have been the cause, and the behaviour disorder may have been caused by some other related trauma or decay. For example, the brain abnormality could have been caused by prolonged drug usage.

✗ **Making the link.** Another limitation is that identifying a brain abnormality and linking it to a disorder does not actually prove that the brain abnormality helped to produce that disorder.

Practice exam questions

1. Outline electroencephalograms (EEGs) as a way of studying the brain. **[4 marks]**

2. Outline one strength and one limitation of electroencephalograms (EEGs). **[4 marks]**

3. Outline event-related potentials (ERPs) as a way of studying the brain. **[4 marks]**

4. Outline one strength and one limitation of event-related potentials (ERPs). **[4 marks]**

5. Outline functional magnetic resonance imaging (fMRI) as a way of studying the brain. **[4 marks]**

6. Outline one strength and one limitation of functional magnetic functional magnetic resonance imaging (fMRI). **[4 marks]**

7. Outline the post-mortem examination as a way of studying the brain. **[4 marks]**

8. Outline one strength and one limitation of a post-mortem examination. **[4 marks]**

9. Outline one difference between the electroencephalogram (EEG) and event-related potentials (ERPs) in recording the electrical activity of the brain. **[2 marks]**

10. Explain two difference between functional magnetic resonance imaging (fMRI) and post-mortem examinations as ways of studying the brain. **[2 marks]**

11. Discuss two or more ways psychologists study the brain. **[16 marks]**

AQA specification for Topic 5: Biopsychology

- Biological rhythms: circadian rhythms.

◆ Introduction

Biological rhythms are the repeated cycles of biological changes that occur in your body. These biological rhythms are regulated by a master 'clock' that co-ordinates the other clocks in your body. The 'clock' is located in the brain, right above where the nerves of the eyes cross. It's made up of thousands of nerve cells that help sync your body's functions and activities. One type of biological rhythm is known as the *circadian rhythm*.

◆ Circadian rhythms

- Circadian rhythms are biological changes in the body that follow a repeated cycle (think of 'circles') – approximately a 24-hour cycle. An example of a circadian rhythm is the *sleep/wake cycle,* which determines when humans (and animals) should be asleep and awake – sleeping at night and being awake during the day. Other circadian rhythms are *body temperature; patterns of hormone secretion; blood pressure; digestive secretions;* and *levels of alertness*.

Endogenous pacemaker and exogenous zeitgebers

- Our circadian rhythms are regulated by endogenous pacemakers, which are internal biological 'clocks' that are found in all cells, tissues, or organs (referred to as *peripheral circadian oscillators*). The clocks are controlled and synchronised to work together by a master circadian pacemaker (master clock) called the suprachiasmatic nucleus (SCN), which is a cluster of nerve cells located in the hypothalamus. The SCN has been identified as controlling our sleep/wake cycle. The peripheral clocks can maintain a circadian rhythm but not for very long. They require the SCN to provide time-co-ordinated signals. Circadian rhythms are also governed by *external cues in the environment,* which set off and reset our biological clock. These external changes in the environment are known as exogenous zeitgebers. The most important exogenous zeitgeber is light, which is responsible for resetting the body clock each day and keeping it on a 24-hour cycle.

Sleep/wake cycle

- One important circadian rhythm is the sleep/wake cycle. The circadian rhythm not only dictates when we should be asleep but also when we should be awake. Exogenous zeitgebers, such as light and dark, are the external signals when we sleep and when we wake up. Light is first detected by the eye, which then sends messages concerning the level of brightness to the suprachiasmatic nuclei (SCN). The SCN then uses this information to co-ordinate the activity of the entire circadian system. Sleeping and wakefulness are not determined by the circadian rhythm alone, but also under the control of homeostatic (body's regulation) mechanisms. Homeostasis tells the body that the need for sleep is increasing because of the amount of energy consumed during the day, in an awake state. This homeostatic drive for sleep increases throughout the day, reaching its maximum in the late evening when most people fall asleep.

Body temperature

- Body temperature is another circadian rhythm that can vary over the course of 24 hours. Human body temperature is at its lowest in the early hours of the morning (36.5°C at 4:30 am) and at its highest in the early evening (37.4°C at 6 pm). Sleep typically occurs when our core temperature starts to drop. Our body temperature starts to rise towards the end of a sleep cycle, promoting feelings of alertness first thing in the morning.

Research studies into circadian rhythms

- **Caveman study.** Michel Siffre (1975), a 23-year-old French caver, subjected himself to living underground in a cave in order to study his own circadian rhythms. In 1962, beginning on July 16, he spent two months in a cave in the Southern Alps. He emerged from the cave on 17 September. While living underground, he was deprived of external cues to guide his circadian rhythms (e.g. no daylight, clocks, or radio) and he simply woke, ate and slept when he felt it was appropriate to do so. The only thing influencing his behaviour was the 'free-running' circadian rhythm of his internal body clock. Siffre found that his natural circadian rhythm became slightly longer from the usual 24 hours to around 25 hours, but he did have regular sleep/wake cycles. This suggests that the internal control (endogenous pacemaker) of the circadian rhythm, can maintain a regular daily cycle, even when there are no external cues.

- **Bunker study.** Aschoff and Wever (1981) studied participants who lived in a World War I bunker for four weeks. The bunker had electric light but no windows, so they were deprived of natural light. The participants were allowed to turn the lights on and off as they wished, so that the light source fitted with their body clocks. Eventually, their body clocks settled into a sleep/wake cycle of 25 to 29 hours. This study (like Siffre's) shows that circadian rhythm persists despite isolation from natural light and demonstrates the existence of an endogenous clock. However, this research also shows that external cues are important because the clock was not perfectly accurate; it varied from day to day.

- **Clock study.** Folkard et al. (1985) conducted an experiment to see if external cues could be used to override the internal clock. A group of 12 people lived in a cave for three weeks, isolated from natural light and other time cues. The volunteers agreed to go to bed when the clock said 11.45 pm and to get up when the clock said 7.45 am. The clock was then adjusted to run quicker (unbeknown to the participants). This meant when 24 hours passed on the clock, only 22 hours had actually passed. In the beginning, the volunteers' circadian cycle matched the clock. As it quickened; however, their circadian rhythm no longer matched the clock and they continued to follow a 24-hour cycle rather than the 22-cycle imposed by the experiment (except for one participant who did adapt to the 22-hour cycle). Overall, this suggests that the endogenous pacemakers may have a stronger influence on our circadian rhythm than the exogenous zeitgebers.

◆ Evaluation

Strength

✔ **Research into a circadian rhythm has real-life applications.** One strength of the research into a circadian rhythm is that it has real-life applications. Recent research has shown that the circadian rhythms of adolescents are fundamentally different from those of adults and children. The onset of puberty lengthens the circadian cycle in adolescents and also decreases the rhythm's sensitivity to light in the morning. These changes cause teens to fall asleep later each night and to wake up later each morning than children and adults. However, early school starts in Britain often force adolescents to reduce their sleep hours. They lose on average 10 hours of sleep per week, which makes them sleep-deprived. This has a negative effect on their education (they lack concentration, feel sleepy, etc) and on their health (Paul Kelly, 2017). Research into circadian rhythms can have real benefits in society, and may shape the future of start times in educational systems.

Weaknesses

✘ **Poor control.** A limitation is that there is poor control in the research studies that investigate circadian rhythm. Participants deprived of natural light often still had access to artificial light. For example, Siffre had a lamp turned on from when he woke up until he went to bed, assuming artificial light would have no effect on free-running circadian rhythms. However, another study suggests that this is not true. For example, Czeisler et al. (1999) adjusted participants' circadian rhythms from 22 up to 28 hours by using dim artificial lighting alone. This finding shows that circadian rhythms are affected by artificial light and that researchers may have ignored an important confounding variable in circadian rhythm research.

✗ **Individual differences make generalisation difficult.** One limitation is that individual differences can influence the results of studies. There are two types of individual differences in circadian rhythm - one is the cycle length. Research has shown that the circadian cycles in people can vary by 13 to 65 hours (Czeisler et al.,1999). The other type is the individual differences relating to cycle onsets. Individuals appear be innately different in terms of when their circadian rhythm reaches its peak. For example, Duffy et al. (2001) found that 'morning people' prefer to rise early and go to bed early (about 6 am and 10 pm), whereas 'evening people' prefer to wake and go to bed later (10 am and 1 am). We cannot generalise the findings from research into the circadian rhythm of the sleep/wake cycle. This is because of the great variation between people, the rhythms do not operate in the same way for everyone. As a result, the credibility of research into circadian rhythms is reduced.

✗ **Methodological issues.** Other limitations with the research into circadian rhythms are to do with methodological issues. The sleep/wake studies tend to use only small groups of participants (e.g. Aschoff and Weaver) or a single person (e.g. Siffre). We need to be cautious about generalising. The people involved may not be representative of the wider population. Siffre's most recent study showed him that his internal body clock was much slower now, as a 60-year-old man, than it was in his younger days. This further highlights the issue that even when the same person is studied, they will change. However, unusual studies (such as Siffre's) offer a rare insight into what happens to our circadian rhythm in the absence of external changes, and therefore play an important role in confirming what experimental studies with larger groups have suggested. As a result, the combined findings from case studies and experiments increase the credibility of theories on the sleep/wake cycle.

✗ **Temperature more important than light.** Although studies have shown 'light' as being the most important exogenous zeitgebers influencing the suprachiasmatic nuclei (SCN), other psychologists have questioned this. For example, Buhr et al. (2010) believed it is temperature, rather than light, which controls our circadian sleep/wake cycle. Buhr claimed that light levels may trigger the SCN and the SCN then transform the light levels into neural messages that set the body's temperature. Buhr found that these fluctuations in body temperature set the timing of cells in the body, and therefore cause tissues and organs to become active or inactive. This suggests more research is needed to fully understand the nature of exogenous zeitgebers and the effect they have on the circadian rhythm.

Practice exam questions

1. Explain what is meant by a 'circadian rhythm' and give an example. **[3 marks]**

2. Describe one study into circadian rhythms. In your answer, explain what the researcher(s) did and what they found. **[4 marks]**

3. Evaluate research into circadian rhythms. **[4 marks]**

4. Discuss research into circadian rhythms. In your answer refer to evidence. **[16 marks]**

AQA specification for Topic 5: Biopsychology

- Biological rhythms: infradian and ultradian, and the difference between these rhythms.

◆ Introduction

Two types of biological rhythms that you will need to know for the exam are infradian rhythms and ultradian rhythms.

◆ Infradian rhythms

- Infradian rhythms are repeating biological cycles that last for more than 24 hours. There are many variations in infradian rhythms. They can repeat in a weekly, monthly, seasonal, or annual cycles. For example, skin shedding in snakes happens *monthly*, while antler shedding in deer and hibernation are seasonal events. The two examples we will look at are the *female menstrual cycle* and *seasonal affective disorder*.

The female menstrual cycle

- The female menstrual cycle is an example of an infradian rhythm that typically repeats itself every 28 days. This cycle prepares the body for pregnancy, and it is generated in the brain by the hypothalamus. The hypothalamus causes the pituitary gland to produce certain chemicals that are important in determining the menstrual cycle. These are the *luteinising hormone* (LH) and the *follicle-stimulating hormone* (FSH), which stimulate the ovaries to produce oestrogen. This encourages the ovaries to develop and release a mature egg so that fertilisation may occur. This is known as *ovulation*. After ovulation occurs, there is an increase in the release of *progesterone* in the ovaries. This helps the womb lining to thicken with nutrients and blood, so it will be able to provide the egg with the support it needs in case of pregnancy (implantation of an embryo in the uterus). If pregnancy does not occur, the egg is absorbed into the lining and the womb lining comes away, leaving the body in the form of a menstrual flow.

Zeitgebers and the menstrual cycle

- The menstrual cycle was once thought to be regulated wholly internally, by the hypothalamus, the endogenous pacemaker. However, there is now evidence that external factors (zeitgebers) can play a role in the timing of ovulation and menstruation. It is thought that women at different stages of the menstrual cycle give off different pheromones. Pheromones are chemical substances released by various animal species that can affect the behaviour of other members of the species. It has been suggested that human females emit pheromones that can influence the menstrual cycles of the women around them.

- Menstruation synchrony study. Stern and McClintock (1998) wanted to show that the menstrual cycle is not totally regulated by the internal biological clock of the hypothalamus. That is, the cycle is not only influenced by an endogenous pacemaker. A sample of 29 females with an irregular menstrual cycle were selected. Pheromones (chemical secreted during sweat) were collected using a cotton pad, which nine of the women wore under their armpits for a minimum of eight hours at different stages of their menstrual cycles. These pads were then cleaned with alcohol and then rubbed on the upper lips of the other 20 females and then their menstrual cycles were monitored over a period of time. They found that 68% of women experienced changes to their cycle that brought them closer in timing to the cycle of the 'pheromones donor'. This shows that infradian rhythms such as the menstrual cycle can be affected by external factors (zeitgebers), in this case, pheromones. This may explain why when a group of women live in close proximity, their menstrual cycles tend to synchronise.

- **Women in caves.** Reinberg (1997) carried out a study on infradian rhythms on women who spent more than three months in a cave, with no external source of light, to see the effect on the sleep/waking cycle and the infradian cycle of menstruation. They found that the women's day lengthened (to 24.6 days), but their menstruation cycle shortened (to 25.7 days.) This showed that infradian rhythm of the menstrual cycle can be affected by zeitgeber (the lack of light).

Seasonal affective disorder (SAD)

- Another infradian rhythm is related to the seasons. Research has found that variations in people's moods are based on the seasons. Some people have depression-like symptoms (a low mood and general lack of activity and interest in life) in the winter when there is less daylight due to shorter days, but symptoms lessen or disappear entirely during the spring and summer. This is known as seasonal affective disorder (SAD). SAD is a *circannual* rhythm, as it is subject to a yearly cycle. However, it can also be classfied as a *circadian* rhythm, as SAD may be caused by the disruption of the sleep/wake cycle due to prolonged periods of daily darkness during winter. Psychologists believe two chemicals are involved in SAD: *melatonin* and *serotonin*. Melatonin (which makes you sleepy) is secreted by the pineal gland in greater quantities when it is dark (during the night) or when the days are shorter. Increased production of melatonin can cause sleepiness and lethargy. During winter, the lack of light in the morning means this secretion process continues for longer. Serotonin production increases with exposure to sunlight. Low levels of serotonin are associated with depression. Shorter days and longer hours of darkness in autumn and winter can increase melatonin levels and decrease serotonin levels, which may create the symptoms of depression.

◆ Ultradian rhythms

Stages of sleep

- Ultradian rhythms are repeating biological cycles that have a duration of less than 24 hours. Probably the most obvious and most researched ultradian rhythm is our sleep pattern. Human beings (and animals) have very regular patterns of sleeping and waking. On average, we spend about eight hours in every 24 asleep. In general, we are very regular in our sleeping and waking times, waking up and going to sleep at about the same time every day. The two basic phases of sleep cycles are REM (rapid eye movement) and NREM (non-rapid eye movement) sleep. A complete sleep cycle consists of five stages; four stages: of NREM sleep before we enter REM (Stage 5) and then the cycle repeats itself. Researchers using electroencephalograph (EEG) scans have demonstrated that sleep progresses through a series of stages: in which different brainwave patterns are displayed.

  - Stage 1 and 2: At stage 1 of sleep, your brain begins to relax and slow down, and slower rhythmic brainwaves are produced known as 'alpha waves' (as identified by the EEG machine). At this stage, you are in a relatively light stage of sleep, which means you are somewhat alert and can be easily woken. This period lasts between 1 to 10 minutes. In stage 2, as sleep becomes deeper, the brainwaves become even slower and more rhythmic, known as 'theta waves'. Eye movements slow down, the heart rate slows, and muscles relax. Stage 2 sleep lasts approximately 10 to 25 minutes.

  - Stages 3 and 4: This is the beginning of deep sleep, as the brain begins producing slower delta waves. You won't experience any eye movement or muscle activity. At this point, the body relaxes further, and it becomes a little harder for you to be awakened, because your body becomes less responsive to outside stimuli. The brain produces even more delta waves and you move into an even deeper sleep. It's most difficult to wake up during stage 4. This is when the body repairs muscles and tissues, stimulates growth and development, boosts immune function, and builds up energy for the next day. Stage 3 lasts only a few minutes, while stage 4 lasts for approximately 20-40 minutes.

  - Stage 5: Rapid eye movement (REM) sleep: You generally enter REM sleep about 90 minutes after initially falling asleep, and each REM stage can last up to an hour. During this final phase of sleep, your brain becomes more active. This is when most dreaming occurs. Your eyes jerk quickly in different directions (hence the name!), your heart rate and blood pressure increase, and your breathing becomes fast, irregular, and shallow. Your brain activity resembles that of an awake person. REM sleep plays an important role in learning and memory function, since this is when your brain consolidates and processes information from the day before, so that it can be stored in your long-term memory. During the initial cycle, the REM period may last only 1 to 5 minutes; however, it becomes progressively prolonged, up to an hour, as the sleep episode progresses.

On average, the entire cycle repeats (going through stages 1-5) itself every 90 minutes and a person can experience up to five/six full cycles in a night. This means on average; an adult has five to six REM cycles each night.

◆ Evaluation

Infradian rhythms

Strength

✔ **Supporting research evidence.** There is research support for the menstruation synchronicity theory. Russell et al. (1980) used a similar methodology to McClintock and Stern's menstruation synchrony study and found similar results. It is unclear why this synchronisation occurs, but one explanation is because it has evolutionary benefits in our ancestral past. The suggestion is that menstrual synchrony was advantageous to our ancestors because if females in social groups got pregnant and had babies together at similar times, they were able to share breastfeeding tasks and other childcare activities. This increased the offspring's chances of survival. It certainly appears to be the case with animals such as lionesses in the same pride. This is a strength because research findings consistently show it is possible to synchronise menstrual cycles in women and therefore, it also shows that infradian rhythm can be influenced by exogenous factors. As a result, theory of infradian rhythms including the role of endogenous and exogenous are backed up with research evidence, which increases the validity of the theories.

Weaknesses

✘ **Methodological issues with synchronisation studies.** One limitation of studies into menstruation synchrony is the methodological issues. For example, there may be confounding variables involved in the research that have not been considered. There are many factors that may influence the timing of a woman's menstrual cycle such as stress, changes in diet, and exercise. Any supposed pattern of the synchronisation effect demonstrated by the studies may have occurred by chance. One researcher (Wilson, 1992) argued that Stern and McClintock's study had a number of errors (small sample and statistical mistakes in the data) and when you corrected these errors in statistical testing, their results were not significant. They could have occurred by chance. As a result, external factors (zeitgebers) such as pheromones may not have much impact on the menstrual cycle of a woman, as the research evidence may be not be valid.

✘ **Animal studies.** One limitation of research into the effects of pheromones on behaviour is that much of the evidence is conducted on animals. The research evidence for pheromonal effects on animals' sexual behaviour is strong. For example, marine creatures such as sea urchins and oysters release pheromones into the surrounding water in order to induce other members of the same species to simultaneously release their eggs or sperm, thereby increasing the likelihood that external fertilization will occur. However, whether we can generalise the results of animal studies to humans remains controversial, due to the more complex nature of human beings in comparison to animals. For example, an ovulating female boar, when exposed to a male boar's saliva, immediately goes into a spread-legged mating posture. Human behaviour is just not that clear cut! As a result, the validity of the research and the ability to generalise the effect of pheromones on human behaviour remains inconclusive.

Ultradian rhythms

Strengths

✔ **Supporting research evidence.** There is research support for the ultradian rhythm theory. For example, Dement and Kleitman (1957) recorded the EEG sleep patterns of nine adults in a sleep laboratory. The researchers were able to wake the participants during each of the different stages of sleep. The participants were asked to report their feelings, experiences, and emotions. The researchers found that people awakened during the REM sleep stage reported dreams 80-90% of the time, and reported an accurate recall of their dreams. This is a strength, because this study into the REM shows at what point people dream during the ultradian cycle. It thus supports the different stages of a sleep cycle. As a result, the validity of the theory of ultradian rhythms is increased.

✔ **Research into SAD has real-life applications.** A strength of research into SAD is that it has real-life applications. For example, Terman et al. (1988) carried out a study on 124 participants using light therapy (i.e. phototherapy), in which the participants were exposed to a bright light box in the morning or in the evening for 30 minutes each day. They found that 60% of those who received the morning light therapy showed marked improvement in SAD symptoms compared to only 5% in the placebo treatment (a negative ion generator that emitted air ions). This is a strength, because light therapy has now become a treatment for SAD and it is easily accessible, cheap, easy to administer, safe to use, and can often replace medication for people with seasonal and nonseasonal depression. As a result, research into SAD has led to an improvement in the quality of some people's lives, However, others have questioned the usefulness of the research and feel that other factors may be implicated in SAD. A genetic vulnerability and stress are major contributors to the disorder.

Weakness

✘ **Sleep differences biologically determined.** There is evidence to show that differences in people's sleeping patterns e.g. how many hours of sleep or time taken to sleep, may not be due to social factors (e.g. lifestyle, habit, temperature) as is often suggested. For example, Tucker et al. (2007) studied a sample of 21 participants who spent eight nights in a controlled laboratory environment. They found a large difference between them in their sleeping patterns, such as time to fall asleep, duration of sleep, and the amount of time in each sleep stage (stages 1 through 4 and REM sleep). This study suggests that the differences between participants were not driven by their circumstances but were at large part, biologically determined, possibly genetic in origin.

Practice exam questions

1. Define what is meant by an 'ultradian rhythm' and give an example. **[3 marks]**
2. Define what is meant by an 'infradian rhythm' and give an example. **[3 marks]**
3. Describe one study that has investigated an ultradian rhythm. **[4 marks]**
4. Describe one study that has investigated an infradian rhythm. **[4 marks]**
5. Discuss research into ultradian rhythms and/or infradian rhythms. **[16 marks]**

AQA specification for Topic 5: Biopsychology

- Biological rhythms. The effect of endogenous pacemakers and exogenous zeitgebers on the sleep/wake cycle.

◆ Introduction

Our body's biological rhythms, such as the sleep/wake cycle, are regulated by endogenous pacemakers, which are the body's internal biological clocks. Exogenous zeitgebers are environmental cues, such as light, which help to regulate biological clocks every day and maintain their co-ordination with the external world. Below we explain the effect that endogenous pacemakers and exogenous zeitgebers have on the sleep/wake cycle.

◆ Endogenous pacemakers

- Endogenous pacemakers are the internal biological 'clocks' that regulate our circadian rhythm, such as the sleep/wake cycle.

The suprachiasmatic nucleus

- The main endogenous pacemaker is the suprachiasmatic nucleus (SCN), which is a tiny cluster of nerve cells that lies in the hypothalamus and is responsible for regulating our circadian rhythm i.e. sleep/wake cycle. The human body has other circadian clocks that are found in the cells of various organs and are referred to as peripheral circadian oscillators (PCO). The SCN is referred to as the 'master clock' as it controls, co-ordinates, and synchronises all the other body circadian clocks. The peripheral clocks can maintain a circadian rhythm but not for very long, they require the SCN to provide time-co-ordinated signals.

- The SCN is connected to the optic nerve of the eye and is therefore directly affected by the light level (which is an exogenous zeitgeber). When light and dark hit the retina of the eyes, a signal sends the message along the optic nerves of both eyes. Where these optic nerves meet from both eyes (optic chiasma), they then pass into the SCN of the hypothalamus. This happens even when our eyes are shut because light penetrates the eyelid.

- The SNC sends signals to the pineal gland, via an interconnecting neural pathway, which triggers the pineal gland to increase the production of the melatonin hormone when it is dark (which tends to be at night). This is a hormone that makes you feel sleepy and thus helps to induce sleep. When it is lighter, the SCN tells the pineal gland to produce less melatonin, thus making us feel more awake. Light, therefore decreases the level of melatonin being released.

◆ Exogeneous zeitgebers

- Exogenous zeitgebers are environmental cues, such as light, that help to regulate and reset our biological clocks, such as the sleep/wake cycle.

- The circadian rhythm is also influenced by exogenous zeitgebers. They can include social cues such as mealtimes, noise, and social activities, but the most important zeitgeber is light, which is responsible for resetting the body clock each day and keeping it on a 24-hour cycle. The process of resetting the biological clock to align it to external cues such as the light-dark cycle is known as entrainment. The opposite of entrainment is free-running – where the biological clock operates freely of exogenous cues such as light, clocks, radios, etc. Without external cues, the free-running biological clock continues to 'tick' in a cyclical pattern. Entrainment is important, because if endogenous pacemakers were totally inflexible, we would cope very poorly when working at night or travelling in different time zones. Such disruptions have potentially negative consequences on our health and behaviour.

Light is an exogenous zeitgeber

- Light is seen as the main exogenous zeitgeber in humans and is the main exogenous factor that influences the sleep/wake cycle. The SCN contains receptors that are sensitive to light as the receptors are connected to the optic nerve of the eye. Light is first detected by the eye, which then sends messages concerning the level of brightness to the SCN. The SCN uses the light level to synchronise the activity of the body's organs and glands. Light resets the internal biological clock each day, keeping it on a 24-hour cycle. Rods and cones in the retina of the eye detect light and visual images. A protein called melanopsin in the eye is sensitive to natural light. A small number of retinal cells contain melanopsin and carry signals to the SCN to set the 24-hour daily body cycle to synchronise with night and day.

- Campbell and Murphy (1998) carried out a study to see the effect of light on the sleep/wake cycle. They carried out an experiment on 15 volunteers who slept in a laboratory for four days and nights. They woke the participants up at various times (2 pm, 9 am, 4 am, etc.), and shone a bright light onto the back of participants' knees for three hours (knees have many blood vessels). The researchers found that they were able to alter their circadian sleep/wake cycle by up to three hours. This suggests that light is a powerful exogenous zeitgeber detected by skin receptor sites and it is not necessary for light to enter the eyes to influence the SCN. The exact mechanism for this is unclear, one hypothesis is that blood chemicals could be a carrier of light signals with information about day length to the master clock in the brain (SCN), which will reset the sleep/wake rhythm.

Social cues

- Social cues such mealtimes, worktimes, and social activities are also seen as influential zeitgebers, and have an important influence on the internal circadian sleep/wake cycle clock – how sleepy or awake a person feels. For example, research into jetlag by Klein and Wegmann (1974) and by others found that the circadian rhythm of air travellers adjusted more quickly if they went outside more (publicly) at their destination, and adjusted their mealtime, sleep time and watch to the local time (rather than responding to their internal biological clock which told them they were sleepy or hungry). This is an effective way of entraining the circadian rhythm and beating jet lag when we travel long distances. It is thought to work because we are exposed to the social cues of our new time, which then act as a zeitgeber.

◆ Evaluation

Endogenous pacemakers

Strength

✔ **Research into endogenous pacemakers.** The strong effects of endogenous pacemakers have been demonstrated in an animal studies. Morgan (1995) conducted research by breeding mutant hamsters so that they had an abnormal sleep/wake cycle of 20 rather than 24 hours. The SCN neurons from these abnormal hamsters were transplanted into the brains of normal hamsters, and as a result the 'normal' hamsters then displayed the same sleep/wake cycle of 20 hours. In a follow-up experiment, the SCN neurons from a normal hamster with a 24-hour sleep cycle were transplanted into the brains of the abnormal hamsters, which resulted in a 24-hour circadian rhythm rather than a 20-hour circadian rhythm. This research shows the importance of SCN as an endogenous pacemaker in governing the body's sleep/wake cycle.

✔ **Research into endogenous pacemakers.** There is research support for the role of melanopsin in setting the circadian rhythm. A study by Skene and Arendt (2007) claimed that most blind people who still have some light perception (they can see light but can't form clear images) have normal circadian rhythms, whereas those without any light perception (total blindness) show abnormal circadian rhythms. This is because in the former case the pathway from the retina (retina cells) to the SCN containing melanopsin is still intact. The study shows the important role of melanopsin in the SCN system that controls the body's circadian rhythms.

Weaknesses

✗ **SCN is more complex than it might seem.** One limitation of the theory of SCN maintaining circadian rhythms is that there is contradictory evidence. For example, peripheral circadian clocks (peripheral oscillators) are found in many organs and cells (e.g. lungs, liver, skin and pancreas). These are regulated and synchronised together by the master endogenous pacemaker, the SCN (e.g. when their physiological activity occurs such as when the liver breaks down fats and produces energy). Although they are highly influenced by the actions of the SCN sleep/wake cycle, the peripheral circadian clocks can also act independently from it. For example, Francesca Damiola et al. (2000) showed how changing the feeding patterns (restricting food intake) in mice altered the circadian rhythm of cells in their livers by up to 12 hours, while leaving the rhythm of the SCN unaffected. The feeding rhythm of the liver (its metabolic activity) was influenced by the peripheral circadian clocks rather than by the SCN sleep/wake cycle circadian rhythm.

✗ **SCN is not completely in control of circadian rhythm.** A limitation of research into SCN is that there is evidence that the SCN may not be in complete control of our sleep/wake cycle. For example, Folkard (1996) studied a university student, Kate Aldcroft, who volunteered to isolate herself for 25 days in the controlled environment of a laboratory without any zeitgebers (e.g. no access to daylight) that may have set the SCN. At the end of 25 days, it was found that though her body temperature rhythm was still at 24-hours, i.e. circadian, her sleep/wake rhythm was on a 30-hour cycle— much longer than our innate 24.9-hour rhythm. This shows the importance of exogenous zeitgebers in influencing endogenous rhythms in the timing of the 24-hour clock.

✗ **The use of animal studies.** A further limitation of research into endogenous pacemakers is the use of animals. For example, Morgan's research findings on hamsters may not be applicable to humans, mainly because of the physiological differences between animals and humans, but also because cognitive factors may be more significant in human biological rhythms. This means it may not be appropriate to generalise the findings from animals to humans. A more disturbing issue involves ethics of such research with the cruel treatment of the hamsters in the study by Morgan (1995). Whether what is learned from investigations on biological rhythms justifies the cruel procedures involved is a matter of debate.

Exogenous zeitgebers

Weaknesses

✗ **The role of exogenous zeitgebers may be overstated.** Another limitation is that the influence of exogenous zeitgebers may be overstated. Miles et al. (1977) noted the case of a man blind from birth with a circadian rhythm of 24.9 hours. His sleep/wake cycle could not adjust to social cues, so he took sedatives at night and stimulants in the morning to align with the 24-hour world. Similarly, a study by Luce and Segal (1966) of individuals who live in Arctic regions (where the sun does not set during the summer months) showed that people still maintain normal sleep patterns despite prolonged exposure to light. Both these examples suggest that there are occasions when exogenous zeitgebers may have little bearing on our internal biological rhythms.

✗ **Methodological issues.** Another limitation is that there are methodological issues in research investigating exogenous zeitgebers. For example, Campbell and Murphy's research findings have yet to be successfully replicated in other studies. Also, their research has been criticised because there may have been some light exposure to participants' eyes, which would be seen as a major confounding variable to the results. Furthermore, isolating one exogenous zeitgeber (light) in this way does not give insight into the many other zeitgebers that influence the sleep/wake cycle. This suggests that some studies may have underplayed the way in which different exogenous zeitgebers interact.

Practice exam questions

1. Define what is meant by an 'endogenous pacemaker' and give an example. **[3 marks]**

2. Define what is meant by an 'exogenous zeitgeber' and give an example. **[3 marks]**

3. Describe one study into the effects of an endogenous pacemaker on the sleep/wake cycle. **[6 marks]**

4. Describe one study into the effects of exogenous zeitgebers on the sleep/wake cycle. **[6 marks]**

5. Mark complained to his friend that he is now sleeping all day and is awake all night. Using your knowledge of research into exogenous zeitgebers, discuss what Mark could do to encourage him to sleep more at night. **[4 marks]**

6. Describe and evaluate research into the effects of endogenous pacemakers and exogenous zeitgebers on the sleep/wake cycle. **[16 marks]**

Topic 6
Psychopathology

AQA specification for Topic 6: Psychopathology (AS and A-level)

- Definitions of abnormality, including deviation from social norms, failure to function adequately, statistical infrequency and deviation from ideal mental health.

- The behavioural, emotional, and cognitive characteristics of phobias, depression, and obsessive-compulsive disorder (OCD).

- The behavioural approach to explaining and treating phobias: the two-process model, including classical and operant conditioning; systematic desensitisation, including relaxation and use of hierarchy; flooding.

- The cognitive approach to explaining and treating depression: Beck's negative triad and Ellis's ABC model; cognitive behavioural therapy (CBT), including challenging irrational thoughts.

- The biological approach to explaining and treating OCD: genetic and neural explanations; drug therapy.

AQA specification for Topic 6: Psychopathology

- Definitions of abnormality, including deviation from social norms, failure to function adequately, statistical infrequency and deviation from ideal mental health.

◆ Key term

- Psychopathology (or abnormal psychology) is an area of psychology concerned with the scientific study of mental, emotional, and behavioural disorders in an attempt to explain, predict, and treat such behaviours. It covers a wide range of disorders such as psychotic, personality, mood, anxiety, suicide, sexual, and eating disorders.

◆ Introduction

- There have been a number of attempts to define abnormality, but none of them has been satisfactory (as you will see below). However, perhaps the best way to define abnormality is to take into consideration all four attempts and identify common features in abnormal behaviour often called the four 'D's. These are: *deviance* (unusual), *distress* (upsetting to see), *dysfunction* (inability to cope with daily activity), and *danger* (can be dangerous and harmful to oneself or others).

  - Deviation from social norms

  - Failure to function adequately

  - Statistical infrequency

  - Deviation from ideal mental health

  We will now look at each definition in turn and its limitations.

◆ Deviation from social norms

- One attempt to define abnormality is when a person's behaviour deviates from the social norms of society. Social norms are expectations or unwritten rules of what is acceptable behaviour laid down by society. Any behaviour that deviates (violates) from the social norm will be seen as undesirable or disapproved of by society and could be considered as being abnormal.

  For example, going shopping naked at your local supermarket is not seen as the normal way to behave because it deviates from society's social norms of how people should dress in the supermarket. Mental disorders, such as people with schizophrenia who display inappropriate behaviour, such as having a conversation with imaginary voices on a bus or beginning to laugh loudly at a funeral, are seen as abnormal since such behaviour is not viewed as the norm.

Weaknesses

✗ **Dependent on social context.** Deviation from social norms as a definition for abnormality has been criticised because whether someone is abnormal or normal can depend on the social situation in which the behaviour occurred. For example, going to the bathroom to urinate is considered normal behaviour, whereas urinating in the middle of a classroom during a psychology lesson would be seen as abnormal. This suggests that, under this definition, behaviour cannot be judged to be normal, or abnormal unless we take into account the social context it occurred in. Arguably, this not a sound basis to define abnormality as it makes abnormality a relative concept – it may or may not actually exist as it depends on the situation in which the behaviour occurred.

✗ Views can change over time. Another limitation is that social norms can change over time and this can determine if a behaviour is abnormal or normal. For example, take the issue of homosexuality. In America up until the 1970s, homosexuality was viewed as an abhorrent 'disease' and these views of American society were reflected by classifying it as a disorder in the diagnostic and statistical manual of mental disorders (DSM II). However, over time, attitudes towards homosexuality changed to become more accepting and subsequently, the disorder was removed in the later 1980 edition of the manual (DSM-III) to reflect the social norms. This suggests that defining abnormality in terms of the deviation of current social norms is inappropriate because it is not reliable (inconsistent,) as it is dependent on the prevailing social norms and moral values, which can change.

✗ Cultural relativism. A further limitation of the deviation from social norms as a definition of abnormality is that the definition can be culturally specific. For example, the age of sexual consent in the UK is 16 years. So, an adult having sex with someone under this age would be seen as abnormal sexual behaviour (i.e. paedophilia), whereas in other cultures this would not be viewed as abnormal. In Angola, for example, the age of consent is 12 for females. This means we do not have a universal definition, as each culture has a different view of what is normal or abnormal behaviour – abnormality can vary from society to society.

◆ The failure to function adequately

- Another attempt to define abnormal behaviour is the failure to function adequately (FFA). An individual's behaviour would be classified as abnormal if it caused personal distress or the inability to cope with day-to-day tasks (functions). Rosenhan and Seligman (1989) identified six characteristics that demonstrate that a person is failing to cope, which all fall under the three categories of:

  - *Maladaptive* behaviour, e.g. behaviour that prevents the person from adjusting to a situation in an appropriate manner, or unpredictable behaviour.

  - *Irrational or dangerous* behaviour.

  - Behaviour that causes *personal distress or distress to others*.

For example, a person with depression may stay in bed all day, someone with social phobia may avoid social situations, and an alcoholic or drug user may be unable to hold down a job. All these examples show personal distress and maladaptive behaviour. Therefore, according to the FFA criteria, they would be considered abnormal behaviour. Or a schizophrenic may display maladaptive behaviour at a funeral service by displaying fits of laughter and causing distress to others.

Weaknesses

✗ Miming abnormal behaviour. A weakness of this theory is that some people who are clearly abnormal may function quite well. For example, the doctor Harold Shipman, Britain's worst serial killer, murdered at least 250 of his patients. He is classified as having an antisocial personality disorder (psychopath), yet he did not display any of the characteristics outlined by Rosenhan and Seligman.

✗ **Subjective judgment.** A limitation is the subjective interpretation of defining someone as failing to function adequately. Clinicians may wrongly classify people as abnormal. For example, a person who displays personal distress due to a bereavement in the family would be having a normal reaction. At what point does the suffering become abnormal personal suffering? The person may see this as part of the process of mourning, which may take longer than expected. This shows that 'functioning adequately' or 'not functioning adequately' can be difficult to diagnose because they are based on the subjective criteria of the clinicians.

✗ **Cultural relativism.** Another limitation of failure to function adequately as a definition of abnormality is that it is prone to cultural relativism. What is considered as 'adequate' functioning behaviour in one culture may not be considered so in another culture. For example, in Muslim cultures, women who remain completely housebound are considered normal or even virtuous. In Western cultures, such behaviour would meet some of the characteristics of FFA such as maladaptive and irrational behaviour, which can indicate mental disorder such as agoraphobia (fear of public places). This means it is difficult to establish a universal definition, as each culture has a different view of what is normal or abnormal behaviour.

◆ Statistical infrequency

- **Statistical infrequency** defines 'normal' and 'abnormal behaviour' in terms of the number of times that behaviour or trait is observed numerically (statistically). Behaviours/traits that are common can be thought of as statistically 'normal'. Behaviour that is uncommon/extremely rare is defined as abnormal – statistically infrequent. For example, about 1 in 100 people suffer from schizophrenia, which makes it statistically rare, and thus seen as an abnormality.

Strength

✔ **Real-life application.** A strength of statistical infrequency being used to define abnormality is that it is able to determine a clear cut-off point between what is normal and abnormal. This makes it useful for clinicians diagnosing some psychological disorders; for example, intellectual disability. When an individual's intelligence is below 70, their intellectual functioning is considered abnormal and is classified as intellectual disability.

Weaknesses

✗ **Desirability of infrequent behaviours.** A limitation of statistical infrequency to define abnormality is that statistical infrequency fails to account for behaviour/traits that are statistically rare but considered desirable. For example, to have a high IQ such as 130+ is rare (and therefore abnormal); however, high IQ is not a bad thing but a quality that is desirable for the majority of people – and not seen as something that requires treatment. Similarly, extremely low scores on the trait of anxiety would be desirable yet classed as abnormal. Therefore, criticism of classifying anything that differs from the majority as abnormal is that this fails to take into account the desirability of the behaviour and so it is not an effective way of diagnosing abnormality as it is reductionist (oversimplified).

✗ **Some abnormal behaviours are not statistically rare.** Another limitation of statistical infrequency is that some behaviours that are clearly regarded as abnormal are not statistically rare. For example, it is estimated that 20-30% of people will suffer from depression during their lifetime. Statistically, then, depression is relatively common, but it is not considered 'normal'.

✗ **Subjective cut-off point.** Some abnormal behaviour is not statistically rare. Another problem with defining abnormality as statistically infrequent behaviour is that the cut-off points of what is normal or abnormal are subjectively determined. For example, does someone need to be more depressed than 90% of the population, 95% of the population or 99% of the population to be diagnosed as abnormal? It is impossible to provide a clear answer to this question. This means that disagreements about cut-off points make it difficult to define abnormality in this way.

◆ Deviation from ideal mental health

- Jahoda (1958) defined abnormality as a deviation from ideal mental health. Jahoda identified six criteria that constitute an 'ideal' state of positive mental health. The presence of these qualities indicates psychological health and wellbeing. The more criteria someone fails to meet, the more abnormal they are in terms of mental health. The six ideal characteristics for positive mental health are:

1. Positive self-attitude: Having a positive view of one's self is a characteristic of a mentally healthy person (e.g. has a high level of self-esteem).

2. Self-actualisation of one's potential: Having the ability to reach and fulfil one's potential in many aspects of life (the best one can be) is healthy for a positive state of mind. Prevention of reaching one's potential can result in an unhealthy mental state.

3. Resistance to stress: the ability to cope with stressful situations.

4. Personal autonomy: to think and act independently, free from others.

5. Accurate perception of reality: seeing life in a realistic way 'as it is' and not in a deluded way.

6. Adapting to the environment: A normal person is able to adapt and adjust to changing circumstances that occur in their social environment, such as work and their personal life.

Weaknesses

✗ **Too idealistic.** A limitation is that the six characteristics of positive mental health are unrealistic as most people would find it difficult to achieve all of the six at the same time. For example, many people may never achieve 'self-actualisation' in their lives, which would suggest then that many people are psychologically unhealthy (i.e. they are abnormal). Therefore, everyone could be described as abnormal to some extent, which doesn't help determine a genuine difference between normal and abnormal.

✗ **Cultural relativism.** A limitation of deviation from ideal mental health as a definition of abnormality is that it is prone to cultural relativism. What is 'ideal' in one culture may not be in another. For example, individualistic cultures ((Western cultures, e.g. UK) place greater emphasis on personal autonomy and self-actualisation, which are Western ideals. Whereas in a collectivist culture (non-Western, e.g. Asian culture), people may see this as unhealthy behaviour, as they emphasise behaviour that shows inter-dependency and collective responsibility. This means some cultures will fall short of Jahoda's criteria of ideal mental health, which may wrongly indicate abnormality when it is really different cultural values.

✗ **Subjective criteria.** Another limitation of deviation from ideal mental health to define abnormality is that some of the concepts in Jahoda's (1958) criteria are vague and difficult to measure. For example, 'accurate perception of reality' will be difficult to measure objectively. This is because 'reality' is different for each person based on their experiences. 'Reality' for a soldier who spent many years in battle will be different from the 'reality' of a middle-class mother living in the suburbs. This shows that some of the concepts are subjective judgements.

Practice exam questions

1. Explain what is meant by 'deviation from social norms' in the context of abnormality.　**[3 marks]**

2. Give two limitations associated with 'deviation from social norms' as a definition of abnormality.　**[3 marks+ 3 marks]**

3. Explain what is meant by 'deviation from ideal mental health' in the context of abnormality.　**[3 marks]**

4. Give two limitations associated with 'deviation from ideal mental health' as a definition of abnormality.　**[3 marks+ 3 marks]**

5. Explain what is meant by 'failure to function adequately' in the context of abnormality.　**[4 marks]**

6. Give two limitations associated with 'failure to function adequately' as a definition of abnormality.　**[3 marks + 3 marks]**

7. Explain what is meant by 'statistical infrequency' in the context of abnormality.　**[4 marks]**

8. Give two limitations associated with 'statistical infrequency' as a definition of abnormality.　**[3 marks + 3 marks]**

9. Fahim lives in London and has a fear of talking the underground trains as he believes he will be stuck in the underground for many days. This means he has to wake up very early, catch three buses, and walk for half an hour just to get to work, which can take up to three hours. He is consistently very late for work.

10. Give one definition of abnormality.　**[1 mark]**

11. Use this definition to explain why Fahim's behaviour might be viewed as abnormal.　**[3 marks]**

12. Describe and evaluate two or more definitions of abnormality.　**[12 marks AS, 16 marks A-level]**

AQA specification Topic 6: Psychopathology

- The behavioural, emotional, and cognitive characteristics of phobias, depression, and obsessive-compulsive disorder (OCD).

◆ Introduction

Psychological disorders such as phobias, depression, and obsessive-compulsive disorder (OCD) have their own certain characteristics. These clinical characteristics can be broken down into three different categories: 'behavioural', 'emotional' and 'cognitive'. We will look at each in turn.

◆ Phobia

- Phobia is an anxiety disorder – an excessive fear, triggered by an object, place or situation. The strong response of fear is irrational and out of proportion considering the stimulus that is causing the fear-response (e.g. pigeon). There is an overwhelming desire to avoid or escape the situation. Having a phobia is maladaptive because it can be disruptive to everyday life – to functioning adequately.

Behavioural characteristics

- Avoidance. People with phobias tend to display avoidance behaviour - they go to a lot of effort to avoid coming into contact with the object or situation they fear. For example, a person with a social phobia will avoid being in large crowds.

- Panic. At times people may not be able to avoid their fears and they may find themselves in front of the object or situation they fear. This will often trigger a 'panic' response. This is a fear response that is so intense, it results in a person 'freezing', which is part of the 'fight-or-flight' fear response. The freezing response is an adaptive response to make a predator think that their prey is dead.

- Disruption of functioning. Anxiety and avoidance behaviour can affect every day functioning, e.g. not going out/interacting or even going to work. For example, a person with a social phobia will find it hard to socialise with others.

Emotional characteristics

- Fear/anxiety. One emotional characteristic of a phobia is fear. When the person is in the presence of, or anticipates, a specific object or situation, they experience fear, which can lead to anxiety.

- Disproportionate reaction. Another emotional characteristic of a phobia is that the fear/anxiety is disproportionate. There is an excessive reaction of fear in relation to the danger that the object or situation may cause.

Cognitive characteristics

- Irrational beliefs: A cognitive characteristic of a phobia is irrational beliefs. A person will have unfounded, often illogical, thoughts or arguments that exaggerate the danger/risk that the situation or object imposes. They will also be resistant to rational arguments about the fear stimulus (such as 'most dogs are friendly and harmless'). However, the person recognises that their fear is excessive and unreasonable.

- Selective attention to the phobic stimulus: If a person with a phobia is presented with an object or situation they fear, they will find it difficult to direct their attention elsewhere. This selective attention will cause them to become fixated on the object they fear, because of their irrational beliefs about the danger posed.

Types of phobias

Phobias can be broken down into three different types.

- Specific phobia: the fear of a particular object or situation/environment e.g. spiders, flying, elevators, pigeons, injections or thunderstorms!

- Social phobia: the fear of social situations. This is because you are worried about what others might think of you (being evaluated). For example, you may have a fear of public speaking or avoiding social gatherings, e.g. parties, eating with others, meeting other people, and so on.

- Agoraphobia: the fear of being in open or crowded places or situations, which often triggers a panic attack/anxiety because the person feels that they are not able to escape or have little control over the situation. This means that the sufferers avoid public and unfamiliar places.

Depression

- Depression is a mood disorder. This mental disorder is characterised by lengthy disturbance of low mood and low energy levels (e.g. diminished interest or pleasure in activities). Depression has been called the 'common cold' of psychiatry because it is the most common psychological problem that people face (Seligman, 1973). Below we focus on unipolar depression (also known as major depression).

Behavioural characteristics

- Low energy level: One behavioural characteristic of depression is an increase in lethargy (lack of energy). Sufferers of depression have reduced energy levels, making them lethargic. In extreme cases, this can be so severe, that the sufferer cannot get out of bed.

- Changes in sleeping and eating behaviour: Another behavioural characteristic of depression is a disruption to sleep. Sufferers may experience reduced sleep (insomnia) or an increased need for sleep (hypersomnia). Similarly, eating may increase (comfort eating) or decrease, leading to weight gain or loss. Sleep disturbances result in tiredness and feelings of lethargy (loss of energy) or restlessness.

Emotional characteristics

- Loss of enthusiasm. One emotional characteristic of depression is loss of interest. Sufferers of depression lose interest and pleasure in activities and hobbies.

- Low mood. Another emotional characteristic of depression negative mood state. Suffers of depression have a constant overwhelming feeling of sadness, hopelessness, emptiness, worthlessness, and/or inappropriate feelings of guilt.

Cognitive characteristics

- Poor concentration. One cognitive characteristic of depression is difficulty in maintaining attention – poor concentration. For example, sufferers may find it harder to stick to a task or make decisions, as they normally would.

- Negative thoughts. Another cognitive characteristic of depression is is a negative thoughts. Sufferers are inclined to have an irrational negative view of themselves, the world, and their future. In some extreme cases, sufferers have thoughts of suicide.

Obsessive-compulsive disorder (OCD)

- OCD is a type of anxiety disorder. It is a common mental health condition where a person has obsessive thoughts (persistent and recurrent thoughts) and compulsive behaviours (repetitive behaviours or mental acts). Obsessive thought often causes distress (e.g. I will catch a virus if I do not wash my hands now), which compels the person to act on their thought and thus help prevent some dreaded event from happening, and this reduces their anxiety.

Cognitive characteristics

- **Obsessive thoughts.** One cognitive characteristic of OCD is obsessive thoughts. These are unwanted thoughts or images that are recurrent (recur over and over again), intrusive or impulsive, and perceived as being inappropriate or forbidden. These thoughts vary considerably from person to person but are always unpleasant and cause anxiety. Some examples of the outcomes of obsessive thoughts are repeated actions of cleaning and hand-washing, checking (e.g. that doors are locked or the gas is turned off), counting, ordering and arranging, hoarding, or repeating words in their head.

- **Self-awareness of irrationality:** Another cognitive characteristic of OCD is the awareness that the behaviour is irrational. Sufferers with OCD acknowledge and understand that their thoughts and behaviours are irrational and are self-created rather than a reflection of reality.

Emotional characteristics

- **Anxiety:** Emotional characteristics of OCD are anxiety and distress. These are created by obsessive thoughts that are inappropriate, forbidden, or excessive and create a high level of anxiety.

- **Disgust:** Another emotional characteristic of OCD is disgust. Obsessional thoughts about cleanliness or contamination can lead to an emotional reaction of disgust ('disgusting'). This drives some people with OCD to wash their hands repeatedly or perform other irrational behaviours to avoid contamination.

Behavioural characteristics

- **Compulsion.** One behavioural characteristic of OCD is compulsive behaviour. This is where a person feels intense and uncontrollable urges to repeat the behaviour or mental act in order to alleviate anxiety. A common example is compulsive handwashing in response to an obsessive fear of catching germs. Carrying out such behaviours helps reduce anxiety.

- **Avoidance.** Another behavioural characteristic of OCD is avoidance behaviour. People with OCD avoid situations/objects that trigger their anxiety. For example, sufferers who are anxious about germs may avoid going anywhere where they may have to use a public toilet.

Practice exam questions

1. Outline two behavioural characteristics of phobias.   [4 marks]

2. Outline two emotional characteristics of phobias.   [4 marks]

3. Outline two cognitive characteristics of phobias.   [4 marks]

4. Outline two behavioural characteristics of depression.   [4 marks]

5. Outline two emotional characteristics of depression.   [4 marks]

6. Outline two cognitive characteristics of depression.   [4 marks]

7. Outline two behavioural characteristics of obsessive-compulsive disorder (OCD).   [4 marks]

8. Outline two emotional characteristics of OCD.   [5 marks]

9. Outline two cognitive characteristics of OCD.   [2 marks]

10. Emma has a fear of bees and has been diagnosed with a phobia. Describe one emotional characteristic Emma might display.   [3 marks]

AQA specification Topic 6: Psychopathology

- The behavioural approach to explaining phobias: the two-process model, including classical and operant conditioning.

◆ The two-process model

- The behaviourists claim that we learn all normal and abnormal behaviour, such as phobias, simply from the experiences we have with our environment – our surroundings. Based on the behavioural approach to phobias, Orval Hobart Mowrer (1947) claimed that phobias are the result of a combination of both classical and operant conditioning. This 'two-process model' states that phobias are acquired (learned) by classical conditioning and then continue (are maintained) by operant conditioning.

◆ Classical conditioning
How phobias are acquired

- Classical conditioning explains how phobic behaviour is acquired. Classical conditioning states that phobias are learnt through the process of association; in other words, when a person links a negative experience with a harmless event/situation (Ivan Pavlov, 1927). This means that if an event or something in the environment triggers an anxiety/fear response that occurs in the presence of something neutral, the person will now 'associate' fear with the neutral event/object, and thus may develop a phobia.

- The behaviourists use specialist vocabulary to explain how phobias are acquired. (See also Topic 3: Attachments, Exam Notes 4.) The process is described below using this vocabulary:

  - *Unconditioned stimulus (UCS):* is anything that is able to trigger a response in person automatically – has not been learnt.

  - *Unconditioned response (UCR):* means the reflex response happens automatically, it is not a learned response, -we do not have to make it happen.

  - *Neutral stimulus (NS):* a stimulus that does not trigger a response.

  - *Conditioned stimulus (CS):* a stimulus that triggers a response because it has repeatedly occurred at the same time with a trigger/unconditioned stimulus.

  - *Conditioned response (CR):* a learned response trigger by a conditioned stimulus.

Examples of applying classical conditioning to psychopathology

- You have taken the elevator numerous times to see your friend who lives on the 10th floor and you think nothing of it. The elevator is seen as a neutral stimulus as it produces no fear. On one occasion, you become stuck in the lift for few hours. Being 'stuck' is an unconditioned stimulus because it has caused a negative emotional experience – a fear response, known as an unconditioned response. You may now 'associate' the elevator with fear, so every time you enter an elevator you will become fearful. The elevator, which once was a neutral stimulus, has now become a learned conditioned stimulus because it now triggers a learned conditioned response - fear.

Often, phobias are not acquired from one single experience (although this can happen), but when the association between a neutral stimulus and a fear response occur together (are *paired*) several times. Here is an example.

- An unconditioned stimulus (UCS) such as a barking dog may trigger an unconditioned response (UCR) – fear in a person. If this stimulus is repeatedly *paired* at the same time with a neutral stimulus (such as seeing a cat), the person will eventually respond to the neutral stimulus in the same way as they responded to the unconditioned stimulus – with fear. This is because the person has associated the cat with fear. The neutral stimulus (the cat) is no longer 'neutral' but a conditioned stimulus and the person as a response to it – fear, known as a conditioned response. This is because person has now been conditioned (learned) to fear cats.

◆ Operant conditioning
How phobias are maintained

- While classical conditioning explains how phobias are acquired, operant conditioning explains how phobic behaviour is maintained. Operant conditioning (Burrhus Frederic Skinner, 1974) states that we learn through the consequences of our actions. When the consequences of our behaviour create a positive experience (a good feeling), we are more likely to repeat that behaviour. This is positive reinforcement. When the consequences of our behaviour *prevent* a negative experience, we are also more likely to repeat that behaviour (i.e. negative reinforcement). For example, if someone gets anxious when they see a dog, they are more likely to avoid places where this might happen. This *avoidance behaviour* reduces their anxiety and by continuing to avoid the situation, they are maintaining the phobia.

◆ The two-process model
Bringing it together

- The first stage of the two-process model is classical conditioning, where phobias are learned through association. This is when an individual associates a negative experience with a harmless neutral situation. For example, an elevator (a neutral stimulus) becomes associated with something that triggers a fear response such as 'being stuck in the elevator' (unconditioned stimulus). Once the person has formed that association, the 'elevator' (now a conditioned stimulus) triggers a fear response (conditioned response) whenever it is presented and thus we develop a phobia of elevators. The maintenance of the phobia is explained by operant conditioning, which is the second stage of the process. When an individual avoids a phobic stimulus, the 'avoidance' behaviour becomes a negative reinforcement, because it helps reduces anxiety or fear. In turn, this makes the person feel better, and thus the phobia is maintained.

◆ Evaluation

Strengths

- ✔ **Can explain how phobias are developed.** A strength of the behavioural approach is that it can explain how people can recall a specific event that led to them developing a phobia. For example, Sue et al. (1994) found that agoraphobics are most likely to explain their phobia in terms of a specific event, which suggest that classical conditioning can be involved in the development of phobias. However, one limitation of the two-process model is that it does not explain the development of all phobias, as some people cannot remember an incident occurring that led to their phobia developing. However, some behaviourists would argue that such traumatic incidents may have been forgotten, especially if this happened when the person was much younger (Ost, 2001).

✔ **Little Albert experiment.** A strength of the behavioural approach is that there is supporting research evidence for the explanation of how phobias are acquired. Watson and Rayner (1920) carried out a laboratory experiment to show that fear could be learned through classical conditioning (association). An 11-month-old boy called 'Little Albert' showed he had no fear of white rats (NS) while playing. When Albert played with a white rat, the researchers then made a loud noise (UCS) by striking a metal bar with a hammer behind Albert's head. This happened every time he went to touch the white rat, which made Albert jump and cry (UCR). This was carried over a number of weeks and before long, Little Albert learned to associate his fear of the noise with the rat. Eventually 'Little Albert' learned a conditioned fear response (CR) every time he came into contact with white rats (now a CS), without the loud noise being present. This study suggests that phobia can be learnt through classical conditioning.

✔ **Effective treatments based on the behavioural approach.** Another strength of the behaviourist explanation is its application to therapy for those suffering from phobias. Behaviourist ideas have been used to develop effective treatments, such as systematic desensitisation and flooding in addressing phobic symptoms. For example, systematic desensitisation helps people to unlearn their fear response, using the principles of classical conditioning, while flooding prevents people from avoiding their phobias and stops the negative reinforcement from taking place. The fact that therapy based on the behaviourist approach is effective in dealing with phobic systems provides support for the validity of the behaviourist explanation as to how phobias are acquired and maintained.

Weaknesses

✘ **Traumatic experience missing.** A limitation of the two-process model is that a phobia does not always develop after a traumatic incident. For example, Davies (1992) found that only 7% of people with a fear of spiders (arachnophobia) recalled having a traumatic incident with a spider, which suggests not everyone who has a negative experience develops a phobia. One possibility is to combine the behavioural explanation with a biological explanation to have a better understanding of phobias. For example, the diathesis-stress model says some individuals inherit a genetic vulnerability to developing phobias. These individuals will only develop a phobic reaction when if it is triggered by a life event, such as being stung by a wasp. This suggests a wasp sting will only lead to a phobia in people with this vulnerability. This criticism reduces the validity of the behavioural approach because it only offers a partial explanation, as conditioning alone cannot explain phobias. It is only when combined with the biological approach that conditioning provides a fuller explanation of how phobias are acquired.

✘ **Cannot explain all types of psychological disorders.** Another limitation of the behavioural approach is that it cannot explain other psychological disorders. Behaviourism may comfortably explain how certain disorders develop such as phobias (and eating disorders) but the approach struggles to explain more severe mental disorders. For example, it is difficult to see how people may learn to behave as schizophrenic (e.g. symptoms of hallucinations, delusions and disorganised thinking) either through conditioning or observational learning. This suggests that the behavioural approach is limited to some extent, as it does not fully explain all abnormal behaviour.

✗ **Ignores cognitive aspects.** A problem of the behaviourist two-process model is that it does not properly consider the cognitive (thinking) aspects of the development of phobias. This is how a person perceives the fear stimulus, which plays an important role in their phobic development. For example, those who suffer from social phobia (a fear of social situation) may think 'I am going to say something stupid and embarrass myself', which may trigger a phobic reaction. This is an irrational thought and it shows that irrational thinking is also involved in the development of phobias. It could explain why cognitive therapies (CBT) can be more successful than behaviour therapies (e.g. systematic desensitisation and flooding) in treating phobias. As a consequence of ignoring cognitive aspects in the development of phobias, the behavioural approach has been criticised for being reductionist because it offers a simplistic explanation for how phobias are acquired and maintained.

Practice exam questions

1. Outline a behavioural explanation of phobias.   **[2 marks]**

2. Explain how classical conditioning can be used to explain how phobias are developed. **[4 marks]**

3. Explain how operant conditioning can be used to explain how phobias are maintained. **[4 marks]**

4. Outline the two-process model of phobias.   **[4 marks]**

5. Giorgio has a phobia of the dark. Because of this phobia, he has problems sleeping and has difficulty getting up in the morning and he is often late to school.

   Use the behavioural approach to explain why Giorgio has a phobia of the dark. **[5 marks]**

6. Adam has suffered a phobia of feathers for many years. He knows it is to do with a bad experience that he had as a child when sitting on the beach. He was three years old at the time, and a seagull swooped down and stole his ice cream. The bird did not hurt him; it was the shock of the incident that actually scared him. The bird lost some feathers as it flew off with the ice cream and it is this that Adam associates with the fear.

   A. Identify the unconditioned stimulus.   **[1 mark]**

   B. Identify the unconditioned response.   **[1 mark]**

   C. Identify the conditioned stimulus.   **[1 mark]**

   D. Identify the conditioned response.   **[1 mark]**

7. Describe and evaluate the behavioural approach to explaining phobias.   **[12 marks AS, 16 marks A-level]**

AQA specification Topic 6: Psychopathology

- The behavioural approach to treating phobias: systematic desensitisation including relaxation and the use of hierarchy; flooding.

◆ Introduction

- There are two behaviourist therapies used to treat phobias, *systematic desensitisation* and *flooding*. Both therapies use the principles of classical conditioning to replace a person's phobia with a new response, one of relaxation.

◆ Systematic desensitisation

- Systematic desensitisation was developed by Joseph Wolpe (1958) and is based on the behavioural approach to understanding abnormality. If you recall, behaviourists see phobias as learned through the principle of classical conditioning; in other words, a person has learnt a fear response.

- In a nutshell, systematic desensitisation (SD) is a behavioural therapy designed to gradually reduce phobic anxiety through the principle of classical conditioning. The aim of the therapy is to help the patient unlearn the conditioned fear or anxiety response and replace it with a learnt response of relaxation instead when encountering the fearful situation or object. This technique is referred to as counter-conditioning.

The process of systematic desensitisation

- The counter-conditioning of systematic desensitisation treatment involves a series of step-by-step procedures to 'desensitise' the person from their fear (hence the word 'systematic'). There are three main steps to systematic desensitisation:
  - Hierarchy of fear
  - Relaxation training
  - Reciprocal inhibition.

Step 1: Hierarchy of fear

- First, the client and therapist work together to construct a hierarchy of fear, where they rank the phobic situation from the least to the most terrifying experience. Below is an example for a person who has a fear of spiders.
  - Seeing a toy spider
  - Seeing video/photos of real spider
  - Seeing a spider from a distance (e.g. garden)
  - Sitting next to a spider in an enclosed setting (e.g. bedroom)
  - Capturing the spider by covering it with a jar
  - Releasing the spider from the jar
  - Putting your finger near the spider for 10 seconds
  - Touching the spider
  - Holding the spider in your hand
  - Spider crawling on your arm.

Step 2: Relaxation techniques

- Next, the client is taught techniques of deep relaxation (e.g. breathing exercises and muscle control strategies or mental imagery techniques) over the course of several sessions. The aim is to teach the client to be able to bring about a state of relaxation when faced with their anxiety.

Step 3: Reciprocal inhibition

- Finally, the therapist now works with the client through the hierarchy of fear starting with the least fearful situation, while the client applies the relaxation techniques they have learnt. This can be either in vivo (confronting the situations directly in real life) or in vitro (using virtual reality, e.g. images). The client only progresses to the next level of the hierarchy when they can face each scenario in a relaxed way, without having a fear response. The step-by-step pairing of feared items with a relaxation response allows the client to tolerate increasingly more fearful situations. If the client becomes upset, they can return to an earlier stage and regain their relaxed state. Systematic desensitisation works due to the principle of reciprocal inhibition. This states that two incompatible emotional states cannot occur at the same time, e.g. you cannot feel afraid/stressed and calm at the same time. Therefore, a person is unable to be anxious and relaxed at the same time and the relaxation should overtake the fear.

A little bit more information about in vivo and in vitro desensitisation

There are two main forms of systematic desensitisation techniques that can be used. **In vivo desensitisation** is a confrontation and exposure to the real situation or object that produces anxiety. **In vitro desensitisation** is carried out though imagery (imagined, pictures or videos) in place of the real feared object or situation. Depending on the type of phobia, there may be practical problems with using in vivo desensitisation. For example, for sexual anxiety disorders, flying phobias, or if very young children are involved, then in vitro desensitisation will often be used. Generally, when practical issues are not a problem, the therapist will often move from in vitro desensitisation to, finally, in vivo desensitisation (experiencing the feared object in real life). It goes without saying that in vivo desensitisation is always more effective than vitro desensitisation.

Evaluation

Strengths

✔ **Effective therapy**. A strength of systematic desensitisation (SD) is that it is an effective treatment for specific phobias. Capafons et al. (1998) carried out a study on 41 people with a fear of flying (acrophobic). SD therapy was given to 20 people and the other 21 acted as the control group (no therapy given). The researchers found that the participants who had received SD therapy showed reduced anxiety about flying in a flight simulation situation, than the control group. This shows that SD is helpful in reducing the anxiety in acrophobic patients. SD is effective for a wide range of phobias. For example, McGrath et al. (1990) reported that about 75% of phobics respond to SD. However, the success of SD appears to depend on actual contact with the feared stimulus. This suggests that SD is more effective if it is used in vivo, rather than using pictures or imagining the feared stimulus (in vitro).

✔ **Diverse range of people**. Another strength is that SD is suitable for a diverse range of clients. The alternatives to SD such as flooding and cognitive therapies are not well suited to some clients. For example, young children, those with certain health conditions, or those who have learning difficulties may struggle to understand what is happening during flooding, or to engage with cognitive therapies which require reflection. For these types of therapy clients, SD is probably the most appropriate treatment.

✔ **Preferred choice of clients.** . A further strength of SD is that it is often the client's preferred choice of treatment. Those given the choice of SD or flooding tend to prefer SD. This is because it does not cause the same degree of trauma as flooding. This may be because SD allows people to make progress in small steps in their own time, which allows them to be in control. Another reason could be the fact that SD includes some elements that are actually pleasant, such as time talking with a therapist. This is reflected in the low refusal rates (number of clients refusing to start treatment) and low attrition rates (number of clients dropping out of treatment) for SD. This makes SD more suitable for a wider range of clients.

Weaknesses

✗ **Problems with using 'in vitro'.** The limitation of in vitro SD, is that it relies on the client's ability to be able to imagine the fearful situation. Some people cannot create a vivid image and thus SD is not effective. Furthermore, in vitro SD may be effective for the client in a therapeutic situation, but there is no guarantee that it will work for them once they face their feared situation in the real world.

✗ **SD may not deal with underlying cause.** A limitation of SD as treatment is that it does not deal with the real underlying causes of the development of phobias and anxiety disorders but only with the symptoms. For example, the psychodynamic approach claims that many phobic symptoms are often the product of repressed unconscious conflict in the mind. So, changing a person's behaviour to deal with the phobia does not eliminate the disorder. This may lead to 'symptom substitution', which means the phobia is removed this time but not the underlying causes, which may lead this to reappear as another behavioural symptom.

◆ Flooding

• Flooding as therapy involves an immediate exposure all at once to the clients most feared phobic situation/object, rather than a gradual build-up, as in systematic desensitisation. The first step in this treatment is for the client to learn relaxation techniques. These techniques are then applied in one session to the phobic stimuli. An example would be a client suffering from arachnophobia, whose flooding treatment involves having a large spider placed on his hand.

This treatment is based on the idea that when a client is continuously exposed to the phobic stimulus it prevents the option of avoidant behaviour, and thus stops the negative reinforcement that maintains the phobia from occurring. Adrenaline is released in the body as a response to fear. This reaction has a time limit and can only be sustained for a certain period. After a while, through the exhaustion of their fear response, the person's adrenaline levels naturally decrease, their anxiety response will subside, and they will learn to feel more relaxed. When an unconditioned stimulus (e.g. spider) no longer triggers a conditioned fear response, this is known as 'extinction' (or Pavlovian extinction), and treatment is completed. Flooding is not unethical, but it is an unpleasant experience, so it is important that clients give informed consent.

Flooding sessions are longer, with one session often lasting two to three hours but this technique requires fewer sessions (than SD) for a cure, depending on the type of phobia. It is vital that a client consents to this kind of treatment.

Evaluation

Strengths

✔ **Quicker treatment.** A strength of flooding as a treatment for phobias is that it is a more cost-effective treatment than other therapies. This is because flooding does not require a hierarchy of fear responses to be constructed. Instead, the therapy involves exposing the client to the most feared situation. This means that the therapy involves less time and is, therefore, less expensive than systematic desensitisation. This is a strength for flooding because if clients are treated more quickly this makes it more cost-effective for health service providers (e.g. NHS).

✔ **Effective.** Apart from being a relatively quick treatment compared to other therapies, there is also supporting research evidence to show that flooding tends to be more effective. Research has suggested that, when compared to other forms of treatment such as systematic desensitisation and CBT, flooding is significantly more effective (Choy et al., 2007). However, another review (Craske et al., 2008) concluded that SD and flooding were equally effective in the treatment of phobias.

Weaknesses

✘ **Can be traumatic.** A weakness of flooding as a treatment is that although it is a cost-effective solution, it can be highly traumatic for clients and cause a high level of anxiety. Although the client provides informed consent, there are many who do not complete their course of treatment. This is because they are placed under an anxiety-provoking situation for many hours and find such an experience too stressful. This means that flooding can be a waste of time and money, if clients do not finish their therapy, and thus may not be a very effective form of treatment.

✘ **Not effective for complex phobias.** A limitation of flooding is that it does not work on all types of phobias and appears to less effective on complex phobias, such as social phobias. One of the reasons is that social phobias have a cognitive element to them, e.g. a sufferer of a social phobia does not just experience anxiety but also has negative thoughts about the social situation. This suggests that, for certain types of phobias, cognitive therapies (such as cognitive behavioural therapy or CBT) may be more beneficial because they tackle the irrational thinking aspect of phobias.

Practice exam questions

1. Describe how systematic desensitisation might be used to treat a phobia. **[6 marks]**

2. Describe how flooding might be used to treat phobias. **[6 marks]**

3. Briefly explain one reason why systematic desensitisation might be a more successful treatment for phobias than flooding. **[2 marks]**

4. Harriet has a phobia of dogs. She has never liked dogs and will always avoid going to friends' homes if they have dogs. She even avoids going to parks where she fears a dog may be off its leash.

   Explain how the therapist might use systematic desensitisation to help Harriet overcome her phobia. **[4 marks]**

5. Describe and evaluate systematic desensitisation as a treatment for phobias. **[12 marks AS, 16 marks A-level]**

AQA specification Topic 6: Psychopathology

- The cognitive approach to explaining depression, Beck's negative triads and Ellis's ABC model.

◆ Cognitive approach to depression

The cognitive approach assumes that depression is the product of cognitive distortions (i.e. illogical irrational thinking processes, not based on logic or reason). Such maladaptive thought processes can lead to emotional and behavioural disorders. We will look at two cognitive theories that examine cognitive distortions.

- Beck's cognitive triad
- Ellis's ABC model.

◆ Beck's negative triad

- Aaron Beck (1979) put forward a cognitive approach to explain why some people are more vulnerable to depression than others. Beck believes that some people are more prone to depression because of faulty information processing (i.e. thinking in a flawed way). is means they are more prone to cognitive biases, such as distorting and misinterpreting information in a negative way and ignoring the positives, and this can lead to depression.

Example of cognitive biases

Cognitive biases	Explanations and examples
Polarised thinking	Seeing things as either black or white - no shades of grey; for example, you may see yourself as a failure or success, clever or stupid, and so on.
Over-generalisation	Making a general sweeping conclusion based on a single experience; for example, one failed relationship may make you think you are inadequate at relationships.
Catastrophising (or awfulising)	Over-exaggerating a situation or event (now or in the future). Using words like 'awful', 'terrible', 'horrible', 'catastrophic' to describe something. 'It's the worst thing that could happen', 'That would be the end of the world'.
Selective thinking	This involves focusing on negative events or memories, while ignoring neutral or positive information or aspects of the situation.
Musturbatory thinking	Holding unrealistic and unachievable beliefs or goals. Such type of thinking is often expressed through the language they use, such as 'I must,' 'I should,' or 'I cannot.' For example, 'I *must* get As in every exam or else I am a failure'. Or, 'For me to be happy and feel worthwhile I must be loved by all.'

- Negative schemas. Beck saw early childhood and adolescent experiences such as continual parental criticism and/or rejection by others (e.g. friends) as the root for why some people are more vulnerable to depression. This is because such early experiences lead to the development of *negative schemas*. Schemas are a collection of stored ideas and information, which we use to make sense of the world around us. Schemas are created from very early on in life and continue into adulthood. Negative schemas from childhood will continue into adulthood providing a negative framework. This means that a person with negative schemas will interpret all information about themselves and the world in a negative way.

Negative schemas and cognitive biases create what Beck calls the negative triad. This is a pessimistic and irrational view relating to *themselves*, the *world*, and the *future*, which makes a person prone to depression. Below, we have listed the three elements of the negative triad with examples.

- Negative view of themselves (self) – 'I feel worthless, no one will like me.'

- Negative view of the future – 'I can't see myself meeting anyone again.'

- Negative view of the world – 'People just don't care about each other.'

These three interrelate with each other and the more negative the thoughts are, the greater the risk of depression.

◆ Ellis's ABC model

Albert Ellis (1962) suggested a different cognitive explanation of depression. He said that good mental health is the result of rational thinking. To Ellis, poor mental health, such as depression, was a result of irrational thinking. He defined these irrational thoughts as illogical or unrealistic thoughts, which can cause emotional distress such as depression. Ellis proposed the A-B-C three-stage model to explain how irrational thoughts could lead to depression.

- **'A' refers to an activating event:** *This is an event that activates the irrational thought process.* For example, a colleague passes you in the corridor without responding when you say 'Hello'.

- **'B' refers to the beliefs:** *The 'belief' is about why that event happened, the interpretation of the event – either rational or irrational.* For example, 'he must dislike me' (irrational belief) or 'he did not hear me' (rational belief).

- **'C' refers to the consequences:** *These are the emotional consequences of holding that belief.* For example, a rational belief leads to healthy emotional outcomes (e.g., 'I'll speak to him later to see if he's OK.'), whereas irrational beliefs can lead to unhealthy emotional outcomes, such as depression or anxiety, for example, or avoidance behaviour such as ignoring that colleague in the future.

Musturbatory thoughts

Ellis saw musturbatory thinking as the cause of irrational beliefs. Musturbatory thinking is holding certain black and white thoughts about yourself and the world for someone to be happy. Musturbatory thoughts are often expressed through the use of words such as 'must' and 'should'. For example, 'I must get an A', 'People must respect me'. Musturbatory thoughts tend to be unrealistic and unachievable beliefs and goals and, as a consequence, give rise to anger, anxiety and frustration, which can lead to depression. For example, if you believe you must always succeed such as getting a grade A in every exam and then you fail to do so, the consequence could lead to depression.

◆ Evaluation

Beck's negative triad

Strengths

✔   **Supporting research evidence.** A strength of Beck's negative triad of depression is that it has supporting research evidence. For example, a study by Grazioli and Terry (2000) assessed 65 pregnant women for cognitive vulnerability (e.g. faulty thinking/biases) and depression, before and after birth. They found that those women judged to have been high in cognitive vulnerability were more likely to suffer post-natal depression. This suggests that Beck's faulty thinking can lead to depression.

✔ **Beck's theory has led to effective treatment.** A further strength of Beck's theory is that it has practical real-life applications. Beck's cognitive explanation has led to the development of effective cognitive behaviour therapy (CBT) for dealing with depression. The components of the negative triad can be easily identified and challenged in CBT. This means a patient can test whether the elements of the negative triad are true. This is a strength of validity of Beck's cognitive explanation because it translates well into a successful therapy, demonstrating that irrational thoughts are probably a cause of depression.

Weaknesses

✗ **Faulty thinking leads to depression or other way round?** A limitation of Beck's cognitive approach to depression is that we can't be sure we can distinguish the cause-and-effect factors of depression. We cannot be sure that faulty thinking (cognitive biases) is the cause of depression. It could be that depression leads to faulty thinking. For example, Lewinsohn et al. (1981) found that people who suffered from depression were not more likely to have negative thoughts than people who have never been depressed. This suggests that Beck's cognitive theory is weakened. As a result, it may point to other factors, such as genes and neurotransmitters, as the cause of depression.

✗ **It ignores biological explanations.** Another criticism of Beck's theory in explaining depression is that it over-emphasises the importance of thought processes as the cause of depression and tends to ignore biological explanations. There is research evidence suggesting that genes and neurotransmitters may be involved in the development of depression. For example, some research has focused on the role of the neurotransmitter serotonin and found lower levels in patients with depression. Furthermore, drug therapies, including SSRI (selective serotonin reuptake inhibitors) that increase the level of serotonin, are found to be effective in the treatment of depression. This means that neurotransmitters also play a role in causing depression, and so a diathesis-stress model could be a better explanation for depression rather than cognitive or biological explanations on their own.

✗ **Over-simplified.** One criticism of Beck's cognitive explanation of depression is that it is over-simplified as it cannot explain all aspects of depression. For example, it cannot easily explain bipolar depression, where people that have 'manic episodes' (having high extreme emotions). A study by Jarrett (2013) found that, very occasionally, depressed patients can suffer from hallucinations and Cotard's syndrome (the delusion that they are dead/zombies), which Beck's cognitive theory of depression cannot easily explain. As a result, it shows that depression is a complex disorder and the validity of Beck's cognitive theory as an explanation of depression is weakened because it doesn't offer a full, in-depth explanation and just focuses on one aspect of the disorder.

Ellis's ABC model

Strengths

✔ **Supporting research evidence.** A strength of Ellis's ABC model of depression is that there is supporting research evidence. For example, Hammen and Kranz (1976) compared 33 depressed females with 34 non-depressed females and found that depressed participants made more errors in logic when asked to interpret written material, than did non-depressed participants. This shows that irrational thinking has impaired their ability to do something which should have been quite simple. This study suggests that irrational thinking may also make people more prone to depression.

✔ **Ellis's ABC model has led to successful cognitive therapies.** A strength of Ellis's ABC model is that it has practical real-life applications. Ellis's cognitive explanation has led to the development of an effective rational emotive behaviour therapy (REBT) for dealing with depression. The irrational thought can be easily identified and challenged in REBT. This means a patient can test whether the elements of their irrational thoughts are true. This is a strength of validity of Ellis's cognitive explanation because it translates well into a successful therapy, demonstrating that irrational thoughts are related to depression.

Weaknesses

✗ **Irrational thinking leads to depression or other way round?** A limitation of Ellis's ABC model of depression is that we cannot be sure that we can distinguish the cause-and-effect factors. We cannot be sure that faulty thinking (cognitive biases) is the cause of depression. It could be that depression leads to faulty thinking. For example, Lewinsohn et al. (1981) found that people who suffered from depression were not more likely to have negative thoughts than people who have never been depressed. This suggests that Ellis's ABC model to explain depression is weakened. As a result, it may point to other factors, such as genes and neurotransmitters, as the cause of depression.

✗ **It ignores biological explanations.** Another criticism of Ellis's ABC model in explaining depression is that over-emphasises the importance of thought processes as the cause of depression and tends to ignore biological explanations. There is research evidence suggesting that genes and neurotransmitters may be involved in the development of depression. For example, some research has focused on the role of the neurotransmitter serotonin and found lower levels in patients with depression. Furthermore, drug therapies, including SSRI (selective serotonin reuptake inhibitors) that increase the level of serotonin, are found to be effective in the treatment of depression. This means that neurotransmitters also play a role in causing depression, and so a diathesis-stress model could be a better explanation for depression rather than cognitive or biological explanations on their own.

Practice exam questions

1. Describe Beck's negative triad as an explanation of depression. **[6 marks]**

2. Describe Ellis's ABC model as an explanation of depression. **[6 marks]**

3. Oliver has just been told by his manager that he is no longer required at work as the company is no longer making any profit. Since he has left his job, Oliver has become depressed.

   Use the cognitive approach to explain why Oliver has become depressed. **[4 marks]**

4. Describe Beck's negative triad as an explanation of depression. **[12 marks AS, 16 marks A-level]**

5. Describe and evaluate Ellis's ABC model as an explanation of depression. **[12 marks AS, 16 marks A-level]**

AQA specification Topic 6: Psychopathology

- The cognitive approach to treating depression: cognitive behavioural therapy (CBT), including challenging irrational thoughts.

◆ Introduction

Cognitive behavioural therapy is based on the cognitive approach explanation of depression. Therefore, the aim of cognitive therapies is to change/modify the client's irrational thoughts, which are causing them depression and replace these negative thoughts with more positive ones. Cognitive behavioural therapy (CBT) involves both cognitive and behavioural elements. The cognitive element aims to identify irrational and negative thoughts and the behavioural element encourages patients to test their beliefs through behavioural experiments and homework. There are two different strands of CBT, based on Beck's theory and Ellis's ABC model.

◆ Beck's cognitive behavioural therapy (CBT)

Beck's (1976) cognitive behavioural therapy (CBT) is based on the view that the way we think about things has an impact on how we feel about things. The aim is to identify, challenge, and change the client's 'negative triad' (faulty thinking). In other words, the therapist works with how the client sees themselves, their world and their future to help them have a more realistic interpretation of themselves and the world around them. The assumption of CBT is that altering a person's negative thought process will lead to healthier emotions and behaviour, and thus remove the depression they are experiencing. There are three main steps to correcting a person's negative thoughts.

- **Client learns to identify irrational thoughts.** An important first step is for the client, with the help of the therapist, to identify when they are having negative or irrational thoughts e.g. 'I feel lonely and unlovable, which means there is something wrong with me.' To do this, the client is set a homework assignment to monitor and keep a *thought record* (e.g. diary) of events that trigger negative thoughts and associated emotional upset and maladaptive behaviour. Often, the therapist will ask the client to complete a Beck Depression Inventory (BDI), which is used to identify how the client is feeling and identify issues that are affecting them.

- **Therapist challenges the client's thoughts.** Once the information is collected and the irrational thoughts have been identified, the next step for the therapist is to challenge these thoughts, by using *logical questioning techniques*. The therapist's aim is to bring about cognitive restructuring to help teach the patients to think differently, e.g. 'Many people do like me'.

- **Validity testing.** As well as challenging these thoughts directly by using cognitive restructuring, the therapist sets the client homework tasks to test the validity of their negative thoughts in real life. For example, the client may perform and record a behavioural task to determine what actually happens when mistakes are made (e.g. 'I believe if I make a mistake everyone will laugh and ridicule me'). This is sometimes referred to as the 'patient as a scientist', because the patient is investigating the reality of their negative beliefs in the way a scientist would. In the follow-up session, the therapist discusses the outcome of such homework task, to prove that the client's statements are incorrect. Over time with cognitive restructuring and behaviour tasks, this approach results in a person's cognition changing to a more positive one and thus alleviating their depression.

A little more about CBT...

There are variations of CBT, and the techniques used will vary, depending on the type of therapy. Typically, sessions are held once a week for approximately 50-60 minutes. CBT is a short-term treatment that can last between six weeks to six months (approximately 5-24 sessions), depending on the type of disorder and severity of the client's symptoms.

◆ Ellis's rational emotive behaviour therapy (REBT)

Albert Ellis (1950s) devised a therapy called rational emotive behaviour therapy (REBT), which is based on his own ABC model for explaining psychological disorders such as depression. The aim of REBT is to help the client identify, challenge, and change their irrational beliefs and replace them with rational ones, which produce new positive feelings. Like Beck, the main idea is to challenge irrational thoughts; however, with Ellis's theory, this is achieved through 'disputing' (arguing) irrational thoughts and beliefs. The REBT process has four steps.

- **Identify the client's irrational beliefs.** The first step is for the therapist to identify the client's irrational beliefs that are causing the emotional and behavioural problems (e.g. depression) and set out the goals for the client to achieve.

- **Irrational beliefs disputed.** The next step for the therapist is to dispute the patient's irrational beliefs and replace them with rational beliefs. The therapist can use three types of disputing questions:

  - Logical disputing – where the therapist questions the logic of a person's thoughts, for example, the client is asked if holding irrational thoughts makes any sense. 'Katie should not reject Philip because he believes he is rich', for example.

  - Empirical disputing – this involves asking the client to provide proof/evidence in the real world for their thoughts they hold e.g. 'Where is the evidence that Katie rejected you, Phillip?'

  - Pragmatic disputing – the client is made to realise that holding irrational thoughts are not helpful or serve no purpose, e.g., 'Philip, how does this irrational belief make you feel?'

  The therapist teaches the client to apply disputing questions to their irrational beliefs in order to look at their beliefs in a more logical and reasonable manner, and thus create more positive feelings.

- **Homework.** Throughout therapy, the client is given a number of behavioural assignments (homework tasks) between sessions. The aims of the assignments are to test and challenge their irrational beliefs, to show how unrealistic they are. The client may also carry out new behaviours/acts (e.g. such as being late for a meeting), so they can test their new way of thinking differently (e.g. deal with the negative emotions of being late). Real-life assignments are designed to strengthen the client's new psychologically healthy mind set, helping them to have having a rational and positive view of themselves and the world.

- **Behavioural activation.** Part of the behavioural therapy is to teach the client different coping strategies to deal with depression. The therapist and client draw up a 'schedule of activity' for the client to undertake on a weekly basis (e.g. going for walks, swimming, going out). The assumption is that increasing activity which is engaging and pleasurable is rewarding and can also help to improve the client's mood.

◆ Evaluation

Strength

✔ **Supporting research evidence for the effectiveness of CBT.** A strength of CBT comes from research evidence that demonstrates it is an effective method of treating depression. For example, research by March et al. (2007) found that CBT was as effective as antidepressants in treating depression. The researchers examined 327 adolescents with a diagnosis of depression and looked at the effectiveness of CBT, antidepressants, and a combination of CBT plus antidepressants. After 36 weeks, 81% of the antidepressant group and 81% of the CBT group had significantly improved, demonstrating the effectiveness of CBT in treating depression. However, 86% of the CBT plus antidepressant group had significantly improved. This shows CBT is just as effective as drug therapy and suggests a good case for making CBT the first choice of treatment in health care systems such as the NHS. This is because CBT is safer, as there is less chance of becoming addicted to drugs, and it deals with the underlying causes of depression (i.e. irrational thinking) whereas drug therapies deal only with treating the symptoms of the disorder. This also means CBT is better for preventing further episodes than drug treatments.

Weaknesses

✗ **CBT not effective for types of depression.** A weakness of CBT is that it may not be appropriate for all cases of depression. For example, those patients suffering from severe depression will find it difficult because they cannot motivate themselves to engage with CBT or even attend the CBT sessions. This is a problem because this treatment will be ineffective in treating these patients. Alternatively, these patients could be treated using antidepressant medication and then potentially continue with CBT when they are more alert and motivated. This poses a problem for CBT, as it cannot be used as the sole treatment for severely depressed patients and consequently, this reduces the credibility of CBT as a treatment for depression.

✗ **Over-emphasis on the role of cognition.** Another criticism of CBT as a treatment for depression is that it may over-emphasise the importance of cognition. For example, McCusker (2014) criticised CBT, because it places too much emphasis on a person's irrational thinking as the primary cause of their depression and does not take into account, or minimises, other important factors that might contribute to a person's depression. For instance, a patient living in poverty or suffering domestic abuse does not need to change their negative/irrational beliefs, but needs to change their social circumstances. Therefore, you could argue that CBT is an inappropriate form of treatment because it may demotivate/prevent people from changing their social situation.

✗ **Therapist- patient quality of relationship important.** A limitation of CBT or REBT is that the outcome could be dependent on the quality of the therapist-patient relationship. Rosenzwieg (1936) believed that all psychotherapies have one essential ingredient, the relationship between therapist and patient. It may be the quality of this relationship that determines success rather than a particular type of treatment. Luborsky et al. (2002) reviewed over 100 studies that compared different therapies. They found that there were only small differences between the therapies in terms of their effectiveness. One possible reason for this is that different psychotherapies share common factors, such as being able to talk to a sympathetic person and having an opportunity to express your own thoughts.

Practice exam questions

1. Explain how cognitive behavioural therapy is used in the treatment of depression. **[6 marks]**

2. Explain how irrational thoughts are challenged in the treatment of depression. **[6 marks]**

3. Eli becomes extremely anxious when she goes to work because three times a week she has to speak in front of her colleagues. She is convinced that she will make a fool of herself by saying something that will embarrass or humiliate her. She has taken many weeks off work and is considering leaving her job because she now feels depressed.

    A. Why might cognitive behavioural therapy be appropriate for Eli? **[3 marks]**

    B. Describe how CBT would be used to treat her depression. **[5 marks]**

4. Discuss the cognitive approach to treating depression. **[12 marks AS, 16 marks A-level]**

AQA specification Topic 6: Psychopathology

- The biological approach to explaining OCD: genetic and neural explanations.
  (The exam requires that you are able to describe and evaluate the biological approach to explaining OCD.)

◆ Introduction

The biological explanation, otherwise known as the medical approach, views abnormal behaviour/mental disorders as being similar to physical illnesses, caused by abnormal biological processes in the body, rather than a psychological or social one. Two possible biological explanations for obsessive-compulsive disorder (OCD) are that individuals inherit specific genes from their parents (genetic transmission) and through damage to the neural mechanisms/neurotransmitter activity in the brain and structures in the brain.

◆ Genetic explanations

- The genetic explanation suggests that OCD is genetically inherited from the parents. That is, the individuals inherit specific genes from the parents which are implicated in the development of OCD.

Candidate genes

Researchers have identified certain genes, which create vulnerability for OCD, called candidate genes. Two genes linked to OCD are the SERT and the COMT genes.

- SERT gene (or 5-HTT) has been implicated in the vulnerability of developing OCD. The SERT gene helps transport and regulate the use of serotonin (hence SERotonin Transporter) in the brain and serotonin is involved in regulating anxiety. Researchers have found a mutated SERT gene that can affect the transport and regulation of serotonin, leading to an increase in the reuptake of serotonin into the neuron that decreases the level of serotonin in the synapse (Murphy, 2003). These lower levels of serotonin cause low moods and anxiety, which may explain the anxious 'obsessional thoughts' in OCD sufferers.

- COMT gene may be involved in the development of OCD. This gene carries the instructions to make an enzyme, called *catechol-O-methyltransferase* (hence 'COMT'), which helps breaks down dopamine (neurotransmitter) in the synapse. Dopamine is involved in many brain activities; for example, it regulates how you perceive and experience pleasure/rewards, controlling the body movement, as well as emotional responses. Research has found that a mutated variation of the COMT gene is found in OCD individuals. This mutated COMT gene lowers the production of the enzyme, and as a result, this *increases* the dopamine in the synapse. High levels of dopamine have been linked to the 'compulsive behaviour' part of OCD.

- In summary, the mutated COMT gene increases dopamine activity in the brain, whereas the mutated SERT gene causes the opposite effect of decreasing serotonin brain activity. However, according to the diathesis-stress model, the presence of genes does not mean you will develop OCD but do leave some people more 'vulnerable' to developing OCD - some environmental stress (experience) is necessary to trigger the condition.

OCD is polygenic

- OCD may be polygenic, which means that OCD is not caused by one single gene, but the result of many (poly) defective genes. Each defective gene increases the risk of developing OCD. Taylor (2013) analysed the findings of previous studies and found evidence that up to 230 different genes may be involved in OCD.

Aetiologically heterogenous

- Some research suggests that OCD is aetiologically heterogenous. This means a certain group of defective genes may cause OCD in one person, but a different group of defective genes may cause the disorder in another person. Heterogeneous means that the origin (aetiology) of OCD has different causes (heterogeneous). There is also evidence to suggest that different types of OCD (e.g. hoarding disorder and religious obsession) may be the result of particular variations.

◆ Neural explanations

Neural explanations of OCD focus on neurotransmitter activity and structures of the brain as the possible cause of OCD.

Neurotransmitters

- Serotonin. OCD has been associated with a low level of serotonin in the brain, which prevents the nerve cells from communicating effectively. Serotonin plays a key role in regulating our mood (e.g. happy, sad, and anxious). In OCD sufferers, some of the nerve cell receptors (i.e. postsynaptic neuron) are thought to block serotonin from entering the cell. This leads to a deficiency (low levels) of the neurotransmitter in key areas of the brain. Pigott (1990) found that anti-depressant drugs that increase serotonin activity have been shown to reduce the symptoms of OCD.

- Dopamine. Excessive dopamine activity is thought to be associated with some of the symptoms of OCD, in particular compulsive behaviours. Szechtman (1998) conducted animal studies and found that high doses of drugs that enhanced levels of dopamine induced stereotyped movements that resembled the compulsive behaviours witnessed in OCD patients.

Abnormal brain circuit

- Frontal lobe. The cycle of obsessive thoughts and compulsive behaviour in OCD might reflect a fault in circuits located in several areas of the frontal lobe of the brain. The orbital-frontal cortex (OFC) is the part of the brain that notices when something is wrong and then converts sensory impulses into thoughts and actions. For example, touching a dirty cup: the OFC will interpret a visual image as possibly having potential hazardous germs and sends a 'worry' signal to the thalamus. This prompts the person to wash their hands and the 'worry' signal lessens, the person stop washing their hands.

- The caudate nucleus (located in the basal ganglia) lies between the OFC and the thalamus, and regulates the signals sent between them. The caudate nucleus acts like the brake pedal on a car, suppressing the original minor 'worry' signals sent by the OFC to the thalamus. This prevents the thalamus from becoming hyperactive. In OCD sufferers, the caudate nucleus is thought to be damaged and cannot 'turn off' signals from the OFC. This causes the thalamus to become over-excited, sending strong signals back to the OFC, which in turn sends it back to the thalamus creating a 'worry circuit' between the OFC and the thalamus. This 'to and fro' between the OFC and thalamus could explain the compulsive and repetitive behaviour performed by obsessive-compulsives. This is supported by positron emission tomography (PET) scans of patients with OCD, taken while their symptoms are active (e.g. when a person with a germ obsession hold a dirty cloth), which show heightened activity in the OFC.

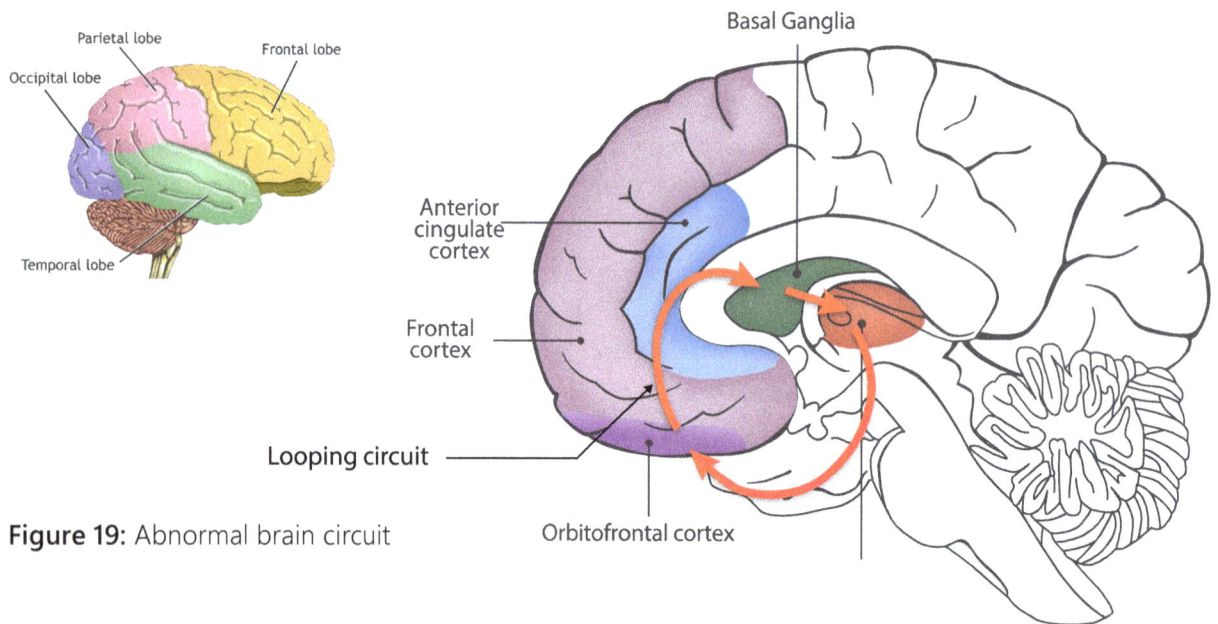

Figure 19: Abnormal brain circuit

Labels in figure: Parietal lobe, Frontal lobe, Occipital lobe, Temporal lobe, Basal Ganglia, Anterior cingulate cortex, Frontal cortex, Looping circuit, Orbitofrontal cortex

- Neurotransmitters, serotonin and dopamine are linked to these regions of the frontal lobe and could also be to blame. Comer (1992) suggested that because serotonin plays a key role in the operation of the OFC and the caudate nuclei, it is likely that low levels of serotonin cause these areas to malfunction. However, Hollander et al. (1990) proposed that damage in other brain areas (e.g. the brain stem nuclei) may be the cause of low serotonin levels. Dopamine is also linked to this system, as the main neurotransmitter of the basal ganglia. High levels of dopamine lead to overactivity in this region (Sukel, 2007).

◆ Evaluation

Genetic explanation

Strength

✔ **Supportive research evidence.** A strength of the genetic explanation for OCD is that there is strong evidence from research studies. Lewis (1936) examined patients with OCD and found that 37% of the patients had parents with the disorder and 21% had siblings who also suffered from OCD.. Further support comes from Nestasdt et al. (2010) who reviewed previous twin studies examining OCD. They found that 68% of identical twins and 31% of non-identical twins experience OCD. These two studies strongly suggest a genetic component to OCD: the closer the genetic similarity to someone suffering from OCD, the higher the risk of the other person developing the disorder as a result of their genetic makeup. As a result, these findings enhance the validity of a genetic explanation (and therefore the biological approach) for OCD.

Weaknesses

✘ **A criticism of twin studies.** A criticism of the evidence provided by twin studies to support that OCD is genetic is that the evidence is unclear. For example, although there is a higher concordance rate for OCD in identical (monozygotic or MZ) twins, compared to non-identical twins, the concordance rate for identical twins is less than 100%. If OCD was due to genetic inheritance, then we should see 100% of both MZ twins develop the disorder. This was not the case, which means that environmental factors must also play a role in OCD. One reason may be that twins very often share the same social environment, so the similarities in abnormal behaviour may be due to environments they share, rather than genetic factors, or it could be both. This suggests that the evidence is inconclusive on the cause of OCD.

Neural explanation

Strengths

✔ **Supported by drug therapy.** A strength of neural explanations for OCD is that it is supported by drug therapy. For example, some antidepressants drugs such as SSRI (Selective Serotonin Reuptake Inhibitors), stop nerve cells that have just released serotonin from absorbing it back into the cell. This therefore increases the levels of this neurotransmitter in the brain and thus helps reduce the symptoms of OCD. Approximately 50% of people show an improvement after taking SSRI, proving that the neurotransmitters do play a part in OCD. However, what about the other 50% of people who don't improve after taking SSRI? This finding reduces support for the abnormal levels of neurotransmitters being the sole cause of the disorder, suggesting that there are psychological and environmental influences in the development of OCD.

However, it could be argued that the success of antidepressant drugs as a treatment does not necessarily mean the biochemicals are the cause of OCD in the first place. This is known as the 'treatment fallacy'. For instance, using headaches as an example, aspirin works well as a treatment, but this doesn't mean the headache was due to an absence of aspirin.

✔ **Brain scans.** There is also research evidence that supports abnormal neurotransmitter levels as an explanation for OCD. For example, brain scans of patients that suffer from OCD show heightened activity in the orbitofrontal cortex. This happens if the scans are taken while their OCD is active, such as someone with a germ obsession holding a dirty cloth. This suggests that obsessional thinking might be caused by damage to the brain circuits.

Weaknesses

✘ **Biological explanations do not distinguish cause-and-effect factors.** A limitation of the biological approach to OCD is that it cannot distinguish cause-and-effect factors. We cannot be sure that low levels of serotonin and activity of the orbitofrontal cortex cause OCD or that OCD leads to low levels of serotonin activity. All that's known is that low serotonin and OCD are related. This means the biological explanation for OCD is weakened because a causative relationship cannot be determined. This may point to other factors, such as psychological and environmental factors.

General

✗ **Reductionist.** A further limitation of the genetic/neural explanations for OCD is that they are reductionist. This is because because they reduce the explanation of a complex disorder to a genetic/ biochemical level and do not consider other potential environmental factors that may trigger or increase the risk of developing OCD, as suggested by the diathesis-stress model. To support this view, Cromer et al. (2007) found that over half the OCD patients they studied had suffered a traumatic event in their past, and that OCD was more severe in those with more than one trauma. This suggests that OCD cannot be entirely genetic or biochemical in origin and we must account for psychological and environmental factors or provide a better explanation for OCD. As a result, the validity of the biological explanations for OCD is reduced.

Practice exam questions

1. Explain the genetic explanation for OCD. **[6 marks]**

2. Explain the neural explanation for OCD. **[6 marks]**

3. Francis says to Ben, 'To be honest, I am not that surprised that you have OCD, because your mum has OCD, doesn't she? She's always washing her hands and arranging things, before she leaves the house.'

   Ben says, 'Are you sure? I read that people with OCD have something in their brains that makes them behave in that way.'

   Using your knowledge of neural and genetic explanations for OCD, refer to the conversation above in your answer **[4 marks]**

4. Outline and evaluate neural and genetic explanations for OCD. **[12 marks AS, 16 marks A-level]**

AQA specification Topic 6: Psychopathology

- The biological approach to treating OCD: drug therapy.

◆ Introduction

The biological approach to psychopathology states that there is an underlying physical cause for abnormal behaviour and mental disorders. One biological explanation for OCD is chemical imbalances in the brain, such as neurotransmitter levels that are too high or too low. Drug therapy attempts to restore the neurotransmitter to a normal functioning level again. The main biological treatments used in biological therapy are *drugs*. The two main drug treatments for OCD are *anti-depressants* and *anti-anxiety drugs*.

◆ Anti-depressant drugs (SSRI)

- Anti-depressant drugs are the most widely prescribed drugs and are mainly used to deal with depression but also with OCD symptoms. The biological explanation is that OCD could be the result of a low level of the neurotransmitter serotonin. Selective serotonin reuptake inhibitors (SSRI) are a type of anti-depressant drug (such as fluoxetine, commonly known as Prozac) that is used to tackle the symptoms of OCD. SSRI work like this:

    - *Presynaptic neuron.* Serotonin is a chemical messenger (carries information) carried by certain types of neurons. Serotonin is released by the presynaptic neuron into the synapse (the tiny gap between each neuron).

    - *Postsynaptic neuron.* The serotonin in the synapse travels to a receiving neuron called the postsynaptic neuron which absorbs the serotonin using receptors. Serotonin that is not absorbed into the postsynaptic neuron is reabsorbed (reuptake) into the presynaptic neuron. Reuptake is a required aspect of neurological activity which regulates the amount of neurotransmitter present in a synapse.

    - *How SSRI work.* To increase levels of serotonin, SSRI drugs work by blocking the presynaptic neuron from re-absorbing (reuptake) serotonin. This means an increase in serotonin levels in the synaptic gap, and as a result, more serotonin is received by the postsynaptic neuron.

- As a result of SSRI increasing the levels of serotonin, this helps reduce anxiety and as a consequence, the person's behaviour should change, becoming less obsessive or compulsive.

Figure 20: How SSRI work

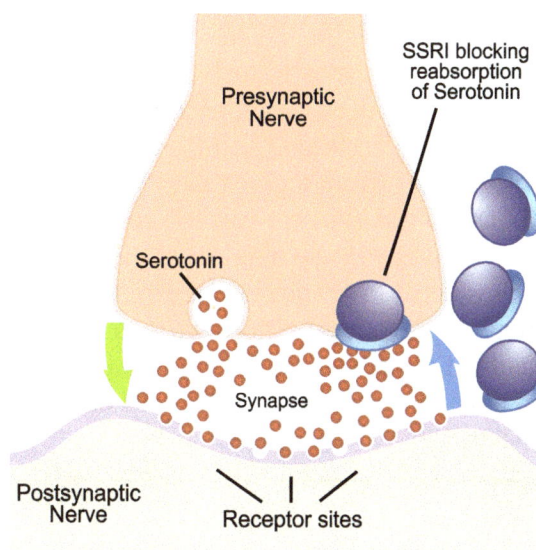

A little bit more information about SSRI

The typical dose of fluoxetine for adults is 20mg; however, this may be increased gradually if it is not benefitting the patient, with a maximum dose of 60mg a day. It usually takes 4-6 weeks for fluoxetine to work and it is available as capsules or liquid. If no improvement is observed within 10 weeks, alternative anti-depressant drugs are considered (e.g. Clomipramine). Most people take fluoxetine for at least 6-12 months. Drugs are often used alongside cognitive behaviour therapy (CBT) to treat OCD. The drugs reduce a patient's emotional symptoms, such as feeling anxious or depressed. This means that patients can engage more effectively with the CBT.

◆ Anti-anxiety drugs

- Instead of anti-depressant drugs, OCD is sometimes treated with anti-anxiety drugs. Benzodiazepines (BZ) is the name given for a group of anti-anxiety drugs (e.g. Valium). BZ work by increasing the levels of the neurotransmitter called GABA (gamma-aminobutyric acid) in the brain. GABA is an inhibitory neurotransmitter, which is released from a 'calming neuron'. This is because when we are faced with fear or anxiety (e.g. fight-or-flight response), it helps slow down neural activity in the brain and the nervous system (e.g. adrenaline, noradrenaline, serotonin), by preventing the neurons from becoming overexcited. This helps reduce the feelings of anxiety experienced by OCD sufferers and as a result, their obsessive thoughts and compulsive behaviour will lessen.

◆ Evaluation

Strengths

✔ **The effectiveness of drugs.** A strength of drug therapy to treat OCD is that there is supportive research evidence to show this is effective. Soomro et al. (2008) found that drugs were more effective than placebos in reducing symptoms up to three months after treatment. This supports the use of biological treatments such as SSRI for OCD. Typically, 70% of patients who use SSRI see a decline in symptoms. However, for the other 30%, alternative drug therapies, or a combination of drug therapy and psychological treatments would be more effective. However, one of the issues regarding the evaluation of treatment is that most studies have only lasted 3-4 months (Koran et al., 2007). This means that we can only know about the short-term effectiveness of drug therapy and very little is known about the long-term effectiveness.

✔ **Comparison with alternative treatments.** Another strength of the use of drug therapy as a treatment for OCD is that it is cost-effective and non-disruptive. Drug therapy is much cheaper compared to other psychological treatment therapies as it requires little monitoring. Therefore, using drugs as a treatment for OCD is better value for the NHS compared to psychological therapies. Furthermore, drug treatment such as SSRI are also less disruptive to patient's lives, compared to psychological therapies. This is because it requires little effort from the user, they simply take the medication until their symptoms are reduced. Therapies such as CBT and REBT require the patient to attend regular meetings and put considerable thought/motivation into tackling their problems. This means drug therapies as a biological treatment for OCD can be seen as a more appealing method of treatment for some patients.

Weaknesses

✗ **Potential side effects.** One potential issue with drug therapy as a treatment for OCD is that it can have unpleasant/severe side effects. Nausea, dizziness, headaches, and insomnia are common side effects of SSRI (Soomro et al., 2008). In some instances, some of the side effects can be more serious, such as disruption to weight (gain), blood pressure, and heart rhythm (irregular heartbeat) and with men suffering erection problems/drop in sex drive. The possible side effects of BZs include increased aggressiveness and long-term impairment of memory. There are also problems with addiction, so the recommendation is that BZ is a short-term treatment and usage should be limited to a maximum of four weeks (Ashton, 1997). As a result of these side effects, patients stop taking their medication, which limits the usefulness of these treatments for OCD.

✗ **Not a cure.** A final criticism of drug therapy for treating OCD is that does not provide a lasting cure, but only deals with the symptoms of the disorder. In the short term, the drugs are effective, but if patients stop taking their medication, then they relapse within a week to having OCD again (Maina et al., 2001). Scientists have an idea of how these drugs work; they don't know why they work. Nor is it understood why they work in some people to some degree but not in other people. Delgado and Moreno (1998) stated that there is no agreement between scientists that serotonin and other neurotransmitters are the cause of OCD. Until scientists know exactly the cause of OCD, drugs will be used to manage the problem as opposed to curing the disorder. This suggests that the drugs are not effective in the long term and psychological therapies, such as CBT, should be used instead (Koran et al., 2007).

Practice exam questions

1. Outline one drug therapy that has been used to deal with OCD.   **[4 marks]**

2. Anthony has been suffering from OCD. Dr Frown prescribes a short course of drugs. Anthony does not like taking drugs and asks Dr Frown to explain the benefits and disadvantages of taking drugs to treat his panic attacks.   **[4 marks]**

   Explain one advantage and one disadvantage that Dr Frown can give Anthony about using drugs to treat his OCD.

3. Outline and evaluate the biological approach to treating OCD.   **[12 marks AS, 16 marks A-level]**

Topic 7

Research Methods

AQA specification for Topic 7: Research Methods

AS-LEVEL SPECIFICATION	A-LEVEL SPECIFICATION
3.2.3 Research methods Students should demonstrate knowledge and understanding of the following research methods, scientific processes and techniques of data handling and analysis, be familiar with their use and be aware of their strengths and limitations: • Experimental method. Types of experiments, laboratory and field experiments; natural and quasi-experiments. • Observational techniques. Types of observation: naturalistic and controlled observation; covert and overt observation; participant and non-participant observation. • Self-report techniques. Questionnaires; interviews, structured and unstructured. • Correlations. Analysis of the relationship between co-variables. The difference between correlations and experiments.	**4.2.3 Research methods** Students should demonstrate knowledge and understanding of the following research methods, scientific processes and techniques of data handling and analysis, be familiar with their use and be aware of their strengths and limitations. • Experimental method. Types of experiments; laboratory and field experiments; natural and quasi-experiments. • Observational techniques. Types of observation: naturalistic and controlled observation; covert and overt observation; participant and non-participant observation. • Self-report techniques. Questionnaires; interviews, structured and unstructured. • Correlations. Analysis of the relationship between co-variables. The difference between correlations and experiments. • Content analysis. • Case studies.

Please note

Some sections within this topic cover both AS and A-level subjects and others cover subjects for A-level only. Check the specifications on this page and the following page for details. A-level only subjects are also clearly marked in the specific Exam Notes.

3.2.3.1 Scientific processes

- Aims, stating aims, the difference between aims and hypotheses.
- Hypotheses: directional and non-directional.
- Sampling: the difference between population and sample; sampling techniques including: random, systematic, stratified, opportunity and volunteer; implications of sampling techniques, including bias and generalisation.
- Pilot studies and the aims of piloting.
- Experimental designs: repeated measures, independent groups, matched pairs.
- Observational design: behavioural categories; event sampling; time sampling.
- Questionnaire construction, including use of open and closed questions; design of interviews.
- Variables: manipulation and control of variables; including independent, dependent, extraneous, confounding; operationalisation of variables.
- Control: random allocation and counterbalancing, randomisation and standardisation.
- Demand characteristics and investigator effects.
- Ethics, including the role of the British Psychological Society's code of ethics; ethical issues in the design and conduct of psychological studies; dealing with ethical issues in research.
- The role of peer review in the scientific process.
- The implications of psychological research for the economy.

4.2.3.1 Scientific processes

- Aims: stating aims, the difference between aims and hypotheses.
- Hypotheses: directional and non-directional.
- Sampling: the difference between population and sample; sampling techniques including: random, systematic, stratified, opportunity and volunteer; implications of sampling techniques, including bias and generalisation.
- Pilot studies and the aims of piloting.
- Experimental designs, repeated measures, independent groups, matched pairs.
- Observational design: behavioural categories; event sampling; time sampling.
- Questionnaire construction, including use of open and closed questions; design of interviews.
- Variables: manipulation and control of variables, including independent, dependent, extraneous, confounding; operationalisation of variables.
- Control: random allocation and counterbalancing, randomisation and standardisation.
- Demand characteristics and investigator effects.
- Ethics, including the role of the British Psychological Society's code of ethics; ethical issues in the design and conduct of psychological studies; dealing with ethical issues in research.
- The role of peer review in the scientific process.
- The implications of psychological research for the economy.
- Reliability across all methods of investigation. Ways of assessing reliability test-retest and inter-observer; improving reliability.
- Types of validity across all methods of investigation: face validity, concurrent validity, ecological validity and temporal validity. Assessment of validity. Improving validity.
- Features of science: objectivity and the empirical method; replicability and falsifiability; theory construction and hypothesis testing; paradigms and paradigm shifts.
- Reporting psychological investigations. Sections of a scientific report: abstract, introduction, method, results, discussion and referencing.

3.2.3.2 Data handling and analysis

Quantitative and qualitative data; the distinction between qualitative and quantitative data collection techniques.

- Primary and secondary data, including meta-analysis.
- Descriptive statistics: measures of central tendency – mean, median, mode; calculation of mean, median and mode; measures of dispersion; range and standard deviation; calculation of range; calculation of percentages; positive, negative and zero correlations.
- Presentation and display of quantitative data: graphs, tables, scattergrams, bar charts and histograms.
- Distributions: normal and skewed distributions; characteristics of normal and skewed distributions.
- Introduction to statistical testing; the sign test. When to use the sign test; calculation of the sign test.

4.2.3.2 Data handling and analysis

Quantitative and qualitative data; the distinction between qualitative and quantitative data collection techniques.

- Primary and secondary data, including meta-analysis.
- Descriptive statistics: measures of central tendency – mean, median, mode; calculation of mean, median and mode; measures of dispersion; range and standard deviation; calculation of range; calculation of percentages; positive, negative and zero correlations.
- Presentation and display of quantitative data: graphs, tables, scattergrams, bar charts and histograms.
- Distributions: normal and skewed distributions; characteristics of normal and skewed distributions.
- Analysis and interpretation of correlation, including correlation coefficients.
- Levels of measurement: nominal, ordinal and interval.
- Content analysis and coding. Thematic analysis.

4.2.3.3 Inferential testing

Students should demonstrate knowledge and understanding of inferential testing and be familiar with the use of inferential tests.

- Introduction to statistical testing; the sign test. When to use the sign test; calculation of the sign test.
- Probability and significance: use of statistical tables and critical values in the interpretation of significance; Type I and Type II errors.
- Factors affecting the choice of statistical test, including level of measurement and experimental design. When to use the following tests: Spearman's rho, Pearson's r, Wilcoxon, Mann-Whitney, related t-test, unrelated t-test and Cap C and cap S test.

AQA specification for Topic 7: Research methods

- Experimental method. Types of experiments, laboratory and field experiments; natural and quasi-experiments.

- Variables: manipulation and control of variables, including independent, dependent, extraneous, confounding. (Note: Operationalisation of variables is covered in Exam Note10.)

- Control: random allocation.

◆ Introduction

There are four different types of experimental methods commonly used in psychological research.

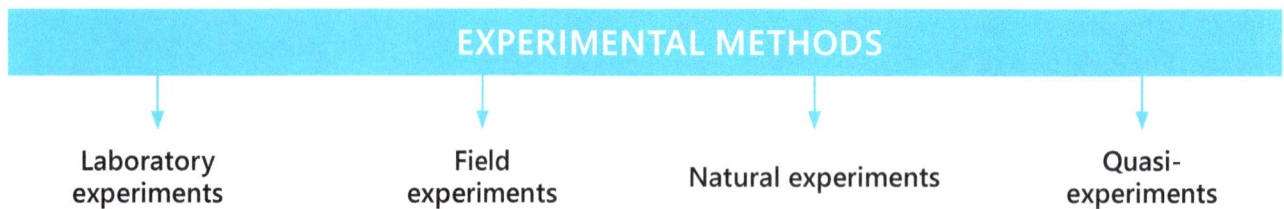

EXPERIMENTAL METHODS

Laboratory experiments   Field experiments   Natural experiments   Quasi-experiments

◆ Laboratory experiments

A laboratory experiment (or true experiment) is seen as the most scientific psychological method a researcher can use when investigating human behaviour. It is a tightly controlled research method conducted in an artificial environment to test a hypothesis.

The purpose of conducting a laboratory experiment is to see if one variable called the *independent variable (IV)* has an effect on or changes another variable called the *dependent variable (DV)*, with the aim of discovering a cause-and-effect relationship (or causal relationship) between the two variables, that is, the change in the IV has an effect on the DV.

The three main characteristics of a laboratory experiment are:

- Manipulation of the independent variable – The experimenter manipulates the first variable (the IV) to observe what effect it has on the second variable (the DV).

- Experimental control – The experimenter ensures, as far as possible, that all other unwanted factors (variables) are controlled (held constant or eliminated). These potential unwanted variables are known as extraneous variables.

- Randomisation – A laboratory experiment allows the researcher to randomly allocate the participants to the different experimental conditions.

◆ Independent and dependent variables

An important feature of experimental research is what we call variables. In a simple psychology experiment, there are usually two variables, the independent variable (IV) and the dependent variable (DV). To understand the difference, let us take this hypothesis:

Independent variables   Dependent variables

Being hungry has an effect on memory recall

- **Independent variable (IV)** – This is the variable that is **manipulated** by the experimenter to see what effect it has on the *dependent* variable. In the example above, *hunger* would be our independent variable. In a research experiment, a group of participants went without food for a day (i.e. the *hungry* lot = the experimental group). The other group of participants had eaten (i.e. the *not-hungry* lot = control group). The two groups can be compared to see what effect hunger has on memory recall (e.g. remembering words). This is what is meant by manipulating the independent variable (i.e. anything that can be varied such as behaviour, items, events, sizes or amounts).

- **Dependent variable (DV)** – This is the variable that is **measured** (a result or score) by the experimenter. We measure the effects that the *independent* variable may have on the dependent variable. In our example above, memory recall would be our DV because we are measuring how good memory recall is (e.g. the number of words remembered), when someone is hungry or not hungry.

Experimental control

In order to establish a cause-and-effect relationship between hunger and memory, the experimenter must *control* – or *eliminate* – other 'interfering variables' known as **extraneous variables (EV)**, that may influence the participant's memory recall.

Extraneous variables can be defined as any *unwanted* variable (other than the IV) that may potentially affect the results (DV) of the study. If an extraneous variable does affect the results, then we say it has confounded (confused) the results. This is known as a **confounding variable (CV)** and it describes a factor in the experiment that was *not* controlled and that affected the research findings. If this occurs, it reduces the validity of the results, which means we can't trust the research findings. Note that some CVs are easier to identify than others!

Two main types of extraneous variables that can affect the validity of an experiment are:

- **Participant variables** – These refer to individual differences and behaviours of the participants themselves that could influence the results of the experiment, such as age, intelligence, gender, ethnicity, social class, experiences, skills, tiredness, mood, and motivation. They can all (unintentionally) influence the outcome of the results. This is only an issue if the experimental design is an *independent group design*. *(See Exam Notes 2)*

- **Situational variables** – These relate to the situational setting of the research, which may affect the participants' behaviour. There might be *environmental factors*, such as the instructions given, the material used, noise levels or temperature, light level and time of day, and even weather conditions! Situational variables could also be features of the experiment that lead participants to behave in a particular way called *demand characteristics* and *investigator effects (See Exam Notes 13)*. There are also *order effects*, whereby the type of *experimental design* can affect the results of the research *(See Exam Notes 13)*.

Example of a study with extraneous variables

In the above example of hunger and memory, the potential situational and participant EVs could be the number of hours they slept the night before the test, their intelligence, and the time of day the test was taken. Let's say we tested the participants at different times of the day, perhaps one group in the morning and the other in the afternoon; the results would then be confounded (i.e. confused). We cannot be sure if the IV (hunger) or the time of day (EV) was the cause of any difference in memory scores among the participants. The time of day would be a confounding variable.

Experimental groups and the control group

In order to see if the IV has an effect on the DV, an experiment must have at least *two groups* (conditions) – one group receives the IV and the other group does not. Then we can compare the results.

- The **experimental group** is exposed to the IV.

- The control group is not exposed to the IV.

If the results differ between the two groups, and we have assured ourselves that we have controlled any EVs, then we can conclude that any difference in the participants was due to the IV. For example, a study on *Revising for an exam while listening to music affects memory recall* might have two groups:

- The participants in the *experimental group* attempt to learn a psychological theory while listening to music.

- The participants in the *control group* learn a psychological theory without listening to music.

The control group is really important because without them it would be impossible to tell whether the music had any effect on learning. With a control group as a comparison, and if the average score of the experimental group is higher than the average score of the control group, we can conclude that music improves learning. If there were no differences between the groups, then we can conclude that that the IV (listening to music) made no difference.

Randomisation

In the above example, participant EVs would relate to *individual differences*, that is personal characteristics of the participants. It is possible, for example, to assign more participants with higher intelligence to one group than the other. If this occurs, their individual differences will confound the results.

- A way to reduce the effect of personal differences is to use random assignment (or randomisation). This is based on the laws of chance. This means that the participants have an equal chance of being selected *either* in the experimental group or in the control group.

- The process of *random sampling* (e.g. tossing a coin or running a computer program to generate random numbers) for each participant will determine which group they go into. This means that any personal differences of the participants would be to some extent equally balanced out between the two groups, and this will increase the internal validity of the study.

Evaluation

Strengths

✔ **High levels of control.** A strength of laboratory experiments is they allow a high level of control over the research environment. This is done by controlling EVs, which means that the researcher can be confident about establishing a causal relationship between the IV and the DV, increasing the validity of the study.

✔ **Easy to replicate.** Laboratory experiments are easier to replicate than many other research methods, which is a strength. This means that the original experiment can be repeated by other researchers, under the same conditions and following the same procedures, to see whether they obtain similar results. The ability to be replicated is important for checking other researchers' work. If the findings are similar, we can be confident that the original results have internal validity and reliability.

Weaknesses

✘ **Artificiality.** A weakness of laboratory experiments is that they have been criticised for being highly artificial, that is they lack mundane realism (because the setting is unlike real life). This means that the results obtained in a laboratory experiment may not be valid because they bear little resemblance to the real world. Therefore, research findings from laboratory experiments are difficult to generalise to the real world.

✗ **Demand characteristics**. Another weakness of a laboratory experiment is that the participants may show demand characteristics because they know they are taking part in the experiment. Participants naturally will be curious and try to guess what the study is about. Any features of the experiment (e.g. tasks, resources, equipment, video clips), and the experimenter themselves, may act as a clue to what the study may be about. The participants may unconsciously respond to such cues and will then change their behaviour. This will affect the validity of the findings because the participants are not behaving as they normally would.

◆ Field experiments

Sometimes experiments are not carried out in an artificial laboratory setting, but in a real-life environment where people are engaged in everyday normal behaviour. Experiments might be conducted in schools or shopping malls, on the streets or in a workplace. Often, the participants do not know they are taking part in a study. Such experiments are called field experiments. In field experiments, the researcher is still able to manipulate the IV in a natural setting, to see the effect it has on the DV.

Example of a field experiment

Sissons (1979) investigated the effect that social class can have on 'helping behaviour' from strangers (helping others out). The confederate (an actor) stood outside Paddington rail station in London and asked people for directions to Hyde Park. In the first part of the experiment, the actor was dressed professionally, in a suit and wearing a bowler hat, and he spoke with a middle-class accent. In the other half of the experiment, the actor changed his clothes into those of a working-class labourer and spoke in a working-class accent. He asked passers-by the same question as before. The findings indicated that people were more helpful towards the man who was smartly dressed, with a middle-class accent, than the labourer, implying that people's perception of each other can alter responses. In this case, it influenced how helpful they were.

Evaluation

Strength

✔ **High external validity.** The strength of field experiments is that they are conducted in the real world, where the participants are often not aware they are taking part in a study, so there is no influence of the investigator effect or demand characteristics. This means that findings of field experiments are often more realistic and true to life than laboratory experiments, and therefore they are high in external validity. Therefore findings from field experiments can be generalised to the real world – something laboratory experiments cannot.

Weaknesses

✗ **More difficult to control unwanted variables.** A problem with field experiments is that the researcher has less control over the natural environment. This means changes to the DV may not be due to the IV, but to other unwanted variables (CV). This makes it more difficult to establish a cause-and-effect relationship, which reduces the validity of the research findings.

✗ **Not easy to replicate.** Field experiments are less reliable than laboratory experiments because they are carried out in a natural environment, where it is difficult to replicate the study under conditions that are the same as the original. This makes the findings from different field experiments difficult to compare.

✗ **Ethical issues.** Field experiments have ethical weaknesses. If the participants are unaware they are taking part in a study, this means they have not agreed to take part (lack of informed consent). In such instances, the researchers should, if possible, attempt to debrief the participant. This means telling the participants the purpose of the experiment at the end of the study, to reassure them that the information collected will be kept confidential and that they have the right to withdraw the data collected on them (if they were not happy being part of the research!).

◆ Natural experiments

A natural experiment is a type of research that collects data from a situation where the researcher does not manipulate the IV. This is because the IV would have changed/occurred naturally by itself.

The DV may be measured in a laboratory or in the field. The key feature of a natural experiment is not *where* it is conducted but *the way* the independent variable is manipulated.

Examples of a natural experiment

Charlton et al. (2002) investigated whether increased exposure to media such as television increases antisocial behaviours like aggression. He studied a small island called St Helena (a remote island in the South Atlantic Ocean), where television had been introduced only recently – in 1995 – to see whether levels of aggression had increased. After five years of television viewing, there was no increase in the children's physical or verbal aggression.

Another example of a natural experiment is that by Hodges and Tizard, who studied the effects of privation on children. They wanted to see how privation affects a child's development. To do this, they compared a group of children in institutionalised care with a group of children who were living at home with their families and assessed each child's development.

Another example is a study that compares football players to rugby players (IV varies 'naturally'). The DV could be an IQ test in a controlled laboratory setting.

Evaluation

Strengths

✔ **Greater external validity.** A strength of natural experiments is that they often involve real-life issues such as the effects of institutionalisation on children. This means the findings are more relevant to real-life situations.

✔ **Avoid investigator effects and demand characteristics.** Another strength is that, like field experiments, the participants are unaware that they are taking part in a natural experiment study. This means that their behaviour will be more normal and not subject to investigator effects and demand characteristics. Again, this increases the ecological validity of the study, which means that the findings can be generalised to the real world.

✔ **Only possible method.** Natural experiments are also good because they allow psychologists to investigate phenomena that would be unethical to manipulate the IV. For example, researcher investigating the effects of teenage smoking cannot randomly assign people to groups of smokers and non-smokers to see whether they develop cancer. This means a natural experiment may be the only way to research some topics.

Weaknesses

✘ **Participants are not randomly assigned.** A weakness of this design is that the researcher has no control over which participants are placed in which conditions as the IV is pre-existing. This may result in uncontrolled variables that affect the IV (confounding variables). For example, the Romanian orphans that were adopted early may have also been the friendlier ones. This reduces the validity of the findings.

✘ **Difficult to replicate.** Another weakness of these studies is that natural experiments tend to investigate a phenomenon that is unique, a one-off situation. This makes it difficult to verify the research findings because it is extremely unlikely that a researcher can replicate the study using the same setting and conditions. Therefore, it is difficult to check the reliability and validity of the results.

◆ Quasi-experiments

There are some studies that resemble a true experiment, because the IV seems to be manipulated in a controlled setting in which the extraneous variables are held constant. However, they may share similar characteristics of a true experiment design, without being truly experimental. These are known as quasi-experiments. Some differences between true experiments and quasi-experiments are:

- In a true experiment, the IV is manipulated in a controlled way and participants have an equal chance of being randomly assigned to either group; whereas in a quasi-experiment, the participants are *not assigned randomly into the different groups*. The experimenter does manipulate the IV.

- The reason why participants cannot be randomly allocated to the experimental/control group is because, in a quasi-experiment, the IV is already established and cannot be manipulated. If the IV is gender, age or ethnicity, this obviously cannot be changed by the experimenter for the purpose of the experiment. Usually this happens when the independent variable in question is something that is an innate characteristic of the participants involved. This also means that natural experiments are deemed as quasi-experiments.

Examples

An experimenter wants to see the difference in the reliability of memory recall of female and male participants after watching a crime scene. (The IV will be the sex of the participants and the DV will be the reliability of information recalled.) The researcher cannot manipulate the sex of the participants and randomly allocate them to be either male or female. So instead, the researcher assigns the participants to one group or the other, depending on whether they are male or female (this is the pre-existing variable).

A psychologist wants to see if personality traits 'extrovert' and 'introvert' have an effect on intelligence. The personality factors are the independent variable. Personality traits are inherent to each person, so random assignment cannot be used. Participants would initially be assigned to one of the groups based on their personality assessment scores.

Evaluation

Strength

✔ **Comparison can be made.** Quasi-experiments are good because they allow psychologists to study the differences in people (gender, developmental disorders such as autism, ethnicity, etc.). This means that a comparison between different types of people or behaviours can be made.

✗ **Cause-effect relationship cannot be inferred.** A weakness of these studies is that because in a quasi-experiment there is no random allocation, there is no control over the participants. This means that individual differences (social background, IQ, education, experience, etc.) might explain the difference in the results between the experimental groups, therefore we cannot be confident in inferring a cause-and-effect relationship.

Practice exam questions

1. Explain what is meant by the term 'laboratory experiment'. **[2 marks]**

2. Give one advantage of using laboratory experiments in psychological research. **[2 marks]**

3. Give two weaknesses of using laboratory experiments in psychological research. **[2+2 marks]**

4. Explain what is meant by the term 'field experiment'. **[2marks]**

5. Give one advantage of using field experiments in psychological research. **[2 marks]**

6. Give two weaknesses of using field experiments in psychological research. **[2+2 marks]**

7. Explain what is meant by the term 'natural experiment'. **[2 marks]**

8. Give two weaknesses of using natural experiments in psychological research. **[2+2 marks]**

AQA specification for Topic 7: Research methods: Scientific processes

- Experimental designs, repeated measures, independent groups, matched pairs.

◆ Introduction

Experimental design refers to how individuals will be allocated to each experimental condition (group) when taking part in an experiment. This is important because there are many ways in which participants can differ from each other, and these differences can act as confounding variables. There are three different ways that participants can be used in experimental design and each has its advantages and weaknesses. These are:

- Independent group design
- Repeated measures design
- Matched-pairs design.

◆ Independent group design

In an independent group design, each participant is randomly allocated and tested in only one experimental condition. If there are two levels of IV, one set of participants experiences only one condition.

Example of independent group design

Forty participants are taking part in an experiment to test the hypothesis that listening to music affects their memory recall. In an independent group design, the participants will be randomly allocated to one group. So, 20 participants will revise while listening to music (experimental group), while the other 20 will revise without listening to music (control group).

Evaluation

Strengths

✔ **Removes order effect.** A strength of independent group design is that it avoids the possibility of order effect because participants have taken part in only one condition. Order effect is when the participants take part in both (or all) conditions and the order this happens can affect the participant's responses. There are two type of order effect. The practice effect is where the participant behaves differently in the second condition because they know what to do (they have practice). The fatigue effect is where the participant's behaviour is different in the second condition because they are tired. Either way, this would act as a confounding variable that would affect the validity of the results. Taking part in only one condition eliminates this possibility.

✔ **Reduces demand characteristics.** Another strength of independent group design is that it reduces the effect of demand characteristics because the participants take part in one condition only. Therefore, it is less likely that they will guess the purpose of the study. If they take part in more than one condition, they are more likely to guess the aim of the experiment, which may affect their performance.

Weaknesses

✗ **Participant variables can still affect results.** A weakness of this design is that even if participants are randomly assigned, we cannot be sure that any individual differences will be balanced between the two conditions. There is still a possibility that the result may be due to individual differences. For example, when investigating the effect of listening to music on memory, any differences between the two conditions could be due to one group having better memory abilities or being more intelligent, rather than manipulation of the IV (the music).

✗ **More participants needed.** Another weakness of this design is that it requires more participants. This means more time spent recruiting which can be expensive.

◆ Repeated measures design

In a **repeated measures design**, the same participants take part in both (or all) of the conditions in the experiment. Two sets of data are produced from the same participants, which are then compared to see the differences.

Example of repeated measures design

If we take the previous example of music and memory recall, in a repeated measures design the same participants (all 40 of them) would be used in both conditions. First, they would revise while listening to the music (experimental condition), then they would revise without listening to the music (control group, or vice versa.

Evaluation

Strengths

✔ **Eliminates participant variables.** A strength of this design is that the participant takes part in both conditions, and has the same characteristics. Taking part in both conditions eliminates the confounding variable of individual differences (e.g. variations in intelligence, experience, motivation mood), which increases the validity of the study.

✔ **Fewer participants are needed.** Another strength is that half as many participants are needed for the repeated measures design. This means less time and expenses in recruiting participants.

Weaknesses

✗ **Possibility of an order effect.** A weakness of this design is that since the participants are taking part in both conditions, they may do better or worse when doing a similar task twice. This reduces the validity of the findings.

✗ **Increases demand characteristics.** Another weakness is that because participants take part in two conditions there is a likelihood that they will guess the aim of the study (demand characteristics), and this is likely to affect their behaviour. This reduces the validity of the results.

Counterbalancing (dealing with order effect and demand characteristics)

One way to minimise order effect and demand characteristics in repeated measures design is by counterbalancing. This is when participants are divided equally between the experimental conditions. Half are randomly assigned to be tested in condition A followed by condition B (A → B). The other half is tested in condition B followed by condition A (B → A) – thus AB and BA, or ABBA (just remember the pop group). In this way, the order of the experimental conditions is not the same for everyone, as some will carry out condition B first and some will carry out A first.

◆ Matched pairs design

In a matched pairs design, different participants are used for each experimental condition. For each person used, there needs to be another person with similar participant variables (e.g. characteristics such IQ, age, etc.). These pairs are then matched, and one participant is assessed in the first condition and the other paired participant is assessed in the second condition.

Example of matched pairs design

If we want to test the hypothesis that IQ level has an effect on memory recall, in a matched pairs design we may select a participant with an IQ of 110, who is 'paired' with another person of the same IQ level. The matched participants are then allocated to the different experimental conditions.

Evaluation

Strengths

✔ **Removes the order effect and demand characteristics.** A strength of this design is that participants are only tested once, so they cannot practise or become bored/tired. If they took part in both conditions, this could affect the participant's responses. Taking part in only one condition eliminates this confounding variable, which increases the validity of the study.

✔ **No participant variables.** Another strength is that differences in participant variables (individual differences) are minimised through pair matching, and thus there is less chance of any variation in the participants across the conditions. This increases the validity of the study.

Weaknesses

✘ **Twice as many participants are needed.** A weakness of matched pair design is that it requires twice as many participants, compared to the repeated measure design. This means it can be time-consuming and expensive.

✘ **Matching difficulties.** Another weakness is that it can be extremely difficult to match all the variables between each pair of participants and it does not guarantee that all participant variables are controlled. This may reduce the validity of the findings.

Practice exam questions

1. A psychologist wanted to investigate whether recall of information is more effective when the context (setting) of the original learning of information is similar at the time of recall. To do this, the researcher asked one group of students to learn and recall a list of 15 words in the same room. The other group of students were tested in a different context, by learning in one room and recalling in another.

   A. What experimental design was used in this study? [1 mark]

   B. Explain one advantage of this experimental design in the context of this study. [2 marks]

   C. Explain one weakness of this experimental design in the context of this study. [2 marks]

AQA specification for Topic 7: Research methods

- Observational techniques. Types of observation: naturalistic and controlled observation; covert and overt observation; participant and non-participant observation.

◆ Naturalistic and controlled observations

Most psychological research uses observation as a way of gathering and recording data on humans. The two main types of observations are *naturalistic* observation and *controlled* observation.

Naturalistic observation	Types of observation	Controlled observation
Observing behaviour in the natural environment without the manipulation of the researcher		The environment has been manipulated or controlled in some manner to observe the effects of such changes

Naturalistic observations

Naturalistic observations involve the researcher observing and collecting data on people's *naturally occurring behaviour* in their *natural environment* without interference or manipulation of the environment. For example, naturalistic observations may take place in a workplace, a hospital ward or a nursery.

Controlled observation

Controlled observations are carried out when the researcher deliberately manipulates or controls the environment in a particular way and observes the effects. For example, Ainsworth (1978) used a controlled observation by bringing children to a laboratory play room and observed and recorded the child's reactions (through a one-way mirror) when separated from the mother, or when introduced to a stranger. The situation was a controlled setting because Ainsworth manipulated the laboratory play room by controlling the behaviour of the mother (having to leave the play room) and the stranger (the appearance of the stranger).

◆ Evaluation

Naturalistic observation

Strength

✔ **High external validity.** A strength of this design is that people are usually unaware they are being observed. If people are unaware they are being watched, they will not be susceptible to demand characteristics. This means findings will be high in validity and more generalisable to everyday life.

Weaknesses

✘ **Observer bias.** A weakness of this design is that in naturalistic observations, the researchers may be selective in what they want to see. They unconsciously filter information, accepting only the information that will confirm their hypothesis. Such an unconscious process leads to the data being biased, which will affect the validity of the findings.

✗ **Cannot establish cause and effect.** Another weakness is that there may be uncontrolled extraneous variables such as participant variables (e.g. intelligence, mood, personality, illness).

This means it is difficult to establish with certainty a cause-and-effect relationship between the variables being investigated.

✗ **Ethical issues.** A further weakness of naturalistic observations is that the participants are unaware that they are being observed, which raises ethical issues regarding the invasion of privacy and lack of informed consent. If participants are informed about the observation, there is a very high possibility that they will behave differently (demand characteristics), which will lower the validity of the findings.

Controlled observations

Strength

✔ **Study can be replicated.** A strength of controlled observations is that the same standardised procedures can be replicated by another researcher. This allows checking the findings if they occur again (reliable).

Weaknesses

✗ **Low external validity.** A weakness of controlled observations is that the participants are aware that they are being observed, so there is a high possibility that demand characteristics will occur, which can lower the validity of the research findings. This means it cannot be applied to a real-life setting.

◆ Observational techniques

Below are some design issues the researcher will need to consider when conducting observational research.

Covert or overt observations

The researcher will need to decide whether the observation is kept 'a secret' from the participants.

- **Covert observation** is when the participants are not aware they are being observed, notably because the researcher's real identity (as a researcher) is hidden. For example, Festinger's (1957) research required him to infiltrate a cult group that prophesied the end of the world (he made out he was a member rather than a researcher).

- **Overt observation** is when the participants know they are being observed and usually they know the reason why. For example, in Zimbardo's (1971) prison simulation study, both the guards and prisoners were aware they were being studied.

Participant and non-participant observation

In observational research, the observer may have one of two roles:

- In **non-participant observation** the researcher does not participate in the activity with those being studied, they remain separate. For example, in Ainsworth's (1971) Strange Situation study, she observed from a distance behind a one-way mirror.

- **Participant observation** is when the researcher becomes part of the group and engages in the activity with those being studied. For example, in Zimbardo's (1971) prison simulation study, Zimbardo himself was actively involved in the study.

Data collection

The researcher will need to decide on how the data will be collected, and whether the observation will be *structured* or *unstructured*.

- Structured observation – The observed behaviour is recorded in a systematic and structured manner by using *behavioural categories*. This type of structured observation produces *quantitative* data, whereby the information gathered can be put into numerical form (numbers) and can be analysed statistically to see whether there is a relationship between the variables.

- Unstructured observation – There are no pre-coded behaviour categories, so the researcher freely writes down random notes on the behaviours they are observing. Unstructured observations produce *qualitative* data, whereby the information is often presented in descriptive form (written). This provides a deeper and fuller picture of the participant's behaviour, enabling the researcher to get a better understanding of behaviour.

Practice exam questions

1. Explain what is meant by the term 'naturalistic observation'. **[2 marks]**

2. Explain what is meant by the term 'controlled observation'. **[2 marks]**

3. Give one advantage of using naturalistic observation in psychological research. **[2 marks]**

4. Give two disadvantages of using naturalistic observation in psychological research. **[2+2 marks]**

5. Give one advantage of using controlled observation in psychological research. **[2 marks]**

6. Give two disadvantages of using controlled observation in psychological research. **[2+2 marks]**

7. Identify one ethical issue that may arise from observational research and suggest how this could be dealt with. **[3 marks]**

AQA specification for Topic 7: Research methods: Scientific processes

- Observational design: behavioural categories; event sampling; time sampling.

◆ Introduction

You should be familiar with observational methods including their advantages and weaknesses *(see Exam Notes 3)*. The researcher will need to make some decisions about design when conducting observational research. Some of these have already been mentioned in *Exam Notes 3;* they are:

- **The type of observation method** – naturalistic or a controlled observation?
- **The role of the observer** – disclosed or undisclosed? Participant or non-participant observer?
- **Data collection** – structured or unstructured observation?

◆ Design issues for observations

One difficulty for the researcher when conducting a naturalistic observation (as well as controlled observation) is how to record the data and what to record. This will depend on whether the observation is structured or unstructured.

Unstructured observation	Structured observation
The observer has no ordered system of collecting data, but merely records the appropriate behaviour when it occurs, using:	The observer uses a systematic and structured manner to record the appropriate behaviour when it occurs, using:
• Written note-taking • Video recordings • Audio recordings.	• Behavioural categories (plus the help of video and audio recording to help with the analysis) • Sampling procedures.

◆ Structured observations

Behavioural categories

If the researcher chooses a **structured observation**, they first need to decide what types of behaviours they wish to record. This is achieved by creating **behavioural categories**. The researcher designs a grid/table with separate columns for each category of behaviour. The observer then records the behaviour in the appropriate category.

Before the researcher can create behavioural categories, the behaviour to be observed needs clear **operational definitions** (to be operationalised). This means clearly defining how the observed behaviour will be *tested* and *how* the behaviour will be *measured*. For example, to investigate physical aggression in children, the concept of *physical aggression* must be operationalised by observing behaviour such as punching, scratching and kicking (the behaviour that is being 'tested') and seeing how often this occurs during playtime (the 'measuring' part).

Different ways that behaviour can be recorded

Tally system	Counting the frequency of the behaviour as it occurs	For example, aggressive behaviour in a school playground could be measured by counting the amount of biting, hitting, pulling and wrestling that takes place, as it occurs.
Rating scale	A point scale system of varying intensity	For example, on a 1 to 4 rating scale of helping behaviour for a person in distress 4 = very helpful; 3 = some help offered; 2 = aware victim needed help but did not offer; 1 = unhelpful and ignored victim.
Coding system	A system that uses letters or numbers to record the observed behaviour	For example, in a coding system for observing peer-play interactions of pre-school children at a nursery: CI = close interaction (children playing closely with each other); H = helping behaviour (children helping other children with a task); W = withdrawn (child not engaged in tasks or with other children).

Example of behavioural categories for observing aggressive behaviour in children within a playground (tally system)

Child	Hits or shoves others with force – unprovoked	Hits or shoves others with force – following peers	Hits or shoves others with force – retaliation	Shouts at others – Unprovoked	Shouts at others – following peers	Shouts at others – retaliation
A	⑁ II	⑁	IIII			IIII
B		⑁ III			II	
C		III		IIII		III
D		I	⑁	II		⑁

Adapted source: Coolican, H. (1999) Research Methods and Statistics in Psychology, Second Edition.

Sampling procedures

It is unlikely that the researcher will be able to record all the observed behaviour continuously. One way to record the behaviour is to take a sample during the observation. There are three main different sampling techniques for observation.

- **Event sampling** – This is when the researcher records a particular behaviour whenever it occurs. For example, when investigating aggression in a classroom setting, the researcher might record every time an aggressive event takes place.

- **Evaluation**

Strength

✔ **May record infrequent behaviour.** A strength of this method is that the researcher will still 'pick' up' behaviour that does not occur at regular intervals. This could be missed if time sampling was used.

Weaknesses

✗ **Complex behaviour over-simplified.** A weakness of this method is that if the event is too complex, important details may go unrecorded and the researcher may lose real insight into the behaviour being investigated. This may reduce the validity of the findings.

- **Time interval sampling** – Time sampling is when the researcher makes a record of the observed behaviour at regular intervals. For example, the researcher may observe children in the playground and record what happens every 30 seconds.

- **Evaluation**

Strength

✔ **Reduces the number of observations.** A strength of this technique is that rather than recording everything that is seen (i.e. continuous recording), the data is recorded at certain intervals.

Weaknesses

✘ **May be unrepresentative.** A weakness of this method is that the researcher may miss important details outside the time scale. This means the recorded behaviour may not reflect the whole behaviour, which makes it unrepresentative.

Practice exam questions

1. A researcher decided to investigate whether children who attend a pre-school day-care centre five times a week are more physically aggressive than those who attend twice a week. The researcher carries out a naturalistic observation at his local pre-school day care centre. The children were observed every morning during their outside play period for one hour.

   A. Suggest two suitable behavioural categories that the researcher could use to record the children's aggressive behaviour. **[2 marks]**

   B. How might the researcher record the children's behaviour during the observation? **[2 marks]**

AQA specification for Topic 7: Research methods

- Self-report techniques. Questionnaires; interviews, structured and unstructured.

◆ Introduction

Self-report techniques involve asking participants to provide information about themselves (hence the term *self*-report) on issues such as attitudes, beliefs, opinions and feelings. The two most well-known self-report techniques are *questionnaires* and *interviews* (often referred to as surveys).

◆ Questionnaires

A questionnaire can be defined as a pre-determined set of written questions. Respondents are invited to fill in their answers and return the questionnaire to the researchers. There are two basic types of questions that can be asked:

- Closed questions – These questions come with a range of answers to choose from that must be circled or ticked as appropriate by the respondent. Closed questions produce *quantitative* data because the answers collected can be summarised in a numerical form (e.g. to find the mean, mode or median), which makes them easy to analyse and draw conclusions.

- Open questions – There are no pre-set answers given to the question, so respondents can freely express themselves however they choose. Open questions produce *qualitative* data because the respondent's answers often involve a detailed descriptive account.

Examples of closed and open questions

Closed: Do you think mothers should stay at home and look after their children? (Respondents choose from Strongly agree / Agree / Disagree / Strongly disagree)

Open: What is your opinion of the latest Harry Potter film? (Respondents answer freely)

Evaluation

Strengths

✔ **Cheap.** A strength of this method is that questionnaires are generally easier, cheaper and quicker to administer (e.g. via email) than other research methods. For example, compared with interviews, questionnaires are easier to use, the researcher does not need any special training to use them or pay the interviewer's expenses. The lower cost also means that a larger sample of people can be obtained.

✔ **More truthful answers.** Another strength is that anonymous questionnaires allow the participants to be more honest with their answers than in a face-to-face interview, especially if there are sensitive or personal issues. The presence of the interviewer may influence the respondents' answers, which will decrease the validity of the data.

Weaknesses

✗ **Biased response.** A weakness of this method is that respondents may not answer the questionnaire in a truthful way. They may lie or deliberately give any false answer just to complete the questionnaire as quickly as possible. Or they may provide information that presents them in a positive light or give answers they think should be given, rather than more truthful answers. This is known as social desirability bias and it can decrease the validity of the data.

✗ **Low response rate.** An additional weakness of self-completing questionnaires is that they suffer from a low response rate (not many people fill them in or send them back). If the response rate is 25% or less, it may have a critical effect on the results, which will be of very little value if the sample is not representative of the population or group from which the sample was taken. Non-response is also a problem because the people who do not return questionnaires differ from those who do. Those who do return them tend to be of a higher social group and more educated, thus introducing bias into the results.

✗ **Wording of questions.** Another weakness of questionnaires is that they are only effective if the questions are sufficiently simple and straightforward to understand. If the words are not understood in the same way by everybody, this will affect how the respondents answer, which may affect the validity of the findings.

◆ Interviews

An interview, like a questionnaire, consists of questions, but this time an interviewer asks the questions when face-to-face with the participant. Interviews can be *structured*, *unstructured* or *semi-structured*.

- **Structured interviews:** All the questions and the range of answers are pre-determined, like in a questionnaire. The only difference is that the questions are read out aloud by the interviewer and the respondent answers verbally rather than writing anything down.

- **Unstructured interviews:** The interviewer introduces a number of research topics for discussion, with very few pre-determined questions. The interview is open and flexible so that respondents can express themselves freely and in greater depth because there are no fixed responses required. The interviewer may raise more questions during the interview based on any information he or she finds interesting.

- **Semi-structured interviews:** These lie somewhere in between a structured and an unstructured interview. The researcher has a set of pre-determined questions but can also ask additional questions depending on the respondent's answers, to probe further for more details or clarification or to open up a new line of enquiry. An example of this is a clinical interview in which the interviewer asks pre-determined questions, but follows up with spontaneous questions depending on the responses of the person being interviewed.

Evaluation

Strengths

✔ **Deeper understanding.** A strength of this method is the flexibility of unstructured and semi-structured interviews, allowing the researcher to explore and probe deeper into the opinions and attitudes of the respondent, which can provide rich and in-depth information. This is something that cannot be done with other research methods, such as close-ended questionnaires or experiments.

✔ **Good for sensitive subjects.** Another strength of this method is that interviews are more effective for sensitive subjects than a questionnaire. Having an interviewer who is sympathetic and understanding towards the respondent is more likely to generate a more truthful response.

Weaknesses

✗ **Social desirability bias.** A weakness of this method is that respondents may give answers that they believe the interviewer wishes to hear. Or they may answer questions in a particular way that portrays them in a positive light (social desirability bias) rather than giving a truthful answer. This will affect the validity of the findings.

✗ **Interviewer effect.** Another criticism is that the interviewer may unintentionally influence the participant's responses by such things as wearing particular clothing, making certain gestures, and using a certain tone of voice. Ethnicity, age, and gender can also play a part in influencing the answers given by the respondent.

✗ **Interviewer bias.** An additional weakness can be caused by the interviewer having a desired expectation or preference about the outcome of the study, so they unintentionally act in a way that may influence the response of the participants. This can also affect how the interviewer interprets the data, making him or her more selective of data that confirms the research hypothesis and more disregarding of data that may not support it. This is usually done without awareness.

Practice exam questions

1. Explain the difference between close-ended questionnaires and open-ended questionnaires. **[3 marks]**

2. Give one advantage of using questionnaires in psychological research. **[2 marks]**

3. Give two weaknesses of using questionnaires in psychological research. **[2+2 marks]**

4. Give one advantage of using interviews in psychological research. **[2 marks]**

5. Give two weaknesses of using interviews in psychological research. **[2+2 marks]**

AQA specification for Topic 7: Research methods: Scientific processes

- Questionnaire construction, including use of open and closed questions; design of interviews.

◆ Introduction

You should be familiar with self-report methods (questionnaires and interviews), as well as the advantages and weaknesses associated with each one *(see Exam Notes 5)*.

◆ Questionnaires

When administering a questionnaire, the researcher will need to make decisions on design issues. The type of data the researcher is seeking will determine the format of the questions (e.g. closed questions or open questions). There are two types of data:

- **Quantitative data = closed questions** such as 'Do you think mothers should stay at home and look after the baby?' YES or NO. These produce quantitative data because the answer can be put into numbers. It makes the data easier to analyse and draw a conclusion.

- **Qualitative data = open questions** such as 'Why do you think some mothers are reluctant to employ a nanny?' Open questions produce qualitative data because the respondent's answers consist of words that offer a detailed descriptive account of the participant's view.

Construction of questions

The researcher needs to ensure that the questions are appropriately worded to minimise misunderstandings that can otherwise affect the reliability and validity of the data. Some things to consider are shown in the list below.

- **Use plain language** – This helps avoid unclear or confusing questions that may be understood differently by different respondents. For example, asking 'How often do you go to the pub?' is an ambiguous question because the word 'often' is open to interpretation. This could be replaced with 'How many times do you go to the pub in a week?'

- **Avoid leading/loaded questions** – These questions can affect how a respondent answers. For example, asking, 'Don't you think that teachers should be paid more money?' is *leading* because it leads the respondent to answer 'Yes'. *Loaded* questions contain emotive language, which may bias the response of the respondent in a particular way; for example, 'Do you think it is right to kill defenceless animals in laboratories, or should it be stopped?'

- **Avoid double-barrelled questions** – These questions have two possible answers. An example is 'Do you think teachers are tired all the time because they don't get enough sleep or because they drink too much?' This question should be rewritten as two separate questions.

- **Avoid complex questions** – Long and difficult sentences that contain jargon (technical words) should be avoided. For example, 'Do you think the rise in psychotic illnesses has been due to the pressure of the individualistic lifestyle people lead now, or have the changes in legislation towards psychotic illness been the contributory factor for the increase?'

◆ Interviews

Again, you should be familiar with interview methods as well as the advantages and weaknesses associated with interviews. The researcher will need to consider certain design issues, such as the type of data the researcher is seeking to collect. This will determine the format of the interview. The types of data yielded by an interview are:

- Quantitative data – If the researcher is seeking basic information (e.g. Very often, Sometimes, Not often, or the Yes or No type) where they can quantify the data into numbers and analyse and draw a conclusion from the information collected, then the researcher will opt for structured interviews (questions are already determined beforehand with a set of fixed possible answers).

- Qualitative data – If the researcher wants to ask 'Why' questions, to find out about beliefs, opinions and attitudes, for example, then unstructured or semi-structured interviews (questions and answers are not determined beforehand) are favoured. They produce qualitative data because the respondent's answers offer a detailed and descriptive account of the participant's view (although it is difficult to analyse).

- Construction of questions – The wording of the questions in interviews is equally as important as it is for questionnaires, therefore all the issues discussed under 'Construction of questions' also apply to interviews.

Interviewer effect

Conducting an interview means that a high level of interaction between the interviewer and interviewee is expected. This means that the interviewer may unintentionally bias the participant's responses, which is known as the interviewer effect, which can affect the validity of the research. In order to minimise bias, the interviewer should:

- Ensure that interviews are standardised.

- Have a formal dress code.

- Express neither approval nor disapproval of the answers given by the respondent.

- Be pleasant and sincere.

- Ensure that the questions are asked in a neutral manner (non-emotive).

- Adopt similar personal characteristics.

Adopting similar characteristics is a way to further reduce the interview effect by matching the interviewer and respondents in terms of their personal characteristics. Research studies have shown that the respondent relates better to someone of the same age, gender, ethnicity and social class.

Practice exam questions

1. Give one example of a closed question.   **[1 mark]**

2. Give one example of an open question.   **[1 mark]**

3. Outline one design issue that researchers need to consider when constructing a questionnaire.   **[2 marks]**

4. Outline one design issue that researchers need to consider when constructing an interview *(other than the answer you have given for question 3).*   **(2 marks)**

AQA specification for Topic 7: Research methods: Data handling and analysis

AS and A-level:

- Correlations. Analysis of the relationship between co-variables. The difference between correlations and experiments.
- Descriptive statistics: positive, negative and zero correlations.

A-level only:

- Analysis and interpretation of correlation, including correlation coefficients.)

◆ Introduction

The term correlation refers to the view (or the aim to see) that a relationship exists between two variables in some way. For example, we can say there is 'a correlation' between the amount of time students spend on the social networking site Facebook and their exam performance.

◆ Correlation research

The purpose of correlation research is to see whether there is a relationship between two variables. We can refer to *non-experimental methods* such as interviews, questionnaires, and naturalistic observations as being correlational research. This is because the researcher has less control over the research conditions with these methods. The best that the research findings can show is a 'relationship' between the two variables, whereas in a laboratory experiment the researcher can manipulate and control the variables in order to establish a cause-and-effect relationship between them.

Example of correlational research

You may carry out a questionnaire survey to see whether there is a correlation between jealousy and the time a relationship lasts; for example, the more jealous you are, the shorter your relationship may be, or the less jealous you are, the longer your relationship will last.

◆ Correlational analysis

The term correlational analysis refers to a mathematical-statistical formula used to analyse data from correlational research. The aim is to discover which type of relationship exists between the two variables (positive, negative or zero), and how strong this relationship is between them.

Positive and negative correlation

There are three possible results of a correlational study: a *positive* correlation, a *negative* correlation, or a *zero* correlation. If we have two variables, x and y, then:

- Positive correlation exists when the two variables *increase* or *decrease* together. For example, a high score in variable x (e.g. frustration) tends to be associated with a high score in variable y (e.g. aggression). We can say that they are positively correlated, meaning that as frustration rises, so do acts of aggression. Equally, when one variable *(x)* decreases, so does the other variable *(y)*.

- Negative correlation exists when one variable increases and the other decreases. For example, a high score in variable x (the amount of alcohol we drink) is correlated with a low score in variable y (the time we can balance on one leg).

- Zero correlation is when there is no relationship between the two variables.

Correlational coefficient (A-level only)

A correlational coefficient is a numerical value (number) that describes the strength and the type of relationship that exist between the two variables. The type of relationship can be positive, negative or zero, and the strength, shown by the number, can vary on a scale from +1 to –1 where:

+1   =   perfect positive correlation

–1   =   perfect negative correlation

0   =   zero correlation

A correlation coefficient cannot be greater than +1 or -1

A negative correlation might have a value –0.49, whereas a positive correlation might be +0.82. The plus or minus sign tells us whether it is a positive or negative correlation.

The nearer the coefficient is to +1 or -1, the stronger the relationship is. So, for example, a coefficient of -0.89 shows a strong (but negative) correlation as the number is close to -1 (as one variable increases the other variable decreases), while a coefficient of +0.62 shows a moderate (but positive) relationship between the two variables (as one variable increases so does the other).

In summary

- A correlation coefficient close to +1.00 indicates a strong positive correlation.
- A correlation coefficient close to –1.00 indicates a strong negative correlation.
- A correlation coefficient of 0 indicates that there is no correlation.

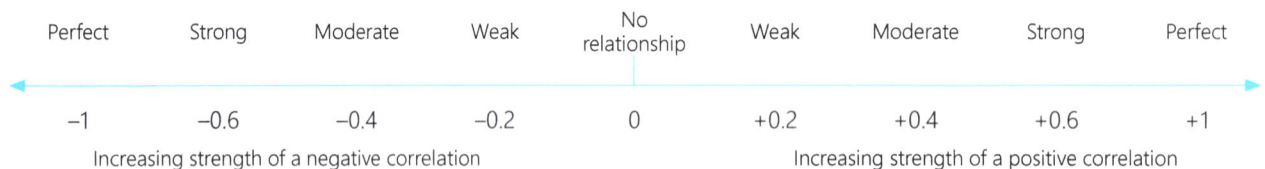

Perfect	Strong	Moderate	Weak	No relationship	Weak	Moderate	Strong	Perfect
–1	–0.6	–0.4	–0.2	0	+0.2	+0.4	+0.6	+1

Increasing strength of a negative correlation   Increasing strength of a positive correlation

Scattergrams (scattergraphs) are used to display correlational data visually. They are covered in more detail in Exam Notes 18.

◆ Evaluation

Strengths

✔ **When experimentation is not possible.** A strength of this method is that correlational research can be used when it would be unethical or inappropriate to investigate human behaviour under experimental conditions. For example, it would be unethical to carry out an experiment to see whether smoking causes lung cancer (we could not make people smoke themselves to death!). Instead, we could use a questionnaire or an interview and then analyse the data to see whether a relationship between the two variables exists. This is far more acceptable and ethical.

✔ **Naturally occurring variables.** A strength of this method is that correlational research is able to study the relationship between two variables that occur naturally in society – for example, exam stress and students getting ill.

✔ **Further research.** A strength of this method is that correlational analysis can identify whether a relationship exists or not between the two variables. If a relationship does exist, it can lead to experiments to see whether a causal relationship may be established.

Weaknesses

✗ **No cause and effect.** A weakness of correlational analysis is that it does not establish a cause-and-effect relationship between the two variables that is, that one variable has caused a change in the other variable. This is because there may be other factors involved. For example, a correlational analysis may show a relationship between violent video games and aggressive behaviour in young children, but this could also be due to another influence such as marital conflict in the home, or divorce, or parenting style. For example, if the parents tend to be aggressive or violent themselves, this will be seen by the child as acceptable behaviour. The uncertainly surrounding correlational evidence reduces the validity of the findings.

✗ **Ineffective curvilinear relationships.** A weakness of correlational analysis is that it is only effective for linear (straight-line) relationship between the two variables – but not for a nonlinear relationship (such as curvilinear). For example, the relationship between environmental temperature and aggression may initially show a positive correlation, because as temperature rises, so does aggressive behaviour but this is only true up to a certain point. When the temperature becomes very high, aggressive behaviour drops and so the relationship becomes a negative one. This kind of relationship is called a curvilinear relationship (inverted U-relationship e.g. ∩). If we calculate the correlation coefficient of the curvilinear relationship, it tends to show a zero correlation, even though this is clearly not the case. This shows that using correlational coefficients can be deceptive in terms of the type of relationship between the two variables, as demonstrated by curvilinear relationships.

Practice exam questions

1. Explain what is meant by the term 'correlation coefficient'. **[2 marks]**

2. A correlation coefficient in a study was found to be –0.84. Explain what this indicates. **[2 marks]**

3. Give one advantage of using correlational analysis in psychological research. **[2 marks]**

4. Give two weaknesses of using correlational analysis in psychological research. **[2+2 marks]**

AQA specification for Topic 7: Research methods: Data handling and analysis

Content analysis and coding. Thematic analysis.

◆ Analysis techniques

As with quantitative data, researchers need to analyse qualitative data to enable them to draw a conclusion. This can be challenging to do as qualitative data often produces a wealth of material, making it difficult to make sense of what the material may suggest. One way to summarise the material in a meaningful way is to use content analysis. Content analysis and thematic analysis are techniques for studying people indirectly via the communication they have produced. For example, this communication may include spoken interaction (transcript of an interview), written material (e.g. books, emails, diaries), and the media (e.g. television programmes, advertisements, music, magazines, and video recordings). Content analysis produces quantitative data and thematic analysis produces qualitative data.

◆ Content analysis

Content analysis can be used to 'analyse' the 'content' of qualitative data (descriptive data providing depth and detail) with the purpose to summarise the material by converting it into numerical form (quantitative data).

Design process of content analysis

Content analysis will need careful planning by the researcher. Just like any other research design, there are stages to follow.

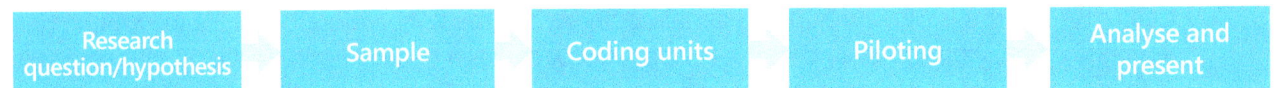

Research question/hypothesis	Sample	Coding units	Piloting	Analyse and present

- **Research question/hypothesis** – You will need to formulate a research question or a hypothesis. This should clearly state the specific question or a statement of prediction (hypothesis) you wish to research. For example, 'Is there a difference in the subject matter depicted on the front covers of male and female magazines?'

- **Sampling** – Select the sample material that is representative of the topic of interest to be analysed (e.g. which magazines). Consider the *quantity* to be sampled (e.g. 20 magazines), *frequency* (e.g. every fortnight), and *length of time* (e.g. over six months).

- **Coding units** – Next, the researcher will need to analyse the material using some form of a coding system in which the information is broken down into 'coding units'. Coding units are 'words' or 'concepts' that are operationally defined (operationalised) and then placed in categories and counted in the issue under investigation. An example of coding units could be all the positive or negative words or phrases related to what mothers think about daycare centres. The column headings in the table below are coding units, for example, for topics of conversation.

	Love	War	Poverty	Drugs	Friendships	Family
Female	37	5	1	1	6	4
Male	24	9	3	7	1	2

- **Piloting** – It is important when developing the categories that they each have clearly defined operational definitions. The researchers (coders) need to know exactly what they are recording in each category.

A way to assess this is by carrying out a *pilot study*. This allows the researchers a 'test run' to ensure that the coders are trained and agree on how to classify the information in the correct category. This can be assessed by having two or more coders independently analysing the material, to see whether there is a high degree of consistency (85%+) of categorising data correctly. If so, we can claim that the way the data is recorded by the coders is reliable (inter-rater reliability), which helps reduce researcher bias. Once any issue is corrected the researcher can begin analysing and recording the data.

- Presentation – Once the material is analysed and recorded into the appropriate categories, this produces quantitative data that can now be counted (e.g. tally scores). Then it can be presented visually using bar-charts, tables, averages and percentages. The researcher also includes a written summary of their conclusions from the results.

◆ Thematic analysis

One way to summarise qualitative material is through the use of thematic analysis. This involves a qualitative analysis where the information is summarised and presented in written form, instead of being reduced into numerical form as in content analysis. So, for example, to examine questionnaires or interview transcripts, the process would involve two stages.

- Coding – The researcher will extract and group information based on themes. Themes are recurring 'ideas' that keep appearing in the material. Themes are broader and more descriptive than coding units. For example, sentences, phrases, and quotations are categorised together if they are similar in theme. The researcher may construct the different types of categories before they examine the data, based on the research purpose (known as *pre-existing categories*). Alternatively, the categories are created after the researcher examines the data to discover any emerging repeating themes they may not have identified initially (known as *emergent categories*).

  - Presentation – The themes may be grouped together under certain headings and 'subheadings' and discussed, supported by the use of examples and quotations, and including some conclusions from the findings.

◆ Evaluation

Strengths

✔ **Conclusions can be drawn.** A strength of this method is that content/thematic analysis is a very useful research technique for analysing and summarising a large body of qualitative material, allowing the researcher to draw a conclusion from the data.

✔ **No researcher effect.** A strength of this method is that content/thematic analysis does not involve the researcher interacting with the participants because the information has already been gathered. This means that the researcher cannot influence the participants' behaviour, which makes the results more valid.

✔ **Reliable.** Another strength of this method is that the data produced from content/thematic analysis is reliable. This is because it can easily be repeated by other researchers using the same content analysis frame to see whether the same results are found.

Weaknesses

✗ **Loss of insight.** A weakness is that content analysis means counting up numbers and then describing the pattern or relationship that these numbers seem to suggest. This can be of limited use as it cannot offer explanations as to why such patterns and relationships occur in the first place.

✘ **Reliability and validity issues.** Another weakness of content/thematic analysis is that it relies on the researcher's subjective interpretation. Different researchers may have different interpretations of the material, which may result in the recorded data being placed in incorrect categories. This inconsistency reduces the reliability and validity of the findings.

✘ **Unrepresentative.** A weakness of content/thematic analysis is that the few selected sample materials may be unrepresentative (e.g. the selection of a few books or an interview transcript), which makes the findings difficult to generalise from.

Summary of the types of data research methods

Quantitative data	Qualitative data
• Experiments	• Unstructured observations
• Structured observations	• Semi-structured and unstructured interviews
• Structured interviews	• Open-ended questionnaires
• Closed-ended questionnaires	• Case studies

Comparing quantitative data and qualitative data

You will realise that the strength of one type is the weakness of the other (and vice versa!)

	Good	Bad
Quantitative data	**Easy to analyse** – summarising numbers makes it easy to analyse the relationship and draw conclusions from the data	**Low in validity** – reducing thoughts and feelings to numbers limits a deeper understanding of human behaviour and experiences
Qualitative data	**High in validity** – as it provides a detailed account into human behaviour and experiences	**Difficult to analyse** – makes drawing a conclusion difficult

Practice exam questions

1. Explain what is meant by the term 'content analysis'. **[2 marks]**

2. Explain one strength and one weakness of content analysis. **[2+2 marks]**

3. Explain the difference between quantitative and qualitative data. **[2 marks]**

4. Explain one strength and one weakness of qualitative data. **[2+2 marks]**

5. Explain one strength and one weakness of quantitative data. **[2+2 marks]**

6. In an observational study, 100 cars were fitted with video cameras to record the drivers' behaviour. Two psychologists used content analysis to analyse the data from the films. They found that 75% of accidents involved a lack of attention by the driver. The most common distractions were using a hands-free phone or talking to a passenger. Other distractions included looking at the scenery, smoking, eating, personal grooming and trying to reach something within the car. Explain how the psychologists might have carried out a content analysis to analyse the film clips of driver behaviour.
[4 marks]

AQA specification for Topic 7: Research methods

- Case studies

◆ Introduction

A case study is a research method that involves studying an individual or a small group of individuals. Case studies enable the researcher to gather a detailed and descriptive account of those being studied.

◆ Case studies

There is no single way to conduct a case study but they often involve a combination of methods such as observations, interviews, and psychological tests to build up a rich and detailed case history of an individual. For example, Koluchová (1972) used a case study to investigate the Czech twin boys and Curtiss (1977) made a case study of Genie. Both examined in great depth the extreme cases of children who were brought up in isolation, with minimal human contact.

How case studies help us

- They help us to explore and describe human behaviour in much greater depth.

- They provide a detailed description of a rare or unusual phenomenon.

- They generate theories or hypotheses that can be further explored through other more controlled research methods.

- They challenge existing theories or studies on human behaviour.

Evaluation

Strengths

✔ **Detailed qualitative data.** A strength of this method is that case studies allow psychologists to study unique behaviours or experiences that could not have been studied any other way. The method allows 'sensitive' areas to be explored where other methods would be unethical, like the effects of sexual abuse.

✔ **Only method possible.** A strength of this method is that case studies can be used to test or contradict existing psychological theories. For example, Koluchová's (1972) case study of the severely deprived Czech twins showed that they made a strong recovery when placed in a caring social environment. This challenges Bowlby's established hypothesis on maternal deprivation (whereby the lack of attachment can irreversibly damage a child's social and cognitive development).

Weaknesses

✘ **Generalisation is an issue.** A weakness of this method is that the findings from each case study are difficult to generalise. This is because each case study is based on single individuals (or small numbers e.g. the twins), whose experience has been unusual and unique. So, whatever was discovered to be true of that one case, we cannot guarantee it will be true of other similar cases – no two cases are alike.

✗ **Prone to researcher bias.** A weakness of case studies is that often rely on a single researcher investigating a single person. Therefore, the attitudes and assumptions of the researcher may have large implications for the results and limit the validity of the study. This is particularly true if the researcher expects particular results and is then leading the participant to produce that data.

✗ **Participant account could be biased.** Another weakness is that case studies often rely on the person's recollections of past events, and these are prone to omission and distortion. The person may leave out or distort important details during the investigation (intentionally or unintentionally) when the information is collected retrospectively. Therefore, the evidence provided may be low in validity.

Practice exam questions

1. Explain what is meant by the term 'case study'. **[2 marks]**

2. Give one advantage of using case studies. **[2 marks]**

3. Give two weaknesses of using case studies. **[2+2 marks]**

AQA specification for Topic 7: Research methods: Scientific processes

- Aims: stating aims, the difference between aims and hypotheses.
- Hypotheses: directional and non-directional.
- Variables: Operationalisation of variables.

◆ Aims

All psychology research investigations start off with an aim. An aim is a general statement that describes the purpose of the study, so people have a general idea of what the research is about and often includes words such as 'investigate', 'examine', or 'aim' in the sentence. So, for example, an aim could be:

> To investigate the influence of sugary soft drinks on memory recall.

◆ Hypothesis

Once you know the general aim of your research project, this will now need to be narrowed down further to formulate a research hypothesis. A hypothesis is a specific and precise *testable* statement that involves making a *prediction* (not a question) between the two or more variables that the researcher wants to investigate. An example of a hypothesis is:

> Participants who drink one pint of sugary drink will do better in a recall word test than those who do not drink a pint of sugary drink.

Types of hypotheses

- **Experimental hypothesis** – The hypothesis is called an experimental hypothesis (H1) when the study is using an *experimental method*.

- **Alternative hypothesis** – In all other *non-experimental research* (e.g. questionnaires, interviews and observations), this is called an alternative hypothesis (Ha). However, the alternative hypothesis is generally used to refer to all types of research methods, whether experimental or non-experimental.

- **Null hypothesis** – The null hypothesis (Ho) is a statement of prediction that the results will *show no relationship* or *no difference* between the variables. The word 'null' means *non-existent*.

Null hypothesis

Psychologists must initially assume when carrying out an investigation that there is no relationship or difference between the variables (e.g. sugary drinks and memory recall). It is the job of the alternative hypothesis to prove that there is a relationship and thus prove that the null hypothesis is wrong! Therefore in a research study there are really two hypotheses that are being investigated: the null hypothesis and the alternative hypothesis (as an alternative to the null hypothesis). Here is an example of a null hypothesis.

> There will be no difference in a recall word test between participants who drink one pint of sugary drink from those who did not consume a sugary drink.

How do we prove which hypothesis is right?

If we found that the results of the memory recall test showed a *very small* difference between people who consumed sugary drinks and those who did not, we would say that the results are not significant, because a small difference was probably due to a chance factor, and not due to the sugary drink itself, but due to something else, like tiredness. This means we would have to accept the null hypothesis – that sugary drinks (the IV) do not have an effect on memory recall (the DV).

However, if the results showed a *large* difference between the groups, we could say that the results are significant enough that the difference could *not* have been down to chance alone, but due to the sugary drink (the IV). We would have to accept the alternative hypothesis, that the sugary drink (the IV) had an effect on memory recall (the DV).

Directional and non-directional hypotheses

A hypothesis can either be:

- A directional (one-tailed) hypothesis – This predicts that there will be a difference in the results and the *direction* the results will go in. An example of a directional hypothesis would be: 'Boys are more aggressive than girls during adolescence.' This tells us there is a difference (i.e. between boys and girls) and direction of the results (i.e. boys are more aggressive than girls).

- Non-directional (two-tailed) hypothesis – This does not predict the direction the results will go in, they can go either way. For example, a non-directional hypothesis for the aggression study would be: 'There is a difference in aggressive behaviour between boys and girls during adolescence.' The hypothesis predicts that there is a difference in aggressive behaviour between the genders but does not predict whether boys or girls are *more* aggressive. Thus, the hypothesis is *not* directed towards either boys or girls and is a non-directional hypothesis.

◆ Which one do you choose – directional or non-directional hypotheses?

Some researchers use a *directional* hypothesis because similar research carried out before has produced results that have gone in a particular direction. A *non-directional* hypothesis may be used when similar research previously carried out has produced unclear or contradictory results, so the researcher is not sure what the outcome will be.

◆ Operationalisation of variables

Once the hypothesis has been established, the researcher needs to put the variables into *operational definitions* – this is operationalisation. It is the process of converting variables so that they can be tested and measured in practical terms (i.e. *how* will you go about doing that?). This means that the researcher will need to define exactly *how* the independent variable will be tested and *how* the dependent variable will be measured.

Consider the following two examples of hypotheses.

Watching violent videos leads to physically aggressive behaviour in young children.

The violent video (the IV) can be operationalised by exposure to three violent 20-minute children's cartoons, shown one after the other. Aggressive behaviour (the DV) could be measured by the number of 'kicks' or 'punches' the child carries out during playtime at school.

Middle-class children are less likely to experience stress than working-class children.

Social class (the IV) can be operationalised by using questionnaires to assess details of the parental occupation, income and housing, and so on, as an indicator of the children's social class. Stress (the DV) could be assessed by a questionnaire using a scoring system.

Why operationalisation of variables is so important

Clear operational definitions are important so that researchers can replicate a study in exactly the same manner as the original. This means that they can compare the results, and thus assess the reliability and validity of the original study.

Practice exam questions

1. A psychologist carried out an experiment to see whether the older you become the less you are able to recall information correctly from short-term memory. In the young group, participants were aged between 15 and 40 years and in the elderly group, they were aged between 75 and 90 years. The two groups of participants were presented with a list of words of everyday shopping items and were asked to recall the words immediately in the correct order.

   A. Write a suitable aim for this study.   [2 marks]
   B. Write a suitable non-directional hypothesis for this study.   [2 marks]
   C. Explain what is meant by the term 'operationalisation'.   [2 marks]

AQA specification for Topic 7: Research methods: Scientific processes

- Sampling: the difference between population and sample; sampling techniques including random, systematic, stratified, opportunity and volunteer; implications of sampling techniques, including bias and generalisation.

◆ Key terms

- **Target population.** The large group of people that the psychologist is interested in researching in order to draw conclusions about their views or behaviour (e.g. mothers, teenagers, children; or more specifically, all single mothers, teenagers from 16-18 years of age, or all children under four years of age.)

- **Sampling frame.** A sampling frame is a list of all names included in the target population from which the sample will be drawn, such as telephone books, registers of electors, school rolls, or lists of patients.

- **Sampling.** The process of selecting a small group of participants from the sampling frame to take part in the study.

- **Generalisability.** How representative the sample is of the larger population and therefore whether conclusions from the research can be 'generalised' to the wider population.

- **Biased sample.** A sample that does not represent the target population.

◆ Introduction

Part of the research process is finding participants to take part in a study. It would be impossible for a researcher to carry out a study on the entire target population as it would be impractical, time-consuming and expensive. So, a small selection of participants is chosen to take part in the study and this is known as a sample.

The aim of a sample is to allow the findings collected from a study to be *representative* (i.e. typical) of the target population. This means it is possible for the researcher to be able to make valid *generalisations* or *conclusions* about the larger group that were *not* included in the study. For example, if the psychologist is interested in the reliability of eyewitness testimonies of very young children, they would ideally want the theory to explain the reliability of eyewitness testimony of all such children, not just the ones in the study.

◆ Sampling techniques

There are different sampling techniques and each technique has its weaknesses, which can lead to having a biased sample. This would affect the generalisability of the findings (as the sample is not reflective of the target population). The sampling techniques covered are:

Random Sampling	Systematic sampling	Stratified sampling	Opportunity sampling	Volunteer sampling

Random sampling

- Random sampling means that *every* person in the target population has an equal chance of being randomly selected for the sample. Random sampling is a way to remove bias in sample selection. The sample can be selected by:

- Manual selection. If the population size is small (e.g. students from a local sixth-form college), the researchers could write the names on pieces of paper, place these in a box or hat, shuffle them (after each draw), and then pick out names until the required sample size is reached.

- Random number generator. For a larger population, a computer program (random number generator) can be used to generate a list of random numbers, which are then matched up with the names (and addresses) to produce the required sample size.

Evaluation

Strength

✔ **Potentially unbiased.** A strength of random sampling is that there is no researcher bias because the researcher has no influence over who is selected. This increases the chances of getting an unbiased and representative sample.

Weakness

✘ **Can lead to a biased sample.** A weakness of random sampling is that there is still a small possibility that you could end up with a biased sample of people (too many females, males, certain social class, occupation, age and so on). In terms of age, you may end up with too many students in the sample compared to non-students (e.g. working adults). This will make the sample unrepresentative of the target population that you are studying and therefore it will be hard to make generalisations from the research findings.

Systematic sampling

- Systematic sampling is when the sample is selected from a fixed sequence by choosing, for example, every ninth name from the sampling frame (a list of people chosen from the population).

So, if we want a 10% sample from 800 students, we could choose every tenth person from the list is (i.e. 80 students) to form the sample.

Evaluation

Weakness

✘ **Can lead to a biased sample.** A weakness of systematic sampling is that it can still result in a biased sample because of a hidden fixed sequence. For example, if every tenth property in a street is a flat occupied by a young person (and the rest are houses), then selecting participants who live there will make the sample unrepresentative, so the findings of the study cannot be generalised.

Opportunity sampling

- Opportunity sampling is when researchers themselves approach anyone who is easily available or easily accessible and willing to participate. For example, a researcher that is based in a psychology department could ask their psychology students if they would like to take part in a study.

Strength

✔ **Quick method.** A strength of opportunity sampling is that it is easy to create and convenient because you just make use of the people who are closest. This makes it one of the most popular sampling methods.

✗   **Can lead to a biased sample.** A weakness of opportunity sampling is that it could lead to the researcher having a biased sample because it may exclude certain people. For example, asking people mid-week during the day will result in a higher percentage of mothers, students or those who are not working. This makes the sample unrepresentative, so the findings of the study cannot be generalised.

Volunteer sampling

- Volunteer sampling (or self-selecting sampling) is when participants have freely chosen to be part of the study by responding to an advertisement in newspapers, leaflets, television, radio, email, social media and word of mouth!

Strength

✔   **Less chance of 'screw you' effect.** A strength of this method is that participants selected themselves, they have given up their time and effort to participate in the study. This means they are less likely to sabotage the study, than in opportunity sampling, for example.

Weakness

✗   **Can lead to a biased sample.** A weakness of volunteer sampling is that it is prone to bias because participants who opt to take part often have certain social or personal characteristics (e.g. more education, more enthusiastic, etc.), which are different from those who do not volunteer. This makes the sample unrepresentative, so the findings of the study cannot be generalised.

Stratified sampling

- Stratified sampling involves dividing the population into strata (categories) depending on the characteristics (e.g. age, class) that are important to the researcher. Then a certain number of people are randomly selected from each stratum in proportion to its representation in the target population.

  For example, if we wanted to carry out a survey on Year 12 and 13 students on cannabis use, we could 'stratify' the sampling into four categories: Year 12 boys, Year 12 girls, Year 13 boys, and Year 13 girls. If 35% of Year 12 students are girls, then 35% from the sample of Year 12 girls are randomly selected e.g. 35% from 120 is 42, thus 42 Year 12 girls are selected as a sample.

Strength

✔   **Can lead to a biased sample.** A strength of this method is that the selection from each stratum (category) is representative from within the target population. This makes the sample more representative, so generalisability is more likely than other sampling techniques.

Weakness

✗   **Potentially biased.** A weakness of stratified sampling is that it requires detailed knowledge of the population characteristics. The problem with this is that this information may not be available, or the strata may not reflect all the ways in which people are different. This means the sample may not be representative, so the findings of the study cannot be generalised.

Sampling and research methods

Research method	Sampling technique (commonly used)
Laboratory experiments	Opportunity sampling, volunteer sampling
Field experiments	Opportunity sampling
Self-report (questionnaires/interviews)	Random sampling, volunteer sampling, opportunity sampling, systematic sampling, and stratified sampling
Observational research	Time sampling, event sampling

Practice exam questions

1. A researcher is interested in studying the experiences of twins raised together and comparing them to twins raised apart. They obtain a register of all the twins in the UK. The researcher chooses all those in the register whose last name begins with H or Z because there are so many names that start with H or Z. The researcher then randomly selects a sample of 20 twins from this list.

   B. The psychologist used a random sampling method. Explain how he could have obtained his sample using this method. **[3 marks]**

   C. Explain the limitations of using random sampling in this study. **[3 marks]**

2. A boys' secondary school has agreed to let a researcher conduct a student survey on bullying. The researcher obtains the school's electronic register with the names of all the students between 11 and 18 years of age. The researcher has decided to select 100 students to answer her questionnaire and is interested in getting a range of views from all year groups.

   A. Suggest one sample method that could provide a range of views. **[1 mark]**

   B. Explain how the researcher could obtain a sample using this method. **[3 marks]**

3. Every January large numbers of people join a gym to get fit, but then stop going after a few months. A team of psychologists decided to investigate why this happens. The psychologists contacted several gyms and asked permission to interview those people who joined during January. They put up posters in each of the gyms, asking for people to take part in their study.

   A. Identify the sampling method used to select participants in this study. Justify your answer. **[2 marks]**

   B. Explain one limitation of the sampling method used to select participants for this study. **[3 marks]**

AQA specification for Topic 7: Research methods: Scientific processes

- Pilot studies and the aims of piloting.

◆ Introduction

Whatever type of research method is chosen, a pilot study is often carried out. This is a technique whereby the researcher carries out a small-scale practice run on a few participants before the real research begins.

◆ Aims of pilot studies

The purpose aims of a pilot study are to reveal any design problems relating to questions, material, procedures, instructions, data handling, and so on, in the research study. Piloting saves a lot of time and money by identifying early on any design flaws so that they can be amended before the 'real thing' begins. Naturally, this helps to *improve the reliability* and *validity* of the design.

Experiments

In experiments, participants can give feedback on the *procedures*. For example, the researcher might want to know whether the instructions were easily understood or confusing to the participants. Was the *experimental task* appropriate? Was there enough time to complete the task? Did the task need less or more time? Did the participants guess the hypothesis of the investigation? If so, the researcher may need to think about redesigning the experimental task to reduce the demand characteristics.

Self-report methods

For self-report methods (questionnaires and interviews), a pilot study could be used to evaluate the construction of the questions, to see whether they are difficult or confusing, relevant to the aims of the study, and all understood in the same way by all the respondents. As a result, the researcher may decide to omit some questions.

Controlled observational research

In controlled observational research, a pilot study helps identify any potential problems with the design of the behavioural checklist. It allows the opportunity to see whether two or more researchers are consistent in the way they record information; in other words, the researchers are interpreting and categorising the observed behaviour in the same way (and not differently).

Practice exam questions

1. Explain what is meant by the term 'pilot study'.   [2 marks]

2. Explain one reason why a pilot study should be carried out in psychological research when using self-report techniques.   [3 marks]

AQA specification for Topic 7: Research methods: Scientific processes

- Variables: control of extraneous variables.
- Demand characteristics and investigator effects.
- Control: random allocation, randomisation and standardisation.

◆ Introduction

Extraneous variables, demand characteristics and investigator effects are all unwanted variables (factors) that can threaten the validity of a study. Part of the design process for the researcher is to identify and control or reduce them as far as possible.

◆ Extraneous variables in experimental research

Extraneous variables (EV) can be defined as anything other than the independent variable (IV) that could affect the dependent variable (DV). One of the reasons why laboratory experiments are viewed as the most scientific method is their high level of control over EV. If such variables are not controlled, or at least minimised, they can confound the results, which will threaten the validity of a study. There are two main types of EV – participant variables and situational variables.

EV: Participant variables

Participant variables can be viewed as differences in the characteristics and behaviours of the participants, which can influence the experiment and thus act as an EV.

- Individual differences: Individual differences and behaviours of the participants themselves can influence the results of the experiment (e.g. age, intelligence, gender, ethnicity, social class, experience, skills, tiredness, mood, and motivation). This is only an issue if the experimental design is an *independent group design*.

Ways to control participant variables

• Randomisation (random allocation)

One way to control individual differences is to use randomisation in an independent group design. The use of random assignment means that each participant has an equal chance of being assigned 'randomly' to any of the two conditions in the experiment. The idea is that any unequal characteristics in their age, IQ or personality, for instance, will be evenly distributed across the groups, thus controlling the unwanted variables. Randomisation makes it less likely that one group will have more unwanted variables than the other group.

• Repeated measures

Another way to control individual differences is to use repeated measures design when it is appropriate.

EV: Situational variables

Situational variables relate to any features of the experiment that may affect the participant's behaviour and thus act as an EV.

- Environmental factors: These relate to the features of the experiment that may affect the participant's behaviour, such as the instructions given, the material used, noise, temperature, lighting, the time of day and so on.

- Demand characteristics: Participants naturally want to guess what the study is about. Any features of the experiment (e.g. tasks, equipment, video clips) may act as a clue. Participants will (consciously or unconsciously) change their behaviour in a way that they think the study 'demands' it. Demand characteristics can affect the validity of the findings because the participant does not behave as they normally would.

- Investigator effects: The investigator can influence the behaviour of the participants. This may be due to the investigator's social and personal characteristics (age, gender, class, ethnicity, attractiveness, mannerisms, friendliness, formality, etc.) or through investigator expectancy. This means that the investigator may act in a way that will influence the participant's responses towards the desired outcome for the researcher *(see page 270 for more detail on investigator effects)*.

- Order effect: If a repeated measures design is used in an experiment, there is the possibility of order effect and demand characteristics. There are two types of order effects. With the practice effect, any improvement in performance in the second condition may be because participants already had practice doing the task in the first condition. Equally, if performance gets worse in the second condition, this might be due to boredom or tiredness, which is known as the fatigue effect. Either way, this would be counted as a confounding variable.

Ways to control situational variables

• Standardisation of instructions and procedures

One way to *control environmental factors* is to ensure that the procedures and instructions in the experiment given to the participants are *standardised*. This means that all the participants are instructed in the same way and tested under the same conditions.

• Single-blind procedure

One way to *control demand characteristics* is to use a *single-blind procedure*. This is when participants do not know the true aim of the experiment (i.e. deception is used), and/or are told something entirely different.

• Double-blind procedure

One way to control investigator effect and demand characteristics is to use the double-blind procedure. This is when the investigator and the participants are both kept in the dark about the true aim of the experiment.

• Counterbalancing

One way to *control order effect* and *demand chrematistics* in *repeated measures design* is to use *counterbalancing (see Exam Notes 2)*.

Extraneous variables: demand characteristics and investigator effects in all research methods

Extraneous variables (EV) such as *demand characteristics* and *investigator effects* are not solely the problem of experimental research, they can occur in all types of research methods used (e.g. interviews and observations).

EV: Demand characteristics

Demand characteristics refer to the research situation in which the participant finds themselves, which can influence how the participant behaves. Demand characteristics can act as an EV because the participant does not behave as they normally would. Examples of different types of demand characteristics are:

- Guessing what the study is about – Participants naturally will be curious and try to guess what the study is about. The participants unconsciously seek clues from any features (characteristics) of the research situation such as the instructions given, the type of tasks or tests performed, or questions asked. Participants may then change their behaviour if they think the study 'demands' a particular response, to what they think is expected of them, hence the term 'demand characteristics'. If this is the case, all the participants are likely to behave in the same type of way because the research situation may have 'invited' (unknowingly) a particular response.

- Participant effects (or participant reactivity) – Some participants in a study may affect the validity of the findings because of their own expectations and attitude. The fact that participants are being observed or evaluated may lead them to not behave as they naturally would. Some types of participant effects are:

  - Social desirability bias – Participants may attempt to present themselves in a positive light to make a good impression (more 'desirable'). For example, in an interview or questionnaire, they may answer in a way that makes them appear more approving towards the researcher but does not truly reflect their opinion or behaviour. Equally, participants may not be helpful towards the investigation (to annoy the researcher or out of frustration) and may deliberately give a wrong answer or behave differently. This is known as the 'screw you' effect.

  - Hawthorne effect – Participants may act differently from how they would do normally, just because of the *attention* they are receiving from the researcher and not because of the manipulation of IV.

Ways to control demand characteristics

- Standardisation of instructions and procedures.
- Single-blind procedure.

EV: Investigator effects

The investigator effect is when the investigator's behaviours and characteristics influence the behaviour of the participants and thus act as an EV on the study. There are two main types of investigator effects – *investigator characteristics* and *investigator expectancy*.

- Investigator characteristics – The physiological and psychological qualities of the investigator, such as age, gender, class, ethnicity and personality type (e.g. friendliness, intimidation) can influence participant behaviour.

- Investigator expectancy – The investigator has specific expectations about the outcome of the study, and may unintentionally or intentionally behave (e.g. mannerisms, body language, the use of leading questions) in a way that influences the participant's responses, which may, in turn, produce the outcome the researcher desired from the study.

Ways to control investigator effects

- Double-blind procedures.
- Standardisation of instructions and procedures.

Practice exam questions

1. Some psychology students wanted to investigate whether people are more likely to recall more happy words than sad words. Forty students took part in the experiment and a repeated measures design was used. The participants were shown a list of happy words, which they then had to recall. Then they were then shown a list of sad words, which they had to recall.

   A. Suggest one possible extraneous variable in this experiment. **[1 mark]**

   B. Suggest one way the researcher can deal with this extraneous variable. **[2 marks]**

2. Explain what is meant by the term 'demand characteristics'. **[2 marks]**

3. Explain what is meant by the term 'investigator effects'. **[2 marks]**

AQA specification for Topic 7: Research methods: Scientific processes

Ethics, including the role of the British Psychological Society's code of ethics; ethical issues in the design and conduct of psychological studies; dealing with ethical issues in research.

The exam requires that you are able to:

- Familiarise yourself with the BPS Code of Ethics.
- Describe and identify ethical issues and ways in which psychologists deal with them when they arise.

◆ British Psychological Society (BPS) Code of Ethics

It is important when considering the design of research to ensure that researchers follow the Code of Ethics and Conduct published by the British Psychological Society (BPS). This publication sets out a number of ethical guidelines for psychological researchers to follow when carrying out research on people (and animals). It aims to ensure that organisations, such as universities and hospitals, which carry out research studies follow certain ethical guidelines. To ensure that they do, these organisations have their own internal ethics committees.

The role of these committees is to assess and advise on ethical matters or issues arising for the researchers within their organisation who wish to carry out a study. Any researchers who break the guidelines may have their licence withdrawn from the BPS, which means that they can no longer practise as a psychologist.

◆ Content of the BPS Code of Ethics

Below are the main themes covered in the BPS guidelines for ethics and conduct. The publication is regularly updated and revised.

Consent

Before agreeing to take part in a study, the participants will need to be fully informed about the purpose of the study. This includes the researcher explaining the aims and procedure and how the data will be used in the study. They should also be informed about their rights, that no harm will come to them, that they can withdraw from the investigation at any time (even if money was given to them for taking part) and that their confidentiality and anonymity will be respected. Only after being fully informed, can the participant give written consent. Children under the age of 16 years need the consent of a parent or guardian.

Deception

The use of deception in a study means that the participants are deliberately misled or lied to, or that vital information was withheld about the true purpose of the study. The BPS states that researchers should try to avoid using deception where possible.

Debriefing

Once the study has ended, the researcher will need to debrief the participants. This involves fully informing them about the purpose of the study, especially if deception was used (and justifying why it was necessary) and reminding them that the information will be kept confidential and their right to withdraw their data at any time. Debriefing also gives the participants an opportunity to have a conversation and ask questions about the study, thus enabling the researcher to ensure that they were unaffected by taking part (and came to no psychological harm).

Right to withdraw

Right from the beginning, when informed consent is given, researchers should also make it clear to participants that they have the right to withdraw from the study. This means participants can leave at any time, regardless of whether a payment was given, or some other form of inducement was offered. Participants are also made aware that they have the right to withdraw any data they have provided, and that it can be destroyed, even when the study has been completed and the data has been collected.

Confidentiality

Participants are guaranteed that all information collected from them during the study will be kept private, unless there are legal, safety, or health obligations. Anonymity is part of confidentiality. If, for example, the study is published, letters, numbers or pseudonym names should be given instead of the participants' real names, so that the information cannot be identified as theirs.

Protection of participants

Researchers have the responsibility to protect participants from any physical and psychological harm (e.g. being anxious, distressed, having feelings of low-esteem or embarrassment) during the investigation. Normally, the risk of harm must be no greater than in ordinary life. This means that participants should not be exposed to risks greater than (or additional to) those encountered during their normal lifestyles.

Observational research

Studies based on observation must respect the privacy and psychological well-being of the individuals during a research investigation. Unless those being observed give their consent to being observed, observational research is *only* acceptable in situations where the observed people would *expect* to be observed by strangers in a normal, everyday environment (like waiting in a bus queue or being served in a restaurant).

◆ How psychologists deal with ethical issues

Even with ethical guidelines like these in place, there are times when carrying out a study may conflict with the rights of the participants. For example, the researcher may need to consider lying to the participants about the real purpose of the study, which is deception. Sometimes there is the possibility of causing distress to participants. Ethical issues may arise when designing a research project, and the researcher will need to deal with these. The three main ethical issues that often arise in psychological research are obtaining consent, the use of deception and the protection of the participants. How psychologists deal with each of these is described in the table below.

Informed consent

The issues

- Although the participants may have consented to take part, they may not have been fully informed about the true purpose of the study. This means deception has been used. Deception is sometimes necessary because explaining the true aims of the study sometimes affects the participants' behaviour (demand characteristics) and thus reduces the validity of the research.

- In field studies (e.g. observational research and field experiments), the participants are unaware that they are being investigated. Therefore, informed consent is difficult or impossible to obtain.

- Young children or people with disabilities or impairments may have limited understanding and therefore they may not fully understand much about the research investigation, even if they have given informed consent.

Informed consent

How to deal with these issues

- Presumptive consent involves asking members of the general population who are similar to the participants in the study whether they would consider the research procedures to be acceptable and whether they would be willing to participate in such an investigation.

- Prior general consent involves telling those who volunteer to take part in the research study that they *may* be deceived about the true nature of the study. Only those who agree with this are selected. In this way, participants have given general informed consent, but they do not know the real aims of the study. This is also known as partially informed consent.

- In studies involving children under 16, consent is obtained from the parents or from those *in loco parentis*, which means 'in the place of a parent' (e.g. a carer or a headteacher in a school).

- For participants who have impairments that limit their understanding, the investigator should consult a person well-placed to appreciate their reactions, such as a member of their family.

Deception

The issues

- Deception means lying to the participants, which is wrong. However, some argue that the use of deception is unavoidable at times, and needs to be used to avoid the participants changing their normal behaviour (e.g. demand characteristics).

- If participants have been deceived, they could not have been fully informed and therefore were unable to consent because they did not know the true purpose of the study.

How to deal with these issues

- If deception has taken place, participants should be debriefed at the end of the research study. This means that they should be fully informed about the true purpose of the investigation and told the reason for the deception. They should also be reminded that the information will be kept confidential and that they have the right to withdraw their data from the study if they wish.

- In general, the aim of debriefing is to restore the participant to the state he or she was in at the start of the investigation.

Protection of participants

The issues

- Some studies require that the participants experience some form of physical harm, such as putting their hands into very cold water. The research cannot always fully predict the amount of harm that this may cause to the participants. Psychological harm may also be caused; however, this is more difficult to measure. It may arise if participants are made to experience undesirable feelings (such as embarrassment), especially if other people are involved and/or watching.

- Probing questionnaires or interviews that involve revealing personal information run the risk of provoking negative feelings (such as lowered esteem and worthlessness) and these may have long-term effects.

How to deal with these issues

- The right to withdraw – Participants who consented to take part in the study should also be made aware that they have the right to withdraw from the research at any point, regardless of any payment received, if they become uncomfortable with it. The data gathered about them will then be removed and destroyed.

Protection of participants

- **Stopping the research** – The researcher should look out for any physical or psychological signs (e.g. negative feelings) and stop any situation that may cause harm to a participant. If they see this occurring with a number of participants, they should stop the entire study to prevent any lasting harm to the participants.

- **Participant information** – Participants must be asked about any factors that might pose a risk, such as pre-existing medical conditions, and must be advised of any special action they should take to avoid risk.

Main ethical issues affecting different research methods

RESEARCH METHODS	MAIN ETHICAL ISSUES
Laboratory experiments	**Deception** – Participants may not know the true purpose of the study (reduce demand characteristics) in order to preserve the validity of the study. **Informed consent** – May not be possible for the participant to be fully informed about the true purpose of the study when deception is used.
Field and natural experiments	**Informed consent** – Consent is very unlikely to be obtained if participants are not aware that they are taking part in a study. **Right to withdraw** – Participants should have the right to withdraw from a study at any time. If they do not know they are part of a study, they will not know about this right!
Correlational analysis	**Problem of interpretation** – Published research findings may reveal socially sensitive information (e.g. regarding ethnicity and crime), which could be misinterpreted by the public as a cause-and-effect relationship.
Observations	**Informed consent** – Consent is very unlikely to be obtained if participants are not aware that they are taking part in a study. **Invasion of privacy** – If participants are not aware that they are being observed (especially if observing in non-public setting such as a school), this raises the issues of invasion of privacy.
Questionnaires and interviews	**Confidentiality** – Questions can reveal personal beliefs, opinions and attitudes. If the researcher cannot guarantee confidentiality, this could be an issue. The participant must be told in advance if this is the case.
Case studies	**Invasion of privacy** – The researcher needs to ensure confidentiality. If the researcher cannot guarantee confidentiality, they must tell the participant in advance.

Practice exam questions

1. A psychologist wants to investigate the effects of day-care on the behaviour of young children. He decides to observe a class of children at a day-care centre.

   A. Identify one ethical issue the psychologist will need to consider **[1 mark]**

   B. Explain how the researcher could deal with this ethical issue. **[3 marks]**

3. Some psychological research requires the use of deception.
   Explain one possible way the psychologist may deal with the use of deception. **[3 marks]**

4. Some psychological research requires the recall of painful memories, such as being a witness to a violent criminal act. A possible ethical issue that might arise during this research is the protection of participants from harm. Explain one possible way in which the psychologist may deal with this ethical issue. **[3 marks]**

AQA specification for Topic 7: Research methods: Scientific processes

- Reliability across all methods of investigation. Ways of assessing reliability, test-retest and inter-observer; improving reliability.

- Types of validity across all methods of investigation: face validity, concurrent validity, ecological validity and temporal validity. Assessment of validity. Improving validity.

◆ Introduction

An important aspect when designing a study or a test (e.g. experiment, interview, questionnaire, observations) is to consider the 'reliability' and the 'validity' of the study. There are different ways of assessing the reliability and validity as well as how they can be improved.

◆ Reliability

- **Reliability.** The ability of a study or test to produce consistent results if it were to be repeated.

Experiments

Assessing reliability.

- **Replication.** The reliability of an experiment can be assessed by replication (repeating). Another researcher repeats the same laboratory conditions and procedures as the original study to see whether similar results occur; if so, the experiment is reliable.

Improving reliability.

- **Standardised procedures.** The use of standardised instructions, experimental designs (e.g. use of random assignment and counter-balancing) or the use of a single or double-blind procedure will minimise experimenter bias and demand characteristics, which will help to improve the reliability of experiments. If the results are conflicting, the design of the study will need to be carefully assessed, such as looking at the procedures and material to see whether confounding variables played a part (e.g. experimental bias, demand characteristics).

Questionnaires/tests

Assessing reliability.

- **Test-retest.** To assess the reliability of questionnaires or tests, a test-retest technique is used. The test is given to the participants at a certain time and repeated at a later date with the same participants. If the results obtained at both times are similar, then there is good reliability. This is measured using a correlation test. A strong positive correlation (test score exceeds +0.8) means the questionnaire/test is reliable.

Improving reliability.

- **Rewriting the questions.** If a questionnaire/test produces low test-retest reliability (low correlation score), the researcher will need to check the consistency of specific questions carefully and identify the parts that did not correlate well on the two occasions the test was given. This may require some questions or items to be modified or removed to improve the reliability. Once this is done, a retest is carried out to see if the reliability has improved. If the correlation test score exceeds +0.8, we say the questionnaire/test is reliable.

Observations

Assessing reliability.

- **Inter-observer reliability.** The reliability of observations can be assessed by having two or more observers using the same behavioural category sheet in a pilot study. The observer should watch the same event or sequence of events, and record the data independently. The scores are compared to see if they are similar. If the data from the different observers show a high level of consistency (e.g. +0.8), we say that the observers have high inter-observer reliability.

Improving reliability.

- **Operationalisation.** If inter-observer reliability is low, this may be due to the operational definitions of the behavioural categories not being clear, leading to confusion when recording the data. Inter-observer reliability can be improved by making sure the behavioural categories are clearly operationalised, e.g. swapping the word 'aggression' for 'kicking' as less open to interpretation. Also, the behavioural categories of each targeted behaviour should be self-evident and not overlap with other categories, otherwise, observers may get confused about what category a behaviour may go in. Training the observers in a pilot study in the use of behaviour categories will allow discussions and clarification on the operational definitions of behaviours until inter-rater reliability is achieved (+0.8).

◆ Validity

Validity. Validity refers to how well a study or test measures what it claims to measure (known as internal validity) and the extent to which the findings can be generalised beyond the research setting (known as external validity).

Internal validity

- **Internal validity** refers to the extent to which the actual study or test correctly measures what it claims to measure ("does what it says on the tin", so to speak). The internal validity can be applied to all research methods, although it is commonly applied to experimental design and procedures.

External validity

- **External validity** is concerned with generalisability beyond the research setting in which it was carried out. Below are different types of external validity:

  - **Ecological validity.** Ecological validity refers to whether the findings of a study can be generalised to human behaviour in the real world – everyday life. Studies that examine behaviour in a natural setting (e.g. naturalistic observation) are said to have high ecological validity, while those placed under controlled (artificial) conditions, such as laboratory experiments, are said to be low in ecological validity. This may not be due to the setting (e.g. lab) – it could be the type of task the participant was asked to perform.

  - **Temporal validity.** Temporal validity refers to the ability to generalise the research findings over time. For example, are Milgram's research findings into obedience in the 1960s still valid in today's society?

  - **Population validity (sample).** Can we generalise the findings obtained from the research sample to the wider population or to a different culture? For example, a study used a sample of 15 male university students. Can we go beyond the findings extracted from these students and apply them to other groups in society or populations, such as elderly men or women of any age? A limited sample may not be representative of the general wider population, and therefore may have low population validity.

◆ Assessing validity

Psychologists use a number of techniques to assess internal validity, including face validity and concurrent validity.

- Face validity. You can assess the validity in a simple way by looking at the research (e.g. questions/items/tasks), and judging if it seems to test what is supposed to measure. For example, if a psychologist wants to examine the relationship between IQ and aggression, then all the questions in the test should relate directly to these two concepts and nothing else. If the test appears 'on the face of it' to measure what it intended, then we say it has face validity. Or by simply 'eyeballing' the experiment, researchers can check that it appears to be measuring obedience (for example) or they might even ask an expert to check. This is a very basic form of validity assessment.

- Concurrent validity. When a new psychological questionnaire or test has been developed, its validity is often assessed by comparison with a similar, well-established test that aims to measure the same thing. Both tests are given to the same participants and a positive correlation should exceed 0.8 for validity. For example, to see if an experiment could be considered a valid (and reliable) measure of attachment, we could compare the results to those produced by a standardised, accepted measure such as the Strange Situation. To be valid, the correlation between the performance on the experiment and the existing measure must exceed +0.8.

◆ Improving validity

- Experiments. The most common method to improve the validity of experiments is to use a control group, which acts as a baseline to compare to the experimental group. This allows the researcher to be more confident that changes in the DV were due to the effects of IV in the experimental group. The use of standardised procedures and single or double-blind procedures will minimise the impact of demand characteristics and investigator effect.

- Questionnaires. One way to improve the validity of questionnaires or psychological tests is to include 'lie scales' within the questionnaire. For instance, one form of a lie scale consists of repetitions of the same or closely worded items, to check for consistency of responses. Also, validity can be further enhanced by assuring the respondents that all the data submitted will remain anonymous (confidentiality).

- Observations. Naturalistic observation, particularly the use of covert observations, tends to produce high ecological validity, as there is minimal intervention by the researcher and the participants are unaware they are being observed so they are more likely to behave naturally. The use of electronic devices, such as camcorders and audio recordings, is one way to increase the validity (and reliability) of observational research, as well as ensuring behavioural categories are thoroughly operationalised (behavioural categories are not unclear or overlapping).

◆ The relationship between reliability and validity

- The findings of the research can be reliable, but not valid. A study that consistently produces the same results when it is repeated does not necessarily mean it reflects an accurate picture of what it set out to investigate. For example, a group of students used a questionnaire to investigate the drinking behaviour of their teachers on weekdays. The results showed that one out of 50 teachers said that they drank during the week. Is this likely to be a true reflection of their drinking behaviour? It is possible that the teachers lied on the questionnaire because they were afraid that the students would disapprove of their drinking habits. The students might administer the questionnaire on other occasions and the teachers may continue to lie, thus producing the same false results consistently. Such findings are reliable, but they lack validity because the study failed to find out about the teachers' real drinking habits.

Practice exam questions

1. A psychology teacher wondered whether there was a relationship between internet use and sociability. The teacher decided to investigate this by asking volunteers from the sixth forms of several local schools to keep a diary. Each volunteer recorded in a diary the number of hours spent using the internet over a four-week period. At the end of four weeks, all the participants were given a test to measure their sociability. A high score on this test indicates that someone is very sociable.

    A. Describe how the teacher could have assessed the reliability of this study. **[3 marks]**

    B. What is meant by internal validity? **[1 mark]**

    C. Describe how the teacher could have assessed the internal validity of the sociability test. **[3 marks]**

2. A pilot study has indicated that boys and girls play differently. Boys have been shown to engage more in rough and tumble play (e.g. pushing, hitting) and girls have been shown to engage in more co-operative play (e.g. clapping games, skipping games). A psychologist wished to study the differences between boys' and girls' play in primary schools. She asked the headteachers of several schools for permission to observe children playing. She observed the children from a window and recorded the ways in which boys and girls were playing.

    A. Explain what is meant by the term 'reliability' in the context of this study. **[2 marks]**

    B. Explain two ways in which the reliability of the observations of boys and girls playing could have been improved. **[2 marks]**

    C. Explain how two factors might have affected the validity of this study. **[2 marks + 2 marks]**

AQA specification for Topic 7: Research methods: Data handling and analysis

Quantitative and qualitative data; the distinction between qualitative and quantitative data collection techniques.

- Primary and secondary data, including meta-analysis.

◆ Primary and secondary sources of data

When deciding on their research method (as listed above), psychologists have a choice of using either primary or secondary sources of data. *Primary data* is information that has been collected by the psychologists themselves for their own purpose. *Secondary data* is information that already exists and has been collected, usually by non-psychologists, with quite different purposes in mind to those of psychological researchers. This type of data may then be re-interpreted and re-analysed by psychologists for their own objectives. The table below shows which research methods use primary and secondary sources of data.

Primary sources of data	Secondary sources of data
• Experiments • Interviews • Questionnaires/tests • Observations	• Meta-analysis • Documents

◆ Evaluation

Advantages and disadvantages of using primary data

Strengths

✔ **Control over the research.** A strength of this method is that the psychologist has complete control of their investigation, which means they can collect the information they want rather than using existing information that may not be completely relevant.

✔ **Original data.** A strength of this method is that often no secondary data exists on a particular issue, which means that the psychologist has no choice but to undertake their own research study.

Weakness

✘ **Cost and time.** A weakness of this method is that psychologists may not be able to carry out their own research investigation because doing so can be time-consuming and costly.

Advantages and disadvantages of using secondary data

Strengths

✔ **Quick and cheap.** A strength of this method is that using secondary data is much cheaper and less time-consuming than carrying out your own research. The researcher does not have to spend money or time collecting their own information as it already exists.

✔ **Only source available.** Another strength is that existing secondary sources may be the only option available for psychologists. This is especially true if they are investigating something that happened in the past.

Weakness

✘ **Different purposes.** A weakness of this method is that secondary information is collected by non-psychologists for very different purposes than those that psychologists have in mind. This means that psychologists may find some of the information unsuitable for what they are trying to find out.

Qualitative and quantitative data

Psychologists may collect or use two types of data while carrying out a research study. We call these quantitative and qualitative data.

- Quantitative data. This refers to information collected in numerical form (i.e. numbers), which is often used in statistics (e.g., percentages, averages, tally scores, etc.). Some research methods allow the findings gathered by the study to be easily quantified and expressed numerically. Research methods that collect quantitative data are referred to as quantitative research methods.

- Qualitative data. This refers to information that is collected in written words (and/or audio and video) rather than numerically. The purpose of gathering qualitative data is to provide a rich and detailed account of the participants' meanings, thoughts and experiences, allowing a deeper understanding of what they mean. Research methods that collect quantitative data are referred to as qualitative research methods.

Research methods that collect quantitative data	Research methods that collect qualitative data
Primary sources • Experiments • Structured interviews • Closed questionnaires • Controlled observations	*Primary sources* • Unstructured interviews • Open questionnaires • Unstructured observations
Secondary sources • Official statistics	*Secondary sources* • Diaries, letters, newspapers, magazines

◆ Evaluation

Advantages and disadvantages of using quantitative data

Strength

✔ **Easy to analyse and interpret.** An advantage of quantitative research methods is that they allow the numbers to be quantified and summarised, which makes it easy to analyse and interpret the data and look for patterns or causal links. This allows us to make generalisations about cause and effect in human behaviour; for example, whether the amount of time young children spend playing violent video games leads to an increase in aggressive physical behaviour at school.

Weakness

✗ **Over-simplified.** A disadvantage of quantitative data is that it reduces thoughts and feelings to numbers, which limits a deeper understanding of human behaviour and experiences. Quantitative data cannot explain why people do things, just identify trends or relationships. For example, psychologists may find a relationship between middle-aged men and high levels of suicide, but fail to explain why middle-aged men are more likely to commit suicide than other age groups.

Advantages and disadvantages of qualitative data

Strength

✔ **Deeper understanding.** One advantage of qualitative research methods is that they provide a deeper understanding of human behaviour, such as experiences, values, attitudes and beliefs, that cannot be achieved by quantitative methods.

Weakness

✗ **Time-consuming.** One disadvantage of qualitative research methods is that information gathered is most often in written form, which is difficult to code, analyse, and interpret. Therefore, it is less easy to form conclusions than when using quantitative data.

Meta-analysis

A research method that uses secondary data is known as meta-analysis. This method allows researchers to combine the findings of different studies (with the same research hypothesis and research method) and treat them as though they were one large study, which provides overall results. By pooling data from multiple studies, this allows the researcher to arrive at an overall conclusion about the topic or issue studied.

Strength

✔ **Cheaper.** A strength of using meta-analysis is that it is a cheaper way to conduct your research as you do not have to pay expenses for carrying out an experiment. The results can provide strong evidence for the hypothesis, which means they become more generalisable.

Weakness

✗ **Publication bias.** A weakness of this method is that meta-analysis has a high chance of being prone to publication bias. This is where the researcher collecting the data will pick specific studies that only provide the outcome that the researcher is looking for. Therefore, the data will be biased because it only reflects some of the data and therefore the conclusion drawn may not be valid.

Practice exam questions

1. Outline two problems of using qualitative data in psychological research. **[2 + 2 marks]**

2. Outline two problems of using quantitative data in psychological research. **[2 + 2 marks]**

AQA specification for Topic 7: Research methods: Data handling and analysis

- Levels of measurement: nominal, ordinal and interval.

◆ Types of quantitative data

- The type of data collected will determine the appropriate way to display the data (e.g. a bar chart or histogram) or which *measure of central tendency* to use (i.e. the mode, mean or median). The four different types of quantitative data that can be collected are nominal, ordinal, interval and ratio. They are known as levels of measurement.

- Nominal data – Nominal data involves recording results in frequencies, i.e. how often something occurs. Each result or item can only appear in one category. For example, how many people prefer Coke or Pepsi? Or for example, a teacher may categorise which month each student was born (e.g. March or December).

  Each category is unrelated because you can only be in one category (you can't be born in both March and December), so the data is referred to as non-continuous data (no connection between the scores). You cannot put the results in order or rank or preference (e.g. first, second, third), just in separate categories (often called discrete categories)

  Evaluation: weakness

  > Nominal data is crude (uninformative). This is because it does not tell us much more than the frequency, e.g. how much each person prefers Coke or Pepsi.

- Ordinal data – Ordinal data involves collecting data and ranking the data in some order. For example, we can rank the winner and runners-up in a singing contest in terms of first (Elena), second (Maria), third (Natasha), and so on.

  Evaluation: weakness

  > Ordinal data is more informative than nominal data, but it still fails to be fully informative. This is because it does not tell us the difference between the scores. For example, in a track event it would not tell us the difference in time between the athletes, so we cannot say whether position 2 is twice as fast as position 4.

- Interval data – Like ordinal data, interval data is ranked in order, but this time the distances (or intervals) between each ranked order are equal to each other (standardised). For example, on a Fahrenheit temperature scale, the interval between 70 and 80 degrees is the same as that between 30 and 40 degrees – namely 10 degrees.

  Evaluation: strength

  > ✔ Interval data is an informative and accurate form of measurement as it uses equal measurement intervals. The interval between 70 and 80 degrees is the same as between 30 and 40 degrees – namely 10 degrees

- Ratio data – This is the same as interval data, but for one difference – ratio data has an absolute true *zero point*. The zero point allows comparisons to be made, such as 'twice as much' or 'half as much'. For example, if you ask three students how rich they are, student A may have £100, student B may have £50 and student C may have £25. So, we can say that student A is twice as rich as student B, and four times as rich as student C. This is possible because the scale starts at zero, which signifies nothing (no money). You can see how this compares to interval data by looking at the Fahrenheit temperature example – 0 degrees does not mean no temperature at all, it is not a genuine zero but a *false* zero, just a point on a scale (because there are more temperatures below zero!).

Evaluation: strength

✔ Ratio data is the most informative. You can see how this compares to interval data by looking at the Fahrenheit temperature. For example, in interval data, 0 degrees does not mean any temperature at all, it is not a genuine zero but a false zero, just a point on a scale (because there are more temperatures below zero!).

AQA specification for Topic 7: Research methods: Data handling and analysis

- Presentation and display of quantitative data: graphs, tables, scattergrams, bar charts, histograms.

The exam requires that you are able to:

» Select the appropriate graphs, scattergrams or tables to illustrate quantitative data.

» Interpret and explain what graphs, scattergrams and tables indicate about the data.

◆ Introduction

The information or results collected from a research study is referred to as data (or a data set). The form of the data can either be quantitative or qualitative. Here we concentrate on quantitative data.

◆ Quantitative data

Research methods that tend to produce quantitative data are:

- Experiments (e.g. reaction times in seconds to complete a task).

- Structured observations (e.g. tally scores on helping behaviour).

- Self-report methods (e.g. a 1–4 rating scale of anxiety levels).

◆ Presentation and interpretation of quantitative data

Once a study has been completed, the researcher will have collected a lot of raw data. The next step is to summarise the data in a way that can easily be understood (analysed and interpreted). Quantitative data can be summarised and displayed using descriptive statistics, either numerically (e.g. mean, mode, and median), or visually (e.g. in a graph). They are called descriptive statistics because they describe the findings from the quantitative data.

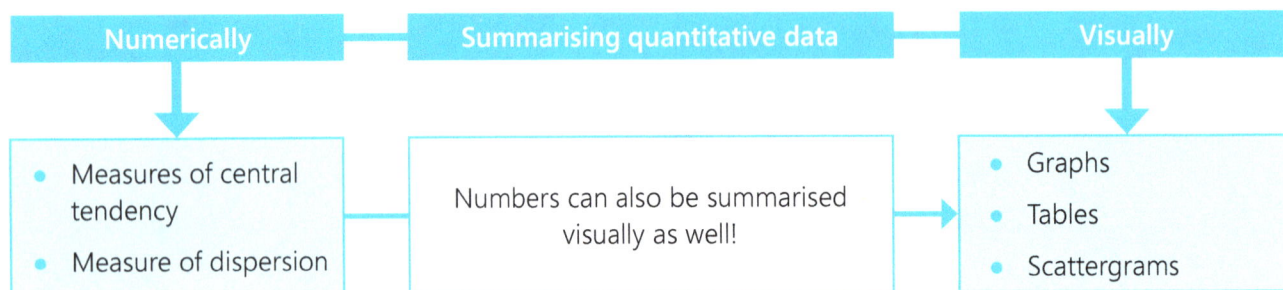

Numerically	Summarising quantitative data	Visually
• Measures of central tendency • Measure of dispersion	Numbers can also be summarised visually as well!	• Graphs • Tables • Scattergrams

◆ Graphs, scattergrams and tables

Graphs and tables are excellent ways of displaying research findings in a clear way that can be easily understood. The type of graph you use will depend on the type of data collected (nominal, interval, etc.). Take care when choosing the right graph to present the data. The wrong graph may present the data incorrectly or be visually misleading. For the exam, you will need to know the following about graphs, tables and scattergrams.

Graphs

Graphs include bar charts, histograms and frequency polygons (line graphs).

Bar charts

- **What are they used for?** Bar charts are used to display *nominal* or *ordinal* data in their various categories. They are also used to show all measures of central tendency (e.g. the mode, mean and median).

- **How is the data presented?** The data is often presented with vertical bars to show individual or groups of scores. The horizontal (x) axis shows the different *categories*. The width of the bars should be the same and there should be a gap between each bar or category. The reason for not letting the bars touch each other is to show that the data is *noncontinuous*. In other words, there is no relationship between each category and the scores are not related. The vertical (y) axis shows the results (frequencies or amounts) of the variable. All the data collected does not need to be presented on the chart – only the most important or average scores.

Figure 21: Bar charts

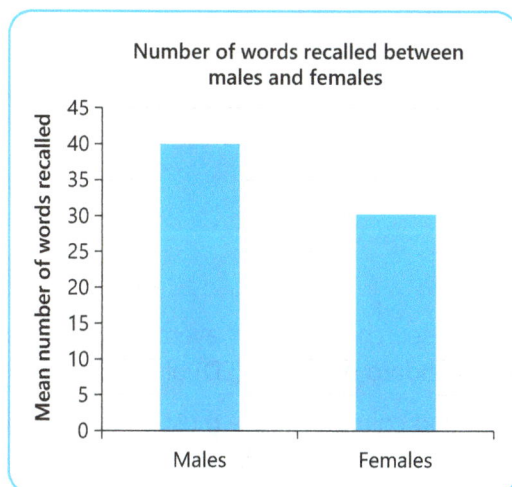

Number of words recalled between males and females

Bar charts are ideal for:	
Type of data:	Nominal, ordinal
Measures of central tendency:	Mean, mode, median

Histograms

- **What are they used for?** Histograms are used to illustrate *interval* or *ratio* data (continuous data such as test scores 0–5, 6–10, 11–15, etc.).

- **How is the data presented?** The *scores or values* are plotted on the horizontal (x) axis and must be arranged in numerical order, usually from smallest to largest (e.g. 0–5 seconds, 6–10 seconds, 11–15 seconds). The vertical (y) axis shows the *frequencies*, that is, how many times something occurs. The bars must all be of equal width but – unlike in bar charts – there must be *no* gaps between the bars. This shows that the data is continuous and related.

Figure 22: Histograms

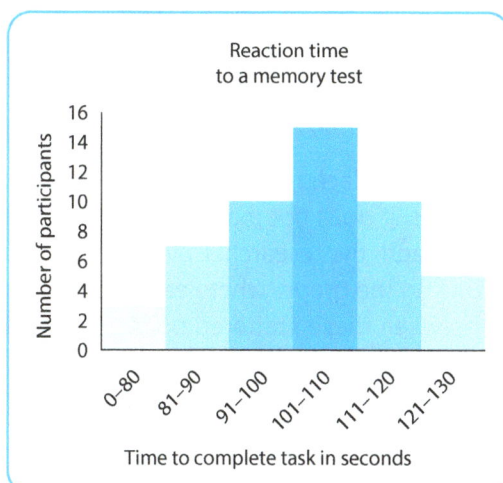

Reaction time to a memory test

Histogram are ideal for:	
Type of data:	Interval/ratio

Frequency polygons (line graphs)

- **What are they used for?** Frequency polygons are an alternative way of presenting the same information as histograms (e.g. for interval and ratio data), but are especially helpful for showing two sets of data at the same time, so that researchers can make comparisons.

- **How is the data presented?** The bars are replaced by lines. The lines connect the *midpoints* of the tops of the bars (as they would appear in a histogram) and when they are joined they form a line.

Figure 23: Frequency polygons (line graphs)

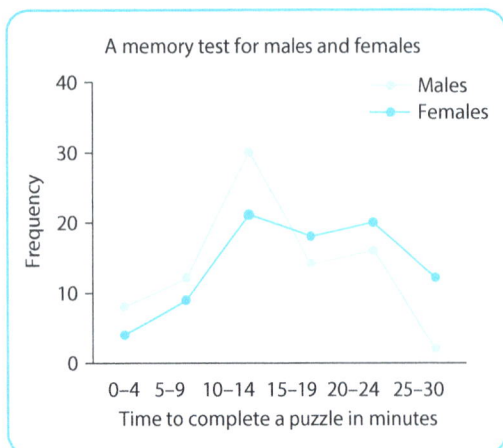

A memory test for males and females

Frequency polygon ideal

Type of data: Interval/ratio

Tables

- **What are they used for?** Tables are used to summarise the research findings of average scores (e.g. medians, means and modes) and to display the range and standard deviation (SD) of scores.

- **How is the data presented?** The data is arranged in tables and columns. There must be a clear title above the table, and each row and column in the table will also need to be clearly labelled.

Figure 24: A table showing the results of memory tests on students at different times of the day

	Memory test scores for students in the morning	Memory test scores for students in the afternoon
Mean score	23	39
Standard deviation	1.7	3.2

Scattergrams

- **What are they used for?** Scattergrams are also known as scattergraphs or scatterplots. They are used to present research findings that produce correlational data. They are plots of the scores of a person or phenomenon under conditions of two different variables, and will show any relationship that exists between them (e.g. poverty and exam results, or stress and heart disease).

- **How is the data presented?** The data from one of the variables is placed on the horizontal (x) axis and the data from the other variable is placed on the vertical (y) axis. It does not matter which variable goes on which axis. Where the two scores intersect (meet) on the graph, the researcher plots a mark. Once all the scores have been placed there will be a scattering of dots on the graph, where each dot represents a single score. The researchers can then draw a best-fit line between these scattered points. Correlational data shows the type of relationship between the two variables as either positive or negative – or no relationship at all. The following scattergrams show the different types of relationship between drinking beer and exam performance.

Figure 24: Scattergrams

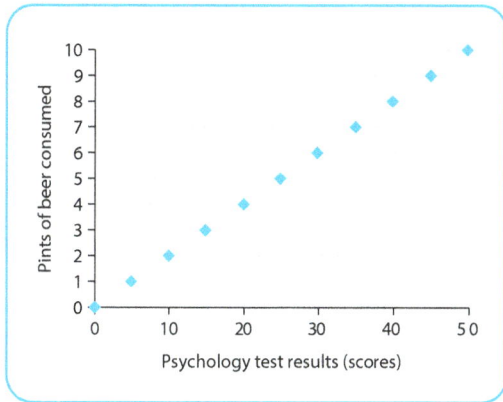

Perfect positive correlaton

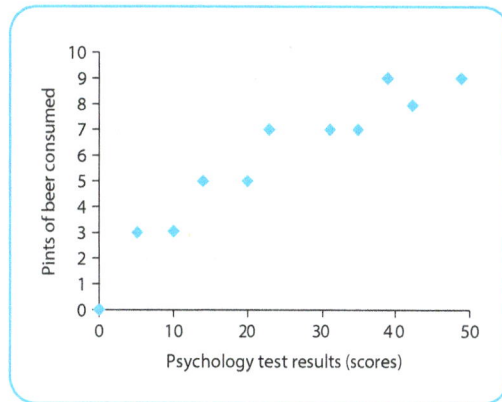

Strong positive correlation

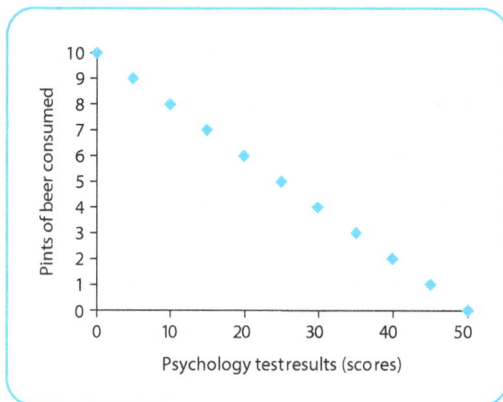

Perfect negative correlaton

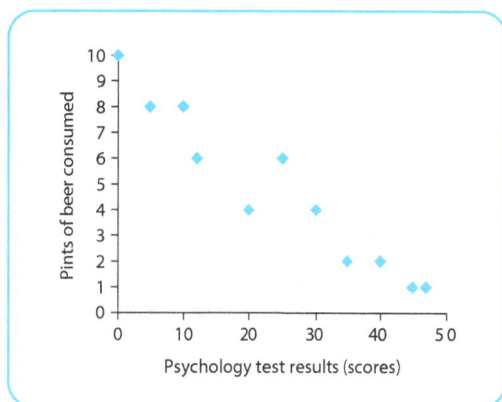

Strong negative correlation

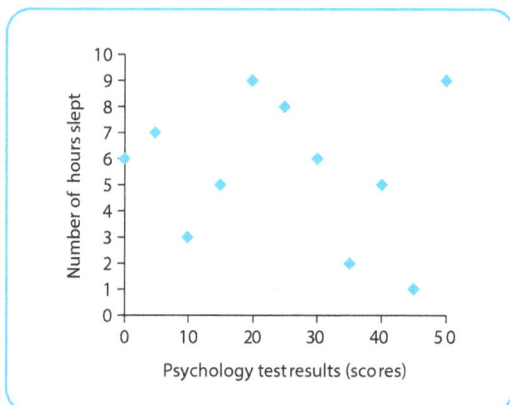

No correlation

Scattergrams ideal for	
Type of data:	ordinal/interval/ratio

1. A psychology teacher, Mr Twirl, was curious to see whether there was a correlation between the time spent on Facebook and exam performance among students. Below are Mr Twirl's findings from 20 students in his AS Level psychology class

The relationship between Facebook and exam performance

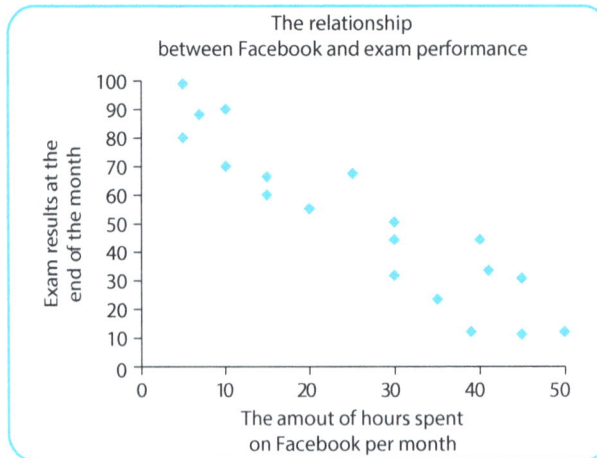

Exam results at the end of the month — The amout of hours spent on Facebook per month

A. Using the scattergram, describe the relationship between Facebook usage and exam performance **[2 marks]**

B. Identify the two variables in this study **[1+1 marks]**

C. Explain one difficulty in drawing a conclusion from this data **[2 marks]**

AQA specification for Topic 7: Research methods: Data handling and analysis

- Descriptive statistics: measures of central tendency – mean, median, mode; calculation of mean, median, and mode; measures of dispersion; range and standard deviation; calculation of range.

◆ Introduction

We can summarise a large set of numbers from quantitative data in two ways. The first is by using a *measure of central tendency* that uses the *mean, median* and *mode* to tell us what the 'average' score is in a set of numbers.

The second way of summarising information is by using a *measure of dispersion* (range and standard deviation). This tells us how far the scores are spread away from the average score.

Summarising quantitative data

Measures of central tendency
(mean, median, mode)

Measures of dispersion
(range and standard deviation)

◆ Measures of central tendency

There are three ways of measuring the average score in a given set of scores: these are mean, median and mode. Together they are called measures of central tendency because they describe the midpoint in a set of numbers. You will need to use the most appropriate measure of central tendency to best sum up the data collected. Using the wrong measure may create misleading results.

Mean

The mean is the most commonly used measure of central tendency. It is the 'average' value of all the scores. To find the mean value of a set of scores, add all the scores together and then divide by the *total number* of scores. The formula can be written like this -

$$\text{Mean} = \frac{\text{total sets of scores}}{\text{number of scores}}$$

For example:
Total sets of scores 5, 8, 9, 3, 12, 16, 17,

$$\text{Mean} = \frac{5, 8, 9, 3, 12, 16, 17}{7}$$

$$\text{Mean} = \frac{70}{7}$$

$$\text{Mean} = 10$$

Evaluation

✔ **Uses all data.** A strength of the mean is that it is the only measure of central tendency that uses all the scores in a set of data.

✘ **Prone to distortion.** A disadvantage of the mean is that the average score can be skewed (distorted) by very high or low scores, which can give a misleading impression of the average score. These extreme scores are called *outliers*. For example, a set of scores obtained for the time taken to do a jigsaw puzzle activity was 5, 6, 5, 7, 5, 6 and 29 minutes. The mean score found for this distribution of scores was 9 minutes. All the participants (apart from one) completed the puzzle in 7 minutes or less, hence the average seems too high if we include the outlier of 29 minutes!

Median

One way to overcome extreme scores in a set of data is to use another method called the median. The median is the *middle score* of a set of data. It is found by placing the scores in order of size, usually from the lowest to highest, and finding the middle number from the list.

For example:

Set of seven scores   17, 5, 8, 9, 3, 12, 16

Arrange them in order, from lowest to highest   3, 5, 8, 9, 12, 16, 17

Count to the middle value (fourth one along out of the seven here), which is 9.

MEDIAN = 9

Some sets of scores will have an even number of scores (the above example had an odd number), which means that there two scores rather than one in the middle position. To work out the median, you would add them together and divide them by two.

For example:

Set of eight scores   19, 5, 8, 10, 3, 12, 16, 17

Arrange them in order, from lowest to highest   3, 5, 8, 10, 12, 16, 17, 19

Count to the two middle values (fourth and fifth along out of the eight here), which are 10 and 12. Add them together and divide by two 10+12 = 22 then 22÷2 = 11.

MEDIAN = 11

Evaluation

✔ **Less affected by extreme scores.** A strength of the median is that it is not affected by outliers (extreme high and low scores). For example, in this set of 13 scores: 2, 2, 3, 3, 3, 3, 4, 4, 5, 5, 5, 6, 47; the extreme outlier is 47. If we include it to calculate a mean, the mean is 7, which does not reflect the typical scores in this range set as 12 of them have a value of 6 or less. However, the median in this set is 4, which seems about right for this set of data.

Mode

Mode refers to the most frequently occurring value (i.e. the most common) in a set of scores. If two values are most frequently occurring, this is called bi-modal. If three or more values are the most frequently occurring, this is called multi-modal. The mode can be used with any type of data, but it is the *only* measure of central tendency that can be used for calculating *nominal* data (e.g. frequency results).

For example:

Set of 11 scores   2, 4, 4, 6, 6, 7, 7, 7, 10, 11, 12
Look for the most frequently occurring number, which is 7. This is the *mode value.*

Now take this set of 14 scores   3, 3, 4, 5, 5, 5, 7, 7, 8, 8, 8, 11, 14, 15
There are two most frequently occurring numbers, 5 and 8. These are the *bi-modal values.*

Evaluation

Strength

✔ **Less affected by extreme scores.** A strength of the mode is that, like the median, it is not affected by extreme scores.

Weakness

✗ **Less accurate.** The weakness of the mode is that it may not reflect the true average of a set of scores, especially if the most frequently occurring scores are either very high or very low. For example, in the set, 3, 3, 3, 34, 37, 42, 44, 50, 55; the mode is 3, however, this does not accurately reflect the otherwise high set of scores.

Which measures to use

The advantages and disadvantages of using the mean, median and mode listed above should give you some indication of why and where you should use them.

Measures of central tendency	Most appropriate type of data	When to use it	Watch out
Mean	Mainly interval and ratio data	When there are no extreme scores (outliers)	The mean cannot be applied to nominal data.
Median	Mainly ordinal data	When there are extreme scores	The median cannot be applied to nominal data.
Mode	Mainly nominal data	When you want to know the frequency (how often something occurs)	The mode is the only one that can be applied to nominal data.

Measures of dispersion

Measures of central tendency may tell us about the average or midpoint score, but they do not tell us much about the rest of the scores. For example, if we look at the table below, the mean scores for Class A and Class B are the same – namely 75 (Grade B). If we only describe the results using a measure of central tendency, it would suggest that both classes are both academically doing really well, when they are clearly not! The test scores for Class B are much more widely spread out than those of Class A. This is where a measure of dispersion is useful. It can tell us how widely the scores are dispersed (spread out) around the average score, or how closely the other scores relate to the average score. This gives a better picture of the overall pattern in the set of data.

Class A test score	Class B test score
73 (grade B)	44 (grade E)
79 (grade B)	56 (grade D)
78 (grade B)	58 (grade D)
70 (grade B)	69 (grade C)
73 (grade B)	99 (grade A)
75 (grade B)	98 (grade A)
77 (grade B)	100 (grade A)
Mean = 75	Mean = 75
Average Grade B	Average Grade B

Finding the dispersion of scores can be done using the *range* and *standard deviation (SD)*. We will look at each one in turn.

Range

The range is the simplest way to work out a measure of dispersion (spread) of a set of scores. It is worked out by subtracting the lowest score from the highest score.

For example:
In Class C, the highest test score is 61 and the lowest is 37. Take the lowest from the highest (61–37) to get the range = 24. Class D's scores are between 87 down to 3, so the range is (87–3) = 84. This shows that the spread of scores in Class D is much greater than that in Class C.

Evaluation

Strength

✔ **Easy to calculate.** The strength of the range is that it is easy to calculate and see the range of scores at a glance.

Weakness

✗ **Distorted by extreme scores.** A weakness of the range is that it can still be distorted by an extreme score, which will be misleading in terms of the real dispersion of scores. For example, in this set of scores – 4, 5, 7, 8, 9, 93 – the range would be 89, which is not a true picture of the scores because the lower scores are clustered together. One extreme score has widened the range disproportionately.

Standard deviation

The standard deviation (SD) is the most precise measure of dispersion. When working out the standard deviation, every score is involved in the calculation by taking the average distance of *each* score from the *mean*. The most important point for your exam is to understand the **significance of the size of the standard deviation.**

- A small standard deviation (number) means the scores are more alike and closer to the mean (average).

- A big standard deviation means the scores are quite different from each other and more spread out from the mean (average). See the table below.

An experiment to investigate the effect of fizzy drink has on memory recall

	With fizzy drink (condition 1)	Without fizzy drink (condition 2)
	27	58
	36	59
	60	60
	60	60
	84	61
	93	62
Mean	60	60
Standard deviation	25.81	1.41

The mean scores in both conditions in the table are the same – therefore we cannot tell whether drinking fizzy drinks has an effect on memory recall. However, the standard deviation tells us a different story. The SD in condition 1 (with fizzy drinks) is larger than condition 2 (without fizzy drinks). This means that the memory recall task had a wider variation of scores from the participants in condition 1 than those in condition 2. We can conclude that some participants performed worse and/or better in the memory recall task after having a fizzy drink than those in condition 2.

Evaluation

Strength

✔ **Sensitive.** A strength of the SD is that it is the most precise measure of dispersion because it uses the spread of all the scores.

Weakness

✗ **Time-consuming.** A weakness of the SD is that it is more time consuming and more difficult to calculate than the range. **Important:** you do not need to know how to calculate SD for the exam.

Practice exam questions

1. A psychologist wanted to find out whether there is evidence that short-term memory fades with increasing age. To test this hypothesis, the researcher carried out a laboratory experiment. In group A, the people were aged between 20 and 40 years. In group B, their age ranged from 60 to 80 years. Both groups were required to learn a list of 20 words (nouns). Then, after a short period of time, they were asked to recall them. The table shows what the researcher found.

Participant	Condition A (20–40 years old) Number of nouns recalled correctly	Participant	Condition B (60–80 years old) Number of nouns recalled correctly
1	14	11	12
2	18	12	13
3	17	13	18
4	15	14	17
5	18	15	4
6	18	16	3
7	12	17	5
8	16	18	14
9	14	19	16
10	13	20	15
Measure of central tendency	15.5		11.7
Standard deviation	2.22		5.62

   A. What measure of central tendency was used in the above data? **[1 mark]**

   B. Explain one strength and one weakness of the measure of central tendency identified in question (1A). **[2+2 marks]**

   C. What does the standard deviation in this study tell us about the data? **[3 marks]**

4. The following scores were obtained in a memory test 10, 15, 12, 15, 14, 13, 49, 11, 14, 12, 47.

   A. Identify and explain which measure of central tendency that would be the most appropriate to use here. **[3 marks]**

3. Explain one strength and one weakness of the measure of central tendency identified in question 2. **[2+2 marks]**

AQA specification for Topic 7: Research methods: Data handling and analysis

Distributions: normal and skewed distributions; characteristics of normal and skewed distributions.

◆ Distributions

Sometimes researchers gather data that tells us about how often something occurs. This is known as frequency data. It is this kind of data that would be plotted on a *histogram* or a *bar chart*. The vertical axis (y-axis) represents the frequency and the horizontal axis (x-axis) represent the item of interest observed. The data displayed on the graph will show some kind of pattern and this provides useful information as it helps us get a better understanding of what is going on. The pattern of the data is called a distribution. Therefore, a 'distribution' is a graph showing frequency data. There are several types of data distributions – see below.

◆ Normal distributions

- A graph that displays normal distribution will show a pattern in the data that is shaped like a bell - a 'bell curve' (diagram below). The 'lump' at the top of the bell is where most of the scores bunch up, the flat ends to the left and the right are where the less common scores spread out.

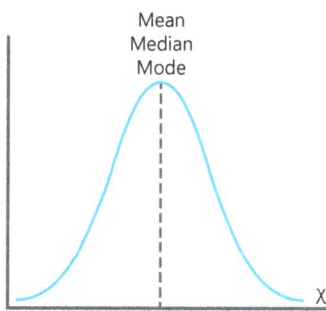

Mean
Median
Mode

The normal bell curve represents perfectly symmetrical distribution

What does this mean?

- In a normal distribution graph, the mean, median, and mode of a normal distribution are identical (or nearly the same) and fall exactly in the centre of the curve – the mid-point at the top. This means most people (e.g., for IQ scores, weight or height) are in the middle. As scores deviate further from the mid-point, they become less frequent giving the distribution a characteristic symmetrical bell shape. These extreme right and left scores from the midpoint are called the 'tails' of the curve, which extend outwards.

- The distribution is symmetrical around the mid-point and the distribution and frequency of scores on the left side match the distribution and the frequency of scores on the right side.

Normal distribution and standard deviation

- All the scores 34% lower or higher than the mean (mid-point) - that's 68% of the total set of scores, are referred to as one standard deviation (1 SD) away from the mean. Being within 1 SD makes the score pretty "normal" statistically speaking. Therefore, for any set of data that is normally distributed, 34.13% (the precise amount) of the people will lie within one standard deviation below the mean and 34.13% will lie one standard deviation above the mean. A total of 68.26% will lie within one standard deviation above or below the mean.

- Two standard deviation (2 SD) means you add another 13.5% lower and 13.5% higher than that (68% + 27%) gives you 95% of all the scores who fall within 2 SD of the mean. Being within 2 SD makes you 'unusual' compare to the mean.

- Then there are the people who fall outside the 95%, the ones in the bottom 2% and the top 2%. These scores are 3 SD away from the mean and count as "very unusual".

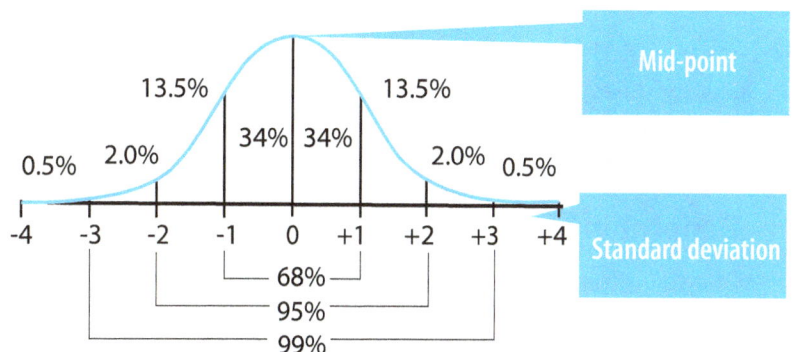

◆ Skewed distributions

- Not all data will result in a perfectly normal distribution. Some scores are not evenly distributed around the mean, which refers to the scores as being a skewed distribution. A skew can be positive or negative.

Negative skew distribution

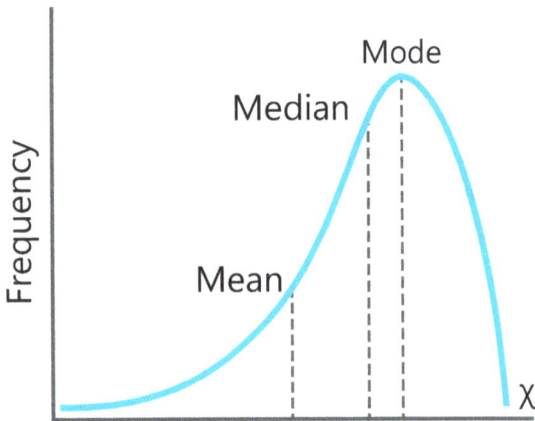

Negative direction

What does this mean?

- Negative skew distribution is when the data is concentrated towards the **right of the graph**, which leaves a long tail on the left.

- Negative skew distribution will contain **more high scores than low scores**. This means many of the scores were higher than the mean compared to a normal distribution. For example, in an exam, many students achieved high scores because the exam may have been too easy, with only a few getting low scores. Therefore, the extreme low scores (outliers) skewed the distribution.

- In a negative skew, the mode is the highest, then the median comes next to the left and the mean is the lowest on the left (if scores are arranged from lowest to the highest).

The 'mean' will be skewed to the left, demonstrating that that mean score in a skewed distribution will not be an accurate reflection of average scores. It will show a low mean score in the test when in fact the real average score was much higher (mode would be a grade B), whereas the mean would be C, for example). The mode is more accurate of the scores.

Positive skew distribution

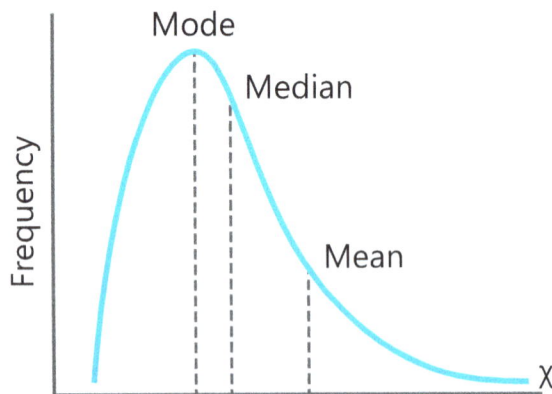

Positive direction

What does this mean?

- Positive skew distribution is when most of the data is concentrated towards the **left of the graph**, which leaves a long tail on the right.

- Positive skew distribution will contain **more low scores than high scores**. This means many of the scores fall below the mean than in a normal distribution. For example, in an exam many students got low scores because the exam may have been too hard, with only a few getting high scores. Therefore, the extreme high scores (outliers) skewed the distribution.

- In a positive skew, the mode is the lowest, then the median comes next to the right and the mean is the highest on the right (if scores are arranged from lowest to the highest).

The 'mean' will be skewed to the right, demonstrating that that mean score in a skewed distribution will not be an accurate reflection of average scores. The mean will show a high mean score in the test, when in fact the real average score was much lower (mode = D, whereas the mean would be B, for example). In this example, the mode is the most accurate of the scores.

General information

- One thing to note with skewed distributions is that they show that the mean is not a very representative score – most scores are either above (i.e. bigger than) or below (i.e. smaller than) the mean. This shows that that mean should not be used as the sole measure of tendency when distributions are skewed.

AQA specification for Topic 7: Research methods: Inferential testing

- Introduction to statistical testing; the sign test. When to use the sign test; calculation of the sign test. **(AS and A-level)**

- Probability and significance: use of statistical tables and critical values in the interpretation of significance; Type I and Type II errors. **(A-level only)**

- Factors affecting the choice of statistical test, including the level of measurement and experimental design. When to use the following tests Spearman's rho, Pearson's r, Wilcoxon, Mann-Whitney, related t-test, unrelated t-test, and Chi-Squared test. **(A-level only)**

◆ Introduction

There are two types of statistics that are used to analyse quantitative data. There are descriptive statistics, which involve *summarising* quantitative data, using charts, graphs, and tables as a measure of central tendency, allowing the researcher to understand and describe the findings from the data. However, descriptive data cannot explain the importance of the results. To determine the significance of the results, the researcher will then need to apply a test called inferential statistics.

◆ Statistical testing

- Once a study has been done, researchers need to analyse the data using statistical tests to see if the results are significant. We use a significance test to determine the probability that the results either occurred by chance/accident or had a real effect. If the results are found to be significant, this means the research hypothesis is true, i.e. there is a difference between the IV conditions (e.g. experimental group and non-experimental) and the effect it had on the DV.

◆ Significance and probability (A-level only)

Significance

The statistical test determines which hypothesis (the null hypothesis or alternative hypothesis) is true, and thus whichever hypothesis we accept means a rejection of the other.

- Significant: If the statistical test shows the result to be significant, this means the null hypothesis is rejected and the research hypothesis is accepted. This means the test shows a very low probability that the findings occurred by chance.

- Not significant: If the statistical test shows the results are not significant, this means the null hypothesis is accepted, and the research hypothesis is rejected. This means there is a probability that the results occurred by chance. Therefore, there is no relationship or difference between the variables of what you were trying to discover.

Note - Null hypothesis means there is 'no difference' or 'no correlation' between the conditions.

Probability

- We can never be 100% sure whether the result of the research did not occur by chance. Psychologists work with 'probability' to determine the likelihood that the 'difference' or 'relationship' occurred by chance. Psychologists use probability levels (referred to as 'significance levels') to determine if the results occurred *by chance or they are real. Significance levels tell us the probability (p) that results are actually significant, that is, beyond the boundaries of chance.

- In Psychology, the generally agreed significance (probability) level to work with is 5%, often written as p=≤0.05 (p= 5%). The means the likelihood of results occurring by chance is equal to or less than 5% (e.g. we are 95% sure the results are true).

- Sometimes, the probability level in psychological research is set at p ≤ 0.01 (p=1%). This is a much stricter level, which means there is a 99% that the results did not occur by chance (or 1% they did occur by chance), giving us greater confidence in the results.

◆ Choosing a statistical test (A-level only)

- The choice of statistical test will depend on three factors concerning your study:

   1. Research hypothesis: Are you testing for a difference or a correlation?

   2. Is the data related or unrelated: How are the participants used in the study?

   3. Levels of measurement: What type of data did you collect: nominal, ordinal, interval, or ratio?

Research hypothesis

When deciding which statistical test to use, you need to determine which type of hypothesis you used – is your hypothesis trying to show a difference or a correlation?

- *Difference.* Some hypotheses are looking for a difference in the two sets of data collected from the two conditions. In an experiment, the researcher manipulates the IV and records the effect it has on the DV. The researcher is therefore looking to see if there is a difference between the two conditions of the IV. Consider the example of Loftus and Palmer's (1974) eyewitness testimony study (see Topic 2: Memory: Exam Notes 5), where the researchers used five different verbs (the IV) to describe a car accident. In this study, there were five experimental conditions (one for each verb) but no control group. For example, in this hypothesis *"teenage females have better memory recall of adjectives than teenage males"*, we are predicting a difference between the two groups (teenage male and female).

- *Correlation.* In a correlational study, the purpose is to see if there is an association (a **link**, not a difference) between the two variables. For example, you may use a questionnaire to see whether there is a correlation between jealousy and the length of a relationship. The suggested correlation would be: the more jealous you are, the shorter your relationship may be – or the less jealous you are, the longer your relationship will last. Here the research is looking for a correlation between two sets of scores.

Is the data related or unrelated to each other?

You will also need to determine if the data collected is from the same person (related data) or from two different people (unrelated data):

- Related data is a repeated measures design - the same participants are used in all conditions.

- Unrelated data is an independent group design - the participants were used in just one condition.

Levels of measurement (type of data collected)

- Nominal data involves recording frequencies – how often something occurs. Each result or item can only appear in one category, e.g. how many people prefer Coke or Pepsi. You cannot put the results in order or rank (e.g. first, second, third place), just separate categories (often called discrete categories).

- Ordinal data involves collecting data and ranking the data in some order, such as finishing positions in an athletic race (e.g. first, second, third place).

- Interval data is ranked in order (like ordinal data), but this time the distances (or intervals) between each ranked order are equal to each other (standardised). For example, on a Fahrenheit temperature scale, the interval between 70 and 80 degrees is the same as that between 30 and 40 degrees – 10 degrees.

Statistical tests for significance

There are different types of statistical tests that are used to determine whether the results obtained from the research are significant or not. They are:

Name of statistical test	The name of the calculated value
Sign test	S
Spearman's correlation	rho
Mann–Whitney	U
Wilcoxon	T
Chi-Squared	X^2
Pearson's	r
related t-test	t
unrelated t-test	t

Use this table to determine which statistical test to use

	Test of difference?		Test of correlation?
	Unrelated design	**Related design**	
Nominal data	Chi-Squared	Sign test	Chi-Squared
Ordinal data	Mann-Whitney	Wilcoxon	Spearman's *rho*
Interval data	Unrelated *t*-test	Related *t*-test	Pearson's *r*

◆ How to determine if your results are significant (A-level only)

- Once you have selected the appropriate statistical test, you can then use it to analyse the set of data from the study. After the calculation, the result from the statistical test will produce a number called the calculated value (or observed value); for example, rho = +0.78. We will use this number to determine if our results are significant or not.

- The calculated value is then *compared* to another number called the critical value. The critical value is found in a statistical table chart called the table of critical values. This determines the probabilities of whether the results are significant or not.

Note for AS and A-level students: For the exam, both AS and A-level students are only expected to be able to work out the calculated value for the **sign test** *(see the next page).*
***A-level students** should also be able to choose the appropriate statistical test and explain their choice.*

How to use the table of critical values

- To find the correct critical value from the table, you must know the following information:

1. Type of hypothesis. Is the research hypothesis a one-tailed hypothesis (directional) or two-tailed hypothesis (non-directional)?

2. Significance level. What is the stated level of significance (probability) selected (e.g. $p \leq 0.05$)?

3. Number of participants. The number of participants used in the study, which is written as **N**. In studies using independent group design, there are two values for N (one for each group of participants: NA and NB). In some tests, such as the t-test and Chi-Squared test, you need to calculate the degree of freedom (df).

Note: The best way to understand statistical tests is to see actual worked examples for each test. Please visit www. psychologyzone.co.uk and download the free PDFs for each worked example.

The degree of freedom (df) is the number of cells in the table, calculated by multiplying (number of rows in your table –1) by (number of columns in your table – 1). For example, if your table has four rows and two columns, the calculation for the df = (4-1) x (2-1) =3. For a two-by-two table (two columns and two rows) , the df is 1. For a three-by-two table, the df is 2.

For the results to be significant, it means you reject the null hypothesis and accept the alternative hypothesis. To see if the study accepts the alternative hypothesis, we examine the critical value.

- For some tests, the calculated value must be equal to or greater than the critical table value.

- For other tests, the calculated value must be equal to or lower than the critical table value.

Remember the 'R'

If there is an 'R' in the name of the statistical test (e.g. Spearman and Chi-Squared), then the observed value should be *greater than* the critical value. If there is no R in the name of the test (e.g. Mann-Whitney and Wilcoxon), then the observed value should be *less than* the critical value.

• See the next page for a worked example of how to use the table of critical values.

◆ The sign test (Both AS and A-level)

As you saw in the tables on page 299, there are different types of statistical tests for significance, depending on the conditions/design of your research methods. One statistical test is the sign test. To use the sign test, your study must have:

• Difference: You are looking for a difference between two sets of data.

• Repeated measures design: The sign test requires two sets of scores from the same person, which can be compared to see if there is a difference (e.g. repeated measures or from matched pairs).

• Nominal data: This is when the data collected falls into a classified category (e.g. Attachment A, B, C, D) and the data is in frequencies (e.g. using a tally system) rather than in scores.

Worked example

A psychologist wants to see if therapy will reduce the levels of depression experienced by people. She asks participants to rate their level of depression by giving a score out of 100 on two occasions, before they start treatment and again after five treatment sessions. These are the results:

Participants	Depressed rating before treatment Condition A	Depressed rating after five treatment sessions Condition B
1	63	58
2	85	22
3	60	33
4	75	78
5	95	75
6	60	60

7	85	46	
8	80	55	
9	90	65	
10	78	72	

STEP 1: Give each pair of scores a plus or minus sign

For each participant's pair of scores, give a plus (+) if the score in column B is greater than the score in column A. Give a minus (–) if the score in column B is lower than the score in column A. Give a zero (0) if the scores are the same (see the completed example below).

Participants	Depressed rating before treatment Condition A	Depressed rating after five treatment sessions Condition B	Depressed rating after five treatment sessions Condition B
1	63	58	–
2	85	22	–
3	60	33	–
4	75	78	+
5	95	75	–
6	60	60	0
7	85	46	–
8	80	55	–
9	90	65	–
10	78	72	–

STEP 2: Find the calculated value

Next, add the total number of plus symbols sign (+) and the total number of minus symbols sign (-).

Ignore all the zeros (same scores).

The calculated value (observed value) is the *total of the less frequent sign*. Give the symbol for the calculated value as 'S'. In this case, $S = 1$ as there is only one +.

STEP 3: Find the critical value

Before you look at the critical values of the sign test, you will need to know the following information:

1. **Number of participants.** Count the number of participants (N) whose scores have changed in either direction (ignore the zeros i.e. scores that remained the same). In the table above, one participant's score remained the same therefore, N=9.

2. **Type of hypothesis.** Identify the type of hypothesis for your study: directional hypothesis (one-tailed test) or a non-directional hypothesis (two-tailed test). In this study, it is a one-tailed hypothesis ("Therapy will reduce the levels of depression experienced by people").

3. **Your chosen level of significance.** The level of significance you could select for your study is usually $p \leq 0.05$ or $p \leq 0.01$. In our study, we will assume $p = \leq 0.05$.

Note: In the exam, you will be told which level of significance to use.

N	One-tailed		Two-tailed	
1	**0.05**	**0.1**	**0.05**	**0.1**
2	–	–	–	–
3	–	–	–	–
4	–	–	–	–
5	–	–	–	–
6	0	-	0	-
7	0	0	0	-
8	1	0	0	0
9	1	0	1	0
10	1	0	1	0
11	2	0	1	0
12	2	1	2	1
13	3	1	2	1
14	3	1	2	1

1. As the study is investigating a directional (one-tailed) hypothesis and the chosen level of significance (probability) is $p = \leq 0.05$, then we select the first column.

2. Now, look down the left-hand column (N) until you reach the appropriate number of participants (which in our case, N=9), then look across the row for N=9 to find the critical value for S which is 1. Compare this with your calculated value of S.

3. The calculated value of the sign test must be **equal to or larger** than the critical value (number shown in in the table), for the **hypothesis to be accepted**.

   If the calculated value is **smaller** than the critical value, then the hypothesis is rejected and the null hypothesis accepted.

4. We know from Step 2 of this worked example (see previous page), that the calculated value is 1. For a one-tailed hypothesis, where $p \leq 0.05$ and N = 9, the table shows that the critical value is 1.

   Since the sign test does not have an "R", then the calculated value should be equal to or lower than the critical value. In this case, both values are the same. This means that we can accept the hypothesis that therapy does have a positive effect on people's level of depression.

This may look complicated but it's an established method for working out whether the results are significant and the hypothesis is accepted.

◆ Type 1 and Type 2 errors (A-level only)

Statistical tests can calculate the probability - but never the certainty - of the results; there is always a possibility the findings were not significant and they occurred by chance. Sometimes the results of statistical tests produce an incorrect decision as to whether to accept or reject the null hypothesis. Possible mistakes based on the results from a statistical test are called Type 1 error and Type 2 error.

- Type 1 error (known as false-positive error) occurs when the null hypothesis is rejected when really it was correct. This can happen even though the statistical test found significant support for the research hypothesis. If this is the case, we have made a Type 1 error. The likelihood of making a Type 1 error is 5% at $p \leq 0.05$ and 1% at $p \leq 0.01$; therefore, it is more likely to occur when $p \leq 0.05$, as there is a larger margin of error, which can lead to wrongly accepting the research hypothesis. When the level of significance is set at 5%, there will always be a one in 20 chance or less that the results are due to chance factors rather than to the influence of the independent variable.

- Type 2 error (known as false-negative error) occurs when the null hypothesis is accepted when really it was wrong to do so. If the statistical test found that the results were not significant when they really were, we have made a Type 2 error. This is more likely to occur when the level of significance is set at $p \leq 0.01$ (1%), as there is a 1 in 100 chance or less that the results were really due to the independent variable rather than chance factors. This is because the margin of error is small, which makes it harder to accept the research hypothesis at $p \leq 0.01$ than it is at $p \leq 0.05$.

Type of errors	Explanation
Type 1 error **Accepting the hypothesis when the null hypothesis is true**	Correction decision should have been… **Do not reject the null hypothesis as it is in fact true**
Type 2 error **Accepting the null hypothesis when the research hypothesis is true**	Correction decision should have been… **Reject the null hypothesis as it is in fact false**

Compromise

Choosing a significance level is a compromise; if we set the significance level to be very strict, such as $p \leq 0.01$, then we lower the chances of making a Type 1 error but increase the risk of making Type 2 error. If we set the significance level $p \leq 0.10$, then we increase the risk of making a Type 1 error. Psychologists work on $p \leq 0.05$ to minimise the risk of Type 1 and type 2 error.

AQA specification for Topic 7: Research methods: Scientific processes

- Reporting psychological investigations. Sections of a scientific report: abstract, introduction, method, results, discussion and referencing.

◆ Introduction

Progress in knowledge depends on communication between researchers. It is therefore important to share the findings with other psychologists. One way to do this is to publish the research (known as 'Research Report') in a scientific journal, where it will be peer-reviewed before publication. To do this, psychologists must follow a certain format when writing up their research report. The purpose of following the correct format is so the researcher can share their findings in a clear and precise manner, so it is easier to understand, which would allow others to repeat the research to check the results. Here is an outline of the format for how to present a psychological research report.

The layout of a psychological research report

The standard format of a research paper in a journal consists of the following elements:

Title: tells the reader what the research is investigating

Abstract: provides the reader with a short summary of the study

Introduction: provides the reader the background literature and rationale of the study

Method: describes how the study was carried out

Results: summarises the findings

Discussion: discusses the findings and their implications

References: informs the readers about all the sources of information the researcher used

Appendices: provide additional material that would interrupt the flow of the research report

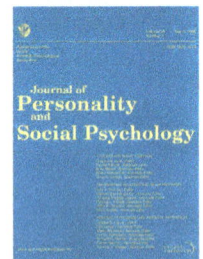

◆ Conventions for reporting psychological investigations

Title

A research report begins with a title page. This needs to be a clear and precise description (usually 12-15 words) about what the research is investigating. This is important because anyone who reads it will know exactly what the report is about before they decide to read further.

Abstract

This is a short summary of the whole study (about 150 to 200 words). The abstract covers the aims/hypothesis, introduction, method/procedures, results and conclusion. Although the abstract appears first, the author usually writes it last, after all the other sections have been written.

Introduction

The introduction is a literature review of theories, concepts, and previous research studies, including the issues surrounding this topic.

The purpose of the introduction is to explain where your hypothesis comes from (i.e. it should provide a rationale for your research study). This section should follow a logical progression, using a funnel technique (inverted triangle). It starts off broadly, with theories and studies surrounding the topic. It then narrows down looking at precise studies related to your study. This then leads to the aims and hypothesis of the study.

Methods

The method section is where the researcher describes how they conducted the study. It should be clear and detailed enough that other researchers could replicate the study by following your 'recipe'. One way to improve clarity is to split the method section into three or four sub-sections: Design, Participants, Materials/Stimuli and Procedure.

Design - This states the chosen research method used: experimental or non-experimental (survey, observation, content analysis, or correlational analysis). If an experiment was carried out; it will need to state the conditions (e.g. experimental and control group) and how the participants were assigned to the different groups - the experimental design used (i.e. repeated measures, independent group design or matched pairs). This sub-section needs to state clearly how the variables were manipulated and measured and what controls were in place (e.g. standard instructions; random assignment; counter-balancing; double-blind technique; environment; time of day).

Participants - This section should provide information about the participants, such as the sampling technique and recruitment used (e.g. advertisement for a volunteer sample), and the number, age and breakdown of gender. It may also be appropriate to describe where the research was conducted and from what country the participants came.

Apparatus/Materials - In this sub-section, the researcher includes the materials they needed in order to carry out their research. Examples of apparatus or materials are: computers, video/audio stimuli, consent forms, standardised instructions, tasks, response sheets, questionnaires, interview schedules, or observation schedule.

Procedure - This section of the report describes a step-by-step procedure for how the investigation was carried out, what the participants did, and in the order in which it happened. Sufficient details need to be provided so other researchers can replicate the study. You will need to include where it took place and any instructions which were given to the participants before (e.g. consents form), during (e.g. standardised instructions) and after (e.g. debriefing) the study.

Results

This section is where the researchers present their results, normally as a summary of data. The data typically includes *descriptive statistics*, where the data is summarised in appropriate tables, averages, and graphs; and *inferential statistics*, where the researcher has used a statistical test to determine the significance of the results and whether their hypothesis has been accepted or rejected.

Discussion

The discussion mainly explains what the results show. This covers a number of elements (although they are not usually organised into sub-headings such as below)

(a)   *Summary of findings.* Key findings are written out here (not in statistical form) and provide a clear answer, whether the aims and hypothesis of the study are supported or rejected by the results. The researcher also provides an explanation of what the findings show and why they occurred (regardless of whether the hypothesis is accepted or rejected).

(b)   *Relationship to previous research.* The researcher compares the findings to other research studies mentioned in the introduction. They also explain the reasons for any differences in results to findings from other previous studies (e.g. difference in design used).

(c)   *Relationship to previous research.* The researcher compares the findings to other research studies mentioned in the introduction. Reasons why differences in results to findings from other previous studies are explained here (e.g. difference in design used).

(d)   *Limitations and modifications.* This is followed by a discussion of the study's limitations by looking at any aspects of the methodology and design that may have affected the validity of the study (e.g. didn't understand the task, lack of controls, poor sampling); and these could be corrected for future studies.

(e)   *Implications.* Finally, there is some discussion of the practical and/or theoretical implications of the research. For example, how can the findings be used in real life? Or, have the findings contributed further knowledge to this topic?

References

The final section is a reference list. This includes the full details of any journal articles, books and websites that are mentioned in the report. This is very useful for those reading the report, as they may be interested to extend their reading to the articles and books indicated by the researchers who wrote the paper.

Examples

Book references take the following format: surname(s) of the author(s) followed by their initials, year published, title of book (in italics), place of publication, and publisher.

Dollard, J. and Miller, N.E. (1950). *Personality and Psychotherapy.* New York, McGraw Hill.

Journal references take the following format: surname(s) of author(s), followed by their initials, year of publication, article title, journal title (in italics), volume/issue number, page range.

Fisher, R.P., Geiselman, R.E., and Amador, M. (1989). Field test of the cognitive interview: Enhancing the recollection of actual victims and witnesses of crime. *Journal of Applied Psychology*, 74, 722–727.

Appendices

An appendix is for additional material that would interrupt the flow of the research report if it were presented within any of the major sections. For example, in the appendices, the researcher would place things like raw data, calculations, standard instructions, lists of stimulus words, questionnaires, observation schedules, and so on.

1. A psychologist was interested in testing a new treatment for people with eating disorders. She put up adverts in several London clinics to recruit participants. Thirty people came forward and they were all given a structured interview by a trained therapist. The therapist then calculated a numerical score for each participant as a measure of their current functioning, where 50 indicates excellent, healthy functioning and zero indicates a failure to function adequately. The psychologist then randomly allocated half the participants to a treatment group and half to a no-treatment group. After eight weeks, each participant was re-assessed using a structured interview conducted by the same trained therapist and given a new numerical score. The trained therapist did not know which participants had been in either group. For each participant, the psychologist calculated an improvement score by subtracting the score at the start of the study from the score after eight weeks. The greater the number, the better the improvement.

Table 1   Median and range of improvement scores for the treatment group and for the non-treatment group

	Treatment group	Non-treatment group
Median	10.9	2.7
Range	2.1	0.8

The psychologist noticed that female and male participants seemed to have responded rather differently to the treatment. She decided to test the following hypothesis:

> Female patients with an eating disorder will show greater improvement in their symptoms after treatment with the new therapy than male patients.

She used a new set of participants and, this time used self-report questionnaires instead of interviews with a therapist.

A. Imagine that you are writing up the report for this study.
   What is the purpose of the introduction section of a report?   **[2 marks]**

B. Imagine that you are the psychologist and are writing up the report of the study.
   Write an appropriate methods section that includes reasonable detail of the design, participants, materials and procedure. Make sure that there is enough detail to allow another researcher to carry out this study in the future.   **[10 marks]**

AQA specification for Topic 7: Research methods: Scientific processes

- The role of peer review in the scientific process.

◆ Key terms

- Peer review (also called 'refereeing'). Peer review is a process whereby a scientist submits their research paper prior to publication, to be critically evaluated by other scientists (hence 'peers') who are experts in the area. The aim is to ensure the quality of the piece of research in terms of research design and validity, as well as the contribution to scientific knowledge it makes.

- Journals. Scientific journals are like magazine publications that publish new research studies that have been peer-reviewed. They may be published weekly, monthly or less frequently. There are thousands of different journals that specialise in different academic disciplines (psychology, physics, chemistry, etc.) and sub-disciplines (e.g. in psychology: *Journal of Personality and Social Psychology, Journal of Cognitive Psychology and Journal of Social Psychology*). Journals are read mostly by practising academic researchers, rather than the general public.

◆ Introduction

Scientific knowledge can only progress if the researchers share their findings with one another and with the general public. Therefore, the final step in the scientific investigation is to write up a concise summary of the study and its findings (See Figure 26 below.) and submit the research article to a journal for publication. Scientific journals represent the most vital means of disseminating (widely circulating) research findings to the scientific community. When articles are submitted to scientific journals, they go through a demanding process known as peer review, whereby other scientific experts in the same field critically evaluate the study's design, data analyses and conclusions, as well as its contribution to scientific knowledge and theory. The sharing of research with other academic peers in the scientific community is an important part of this scientific process as it is a form of scientific 'quality control' before new knowledge is validated. The intention of peer reviewing is to ensure that any research conducted and published is of high quality. It is generally agreed that that journal articles published after a process of peer review have greater merit than those published in journals not subject to peer review.

Figure 26: The layout of a psychological research report

The standard format of a research report in a journal consists of the following elements

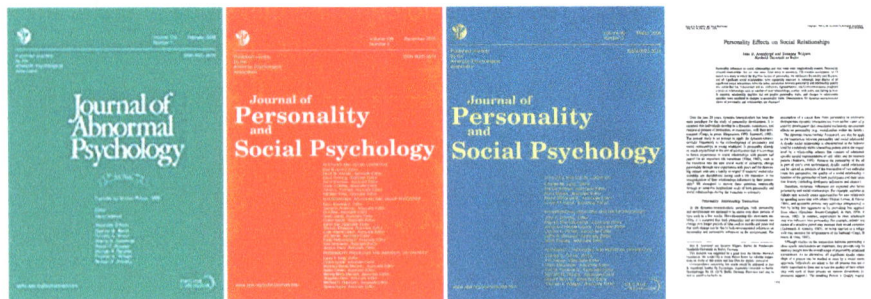

Author	Method
Title	Results
Abstract	Discussion
Introduction	References

◆ How the peer-review process works

- After a researcher has conducted a study, they document the details as a research paper (article) and then submit this to the editor of the appropriate scientific journal in which the researcher wishes to publish it.

- The editor of the journal then selects two or three researchers, who are experts in the field covered by the study. They independently review the research to see if it is worthy of publication in the journal.

- Generally, the editor will remove any personal information about the author, such as his or her name, so the reviewers do not know the identity of the submitting researcher. The submitting researcher will not learn the identity of those doing the peer review either, in order to reduce any form of bias or prejudice.

- The reviewers independently critically assess the quality of the research paper, to ensure that the study is methodologically sound (i.e. its design, analysis and interpretation of the data collection, and written quality). The reviewers provide feedback to the editor, who makes a decision whether to:

    1. Immediately accept the research paper for publication (incredibly rare)

    2. Request that the author 'revise and resubmit' the article based on the reviewers' comments

    3. Reject the article (e.g. due to errors, poor research design or poorly interpreted results).

    The editor, using the feedback provided by the reviewers, will decide whether the research article should be *accepted* for publication, or if the article requires *revision* (e.g. poorly written, clarification or further detail required) prior to publication. The researcher then has an opportunity to change or improve the research paper before it is approved for publication. Alternatively, the research paper may be *rejected*.

◆ Why peer review is important in the research process

Peer review is an important part of this scientific process because it provides a way of checking the overall quality of the research, helping to ensure that poorly conducted studies do not make it into the scientific literature. The reviewers will assess the research paper by looking at:

- **Quality of the research.** It is very unlikely that the researcher will have spotted every mistake, so asking other academic to review it increases the probability that weaknesses will be identified and addressed. The reviewers will scrutinise the quality of the research and the way it was reported (language), in order:

  - To look at the design of the study to ensure adequate controls have been used to eliminate extraneous variables as far as possible.

  - To see if potential sources of bias may have entered the research (e.g. the method used to collect data). If there are weaknesses in the design, then the findings and conclusions would lack validity.

  - To identify any ethical or sampling issues – whether the sample was small or was based on a small part of the general population (e.g. gender, ethnicity, or social class).

  - To assess that the data has been correctly analysed and accurately reported.

  - To assess the interpretation of the findings and the appropriateness of any conclusions drawn from the study.

- **Peer-reviewed has higher integrity.** The peer-review process is a major strength of a scientific approach because it helps to ensure that any research paper published in a reputable journal will be viewed with high integrity, and it reduces the likelihood of publishing erroneous findings. This means the study will be taken seriously by other researchers and the public.

- **Replication.** Replication is another way of validating a research study. Studies published in journals allow other researchers to replicate the study to verify that similar results are recorded. It is possible that the researcher has made errors in their study or, in some (rare) cases, may have deliberately falsified the results (i.e. fraud), which may not have been picked up during the peer-reviewing process. If a study has been replicated by other researchers and the findings are supported, the scientific community will have greater confidence in the results because they are viewed to be valid and reliable.

◆ Evaluation

✗ **Publication bias.** One criticism of the peer-review process is that it tends to favour studies that have positive (significant) results and are therefore more likely to be published in a journal, than those studies with findings that are non-significant. This selective form of publication gives a misrepresented understanding of the topic as it tends to ignore any research with non-significant results.

✗ **Bias in peer review.** One of the weaknesses of peer reviewing is that peer reviewers may have their own biases. For example, the reviewers may be prejudiced against studies that contradict their own research or views, and therefore less likely to give approval for submission for publication (especially if the reviewers are to remain anonymous). Or they may be biased towards publishing studies in support of their own research or views. However, using multiple reviewers is supposed to balance out this form of bias.

✗ **Peer reviewing can be inconsistent.** A weakness of peer review is that it has been accused of being an inconsistent process because the comments provided by the independent reviewers can be so different from each other. They can even differ on whether or not the article should be published. This is because the review process is based on the subjective interpretation of the reviewers. The low reliability of peer reviewing and the low level of agreement among reviewers about the same research paper, mean that many have questioned the effectiveness and usefulness of peer reviewing.

Practice exam questions

1. Outline what is meant by the term 'peer review' in psychological research. **[2 marks]**

2. A research paper was subjected to peer review before it was published in a journal. Explain why peer review is important in psychological research. **[5 marks]**

3. Explain two criticisms of peer review in psychological research. **[3 marks + 3 marks]**

AQA specification for Topic 7: Research methods: Scientific processes

- Features of science: objectivity and the empirical method; replicability and falsifiability; theory construction and hypothesis testing; paradigms and paradigm shifts.

◆ Key terms

- **Science:** The pursuit and application of acquiring valid knowledge and understanding of the natural and social world using the scientific method.

- **Scientific method:** The research process that scientists follow to gather valid and reliable knowledge; by observing a phenomenon, formulating a testable hypothesis, collecting data using empirical research and drawing a conclusion from the data.

  As a note, 'scientific method' is not to be confused with 'scientific methods' (plural), which refers to the different 'tools' used (e.g. experiments, observation, questionnaires, correlational analysis) to collect data.

- **Objectivity:** A view that scientific research and evidence must be free of (not influenced by) the researcher's own private values, opinions, expectations, and bias.

- **Empirical method:** (or empirical research) is the view that data collection can only be obtained based on what is observable through our senses (e.g. through experimentation and observations).

- **Replicability:** (replication) is being able to repeat a study in exactly the same manner as the original study to see if similar results are found.

- **Falsification principle:** Any hypothesis/theory that is tested must have the ability to be proven wrong using empirical methods.

- **Hypothesis testing:** As the name suggests, this means testing the hypothesis by designing an empirical research study to examine whether it is right or wrong (falsifiable) as indicated by the data collected.

- **Theory construction:** refers to how theories are developed and tested through the scientific method (inductive and deductive approach) in order to explain an observed phenomenon.

◆ Definition and goals of science

- **Science** is the pursuit of acquiring credible knowledge and understanding of the natural and social world using the scientific method. The **scientific method** is a particular research process (procedure) that scientists follow to gather valid and reliable knowledge based on observable, measurable evidence. For disciplines such as biology, physics, or psychology to be classified as a 'science', the scientific method must be applied when gathering knowledge.

Psychology is generally viewed as a science as it attempts to study behaviour (actions and responses) and mental processes (thoughts and feelings) using the scientific method. Many of the topics that you have studied at AS and A-level have been investigated using the scientific method (memory, stress, relationships etc.).

Below are the four goals that the psychologist as a scientist (and all scientists) aims to achieve when studying behaviour and the mind.

- **Description** – The first goal of science is to *describe* the phenomenon observed by giving an account of it by naming, classifying, identifying or detailing what is being observed. In terms of psychology, the researcher may attempt to describe the behaviour and mental processes they are interested in. For example, they may have noticed that some infants display clingy behaviour towards their mothers while others do not.

- Explain – The next goal of science is to be able to *explain* the phenomena (the 'why' question). In terms of psychology, the researcher attempts to explain the causes of behaviours and mental processes – why this is happening. For example, Mary Ainsworth (1978) suggested that infants who display clingy behaviour towards their mothers have an insecure attachment (i.e. emotional insecurity), because the mother has provided inconsistent or neglectful care towards the infant (known as the *maternal sensitivity explanation*).

- Prediction – Once explanations are given, scientists can then go on and attempt to *predict* (hypothesise) when this phenomenon is likely to occur, and under what conditions/context. For example, psychologists can predict when an insecure child-mother attachment is likely to occur (e.g. infant or mother is hospitalised, the death of the mother, institutional care, day-care and so on). They can also predict that insecure attachment may cause emotional problems later in life (e.g. poor relationships in adulthood) as predicted by Bowlby (1951).

- Control – Finally, if the scientist can predict an event, they can then move onto the next stage – the ability to *control* that phenomenon, what causes something to occur. In the context of psychology, 'control' means manipulating/altering certain factors or conditions that affect the behaviour in order to bring about the desired outcome. The aim is to bring an improvement in the quality of life in humans. For example, we can 'intervene' in the quality of parenting by offering parenting intervention programmes aimed at improving the infant-mother attachment relationship.

◆ The major features of science

For a discipline such as biology, physics, or psychology to be classified as a 'science' the scientific method of research must be applied when gathering knowledge. Below are the main features of the scientific method.

Objectivity

- Scientists are required to be *objective* when carrying out research. This means that the researcher's own private values, opinions, emotions, expectations, political bias, and religious views should not influence or contaminate the research at any stage (from beginning to end). The researcher must remain 'unbiased' and 'neutral' in the research process. This means that any theory or explanation that has been carried out in an objective manner will be trusted more than research that is subjective or biased.

Example of objectivity

Psychologists can attempt to be objective when conducting research. For example, they can use strategies such as the double-blind procedure in experiments, when the researcher and the participants are both kept in the dark about the true aim of the experiment in order to eliminate any possible bias and expectations (whether 'intentional' or 'unintentional') the researcher may have. The use of standardised instructions and procedures in the study means all the participants are instructed in the same way and tested under the same conditions; again the psychologist is striving for objectivity. In the process of sampling, the psychologists can select research participants using a computer program to generate a random sample, to avoid biasing factors (age, gender, beauty, friends, etc.). Researchers usually make their measurements with instruments (e.g. psychological tests, questionnaires, content analysis and observational techniques - behavioural categories) in order to maintain objectivity.

Empiricism

- *Empiricism* is the essential element of the scientific method. Empiricism basically means that the information collected (e.g. data) to develop/support a theory can only be obtained directly from our senses. Empirical methods refer to the type of methods used to collect empirical evidence such as experiments (lab, field, natural), observational techniques (naturalistic, controlled), questionnaires, interviews, psychological tests and case studies. The use of empirical methods is important in the scientific research process because other researchers can repeat the study to check the reliability or validity of the findings. This means all other information that is based on speculation, intuition, reasoning, common sense, belief, faith old wives' tales is excluded as unscientific!

Example of empiricism

Most of the studies you have learnt in Psychology are based on collecting empirical evidence. For example, in the topic on Memory, the Peterson and Peterson (1959) experiment on duration (how long information remains in short-term memory (STM) without verbal rehearsal) collected data from the participants' test, which helped them draw conclusions about the duration in STM. Another example is Ainsworth's (1978) Strange Situation study where she collected data based on observations to test and classify the different types of attachment that exist between a mother and infant. However, not all psychology theory is based on empiricism. If you recall, the psychodynamic explanation (Freud's theory) for psychopathology is based on concepts such as the 'unconscious', 'ego', 'superego' and 'oral stage' which cannot be tested either by observation or experimentation. This makes Freud's theory unscientific because it is not supported by empirical evidence.

How do psychologists collect empirical evidence?

Psychologists can investigate human behaviour empirically through collecting data on people they are researching. The data gathered is classified as empirical evidence. Data is collected via the different research methods and techniques such as observational techniques, experimentations, interviews, questionnaires and psychological tests. Some empirical evidence may be directly observable to the researcher such as when carrying out observational studies or experimentation (and quantitative data is collected, e.g. scores). At other times, human behaviour may be 'invisible' to the researcher — not directly observable to our senses. So, the researcher may use a questionnaire to collect data on a person's preferences, attitudes and beliefs that would otherwise be indirectly observable to the psychologists.

Replicability

- Another key feature of the scientific research method is *replication*. That is the ability for another researcher to repeat a study in exactly the same manner as the original study to see if similar results are found. This means all the details of the original study need to be clearly reported (e.g. procedures and results). Replication allows us to see if the original findings were deliberately manipulated by the researcher (fraud) or the results were a one-off. More importantly, replication allows us to see if the results are consistent (i.e. reliable). If the repeated findings are reliable this would give validity to the theory they support. If a study cannot reproduce the same result then the theory may have little value. Therefore, research findings must be replicated before they are incorporated into the body of scientific knowledge.

- Some research methods, such as controlled laboratory experiments, are easier to replicate than others. That is why the findings from laboratory experiments tend to be more reliable. It is more difficult to replicate a study that is carried out in natural settings, such as in the field, or through natural experiments and naturalistic observations because it is difficult to achieve the same conditions as in the original study. The results can therefore be unreliable in these types of research methods.

Example of replication

The research findings into the capacity of short-term memory (STM) suggest that we can hold between five and nine items. This is because the studies were based on laboratory experiments, which meant the original study could be replicated by other researchers, using the same experimental conditions and procedures to see if they got similar results. Their results were indeed similar, proving that this explanation of the capacity of short-term memory is valid.

Falsification principle

- Another main feature of science is the *falsification principle*. Karl Popper (1902-1994) argued that for a theory to be classified as 'scientific', it must meet the criteria of falsification. This means the theory must be capable of being proved wrong (falsified). Scientific research requires that any theory/hypothesis that is tested must always have the 'ability' to be incorrect empirically (through observation or experimentation). Any theory that cannot be proven wrong empirically does not meet the criteria of science and therefore is not classified as scientific knowledge. Falsification is important as it allows for the theory to be modified, revised and improved upon, which is a hallmark of good scientific practice.

Example of falsification

For example, we can test the hypothesis that 'all ravens are black' empirically. If, however, we find a 'white raven', we can challenge this statement and say it is not a scientific truth, the hypothesis has been falsified. The point is not whether all ravens are black or not, but the fact that the hypothesis met the criteria of the falsification principle through empirical observation. Some critics argue that the study of parapsychology is a pseudoscience (not real science) because many of the explanations and research evidence are beyond being falsified. For example, a psychic who is asked to demonstrate his powers in a controlled laboratory setting and subsequently cannot do so may offer numerous explanations, such as the scepticism of the researchers interferes with the 'psychic forces', or the time of the day is wrong, or the subject was just having a bad day, etc. The psychic wins either way. His powers are proven when he demonstrates evidence of psychic ability, but his powers are not disproved when he does not. This inability of some psychical research to be proven wrong, under Popper's definition, would be deemed unscientific knowledge.

Consider Freud's theory about repression. The assumption is that psychological problems (e.g. depression, neurosis) of adults are rooted in childhood trauma. If the adult can recall and describe the childhood trauma, then Freud's theory will conclude that his or her current problems developed because of that early trauma. If the adult cannot recall any trauma, then the theory concludes that he or she has repressed the events into his or her unconscious mind. This hypothesis cannot be proven wrong.

◆ Theory construction

The main purpose of scientific research is to collect data to *construct* (develop) theories, as well as to continue to test existing theories in order to strengthen, modify or reject them. A theory is a set of inter-related (connected) explanations of a phenomenon that has been observed. Theories can be constructed in two ways through the processes of *inductive* research and *deductive research*. In reality, both approaches work together in a complementary manner in theory construction and testing. With inductive research, initial observations are made and a theory is developed from them, whereas a deductive process generates a hypothesis/theory, which is then tested by experiments and observations.

Inductive research

The inductive approach puts theory construction at the end of the research process.

Step 1:   **Observation** – Initially, a scientist observes a specific phenomenon where a pattern or trend has been identified.

For example, a scientist finds that if a particular part of the brain is stimulated with electrodes the person often experiences an 'out-of-body sensation', i.e. seeing themselves while floating above the ground.

Step 2:   **Carry out study** – The next stage is for the scientist to carry out a study to collect data on the observed phenomenon using empirical methods. The scientist will analyse the results to see if they can find a pattern or trend in the data.

For example, the scientist collects data from case studies, questionnaires and interviews with patients who have an out-of-body experience when a specific part of the brain is stimulated.

Step 3:   **Develop theory** – If enough information/data is accumulated to demonstrate a pattern or trend, then the scientist will construct a theory to provide an explanation for the observed phenomenon. If the data does not support the theory, the theory is rejected or modified.

For example, out-of-body experiences are not real and can be explained by the malfunctioning of electrical activity or malfunctioning of the temporal-parietal junction (TPJ) in the brain.

Inductive research is particularly useful when psychologists are beginning to investigate a new area where no existing theory has been developed. The inductive process provides a theoretical framework that can, if appropriate, be investigated further using the deductive approach (see below), which is more akin to theory testing than theory construction.

The inductive approach to theory construction

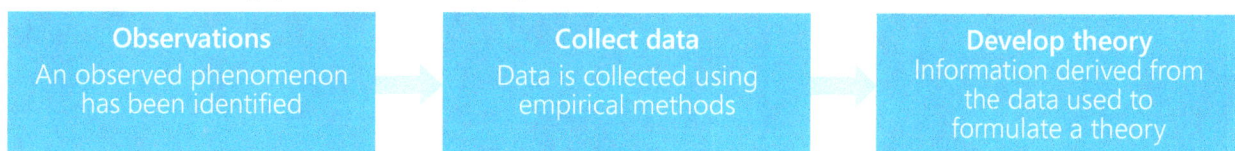

Observations	Collect data	Develop theory
An observed phenomenon has been identified	Data is collected using empirical methods	Information derived from the data used to formulate a theory

Deductive research

Deductive research (known as the *hypothetico-deductive approach*) is recognised as the 'scientific method' of research investigation. The deductive approach puts theory construction at the beginning of the research study. The researcher then investigates by formulating a *hypothesis* derived from a theory that they can test. Initially, the theory may be an existing theory that is based on research carried out by others or it may have developed through the inductive process, by observation. Either way, hypothesis testing allows the validity of the theory to be strengthened, or the theory to be rejected. It also allows the theory to be tested further, under different conditions, enabling us to refine and revise the theory and expand our scientific knowledge.

Step 1:   **Theory development** – A theory is formulated based on observations of a particular phenomenon—a pattern or trend has been identified, or an aspect of an existing theory is being tested based on previous research studies.

Step 2:   **Hypothesis testing** – The scientist then formulates a hypothesis that is derived from the theory. The hypothesis makes a prediction about what will happen in a particular situation.

Step 3:   **Carry out study** – The scientists then carry out a study (using empirical methods) in which the hypothesis is testable and falsifiable.

Step 4: Draw a conclusion – If the results support the hypothesis (assuming replication has been achieved and the study was designed well), then the scientists develop a new theory or strengthen or modify an existing theory to accommodate the new findings. If the results do not support the hypothesis, this can lead to the theory being challenged (rejected) and an alternative theory being provided.

The research process does not have an end. When the results support the hypothesis, additional hypotheses are developed to test the theory further under different conditions. If new supporting evidence is found, the theory is modified and further hypothesis testing is carried out, and so the whole process is repeated again and again—in a cycle.

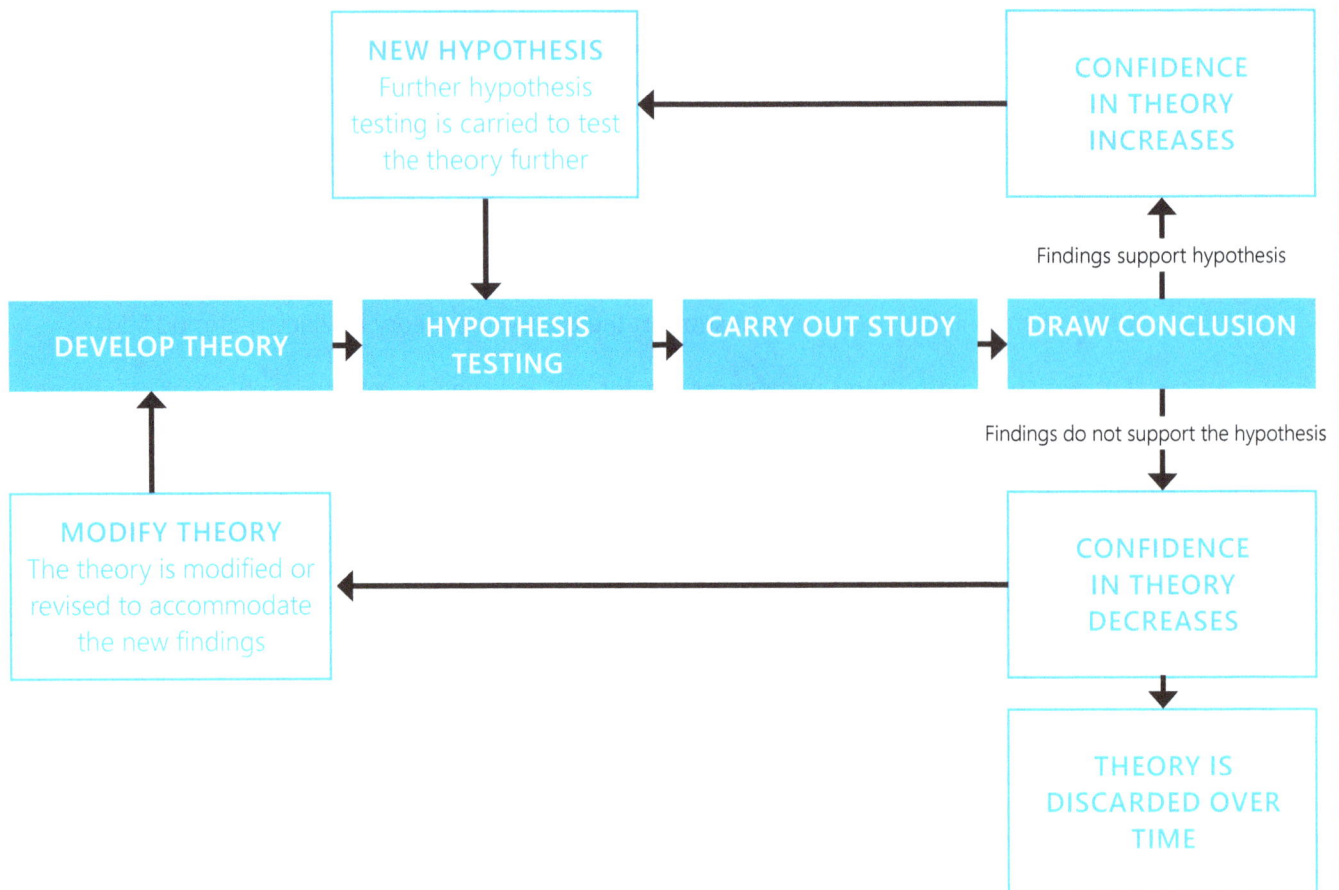

The cycle of theory construction and testing

A good theory will generate a number of testable hypotheses. In a typical study only one or a few of these hypotheses can be evaluated. If the evidence supports the hypotheses, confidence in the theory they were derived from generally grows. If the hypotheses are not supported, confidence in the theory decreases, and the theory may be revised to accommodate new findings. If the hypotheses generated by a theory consistently fail to provide support for the theory, the theory may be discarded. Thus, theory construction and testing is a gradual process.

◆ Hypothesis testing

- Scientific research often starts off by identifying a topic of interest to be tested, which may be based on observation or to test an existing theory. A hypothesis is developed to test the observed phenomenon/ theory. A hypothesis is a precise, testable statement that involves making a prediction about the expected outcome of the study. *Hypothesis testing*, as the name suggests, aims to test the hypothesis by designing a research study by which the hypothesis can be proven right or wrong (falsified) empirically.

Hypothesis testing is an important element in research as it helps us to develop a theory or strengthen, revise, or reject existing theories. We need to ensure that the variables are clearly operational in measurable terms when we test a hypothesis. In hypothesis testing, there are two opposing hypotheses that are being tested the *alternative hypothesis* (Ha) and the *null hypothesis* (Ho). For example, take the study below about whether sugary drinks have an effect on a memory recall test

- Null hypothesis – The null hypothesis is a statement of prediction that the results will *show no relationship* or *no difference* between the variables. For example:

  There will be no difference in a recall word test between participants who drink sugary drinks from those who do not consume a sugary drink.

- Alternative hypothesis – The alternative hypothesis is one in which there is a difference (or an effect) between two or more variables as predicted by the researchers. For example:

  Participants who drink sugary drinks will do better in a recall word test and those who do not drink sugary drinks.

In hypothesis testing, you will test to see which of the hypotheses will be accepted and which will be rejected. If the *alternative hypothesis* is correct (the findings support your prediction) then you would reject the null hypothesis. However, if the alternative hypothesis was not supported in the findings, then you would accept the null hypothesis and reject the alternative hypothesis. Deciding which hypothesis to accept requires a statistical test to analyse the data. If the results support the hypothesis, the theory gains credibility. If the results do not support the hypothesis, this suggests the theory is incorrect or needs modification/revising.

A little bit more information on the 'null hypothesis'

Psychologists must initially assume when carrying out an investigation that there is no relationship between the variables (e.g. sugary drinks and memory recall). It is the job of the alternative hypothesis to prove that there is a relationship and thus prove that the null hypothesis is wrong. Therefore in a research study there are really two hypotheses that are being tested   the null hypothesis and the alternative hypothesis (so-called because it is an alternative to the null hypothesis).

◆ Paradigms and paradigm shifts

- Kuhn (1970) said that what distinguishes scientific disciplines from non-scientific disciplines is that the scientific community has a *framework* of agreed assumptions and methods of how to conduct scientific research, in what Kuhn calls a 'paradigm'. In other words, this is a particular 'mindset' for how a scientist should think and carry out research. The scientific community all agree on the features of science in carrying out investigations, therefore science works on a single paradigm.

- Kuhn argued that social sciences, including psychology, do not work on a single paradigm and therefore can be seen as pre-scientific (pre-paradigmatic). This is because psychologists have a number of paradigms (e.g. behaviourist, humanistic, psychodynamic, etc.), and they do not all agree on what and how to study human behaviour. Some accept the features of science, others do not. For psychology to become a science it must resolve its differences.

- According to Kuhn, occasionally a paradigm is replaced with a new paradigm, this often occurs when there is a scientific revolution. This often starts with a minority of researchers that begin to question the accepted paradigm, when there is too much contradictory evidence to ignore. As a result, a new "revolutionary" paradigm begins to emerge which can better explain inconsistencies than the old way of thinking. The replacement of one paradigm with a newer one is called a paradigm shift. An example of a paradigm shift is Newton's theory of gravity giving way to Einstein's theory of relativity.

Practice exam questions

1. Explain what is meant by the term 'replication' in research investigations and why replication is an important feature of scientific research. **[2 marks + 3 marks]**

2. Explain what is meant by the term 'objectivity' in research investigation. **[2 marks]**

3. Explain what is meant by the term 'hypothesis testing' in a research investigation. **[2 marks]**

4. Explain what is meant by the term 'theory construction' in a research investigation. **[2 marks]**

5. Some people believe they have 'psychic' abilities, such as telepathy. We can define telepathy as the ability to acquire the thoughts of another person (i.e. what they are thinking about) without having any physical or verbal contact with them. Many studies into telepathy are now held in tightly controlled conditions that can be easily repeated by other psychologists. For example, to test the existence of telepathy, a participant looks at an image that has been randomly selected by a computer, while the person who claims to have psychic abilities attempts to pick the same image in another room. Some sceptics argue telepathy does not exist because it does not really meet the criteria of scientific investigation and therefore falls under the term 'pseudoscience' (false science).

    Explain why the above study of telepathy does meet the criteria of scientific investigation. Refer to some of the major features of science in your answer. **[6 marks]**

www.ingramcontent.com/pod-product-compliance
Lightning Source LLC
Chambersburg PA
CBHW080901030426

42336CB00016B/2974